Letters and Sketches of Sermons, in Three Volumes

John Adams, John Murray

Copyright © BiblioLife, LLC

This book represents a historical reproduction of a work originally published before 1923 that is part of a unique project which provides opportunities for readers, educators and researchers by bringing hard-to-find original publications back into print at reasonable prices. Because this and other works are culturally important, we have made them available as part of our commitment to protecting, preserving and promoting the world's literature. These books are in the "public domain" and were digitized and made available in cooperation with libraries, archives, and open source initiatives around the world dedicated to this important mission.

We believe that when we undertake the difficult task of re-creating these works as attractive, readable and affordable books, we further the goal of sharing these works with a global audience, and preserving a vanishing wealth of human knowledge.

Many historical books were originally published in small fonts, which can make them very difficult to read. Accordingly, in order to improve the reading experience of these books, we have created "enlarged print" versions of our books. Because of font size variation in the original books, some of these may not technically qualify as "large print" books, as that term is generally defined; however, we believe these versions provide an overall improved reading experience for many.

LETTERS,

AND

SKETCHES OF SERMONS.

IN THREE VOLUMES

BY JOHN MURRAY.
SENIOR PASTOR OF THE FIRST UNIVERSAL SOCIETY IN BOSTON

"But sanctify the Lord God in your hearts, and be ready always to give an answer to every man that asketh you a reason of the hope that is in you with meekness and fear.

"Having a good conscience, that, whereas they speak evil of you, as of evil doers, they may be ashamed that falsely accuse your good conversation in Christ.

"For it is better, if the will of God be so, that ye suffer for well-doing than for evil-doing."   1 PETER, iii. 15, 16, 17

VOL. III.

BOSTON
PUBLISHED BY JOSHUA BELCHER
1813

CONTENTS.

Introduction - - - - Page 3
Sketches upon various passages in the book of Exodus 17
Subject of the three immediately preceding sketches, examined and considered, together with reflection, serious, solemn, and consolatory - - - 19
Conversation - - - - - 47
Sketches upon the book of Exodus concluded - 50
Sketches upon the book of Leviticus - - 52, 54
Reflections upon the Sabbath day - - - 57
Sketches upon the book of Numbers 69, 71, 75, 79, 85, 87, 88
Question proposed - - - - - 91
Answer attempted - - - - - 92
Sketches upon the book of Numbers resumed and concluded - - - 94, 99, 103, 104, 105
Sketches upon the book of Deuteronomy 107, 108, 110, 113, 114, 116, 117, 119, 120, 122
Sketches upon the book of Joshua 123, 124, 125, 127, 128, 130, 131, 133, 135, 137, 138, 140, 141, 143, 144, 146, 150, 152
Sketches upon the book of Judges - - 153, 155, 156
Sketches upon some passages of Samuel, first and second books - - - - 158, 163, 165
Sketches upon the book of Psalms 166, 169, 170, 171, 172
Sketch upon a passage in the book of Proverbs - 173

CONTENTS.

Sketches upon the prophecy of Isaiah   174, 176, 179, 181, 184,
                                          185, 186, 188
Sketch upon a passage in the prophecy of Hosea   -   169
Sketch upon the prophecy of Micah   -   -   -   191
Sketch upon a passage in the prophecy of Zechariah   192
Sketches upon St. Matthew's Gospel   193, 198, 199, 201, 202
Reflections upon the Lord's prayer   -   -   -   203
Sketches upon St. Matthew's Gospel resumed and con-
        cluded   210, 211, 212, 214, 216, 217, 219, 221, 226
Sketch upon a passage in the Gospel by St. Mark   -   228
Sketches upon St. Luke's Gospel   234, 235, 236, 238, 239, 240,
                                          241, 243, 248
Sketches upon St. John's Gospel   249, 251, 253, 254, 264, 267
Sketch upon a passage in the Acts of the Apostles   -   269
Sketches upon Paul's Epistles to the Romans   270, 274, 275
Sketches upon passages in the first and second of Corin-
        thians   -   -   -   -   -   277, 280
Sketch upon a passage in the Epistle to the Galatians   281
Sketch upon a passage in second Thessalonians   -   283
Sketch upon a passage in the first Epistle to Timothy   286
Sketch upon a passage in the Epistle to Titus   -   288
Sketches upon a passage in the first general Epistle of
        Peter   -   -   -   -   -   297, 298
Sketches upon the book of Revelations   301, 303, 304, 305,
                                          306, 307, 309, 311, 312, 313, 316
Reflections upon Romans ix. 27.   -   -   -   318
Reflections upon John i. 45—51.   -   -   -   325
Reflections upon James v. 20, 21.   -   -   -   331
Letter to a friend   -   -   -   -   -   336
Thanksgiving Sermon   -   -   -   -   365
Extracts from papers containing memorandums of the Au-
        thor's life   -   -   -   -   -   384

INTRODUCTION.

Boston, Franklin Place, 1800.

As from my time of life and accumulating infirmities, I indulge a hope, that the hour of my emancipation draweth nigh; and as my labours must, of course, close with my life, I do, upon this sixth day of June, one thousand and eight hundred, commence a plan of noting and preserving as often as my leisure, my health, and my mental feelings shall permit, the heads of those discourses which I may yet be permitted to deliver. When I am no more with the dear people of God in this place, these hints may be amplified and improved, to the glory of the only-wise God our Saviour, and the comfort and edification of my much loved congregation; and if God should spare the life of my faithful friend, she may so arrange these hints as to render them generally useful. She has long been an attentive hearer of the word of God, and she is sufficiently acquainted with the foundation laid in Zion to rejoice in the superstructure, to echo the divinely inspired voice, which emphatically cries upon the elevation of the top-stone, GRACE, GRACE UNTO IT.

This faithful friend will not, as I believe, be at a loss, while perfecting or filling up the outlines of discourses delivered, even when she was not present; and should she find leisure and inclination, she may collect these scattered materials, and connecting them together, compose a volume that may contain instruction and consolation, both to preachers and hearers.

Those who have, from time to time, listened with admiration, delight, and gratitude, to the volume of inspiration, will be gratified when they recognize these glorious truths, presented in this concise manner to their view; they will thus be reminded of what they before so well knew, and they will not readily let those divine discoveries pass from their recollection.

I have another motive for wishing to preserve these outlines of sermons; it appears to me they will clearly manifest, that *scripture is the best expositor of scripture;* and they will impress upon the serious and attentive mind, a veneration for the testimonies of divine truth.

Placed in their own proper light, the sacred records will appear to be what they really are, a *consistent* and a *luminous revelation*. I confess I have only caught a glimpse of the glory of these divinely consolatory truths; but I have seen more of their divinity, when consulting no other testimony, than while encompassed by a *crowd of commentators*.

In taking these minutes, order makes no part of my calculation. The idea of preserving these small scrips of paper, on which a few texts of scripture will appear, primarily intended merely as a direction to my own mind, since I have suffered from the failure of my memory; this idea, I say, is of recent birth, many are lost, and those which remain are more indebted for preservation to accident, than to design. To dates I have had no regard, having devoted the greater part of my life to the study of the scripture, and possessing some strength of memory, I have not, until lately, found it necessary to note upon paper a single text; and being confident, that I was designed rather for a speaker than a scribe, I have, perhaps too much indulged a natural aversion from writing.

But should my friend continue her mortal career after I am called out of time, she may derive essential advantage from compiling and arranging these minutes; they will aid in forming the mind of our precious child; they will lead her to the study of those scriptures, which are able to make her wise unto salvation; they will, as her youthful faculties expand, *point* her to the rock of ages, whence she is to derive support, protection, and consolation; they will teach her, at all times, (and especially when her earthly parents shall be removed,) on whom she is to repose her brightest hopes of happiness; they will teach her, while a sojourner in this weary land, to take shelter under the overshadowing wings of her ALMIGHTY FRIEND, *of that everlasting Father who can never die;* they will teach her to come up from this wilderness leaning upon the Beloved; in one word, they will give her joy and uninterrupted peace, in believing the true sayings of her God.

From my long acquaintance with, and close study of the sacred pages, I am persuaded their worth is very little known. The volume of inspiration exhibits, in its connexion, a complete view of the redemption of the human family. The splendid truths contained in the Old and New-Testaments, have, even from the early days of christianity, been *obscured* by *commentators;* but the doctrines of revelation are *consistent doctrines;* and this is, as I conceive, a strong proof of the divinity of the oracles of our God; and I repeat, that an *accurate investigation* and *comparison* of scripture testimonies, will abundantly elucidate and confirm this fact.

I am persuaded I shall not proceed far in this vast undertaking, but the hints I may collect, when the passages to which I shall refer, are fairly transcribed, and placed in their own natural and luminous order, may produce reflection, reflection may produce inquiry; persons possessing superior abilities may engage in the subject, new paths of light may open, and the religious world may be enriched by new discoveries.

SKETCHES OF SERMONS.

SKETCH I.

Exodus, xv. 7, 8.

And in the greatness of thine excellency thou hast overthrown them that rose up against thee: thou sendest forth thy wrath, which consumed them as stubble, and with the blast of thy nostrils the waters were gathered together; the floods stood upright as an heap, and the depths were congealed in the hearts of the sea.

First, Who were they who rose up against Israel? The adversaries of God's people were many. All those who were round about them combined for their destruction, but the enemies particularly alluded to in this passage are described in the context, Pharaoh and his host. Pharaoh, as the enemy of Israel, may be considered as a type of the grand adversary.

Secondly, Of whom was Israel a figure? Israel is considered as an epitome of mankind; the Jews of the elect, the especial inheritance of God. The Gentiles we know *were* without, but the middle wall of partition is broken down and the Jew and Gentile are made one. Zechariah, ii. 8, "For thus saith the Lord of hosts, After the glory hath he sent me unto the nations which spoiled you: for he that toucheth you, toucheth the apple of his eye." Thus thinks and thus speaks the Lord of hosts, in every age and in every place, of those whom he hath selected as his inheritance. But in the eleventh verse of this chapter, Zechariah decidedly alludes to the abolition of the then existing distinctions. "And many nations shall be joined to the Lord in that day, and shall be my people, and I will dwell in the midst of them."

Thirdly, Wherein is the greatness of the divine excellency displayed? In overthrowing those that rose up against us, the context is full to this purpose. The LORD is a man of war, the LORD is his name. God spake the word, and the horse and his rider were thrown into the sea. When the God of Israel girded the loins and strengthened the arm, Gideon with his little company, with his trumpet, his pitcher, and his lamp, chased his thousands; Sampson, with the jaw bone of an ass, proceeded conquering and to conquer; and, nerved for the combat by the God of heaven, the son of Jesse, with a sling and a stone, became victorious over Goliah of Gath. It is remarkable that the stone of the brook, chosen by the youthful warrior as his weapon of defence and attack, entered the head of the Giant. *Thus did the seed of the woman bruise the head of the adversary.*

Fourthly, Did God accomplish the destruction of the enemy by the manifestations of his wrath? The enemies of mankind, of Israel, who are the inheritance of God, are destroyed by the breath of the LORD. "By the blast of God they perish and by the breath of his nostrils are they consumed. Thou hast broken the yoke of his burden and the staff of his oppressor, as in the day of Midian. For every battle of the warrior is with confused noise and garments rolled in blood, but this shall be with burning and with fire."

The vauntings of the enemy, in the ninth verse of the chapter which contains our text, are truly in character. " I will pursue, I will overtake, I will divide the spoil, I will draw my sword, my hand shall destroy them." The description of the catastrophe, as given in the tenth verse, is (beyond expression) beautiful: perhaps it is hardly surpassed by that oft cited passage in Genesis, i. 3, " An God said, Let there be light, and there was light." Let us attend to this tenth verse: " Thou didst blow with thy wind, the sea covered them: they sank as lead in the mighty waters." This corresponds exactly with another divine testimony: " Thou wilt cast all our sins, as a stone, into the depths of the sea;" and in the book of Revelations we are told, " That the abominations of the earth were as a great millstone cast into the depths of the sea."

Thus gloriously victorious is the Redeemer, in the cause of his people. In all their afflictions he was afflicted, and the angel of his presence saved them. In his love and in his pity he redeemed them, and he bare them and carried them all the days of old. But they rebelled and vexed his holy spirit; therefore he was turned to be their enemy, and he fought against them. Then he remembered the days of old, Moses, and his people, saying, Where is he that brought them up out of the sea, with the shepherd of his flock? that led them through the deep as an horse in the wilderness, that they should not stumble? Look down from heaven, and behold from the habitation of thy holiness and of thy glory. Doubtless thou art our Father, though Abraham be ignorant of us and Israel acknowledge us not: thou O Lord art our Father, our Redeemer, and thy name is from everlasting.

SKETCH II.

Exodus, xxviii. 2.

And thou shalt make holy garments for Aaron thy brother, for glory and for beauty.

First, Although Aaron was the brother of Moses, yet Moses was appointed to act as a God unto Aaron. Exodus, iv. 16. "And he (Aaron) shall be thy spokesman unto the people; and he shall be to thee instead of a mouth, and thou shalt be to him instead of God."

Secondly, Aaron was the Priest, the high Priest, whose office is pointed out. Leviticus, xvi. 2. "And the Lord said unto Moses, Speak unto Aaron thy brother, that he come not at all times into the holy place within the veil, before the mercy-seat which is upon the ark, that he die not; for I will appear in the cloud upon the mercy-seat."

Thirdly, The garments of this high Priest were holy garments. The term *holy* is, in the sacred volume, occasionally applied to inanimate matter, as to the temple and the consecrated vessels. It is sometimes used to designate the whole Jewish nation. Exodus, xxii. 31. "And ye shall be holy men unto me." Leviticus, xi. 44. "For I am the Lord your God; ye shall therefore sanctify yourselves, and ye shall be holy." Numbers, xvi. 3. "Ye take too much upon you, seeing all the congregation are holy."

Fourthly, Christians will never forget that Jesus Christ, of whom Aaron was a luminous type, is their high Priest. Hebrews, ii. 17. "Wherefore in all things it behoved him to be made like unto his brethren, that he might be a merciful and faithful high Priest in all things pertaining to God, to make reconciliation for the sins of the people."

Fifthly, By the appointment of God, the high Priest was to be clad in holy garments when ministering before the LORD, and a view of these symbolic garments leads to an important inquiry.

Sixthly, What were the garments of the glorious high Priest of our profession? The prophet Isaiah, our ever-ready, our evangelical expositor, gives us (chap. xlix. verse 18,) an answer to this question. "Lift up thine eyes round about and behold; all these gather themselves together and come to thee. As I live, saith the LORD, thou shalt surely *clothe thee with them all as with an ornament, and bind them on thee as a bride doeth.*" And are we not assured by the volume of inspiration, that Emmanuel passed by the nature of Angels and took upon him the seed of Abraham—*clothed himself in humanity?*

Seventhly, These garments are holy garments! Astonishing! Is the fulness of human nature, fallen from rectitude, fallen from righteousness, is this nature holy? Assuredly. For the Being who called the human family into existence, and who so loved them as to give them his son, has made this son unto them *wisdom, righteousness,* and *sanctification;* thus presenting them with that holiness which renders them blameless before the LORD.

Eighthly, These garments shall be for glory and for beauty? Isaiah is again ready with his luminous comment. lviii. 8. "Then shall thy light break forth as the morning, and thine health shall spring forth speedily; and thy righteousness shall go before thee, the glory of the Lord shall by thy re-reward:" and thus clothed in garments of spotless purity, the Redeemer of the world shall say, "Behold thou art fair, my love, thy beauty is without a cloud, I see no spot nor wrinkle in thee."

SKETCH III.

EXODUS xxviii. 3, 4, 5.

First, IT is observable that Moses was directed to speak unto all who were wise hearted, whom God had filled with the spirit of wisdom. It was not sufficient that they were wise hearted: previous to their possessing ability to make those holy garments, God must give them the spirit of wisdom. The thirty-first chapter and sixth verse of this book corroborates, if it does not illustrate this clause in our text. "And I, behold I, have given him Aholiab the son of Ahisimach of the tribe of Dan, and in the hearts of all that are wise hearted, I have put wisdom, that they may make all that I have commanded thee." Isaiah, xxviii. 26. "For his God doth instruct him to discretion, and doth teach him." Again, verse twenty-ninth. "This also cometh forth from the LORD of hosts, which is wonderful in counsel, and excellent in working."

Secondly, The garments which were to be made. A breastplate, Leviticus, viii. 8. Urim and Thummim. The breastplate is a piece of defensive armour, 1 Thessalonians, v. 8. But let us who are of the day be sober, putting on the breastplate of faith, and love, and, for an helmet, the hope of salvation.

Thirdly, The Ephod. A coat or upper garment. To be made of gold, blue, and purple, and scarlet, and fine twined linen. Each of these colours is expressive of the grace and truth which were brought to light by our great high Priest, who is the author and finisher of our faith. Gold was, and is considered the most precious metal, and therefore it is selected to convey an idea of the inestimable value of the Redeemer of the world. Isaiah xiii. 12. I will make a man more precious than fine gold, even a man than the golden wedge of Ophir. Blue is emblematick of faithfulness. Scarlet of courage or heroism; and a mixture of these colours, blue and scarlet, becomes purple. The fine linen is a figure of that garment of unspotted righteousness, wrought out by Jesus Christ for the saints. These were the colours, and such the quality of the *finished* Ephod, or the outward coat or garment, prepared for the high Priest, which demonstrates that he was clothed with the garments of salvation, and covered with the robe of righteousness. It is remarkable that the Evangelist Luke, xvi. 19, describes the rich man as clothed in purple and fine linen, which is one proof that the parable of the rich man and the beggar was intended as a representation of the two nations, Jews and Gentiles. The Jews fared sumptuously every day, while the person of Lazarus is a striking figure of the Gentiles.

We pass, *for the present*, the broidered coat, the robe, and the mitre, dwelling with ineffable pleasure upon the girdle. In the eighth verse of this chapter, this girdle is called the curious girdle of the Ephod. The prophet Jeremiah, xiii, 11, gives us the design of this memorable girdle, the formation and texture of which was directed by Omnipotence. "For as the girdle cleaveth to the loins of a man, so have I caused to cleave unto me, the whole house of Israel, and the whole house of Judah saith the LORD, that they might be unto me for a people, and for a name, and for a praise, and for a glory: but they would not hear."

As a further illustration of our subject, we present the last verse of the thirtieth chapter of Deuteronomy. "That thou mayest love the LORD thy God and that thou mayest obey his voice, and that thou mayest cleave unto him; for he is thy life, and the length of thy days: that thou mayest dwell in the land which the LORD sware unto thy fathers, to Abraham, to Isaac, and to Jacob, to give them." Twenty-ninth 5th, "And thou shalt take the garments and put upon Aaron, the coat, and the robe of the Ephod, and the Ephod, and the breastplate, and gird him with the curious girdle of the Ephod. Compare this direction with Revelations i. 13, "And in the midst of the seven candlesticks one like unto the son of man, clothed with a garment down to the foot, and girt about the paps with a golden girdle." Can we view the divine substance of these figures, and not feel our bosoms glow, as if touched with a coal from the sacred altar of God? Can we view this son of man, thus girt about, without rendering him the devout homage of gratitude, of the purest adoration?

SKETCH IV.

Exodus, xxviii, 9—12.

First, THE names of the people of God were to be engraven upon onyx stones. The onyx stone is a gem as transparent as chrystal. Moses was directed to select two stones, on which were to be engraven the names of the people of God, and these stones, thus engraven, were to be set in ouches of gold—small golden frames.

Secondly, These stones, thus engraven, and thus set, were to be for a memorial. What are we to understand, in this place, by a memorial? Joshua iv. 7, "Then ye shall answer them, that the waters of Jordan were cut off before the ark of the covenant of the Lord; when it passed over Jordan, the waters of Jordan were cut off: and these stones shall be for a memorial unto the children of Israel forever.

Thus, these stones were to be a standing memorial of the love of God to the people; and these precious stones set in gold, and engraven with their names, were continually reminding them of the love wherewith he loved them. This memorial is an abiding memorial. Psalm cxxxv. 13, "Thy name, O Lord, endureth forever, and thy memorial, O Lord, throughout all generations."

Thirdly, and lastly, Aaron shall bear their names before the Lord for a memorial. Thus both the high Priest and the people were to behold these names, thus arranged, thus engraven, as a perpetual memorial: the people that they may never be unmindful of the necessity of such an high Priest, and the high Priest that he may forever live for the people. Hebrews, vii. 25, "Wherefore he is able always to save them to the uttermost that come unto God by him, seeing he ever liveth to make intercession for them." Yea, verily, the God-man of whom the Jewish high Priest was a figure, is able to save unto the uttermost, for when he ascended, the people ascended with him, they came unto God by him, in their elder brother, in their common head, in the head of every man.

But the high Priest must bear the names of the people upon his shoulders. Isaiah, ix. 6, "For unto us a child is born, unto us a son is given, and the government shall be upon his shoulder." God so loved the world, that he gave them his son. I introduce this precious passage in this place, because it is frequently made a question, indeed a subject of violent contention, to whom this son was given. But John, the beloved disciple, decidedly says, "God so loved *the world* as to give them his son," and upon the shoulders of this son, thus given, the government shall be placed. How various, and how comprehensive are the names of the Redeemer! Wonderful, Counsellor, the mighty God, the everlasting Father, the Prince of peace.

I confess I am so fond of this passage, that I rarely pass an opportunity of giving it in full, even when it may not appear, in every part, perfectly apposite. But indeed I am inexpressibly delighted with every testimony penned by the spirit of truth, and the permission frequently to reiterate passages from sacred writ, is to me a divine indulgence. How delightful the study of the sacred oracles! How refreshing to slake our thirst at the never failing fountain of truth! The spirit of God, by the prophet Isaiah, xxii. 22, presents us with another glorious passage, which is full to our present purpose. "And the key of the house of David will I lay upon his shoulder; so he shall open, and none shall shut; and he shall shut, and none shall open." I cannot forbear proceeding onward, even to the close of this chapter.

"And I will fasten him as a nail in a sure place; and he shall be for a glorious throne to his father's house. And they shall hang upon him all the glory of his father's house, the offspring and the issue, all vessels of small quantity, from the vessels of cups, even to all the vessels of flagons. In that day, saith the LORD of hosts, shall the nail that is fastened in the sure place be removed and be cut down and fall; and the burden that was upon it shall be cut off: for the LORD hath spoken it."

Of what is this nail fastened in a sure place figurative? Doubtless of the Lord Jesus. He was indeed fastened in a sure place, his abode was the heaven of heavens, and he was truly for a glorious throne in the house of his Father. All the glory of his father's house hangeth upon him; the offspring and his issue, all vessels of small quantity, from the vessels of cups, even to all the vessels of flagons. What is designed by those vessels? The human family are compared to vessels; some individuals are said to be vessels of wrath, fitted for destruction. But they shall be emptied of wrath, and rescued from destruction.

When was this nail removed? In the day of the LORD; in the day which burnt as an oven, when all that were proud and who did wickedly became as stubble. When Christ Jesus suffered upon the cross, the intense fire of that indignation which burned furiously against the transgressions of mankind; when so exquisite were his agonies that he was removed, he was cut down, yea, although fastened in a sure place, *united to, and one with the* divine nature, he expired, and the burden that was upon him, by which he had been thus sorely oppressed, thus weighed down, the iniquities of the people were cut off. Merciful God, can language be plainer? Yes, he was indeed, and in truth, the immaculate Lamb of God, who taketh away the sin of the world. These are, to the wretched, wandering, undone children of men, blessed discoveries. These are glad tidings of good things, and this intelligence, eternal praises be to God, this intelligence is sent to you, my beloved hearers, to me, and not to us only, but to all mankind. And, moreover, it is sent by one who cannot lie, who is no deceiver. Verily, verily, we may at all times trust in the Lord, not being afraid, for in the Lord Jehovah is everlasting strength.

SKETCH V.

Exodus, xxviii. 36, 37, 38.

First, The high Priest.

Secondly, The furniture of his head—a mitre. Upon this mitre is placed a plate of pure gold, which plate of pure gold appears upon the fore front of the mitre.

Thirdly, Upon this plate was engraven Holiness to the Lord. Holiness consists in a conformity to the nature and will of God. Hebrews xii. 14 " Follow peace with all men, and holiness, without which no man shall see the Lord." Why was not the plate and its engravings fixed upon the breastplate, upon which were engraved the names of the different tribes? Because this high Priest was a figure of the Saviour, of that Saviour who was made of God unto us, sanctification; and he only is holy : our holiness is in our head ; all who are taught of God will devoutly say, Jesus shall be our constant theme, the one object of our unceasing adoration. It is the joy of the christian that Jesus is holy, and that this Holy One is the Holy One of Israel. Our high Priest is the Holy One of Israel. A prophet shall the Lord your God raise up unto you, of your brethren, like unto me. Him shall ye hear. This holy One God hath given to the unholy ! God so loved the world that he gave unto them his holy One, and this that they may be accepted in the beloved, in his holiness. Hebrews iii. 1. " Wherefore, holy brethren, partakers of the heavenly calling, consider the Apostle and high Priest of our profession, Christ Jesus :" In this passage those are denominated holy, who were, as they themselves confessed, remarkably unholy. Hence it is plain their holiness was only to be found in their head, in the Apostle and high Priest of their profession, in Christ Jesus.

Fourthly, This plate was to be fastened to the head of the high Priest with a blue lace. We have before seen that this colour was emblematic of faithfulness and truth ; and it was thus fastened that it might be upon the mitre.

Holiness is perfection. In the present state of things, the people of God are unquestionably imperfect ; they are in themselves decidedly unholy. The oracles of God in, I had almost said countless passages, bear the most unequivocal testimony to this truth. Yet the family of man, although depraved and polluted, were beloved by their God, so much beloved that he gave them his Son, and as, in this Son, it pleased the Father that all fulness should dwell, in giving unto the people this son, he gave them himself. Every record, both in the law and in the gospel, combines to assure us for what purpose this arrangement was made, that the people of God might be saved from their sins, that their transgressions might be taken away in and by Christ Jesus, that individual members might be presented in their head, without spot and blameless, and that they might ultimately be without sin, even in their own characters. Psalm xciii. 5. "Thy testimonies are very sure : holiness becometh thine house, O Lord, forever." Zechariah xiv. 20. "In that day shall there be upon the bells of the horses, HOLINESS UNTO THE LORD ; and the pots in the Lord's house shall be like the bowls upon the altar." There are, in the house, vessels of honour, and vessels of dishonour , but they are all *in* the house of the Lord ; and, says the prophet Zechariah, in that day the pots in the Lord's house shall be like the bowls upon the altar. Those vessels of dishonour, those vessels of wrath, shall, in God's time, be broken, and of course emptied of their wrath, but they shall be made over again nobler vessels, fitted for the master's use, and instead of being filled with wrath, they shall be filled with the knowledge of the Lord. Bishop Lowth, commenting upon this passage, says, it seems to imply the promise of universal peace, a blessing which he acknowledges to be often mentioned in the prophets as a concomitant of the flourishing state of Christ's kingdom. Doth not every faculty of our souls ardently supplicate ? Hasten, good God, this glorious era. Come, Lord Jesus, come quickly, for thine, and thine only, is the right to reign.

The subject of the preceding Sketches critically examined, copiously dilated, and considered with a single eye; together with reflections, serious, solemn and consolatory.

CONSIDERING the sacerdotal garments made for the Israelitish high Priest, under the especial direction of Almighty God, I may be excused if I indulge myself by expatiating particularly upon those emblematick vestments, which I consider as a striking compendium of that grace and truth, which was brought to light by the gospel.

It appears to me that the different parts of these heaven directed garments contain information which is indisputably worthy of all acceptation.

The character priest. The very name priest—it is another term for advocate. The priest under the Mosaic law was never considered as an adversary. He was a peace maker, who brought near the offended and the offender. In 2 Chronicles, vi. 41, Solomon emphatically says, "Now, therefore, arise, O LORD God, into thy resting place, thou and the ark of thy strength: let thy priests, O LORD God, be clothed with salvation." How tremendously would our situation have been reversed, had Solomon said, let thy priests be clothed with damnation! The Apostle Paul dwelleth impressively upon the priesthood. In the first verse of the sixth chapter of the Epistle to the Hebrews he thus expresses himself; "Therefore leaving the principles of the doctrine of Christ, let us go on unto perfection; not laying again the foundation of repentance from dead works and of faith toward God."

There is unquestionably a growth in grace, and in the knowledge and love of God, and, leaving those things which are behind, we should press forward to the prize of our high calling, which is in Christ Jesus. Paul describes himself, and his brethren, in the ministry, in his Epistles to the Colossians, i. 28, as preaching Christ Jesus, warning every man, and teaching every man in all wisdom; that they might present every man perfect in Christ Jesus. Indeed it is impossible a merely human being can be presented perfect any where but in Christ Jesus; perfection can only be found in the Redeemer of men. Indeed, this arrangement in the divine economy is perfectly accommodated to the nature of man; were the individuals of mankind, during their continuance in this changeful state, entrusted with that which is eventually to constitute their felicity, they would as probably forfeit heaven, as did their first parents their high standing in the garden of Eden.

We indulge a hope, and it is a blessed hope, a hope which is full of immortality: we indulge, I say, a hope from the testimonies of sacred writ, that the glorious high Priest of our profession presents us before the divine nature as his fulness, as complete in him.

The ceremonial law abounds with striking figures of grace and truth. The books of Exodus and Leviticus are a rich treasury of emblems, calculated to illustrate the grand plan of redemption. And yet, strange to tell, there are men, men famed for learning and for piety, professing christians too, who have not only regarded the law of ceremonies with sovereign contempt, but have spoken of it as ludicrous and lamented that it had obtained a place in the Bible!!

A celebrated preacher, a Doctor Foster, who was contemporary with Doctor Watts, boasted his infidelity respecting the ceremonial law. The christian poet frequently held converse with him, and in one of those interviews, he requested Mr. Foster to accompany him in a walk, engaging to introduce him to a friend of his, an old friend, possessing great excellence, but far advanced in life, for which reason, as he might soon be called home, he embraced every opportunity of visiting him. Doctor Foster readily consented to make the visit, and on their way to the residence of the old gentleman, Foster was prepared to meet an extraordinary person, by learning from Doctor Watts, that he was singular in his manners; but, continued the Doctor, I never interrupt him, I respect him too highly to counsel or direct him, yet, it must be confessed, there are times when, to a stranger, he would appear a complete idiot.

When our visiters reached the mansion of the sage, Watts would not permit the servant to announce them—No, said he, your master is acquainted with me, he is in his study, I presume? Yes Sir. Very well, we will walk up, but softly if you please, lest we surprise him. It happened that the old gentleman was seated with his back to the door, at a table, on which was placed an apparatus, to which Foster was a stranger. As they entered without noise, and the sage was wrapped in contemplation, they remained unobserved, and he pursued his purpose. Watts held up his finger to his friend, as a token of silence, and Foster beheld him with sensations in which *pity* was a prevalent ingredient. After regarding him a considerable time, they turned about, making their exit as silently as they had entered. Immediately on their reaching the street, well, said Watts, what do you think of my friend? Alas! Sir, said Foster, my sensations were truly melancholy. The appearance of human nature, in such a state of degradation, cannot but give pain. I regarded the old gentleman with compassion, with pity; a view of man reduced to a state of second childhood, is a sad spectacle, and we are doubly mortified, when the character has been such as you represent that of your friend, highly respectable.

Yes, Sir, respectable indeed—But, my dear Sir, my sole object in attending you to his house this morning, was to give you an opportunity of detecting your own folly, in the remarks you have occasionally thrown out, upon the books of Moses, especially that law of ceremonies which those books record. You saw the old gentleman we have visited with pity; you beheld his cups and straws, and breath blown bubbles, and you *imagined a derilection of his understanding;* you *supposed he was in a state of second childhood.* Nothing can be farther from the truth; he was at the moment you beheld him, making experiments in science, which may probably conduce to the good of mankind, and astonish the world. Sir, it is the far-famed, and justly celebrated Sir Isaac Newton, whose pursuits we have this morning witnessed.

Sir Isaac Newton! you astonish me! I am confounded! Hasten. take me back immediately, that I may supplicate his pardon—Rather, returned Watts, go home, and supplicate pardon of your God, for thinking and speaking so unworthily, so contemptuously, of his directions to Moses, respecting the tabernacle, the priest, the sacerdotal garments, &c. &c. Spare me, Sir, I do assure you I deeply feel. So indeed you ought, and so I knew you would, when once the eyes of your understanding were open. I have long wished you to render to your Creator the homage which was his due—I thank you, my friend, you have gained your point; I will, in future, learn to respect what I cannot understand, especially if it is sanctioned by divine authority, and I will learn to regard the regulations of my God as sacred.

In Exodus thirty-ninth, the sacerdotal garments are with great accuracy described, and the delineation exactly corresponds with that in the twenty-eighth. The twenty-ninth gives us the manner in which Aaron and his sons were to be arrayed in the holy garments, the anointing which was to succeed, and seems to present a kind of close to many particulars required by the ceremonial law, according as the Lord commanded Moses, for Moses was, as a servant faithful in all his house.

In the first verse of the thirty-ninth chapter, we are informed that of the blue, and purple, and scarlet, they made clothes of service to do service in the holy place, and made the holy garments for Aaron, as the Lord commanded Moses.

The grand and principal material in those garments was linen. Linen was figurative of the righteousness of the saints, this is evident from various scripture testimonies.

The people of God were forbidden to construct a garment of linen and woollen; they should not mingle their own imperfect deeds with the immaculate robe of righteousness, wrought out for the saints by their common head, the man Christ Jesus. But these linen garments were ornamented with gold, the most precious of all metals, and with the most precious stones. But what were the colours of the clothes of service? blue, purple, and scarlet. Those who are learned in Hebrew lore, assure us that blue has, from the earliest times, been regarded as the figure of faithfulness. Purple is a mixture of scarlet and blue, and scarlet is a symbol of courage or true heroism. Thus the figurative garments seem complete in their base, and beautiful in their ornaments. We are told in the third verse of this chapter, that they did beat the gold into thin plates, and cut it into wires to work it in the blue, and in the purple, and in the scarlet, and in the fine twined linen.

The robe of the ephod was a short coat, made of blue, and purple, and scarlet, and fine twined linen. They made shoulder pieces for it, to couple it together, by the two edges was it coupled together. And the curious girdle of his Ephod, that was upon it, was of the same materials, according to the work thereof; of gold blue, purple, and scarlet, and fine twined linen, as the Lord commanded Moses. The next article to which our attention is led is the girdle. And the curious girdle of his Ephod, that was upon it, was of the same, according to the work thereof, of gold, blue, purple, and fine twined linen, as the Lord commanded Moses.

This girdle was to bind the garments to the high Priest. The breastplate was, and indeed considering the materials of which it was constructed, could not be otherwise than very weighty ; and as the high Priest, when he entered into the holiest of all, clad in these garments, for the purpose of worshipping the supreme Being, did obeisance before the mercy seat, that mercy seat on which the God of Israel took up his rest, lest while bending before this mercy seat the plate on which the names of the children of Israel were engraved, should quit its station near the heart of the high Priest, it was fastened to his breast with a *blue* lace, so that in faithfulness and truth, they may be forever secured. And to testify the value which the God of Israel set on the people, their names were engraven upon precious stones, set in ouches of gold, as diamonds are set in a ring. We are not to form a judgment of the affection of the Creator, for the creature whom he hath called into being, from the character given by the spirit of truth, of the human family: but from the estimation in which they appear to be held, by their Almighty Parent, as thus manifested in this symbolic breastplate. They shall be mine, saith Jehovah, in the day that I make up my jewels. Be it known to you, not for your sakes do I do this, but for mine own name sake, saith the God who made us.

When I look at this part of the heaven directed dress, and compare it with Isaiah, xi. 5, " And righteousness shall be the girdle of his loins and faithfulness the girdle of his reins," and with the twenty-fifth chapter and first verse of this prophecy " O Lord, thou art my God; I will exalt thee, I will praise thy name, for thou hast done wonderful things, thy counsels of old are faithfulness and truth ;" when I compare and consider these testimonies, gratitude, eternal and never ending gratitude, glows in my bosom. One of the characters of my God is faithfulness, even when adversity gets hold of me ; it is in faithfulness, in very faithfulness, that God, the faithful God, afflicts the faithless children of men.

The spirit of God, by the prophet Jeremiah, informs us, xiii. 11. "That as the girdle cleaveth to the loins of a man, so saith the Lord, have I caused the whole house of Israel and the whole house of Judah, to cleave unto me, that they might be unto me for a people, and for a name, and for a praise, and for a glory." Psalm lxxxix. 8. "O Lord God of hosts, who is a strong Lord like unto thee ? Or to thy faithfulness round about thee ?"

Every one of these stones, these precious stones, were enclosed in ouches of gold, and when the high Priest entered into the holiest of all and stood before the mercy seat, the God who filled this seat of mercy saw and acknowledged the names, precisely in the order which he had directed; and lest it should, in process of time, be thought, by any of his family, that they were accepted in their own individual names, they were obliged to appear before the LORD, *in* and *with* the high Priest. Thus it is *in the beloved* that we are accepted.

But the names of the people were placed also upon the shoulders of the high Priest; here it is difficult to avoid a recurrence to the word of the LORD by Isaiah, ix. 67. "And the government shall be upon his shoulders." My attention is also powerfully turned to the evangelist, Luke, xv. 4, 5, 6, where the redeemer speaking of the lost nature under its appropriate figure, sheep, represents the good shepherd, after having sought for and found this lost sheep, as laying it upon his shoulders rejoicing, calling together his friends and his neighbours, and saying, rejoice with me, for I have found my sheep which was lost. Well then, if the lost sheep was found, *his number was again complete.*

When I see the same materials that were on the breastplate, with the names of the children of Israel, placed also upon the shoulders of their high Priest; when I follow this figure to the New Testament and behold the lost nature upon the shoulders of the true high Priest of our profession, carried home rejoicing; when I hear the Redeemer calling upon those whom he met on his return, to rejoice with him inasmuch as he had found that which was lost; when I consider that our Emmanuel *ultimately lost nothing,* (*if we except the son of perdition;*) a view of this consistent plan, of this complete whole, satisfies my understanding, and my soul magnifies the LORD and rejoices in his finished salvation.

It seems to be the design of God to teach the people, by a multitude of figures, that he will lose nothing which he hath made. The woman possessing ten pieces of silver, is another figure, another proof, she had lost one of them, but with a lighted candle she diligently searched the house, *until she had found it;* when she called her friends and her neighbours together requiring them to rejoice with her, for she had found that which was lost. Thus were her *riches restored as at the beginning,* and her real friends could not but congratulate her on the success of her diligent search.

Thus will the Lord of all worlds gather home that which is his, thus will he seek and save that which was lost. Placed by the restitution of all things, in the situation which he filled in the beginning. In such a catastrophe, his friends will have great occasion for rejoicing ; yea, and they will rejoice, and be exceeding glad, uniting in full chorus, to say, Thine is the kingdom, and the power, and the glory forever, and ever, Amen and Amen.

" And he made the breastplate of cunning work, like the work of the Ephod ; of gold, blue and purple, and scarlet, and fine twined linen.

" And the stones were according to the names of the children of Israel, twelve according to their names, like the engravings of a signet, every one with his name according to the twelve tribes.

" And they made upon the breastplate, chains at the ends of wreathen work of pure gold.

" And they made two ouches of gold, and two gold rings, and put the two rings in the two ends of the breastplate.

" And they put the two wreathen chains of gold in the two rings, on the ends of the breastplate. This breastplate, thus engraven, could not, as we have observed, be removed, and therefore the names of the people could never lose their places." This is indeed a soul satisfying consideration, they never did, they never can, they never will lose their places. For although Aaron and his lineal successors are now no more, although the symbolic plate, with its precious stones, having done their office, have long since become private property. Yet the antitype of this figure, our great high Priest, ever lives for the people, and they are still near his heart, within the veil, where he hath entered for us, ever living to make intercession for the people.

" And they did bind the breastplate by his rings upon the rings of the Ephod, with a lace of blue, that it might be above the curious girdle of the Ephod, and that the breastplate might not be loosed from the Ephod ; as the Lord commanded Moses

" And he made the robe of the Ephod of woven work, all of blue."

The Ephod being a short garment, this robe hung over it, and was made all of blue. We have seen of what this colour was figurative.

" And there was an hole in the midst of the robe, as the hole of an habergeon, with a band round about the hole that it should not rend.

"And they made upon the hems of the robe, pomegranates of blue, and purple, and scarlet, and twined linen.

"And they made bells of pure gold, and put the bells between the pomegranates upon the hem of the robe round about, between the pomegranates.

"A bell and a pomegranate, a bell and a pomegranate, round about the hem of the robe, to minister in ; as the Lord commanded Moses."

These bells, and these pomegranates, are replete with information which is truly divine. When the high Priest, habited in his holy garments, including in figure all the people of God, entered within the vale, as much, very much depended upon the reception given to the high Priest, and as being within the veil the people without, however deeply interested, could not by the testimony of their sight, ascertain the situation of their priest whether he existed or not, and as their lives depended upon the event, their torturing apprehension must have been extreme. But although they could not behold his person, they could listen to the report, which the bells upon the hem of his garment made, as he moved, thus announcing his safety, and the people upon hearing these bells, shouted with exceeding great joy.

The fruit too, mixed with the bells, is strikingly symbolic. The pomegranate is not a beautiful fruit, it is rough and unpromising in its appearance, but when opened it is truly delicious ; it is filled with seeds, which are connected and united together by a thick glutinous pulp, which seems to confine the seeds: this pulp is of a sanguine hue, and the whole strikingly describes the many gathered into one, and in that one preserved, and presented.

Thus, as we have already observed, when the high Priest passed before the mercy seat, the motion of his body caused the bells to sound, this sound the people both heard and felt, it was a joyful sound ; the intelligence it conveyed, revived their hopes, and banished their apprehension. It seemed to say, "Because I live, ye shall live also," they knew that they were accepted in the person of their high Priest.

And our glorious high Priest hath entered into the holiest of all for us : he hath ascended far above all heavens, that he may fill all things. The gospel trumpet is blown with a steady sound, its bells make a joyful noise, there is nothing equivocal in its report. and when we hear, and hearing receive, when we believe the glad tidings with which it is replete, viz. that the high Priest of our profession hath entered the holiest of all, that he hath entered for us with his own blood, it is then that our souls do indeed revive, that our spirits rejoice, that we unceasingly magnify God our Saviour.

The holy crown too, proclaims to my understanding, more than at any period of my life, I have ever been able to find words to express. Its description is contained in the thirty and thirty-first verses of this thirty-ninth chapter. " And they made the plate of the holy crown of pure gold, and wrote upon it a writing, like to the engravings of a signet, HOLINESS TO THE LORD.

" And they tied unto it a lace of blue, to fasten it on high upon the mitre, as the LORD commanded Moses."

It is observable that this plate, with this engraving, HOLINESS TO THE LORD, was placed upon the head of the high Priest; the engraving, HOLINESS TO THE LORD, was not wrought upon the plate, that contained the names of the tribes; yet it was as *effectual*, for the head and the breast are connected, and hence it is written, that the head of every man is the holy one of Israel. The high Priest could not enter the holiest of all, without this holy crown, without holiness, no man can see the LORD God, our God, the God of the whole earth, in thus teaching us, gives us to know that Jesus Christ is the high Priest of our profession, that he is indeed made of God unto us, not only wisdom, and righteousness, but sanctification also. Yet the doctrines and traditions of men, taking place of the doctrines of God our Saviour, with unwarrantable licence, put asunder what God, in those sacred writings, the testimony of which is worthy of all acceptation, hath joined together.

The assembly of divines, in their catechism, speaking of justification, assert that it is an act of God's free grace, that it is *perfect*, and becomes ours upon believing, because it is the righteousness of Christ. But sanctification is the work of God's spirit upon the heart of the creature, rendering him more like God in himself. Is not this putting asunder what God hath joined together? I do not deny a work of the spirit upon the heart, I believe that the spirit, takes of the things of Jesus, and shows them unto the believer, and I am confident, that the spirit influences the genuine believer, to conform his life, as much as possible, to the rules and directions, so plainly given in sacred writ; but as all creative excellence, while in this *imperfect* state, must of necessity be *imperfect*, I am impelled to deny, that this work of the spirit is *sanctification*, or *that holiness*, without which no man can see the LORD.

We frequently hear of being sanctified in part, and many a sincere preacher believes this doctrine, *sanctification* in *part*, to be a scripture doctrine. Thus I once believed, and I once taught. But from the period when, by the grace of God, I was permitted to turn aside from the traditions and doctrines of men, from the moment when I beheld the figure of the true high Priest, entering into the holiest of all, in his sacerdotal habit, according as the LORD commanded Moses, I have continued steadfast in the faith, constantly believing, that we were accepted in the beloved, as made of God unto us sanctification, and that sanctification *in part*, was a solicism in language, especially when we attempted the delineation of scripture testimonies.

We are no more *sanctified* in part, than we are *justified* in part. In fact our Saviour was, and is, a *complete* Saviour, made of God unto us, who are in our best estate vanity, prone, constantly prone, to evil ; yet the immaculate Redeemer is made of God unto us righteousness, and sanctification.

The people of God were accepted in their high Priest, and, saith the Apostle Paul, Colossians, ii. 10, " Ye are complete in him, which is the head of all principality and power."

I say again, the children of Israel were accepted in their high Priest, who was appointed an illustrious figure of the holy one of Israel, they were complete in him ; he was exhibited as their holiness ; HOLINESS TO THE LORD was not, I repeat, inscribed upon the breastplate, where the names of the people were engraved, but the intimate union of the head and breast, is my authority, for declaring that the *holiness*, without which no man should see the LORD, is found in the head, and hence it cannot be remembered with too much gratitude, that the head of every man, is the *holy one* of Israel, and that although Israel may be as the sands of the sea for multitude, yet, is this exalted head the holiness of every individual. Nor can the most excellent created being, say unto this glorious head, *I*, for *one*, have no need of thee.

Such was the gospel preached unto the people in the law of ceremonies, and those who are taught by the spirit of God, will see it, and seeing it, will believe it, and believing it, will be saved from all the misery which is consequent upon unbelief.

But the plate and its engraving, was not only placed upon the head of the high Priest, but fastened upon his head with a lace of blue. The same God which directed the figurative plate, directed also that it should be secured upon the head, that the people with lifted eye might always behold that holiness, without which it was impossible they should see God.

Be ye holy as God is holy. Be ye perfect as, as whom ? As Moses, as Peter, as John ? No, no ; but be ye perfect as your Father who is in heaven, is perfect.

Nothing short of the holiness of God, can gain us admittance into that state, where nothing that defileth can enter. *Perfection in part, sanctification in part.* Nonsense, errant nonsense ; perfection in part, sanctification in part can have no existence. Who so offendeth in one point, is guilty of all. When we hear of holy men, without turning with a single eye to the *holy one* of Israel, when we hear christians describing men as *good men*, good men even in the sight of God, and yet admitting they have stopped short of perfection, when we compare this testimony with the testimony of that man, that Redeemer, who spake as never man spake, and who pronounces positively, that a corrupt tree cannot bring forth good fruit, What can we say to these things? Surely we must acknowledge that the great master was full of grace and truth.

But, why did the Saviour of the world thus teach his disciples? Assuredly that they might turn unto him, in the complicated character which he sustained, and say with the royal prophet, Whom have I in heaven but thee ? And there is none on earth I desire beside thee. Such will indeed be the language of every christian, in every place, and every age ; they will count all things but loss, for the excellency of the knowledge of Christ Jesus their Lord ; all the righteousness of men, in every age and place is, when viewed as the matter of our justification or sanctification, in the sight of God, nothing, and worse than nothing, it is a rag, a filthy rag. Such was the language of the pupils of the old school, until it was believed, good morals were not sufficiently inculcated, that it was better to lay these doctrines aside as obsolete, or at least to relax in our tenacious adherence to these antiquated testimonies ; it savoured too much of bigotry, to be thus wedded to a sentiment.

When we say the scriptures declare thus, and so, this is agreeable to the testimony of Moses : thus spake God by his prophets, thus saith the Redeemer of the world, and thus, and thus, declared the apostles of our Lord; a company of weeders start up, to oppose us, "It is necessary," say they, " *to weed this same Bible ; it is an old book, and may contain some good things, but we have been long enough schooled with these old sayings, we should dare to think for ourselves. The men who wrote the scriptures were perhaps well meaning, well disposed men, and we ought to have charity for them; but they were but men, and we are men, and we will not give up our reason to any of them. We will judge for ourselves, we will act as becomes reasonable creatures. This is a day of light and liberty; must we be always children ? The writers of what you call divine Revelation, have written as they felt, they were true to their own judgment, and so were those who came after them; and they were wise enough to say, let every one be persuaded in their own minds.*"

But I must be excused for believing the Bible to be the word of God, written by the pen of inspiration, by men under the especial influence of Deity, and while I thus think these sacred oracles must continue to be my standard, and I must say to every *system maker*, to the law, and to the testimony, if you speak not according to the things written in the book, it is because there is no light in you. I do not set about *weeding* the Bible, it is highly acceptable to me, precisely as it stands, my understanding does not object to a single passage which it contains, my method is to explain passages by corresponding, or explanatory passages, and thus is my comment as infallible as my text, and when I have not a perfect comprehension, still I do not object, I take refuge in an unwavering assurance, that the testimonies all *consist* in the character of Christ Jesus, and that his words, all his words are full of grace and truth.

I do not deny that every man should be persuaded in his own mind, and so, blessed be God, are they who take, and hold fast the testimony of divine truth, as the form of *sound words*.

Yes, we should be in the exercise of charity, and while in the exercise of charity, we should not deal damnation round the land, to all *we* judge the foes of God.

I acknowledge that every man has an unalienable right to think for himself, he who differs from me, may be as meritorious, and perhaps abundantly more so than I, myself am. Yet I will not, in complaisance to any man, relinquish my own faith, my own reason; I will endeavour to hold fast the profession of my faith, without wavering, and I will be ready on all occasions to render unto every one that asketh me, a reason of the hope that is in me, with meekness and fear. But I would say, Now abideth faith, hope, charity, these three, but the greatest of these is charity.

It is the wish of the christian, to do unto others at all times and upon all occasions, as he is desirous that others should do unto him : but, alas ! in this and in every thing else, we all, in many things offend ; so that we are constantly necessitated to turn to our strong hold, and as we have received the Lord Jesus, so to walk in him.

But to return to the tabernacle ; we have seen the holy crown, and its engraving; the lace of blue by which it was fastened to the mitre, we have seen the whole bound upon the forefront of the head of the high Priest. We have seen why it was thus, and if we consult our luminous commentator, the apostle Paul, we shall hear him affirm, Hebrews, vi,

" When God made promise to Abraham, because he could swear by no greater, he swore by himself,

" Saying, surely blessing, I will bless thee, and multiplying, I will multiply thee.

" That by two immutable things, in which it was impossible for God to lie, we might have a strong consolation, who have fled for refuge to lay hold on the hope set before us.

" Which hope we have as an anchor of the soul, both sure and steadfast ; and which entereth into that within the veil

" Whether the forerunner is for us entered, even Jesus made an high Priest forever after the order of Melchisedec."

Is it not a blessed consideration, that what the Redeemer was, when this epistle was written, he now is, and will continue to be, worlds without end ? For he 'was made a *Priest forever after the order of Melchisedec.* And what, and who is Melchisedec ? *The same yesterday, to day and forever ;* he was King of Salem, and Priest of the most high God, without beginning of days, or end of time , his name, by interpretation is King of righteousnes, King of Salem, King of peace.

Without father, without mother, without descent, but made like unto the son of God, abiding a Priest continually.

Doth not this illustrious figure, correspond exactly with his antitype, the glorious high Priest of our profession, who with respect to his human nature was without father, and with respect to his divine nature, without mother.

It is notorious that perfection was not to be found in the Levitical priesthood. Nor did God expect to find undeviating rectitude either in Aaron or his successor. An omnipotent and prescient being can never make erroneous calculations. God, according to his own good pleasure, instituted another order, selected from another tribe, in whose line the priesthood was not found. It is evident from the genealogical table, regularly and distinctly preserved in scripture, even to the birth of our Saviour, that he was not of the house of Levi, he was a lineal descendant of Judah, whose posterity was not consecrated for the priesthood. The Apostle, from these considerations, leads us to conclude, that as a priest of a very different order was now ordained, not after the carnal commandment, but after the power of an endless life, that there is verily a disannulling of the commandment, going before for the weakness and unprofitableness thereof, Hebrews, vii. 11, 18.

How incalculably great, to the human family are the advantages A Priest forever, says the Apostle to the Hebrews, after the order of Melchisedec. This is assuredly a royal priesthood, a royal order; here church, and state, are indeed united, here therefore, on all our glory there is a defence. Both Priests and Kings have been found among men very injurious to their species; but those Priests and Kings were not of this order, but they shall be brought in, for all Kings shall serve him, Psalm. cxxxviii. 4, " All the Kings of the earth shall praise thee, O Lord, when they hear the words of thy mouth." Again, Isaiah, lx. 3, "And the Gentiles shall come to thy light, and Kings to the brightness of thy rising." And lxii. 2, " And the Gentiles shall see thy righteousness, and all Kings thy glory : and thou shalt be called by a new name, which the mouth of the Lord shall name." This is glad tidings of good things, even unto Kings, and if the Neroes and other blood-thirsty monarchs, who have slaughtered mankind, are to be saved, their suffering victims can have little reason to fear.

The Apostle Paul informs us, Hebrews, vii 24, " That this man, because he continueth forever, hath an unchangeable Priesthood," and again,

" Wherefore he is able to save unto the uttermost, them that come unto God by him, seeing he ever liveth to make intercession for them."

But who are they who are thus blessed ? Certainly all those to whom this Priest was given, and certainly this everlasting Priest was given to every one, to whom the passing, dying Priests, under the Levitical institution were given, and surely Aaron was given to all the people of Israel, and most certainly all the people of Israel came unto God by their high Priest; they were his fulness, as we have seen in the high Priest we have been contemplating. Many of the people might have been, and no doubt were, at the moment when Aaron entered within the veil, otherwise engaged, without a recurrence even in thought, to their high Priest ; yet undoubtedly they came to God by him : and so far were they from being parties concerned with their high Priest, either in thought, word or deed, that no one of the tribes were suffered even to look into the holiest within the veil, yet they all entered with him. The children of Israel were, according to scripture testimony, an epitome of the human race. The house of bondage, in which they were retained, was a figure of the thraldom of sin. Pharaoh is a type of the grand adversary ; Moses and Aaron are figures of the Redeemer in his different offices ; the deliverance of the Israelites is the redemption of mankind ; the pursuit and overthrow of Pharaoh, is the victory obtained over the Prince and power of the air, and his legions, &c. &c. &c.

When our glorious high Priest entered into the holiest, within the veil, the people entered with him and were accepted in the beloved, so that being crucified with Christ, they were buried with him, they have risen with him, and they have ascended with him, and they are seated together with him in heavenly places, in Christ Jesus, and thus having entered with him as his fulness within the veil, he ever liveth for them, and they will be saved to the uttermost, thus coming to God by him. No wonder, therefore, that we hear this high Priest saying, *" Because I live, ye shall live also."*

Another special benefit attendant upon this change is, that the high Priest of our profession is holy, harmless, undefiled, separate from sinners, and made higher than the heavens; yea, and he will always thus continue, and indeed, indeed such, exactly such an high Priest, became us so perfectly accomodated at all points to our infirmities.

Moreover, it is not necessary to repeat this sacrifice, as did those high Priests who daily offered sacrifices, first for their own sins and then for the sins of the people, for this he did once when he offered up himself. And as when he was lifted upon the cross, he drew all men unto him, we were thus crucified with him. Hence, saith an Apostle, " *The love of Christ constraineth us, because we thus judge, that if one died for all, then were all dead.*"

The law maketh men high Priests which have infirmity; but the word of the oath which was since the law, maketh the son, who is consecrated forever more. He will ever continue blameless, offending in no one point, either with respect to God or to the people, with respect to the human or to the divine nature: he will be forever faithful to both, and in these characters he is consecrated forever more.

These are the true sayings of God. Surely we should never lose sight of this glorious, this divine high Priest. We were gratified and astonished, by a view of the figure, in his sacerdotal habit, entering within the veil. But now, when the veil of the temple is rent from the top to the bottom, we see our high Priest, who hath entered for us within the veil, seated upon the throne of his glory, and if we have not heard the golden bells, we have heard the glad sound of the gospel, we have heard our great high Priest say, "*Because I live, ye shall live also.*" Moses turned aside to see the great sight, when he saw the bush burning and not consumed. But this is an infinitely greater sight than ever was exhibited upon mount Horeb or mount Sinai. It is the living God clothed in garments of flesh.

The ninth chapter of Hebrews is full to our purpose, and in Exodus, xxiv. 7, 8, we read,

" And he took the book of the covenant, and read in the audience of the people : and they said, All that the Lord hath said will we do, and be obedient.

" And Moses took the blood, and sprinkled it on the people, and said, Behold the blood of the covenant, which the Lord hath made with you concerning all these words."

Exhibiting blood as the sanction of leagues and covenants, was an ancient rite, and probably intended to show that the parties entering into covenant, pledged their lives for the fulfilment of the covenant, for the blood is said to be the life of the creature, and the words added to the action were, This is the blood of the covenant, that is, this is the blood by which the covenant is confirmed between God and the people. It is called the blood of the covenant, because it was a sign of the covenant, and a seal in confirmation of its validity.

The new covenant was confirmed by blood, so said the Saviour, this is my blood of the New Testament, shed for you and for many; without the shedding of blood there can be no remission of sins. If the blood of Christ had not been shed, not all the tears that the sinner could shed, nor all the confessions he could make, would avail to procure his salvation. These, no more than the blood of calves or any other sacrifice, could take away sin, or obtain the remission of sins. But, says the Apostle, Christ is not entered into the holy places made with hands, which are the figures of the true; but into heaven itself, now to appear in the presence of God, for us.

Nor yet that he should offer himself often, as the high Priest entereth into the holy place every year with blood of others.

For then must he often have suffered since the foundation of the world: but now, once in the end of the world hath this, our glorious high Priest, appeared to put away sin by the sacrifice of himself.

It is a most consolatory, nay, it is a transporting consideration, that Jesus Christ came in the end of the world to put away sin, by the sacrifice of himself.

We know he did not then display his almighty power by producing a physical change in the creature. This he could assuredly have done, yet this he did not do, but he put away sin by the sacrifice of himself, thereby evincing that he was indeed the Saviour of the world.

When the sacrifices under the law were offered up, for the sins of the people, their sins being first laid upon the appointed victim; although this memorable transaction wrought no physical change in the people; yet God, that God whose law was broken, beheld them as sinless as though they had never transgressed. But these sacrifices could not so effectually take away sin, as to render their continuation unnecessary; hence, their repetition; hence, the superiority of the substance of these figures, who now, once in the end of the world hath appeared to put away sin by the sacrifice of himself. Do not let us repeat the question. Whose sins hath he taken away? Are we not called upon to behold the Lamb of God that taketh away the sin of the world? And did not this fundamental truth, furnish the Apostle with a reason for exhorting the people to whom he preached, to reckon themselves indeed dead unto sin, but alive unto God by Jesus Christ our Lord? Romans vi. 11. Thus, while according to the testimony of their senses, they were dead to a life of holiness, they were according to the testimony of God, and as living by faith, to conclude they were dead indeed unto sin, and alive unto God by Jesus Christ.

O! how vast the difference between *faith* and *sense*, between the believer and the unbeliever, between him who gathereth with Christ, and putting on the Lord Jesus, walketh in him, as he hath received him, and those who judge themselves by themselves; so did not the man of Tarsus, but he was a christian, God had revealed his son in him, and his first wish was to be presented complete in the God man.

The Apostle concludes the ninth chapter of his Epistle to the Hebrews, by observing, that as it was appointed for all men once to die, but after this was the judgment; so Christ was once offered to bear the sins of many; upon this clause in the passage unbelievers thus remark and thus question; *to bear the sins of many*. Who were the many, whose sins he bore? If you can answer this question in our favour, you will indeed give us consolation. How abundant is our happiness, who can boldly assert, that God himself has given a full answer to this all important question; and an answer from which there can be no appeal. Isaiah, liii. 6, " All we like sheep have gone astray; we have turned every one to his own way, and the Lord hath laid on him the iniquity of us all" But the prophet Isaiah is not a solitary witness. The immediate harbinger of our Lord, called upon the multitude, to behold the Lamb of God, who taketh away the sin of the world. Yes, we can determine to a single individual, how many there are whose sins he bore in his own body on the cross, for we can say, that for whomsoever Christ died, their sins he bore, their sins are taken away, and, saith the spirit of truth, Jesus by the grace of God tasteth death for every man.

But the text concludes by an affirmation, that unto them who look for the appearance of our Saviour, he shall appear the second time without sin unto salvation.

It could not be the design of our Apostle, to teach the people, that on the second appearance of our Saviour, he should be more perfect, but that he should appear without those sins, which he had borne in his own body on the accursed tree, and the reason is obvious, he had previously put them away, by the sacrifice of himself.

The Apostle Paul, in the tenth chapter of this same Epistle to the Hebrews, proceeds to say, " For the law having a shadow of good things to come, and not the very image of the things, can never, with those sacrifices which they offered year by year continually, make the comers thereunto perfect." It is upon this insufficiency of the law, that the Apostle bases his assertion, that by the deeds of the law no flesh living can be justified. Our Lord commencing his humiliation saith, " Sacrifices and offering thou wouldest not, but a body hast thou prepared me."

And this body, prepared for the Redeemer, was the body, the head of which was sick, and the whole heart faint. This body is that very identical body, which having sinned, and come short of the glory of God, *fell in* the first Adam, and was prepared for the second, that he might take away its sinful character, that he might heal its wounds, that he might cure its diseases, that he might remove all its infirmities, and restore it to primeval rectitude. The royal Psalmist faithfully says, speaking by the spirit of God; yet have I set my King upon my holy hill of Zion, I will declare the decree: the Lord hath said unto me, thou art my son; this day have I begotten thee. And says David, ask of me, and I will give thee, the heathen for thine inheritence, and the uttermost parts of the earth for thy possession. But David is not alone in his testimony, the magnitude of God's kingdom is a theme of rapture, both to prophets and apostles. It is said to be a holy kingdom. The prophet Daniel, ii. 44, speaks energetically, " And in the days of these kings shall the God of heaven set up a kingdom, which shall never be destroyed: and the kingdom shall not be left to other people, but it shall break in pieces and consume all these kingdoms, and it shall stand forever." Again, vii. 14, " And there was given him dominion, and glory, and a kingdom, that all people, nations and languages, should serve him: his dominion is an everlasting dominion, which shall not pass away, and his kingdom that which shall not be destroyed."

From the Epistle to the Hebrews, we learn, that although the God of Israel had himself established the ceremonial law, yet, having done its office, performed its figurative part, and being incompetent to the accomplishment of his will, which will was the salvation of mankind, he had no pleasure therein. In burnt offerings and in sacrifices for sin thou hast no pleasure; although they are offered by the law.

But Jesus came to do the will of God, by the which will we are sanctified through the offering of the body of Christ Jesus once for all. This offering was effectual, both as to *quality* and *quantity*, for although our illustrious high Priest, was offered but once, yet having been offered up to death, he dieth no more; under the law, the high Priests continued daily ministering in the sanctuary, and offering those self-same sacrifices which can never do away sin; how soul satisfying the contrast. This man, after he had once offered himself a sacrifice for sin, set down on the right hand of God, expecting until his enemies should be made his foot-stool. Yea, verily by one offering he hath perfected forever those who are sanctified. Sanctification is as we have frequently said, strictly speaking, purification. It would be idle to talk of a sanctified sinner; people do not sufficiently consider, they would be shocked were we to tell them of a sanctified murderer, or a sanctified thief; yet we are taught to think, and to say, that *whoso offendeth in one point, is guilty of all,* and why indeed should we consider the breach of the sixth, seventh, or eighth commandment, as a more heinous crime, than the breach of the ninth or tenth? Yet we tolerate him who slandereth his neighbour, and him who coveteth his possessions, assigning him a place among those who are sanctified.

But this man, after he had offered one sacrifice for *sins*, (not simply for *sin*, but for *sins*, for all *sins*, committed by all sinners, at all times, and in all places,) forever set down on the right hand of God; on the right hand of the divine nature. The right hand is the place of honour and trust; sitting is an attitude of rest, therefore as God delighted in mercy, he called the place of his rest, the *mercy seat*. On the mercy seat God fixed his rest. Here, said he, I will abide forever. Mercy shall be built up forever Divine attribute of my God, thou art indeed the helpless sinner's theme, his daily plea, and thou shalt be my abiding plea, until my latest breath, until my soul escapes to the world of spirits, and then, and there, I will carry on the song, and it will be forever new.

Yes, he hath perfected forever them that are sanctified. If he, as the Lamb of God, took away the sins of the world, then in the same place, and in the same manner, the world of mankind were sanctified We pronounce every individual, whose sin by the grace of God, is taken away, completely sanctified; we do not hesitate to say, that all such individuals are perfect, even as their father who is in heaven is perfect, and the excellency of this salvation, of this sanctification, is its *durability;* for those who are sanctified, those who are saved, are *perfected forever,* for they are saved with an everlasting salvation; and although they are not as *happy,* they are, however, as *secure* as if they were already in heaven. To this truth, the Holy Ghost beareth witness; let us seriously attend to his testimony; it is our interest so to do, for it is altogether in our favour. Thus runs his evidence, and as it is the Holy Ghost who thus testifieth, we are assured he cannot bear false witness. Jeremiah xxxi. 31, 32, 33, 34:

" Behold, the days come, saith the Lord, that I will make a new covenant with the house of Israel, and with the house of Judah :

" Not according to the covenant, that I made with their fathers in the day that I took them by the hand to bring them out of the land of Egypt; which my covenant they brake, although I was an husband unto them, saith the Lord :

" But this shall be my covenant, that I will make with the house of Israel; After those days, saith the Lord, I will put my law in their inward parts, and write it in their hearts; and will be their God, and they shall be my people.

"And they shall teach no more every man his neighbour, and every man his brother, saying, Know the Lord : for they shall all know me from the least of them unto the greatest of them, saith the Lord : for I will forgive their iniquity, and I will remember their sin no more." *I will remember their sins no more.* There is, in the language of revelation, a divine benignity. My Bible is my treasure; I cannot for a moment relinquish it; it is my life; its words are pure words; I contrast its excellency with the doctrines and traditions of men, and I stand astonished at its immeasurable superiority. Should it be asked, if the writers of holy writ were not men, I answer, yes, but they were men divinely inspired; they spake as moved by the Holy Ghost. " But how are we to know they were moved by the Holy Ghost? Are there not thousands whose testimonies are at variance with the doctrines of scripture?" There is one evidence of the divinity of the sacred writings, that I confess, has great weight with me. The sacred writers preached not themselves, but Christ Jesus the Lord. God made choice of the prophets and apostles, as his servants to deliver his mind to the children of men; and he gave them power to say, to do, and also to suffer for his name sake. "Aye, so they said, and so may others say." Yes, but there was power given them *to do* what no one else did, and to these deeds they appealed. " They are gone, and we see not the evidences of which you speak." Their testimony continues, and will continue to the end of time; and when we reflect upon the characters of those who have assisted to preserve this sacred Book, who have translated and handed it down to us; when we recur to the natural and deep rooted enmity, which they so strongly evince to the leading doctrines of the sacred Oracles, I am constrained to say, that I think the holy writings contain no miracle more wonderful than their preservation; and, blessed be God, there is an internal conviction of the truth and divinity of holy writ, that bestows upon the distinguished individual, by whom it is possessed, enduring peace.

Much is said of prejudice and bigotry, and as an old man, I beg to be forgiven, if I again declare, I am prejudiced in favour of those divinely inspired pages, which constitute the volume of my treasures. I am pained, whenever I hear professors of faith in the christian religion, speaking lightly of the Bible, or doing or saying any thing which may directly or indirectly, contribute to weaken its authority.

It is said, there are various opinions formed of the Bible, even by those who consider its divine origin as unquestionable; and I have conversed with many who have professed to believe in the Bible, but then they have taken leave to make it speak their own language. " A great part of the Bible, it is asserted, will not admit of being taken literally, and what upon such occasions are we to do?" Search the scriptures carefully, diligently search them; compare scripture with scripture ; let one passage explain another, and you may then give them a literal reception; they will support each other.

" Why, this may do for private individuals. But you will never see all men of one mind; men will not agree." Well then, if they be wise, they will agree to differ.

But we will return to our blessed Apostle, our unerring expositor, who, having pointed out to the Hebrews the incalculable advantages they derived from the change of their dispensation; having dwelt upon the superiority of the new and living way to these paths of death, to which the administration of condemnation under the law immediately tended, proceeds in language beautifully and solemnly impressive, thus to exhort his brethren—" Let us draw near with a faithful heart," not deceitfully professing to believe the testimony of God, that it is the only rule given for our direction in religious matters, while we refuse to abide by its decision. Let us draw near with a *true heart*, with a heart established in the belief of the truth as it is in Jesus, in the full assurance of faith.

Much has been said, and much will be said of the faith of assurance; and as it relates to the faith generally brought into view, I wonder not, that this faith of assurance is so rare. But the christian's faith is a faith which admits not of doubt, and such who are acquainted with, and have this faith, never doubt. *The faith of the christian is the faith of God, which is as perfect as his words and works.*

Although we cannot read the Bible without reading much of the *faith of God*, *the faith of Christ*, yet is the value, the importance, the perfection of these faiths rarely contemplated. The promises, we are told, were made to Jesus, and if they were, he either believed these promises, or he did not. But if they be made to him, and he believe them, and if he be indeed the head of every man, then eternal praises be to the God who created, who redeemed, and who preserveth us. We have a full assurance of the performance of these promises; we are exhorted to run with patience the race set before us; we are directed to look unto Jesus *the author and finisher of our faith, who for the joy that was set before him,* endured the cross, despising the shame, and is set down at the right hand of the throne of God.

If the Apostle by *our* faith, intended the *faith* of *our minds* individually, then this faith could not be finished until our death. When we are said to believe in Christ, we believe in him as a *faithful* high Priest, in things pertaining both to God and to the people. Faith, whether existing in the *Saviour* or the *saved*, is the evidence of things not seen; and surely if God so loved the world as to give them his beloved Son to be the Saviour of the world, he certainly believed the ransom was complete; he believed he would be the world's Saviour. When Jesus laid down his life a ransom for sinners, he certainly believed they would be ransomed; and it was, therefore, that he endured the cross. Wherefore? For the joy that was set before him. When the divine Nature promised the human Nature, that he would give him the heathen for his inheritance, and the uttermost parts of the earth for his possession, he believed it; and he spake in firm faith when he said, all that the Father hath is mine, and all that the Father hath given unto me, shall come unto me.

Yes, there is the faith of God and the faith of Christ. Indeed the faith of Christ is that faith by which we are justified. Hence, saith the Apostle, Galatians ii. 16, " Knowing that a man is not justified by the works of the law, but by *the faith of Jesus Christ, even we have believed in Jesus Christ, that we might be justified by the faith of Christ.*" Here there is an evident distinction between the faith of Christ, and the faith of men. Assuredly there is a faith of God and a faith of Christ, and all this is *ours*. Let us, therefore, said the Apostle, hold fast the profession of our faith without wavering. The Apostle proceeds to render a reason, why we should hold fast the profession of our faith without wavering; because he is *faithful* who hath promised. We are greatly blessed, for we have in the divine Nature, and we receive from the hands of the bountiful, not only *works*, but *faith ;* yea, we have in Christ Jesus all spiritual blessings. The inference of the Apostle is acknowledged by reason, judgment, and gratitude. Let us, says he, consider one another, to provoke one another unto love and unto good works.

We are frequently called upon to attend to and prepare for the day of the Lord, that when the Redeemer cometh, he may find us in the paths of duty; for if we sin wilfully, after we have received the knowledge of the truth, there remaineth no more sacrifice for sins.

But a certain fearful looking for of judgment and fiery indignation which shall devour the adversaries. The Apostle, in the next verse, turns the attention of the Hebrews to that law, which he had been leading them to contrast with the present dispensation, and he reminds them that the people of God, (at that time convicted of disobedience to the precepts of the law) died without mercy; that is, they could not escape the sentence of death.

The Apostle proceeds, Of how much sorer punishment, suppose ye, shall he be thought worthy, who hath trodden under foot the son of God, and hath counted the blood of the covenant, wherewith he was sanctified, an unholy thing, and hath done despite unto the spirit of grace?

For we know, who hath said, vengeance belongeth unto me, I will recompense, saith the Lord. And again, the Lord shall judge his people.

Many of God's chosen people fell in the wilderness, consequent upon their loathing the manna with which they had been fed, and for their murmuring, frequent discontent, and marked disobedience. Numbers, xiv. 20—23.

"And the Lord said, I have *pardoned* according to thy word:

"But as truly as I live all the earth shall be filled with the glory of the Lord.

" Because all those men which have seen my glory, and my miracles, which I did in Egypt and in the wilderness, have tempted me now these ten times, and have not hearkened to my voice;

"Surely they shall not see the land which I sware unto their fathers, neither shall any of them that provoked me see it."

Thus, *God pardoned these people according to the supplication of Moses.* "But as for your carcases," saith God, verse 32, "*they shall fall in the wilderness,*" yet God *had pardoned them although they fell in the wilderness;* they suffered the death denounced by the law upon the disobedient, but as God had pardoned them, they will, no doubt, be in God's own time, again restored, agreeably to which saith the prophet Ezekiel,

"When I shall bring again their captivity, the captivity of Sodom and her daughters, and the captivity of Samaria and her daughters, then will I bring again the captivity of thy captives in the midst of them:

"When thy sisters, Sodom and her daughters, shall return to their former estate, and Samaria and her daughters shall return to their former estate, then thou and thy daughters shall return to your former estate." Signal vengeance was poured down from heaven upon these people, particularly Sodom and her daughters. Yet they, as Gentiles, will be brought in with the fulness of the Gentiles, at which period all Israel will be saved. My spirit is beyond measure elevated, it seems as if it would leap from its clay built tabernacle, when tracing the divinely beautiful correspondence in these sacred testimonies; an instance in point this moment presents, Isaiah xix. 19—25, " In that day shall there be an altar to the LORD in the midst of the land of Egypt, and a pillar at the border thereof to the LORD.

" And it shall be for a sign and for a witness unto the LORD of hosts in the land of Egypt: for they shall cry unto the LORD because of the oppressors, and he shall send them a Saviour, and a great one, and he shall deliver them.

" And the LORD shall be known to Egypt, and the Egyptians shall know the LORD in that day, and shall do sacrifice and oblation ; yea, they shall vow a vow unto the LORD, and perform it.

" And the LORD shall smite Egypt: he shall smite and heal it: and they shall return even to the LORD, and he shall be entreated of them, and shall heal them.

" In that day shall there be a highway out of Egypt to Assyria, and the Assyrian shall come into Egypt, and the Egyptian into Assyria, and the Egyptians shall serve with the Assyrians.

" In that day shall Israel be the third with Egypt and with Assyria, even a blessing in the midst of the land:

" Whom the LORD of hosts shall bless, saying, blessed be Egypt my people, and Assyria the work of my hands, and Israel mine inheritance."

By the mouth of two witnesses, saith the sacred historian, a report shall be established. But the christian can produce, from the treasury of his God, a cloud of witnesses to support and justify his faith. Nay, so connected and so consistent is the mass of evidence, that the wonder is, that there should exist a dissenting individual.

It is observable that both Isaiah and Ezekiel place the restoration of Israel in the third *class*, and it is remarkable that Sodom and her daughters were destroyed by fire from heaven. This fire, descending from heaven, was unquestionably eternal fire. These Sodomites suffered the vengeance of eternal fire; very well, this is granted; but when we learn from the prophet Ezekiel that they are to be restored, and even to take rank before the children of Israel, we are under the necessity of confessing, that though they suffered the vengeance of this *eternal fire*, it was not designed by God they should *eternally suffer under this vengeance, that they should forever experience the vengeance of this eternal fire.*

But if offenders before and under the Mosaic dispensation were thus chastised, of how much sorer punishment, suppose ye, shall he be thought worthy, who hath trodden under foot the son of God, and hath counted the blood of the covenant wherewith he was sanctified an unholy thing, and hath done despite to the spirit of grace?

Is there any sorer punishment than death? undoubtedly there is. Let us figure to ourselves for a moment, a person who has embraced the truth, who has tasted that the LORD is gracious—He hath hailed his Creator, not only as his maker, but as his Redeemer, and preserver, and he hath reposed in him, both for time and for eternity, unbounded confidence; when suddenly he falls from this grace, he accounts this blood of the covenant an unholy, an unprofitable thing! To whom now can he go for comfort, since he hath quitted him who alone hath the words of eternal life—He no more looketh unto Jesus, he looketh unto the law; his expectations are dreadful; nothing remaineth but a certain fearful looking for of fiery indignation, which shall devour him; he anticipates the hour when he shall call upon the rocks and mountains to fall upon him, and hide him from the wrath of the Lamb. Who can describe the terror, the anguish of his darkened, his despairing mind, when he exclaims, "It is a fearful thing to fall into the hands of the living God?" Say my soul, my emancipated soul, is not such a situation as this, worse, infinitely worse than death? Yes, this darkness, this despair, is indeed a calamity infinitely sorer than death.

But was the *spirit*, was the *soul*, of this suffering Apostle, *sanctified by the blood of the covenant*, by that very blood which his *conduct* now demonstrates, he accounts an *unholy thing?* Was the spirit to which he hath done despite, a *spirit of grace?* And is this subject of the judgment, an individual who *belonged to, and was one of the people of God?* Well then, when Sodom and her daughters are restored, he may be restored also, nay, he absolutely will be restored, for the restoration of all things has been preached by all God's holy prophets, ever since the world began.

We know who hath said, Vengeance belongeth unto me; I will recompense; and again, the Lord shall judge his people. Men, mortal men, if they be yet in the way of the transgressor, in whose ways are misery and destruction, read the testimonies of God with a veil upon their hearts; and hence, they cannot behold mercy and truth meeting together, righteousness and peace embracing each other. Hence, they are ever setting at odds the attributes of heaven. They produce discord, jarring discord, even in the regulations, and plans of the fountain of light, harmony and order, and with one perfection of Deity they are constantly aiming to wound another! Yet, notwithstanding the combining efforts of men and devils, mercy and truth can, and will, as they have always done, meet together, righteousness and peace shall, as they have hitherto done, embrace each other.

Such is the result of the dealings of our God. When the Lord judgeth his people, when the day of vengeance of our God shall arrive, it will terminate in comforting all that mourn. This shall be the conclusion of the matter. The top stone will be brought forth with joy, and every one will unite with shouting, and with exclamations of rapture, crying grace, grace unto it.

Yea, every creature in heaven, and on earth, and under the earth, and in the sea; yea, all of them shall, with one voice say, "Thou art worthy, for thou wast slain, and hast redeemed us to God by thy blood; therefore I will praise thee, O Lord, while every faculty of my soul shall devoutly echo the loud Amen, and Amen."*

---

* These reflections, confined at first to the sacerdotal vestments of the Israelitish high Priest, proved in their progress miscellaneous, and were unexpectedly enlarged. The reflections were dictated by the author a few days since, more than eighteen months having revolved since the period which he has impressive called the *day of his death*.

The melancholy event which deprived him, by a paralytic stroke of the use of his limbs, took place on the 19th of October, one thousand eight hundred and nine.

But, for the happiness of his friends, he still continues to possess enough of mind, to console and inform those, with whom he is intimately connected.

The same energy, the same evangelical faith, the same lucid discrimination of doctrines, the same devout homage, and pious gratitude to the

CONVERSATION.

A gentleman entered my study, and fixing his eyes upon me, said, I suspect you do not know me Sir?

Murray. I cannot recollect your name Sir.

Gentleman. Thirty years ago I saw you, and, Sir, I felt you too, and in consequence of feeling you, I visited you, nor have I ever since lost sight of you.

M. You do me honour, Sir.

G. I honour your Creator, Sir, for to him both you, and I, are indebted for every good.

M. Your observation becomes the mouth of a gratefully dependant being. All praise, and every acknowledgment is unquestionably due to the God by whom we were made.

G. To convince you how deeply I was impressed by the first discourse I heard you deliver, although thirty years have since elapsed, I will delineate it to you, nor do I believe that I shall deviate, in point of doctrine, in a single particular. To confess the truth, I rarely pass a day without rehearsing this same sermon, for it was the instrument by which I received *a hope full of immortality*. Are you willing to hear me, Sir?

M. I am all attention, Sir.

G. Well, Sir, interrupt me if I should be wrong. It was about thirty years ago, more or less, that I entered a church with a number of other triflers, merely to hear what the stranger, the babbler, as we licentiously styled you, could say for himself; but never, in the whole course of my life, was I so much astonished; never was I so completely confounded. Your prayer was impressive; I was awed and solemnized. You named your text, Matthew iii. 10, "And now also the axe is laid to the *root* of the

---

Redeemer of the world, which has, through a series of years so strongly marked his career, characterizes and distinguishes the reflections, but perhaps the multiplied remarks and investigations, are not altogether as methodical, and luminous, as he could have rendered them, had they been the result of those happy hours, when he was blest by the full enjoyment of intellectual vigor. Editor.

trees; therefore every tree which bringeth not forth good fruit, is hewn down and cast into the fire." Do you remember the evening, Sir?

M. Not particularly, Sir; but I have frequently considered that passage.

G. Well, Sir; you read your text, and having thus done, you paused, remarked, and questioned. " *Stop, indulge me once more; did we read correctly? Is the axe laid to the roots* of the *trees,* or is it laid to the *root* of the trees? Yea, verily, we have rendered the passage verbatim; it is *root* in the *singular,* it is *trees* in the *plural.* " This caught and fixed my attention; I was roused; I began to *feel* as well as to *hear.* You forcibly entreated your audience to *observe* the axe was not laid to the *roots* of the trees. I started; what can this man mean? *Root* in the *singular, trees in the plural!* What is it? You proceeded. Every tree which bringeth not forth good fruit is hewn down and cast into the fire. I listened with all my soul to every word you uttered. You informed us, that men were compared to trees; that there could be but two sorts of trees, *good* and *bad;* and that a *good tree* could not bring forth *bad fruit,* neither could a *bad tree* bring forth *good fruit;* you proceeded to demonstrate, that nothing could be good which did not, in every particular, correspond with the perfection of God's holy law; and I remember you derived all your authorities from scripture, by which sacred writings, you proved incontrovertibly, that whoso offended in one point was guilty of all; and it was made evident to my understanding, and that from the same divine source, that there was none good; no, not one. I was exceedingly, and I will confess, distressingly alarmed. Bless me, thought I, where are we now? I came into this church to hear a Universalist; yes, he is a Universalist with a vengeance; but it is universal damnation which he preaches. I promise you my sensations were truly horrible; for although I had united with the multitude to ridicule you, I still cherished a *secret* hope, that I might derive consolation from your teaching; yet you had precipitated me to the brink of despair! But while my astonishment momently augmented as if you had read my thoughts, and it appeared to me you looked full in my face, you proceeded to say, " but it will be asked, who then can be saved?" You answered this most important question, and your answer removed a mountain from my bosom. If, said you, the axe had not been laid to the *root* of the trees, no individual could have been saved. It was then, that you began to preach unto us, Jesus, the *root* as well as the *offspring* of David, the bright and morning star, who, when lifted up from the earth, drew all men unto him, so that the love of Christ constrained the Apostle to say, if one died for all, then were all dead; and you proved from the sacred volume, that one did indeed die for all. It had been said, you remarked, that in many places the word *all*, did not mean *all;* but if all did not mean all, *every one* must assuredly mean all and *every one ;* and if the axe be laid to the *root* of the *trees*, and if the prophet Malachi in the first verse of his fourth chapter of his prophecy was correct; if in that day, that burned as the oven all the proud, and all that did wickedly were as the stubble burned up, leaving them neither root nor branch, then the prophet showed us what has since been accomplished. It was, said you, in this day of the LORD which burned as an oven, when the head of every man being lifted up, drew all men unto him, that this head of every man finished transgression and made an end of sin. I recollect you summoned the prophet Daniel to your aid. After three score and two weeks shall Messiah be cut off, but not for himself: and the people of the prince shall come, shall destroy the city, and the sanctuary, and the end thereof shall be with a flood, and unto the end of the war desolations are determined. When Messiah was cut off, then was the axe laid to the *root* of the *trees ;* and when he came to the close of his sufferings, when he pronounced, it is finished, and bowing his head, gave up the ghost, then did the Lamb of God take away the sin of the world. Then as the *root* was holy, so were the *branches*. Romans xi. 16.

It was upon that, to me, memorable evening, that the scriptures broke forth upon me in all their beautiful consistency. The testimony was most glorious ; never can that evening be blotted from my memory. From that moment I have perused the sacred volume with pleasure, with gratitude. It hath become a source of information, a source of constant delight. But, Sir, now we are upon this subject, permit me to say, as I may never again be indulged with an opportunity of seeing you, that I wish to make a request ; have I permission ?

M. Undoubtedly, Sir.

G. I have heard, that you write your sermons before you deliver them, and then commit them to memory. If my information be correct, I presume you preserve those productions. The second time I heard you was upon the dress of the Jewish high Priest, and from that moment I have been charmed with Aaron's dress. Will you favour me with a copy of that discourse?

M. You have been misinformed, Sir; I have never yet been in the habit of writing down even my text. I frequently search for it after I reach the pulpit; and I have often found it chosen for me by an unknown hand, and pinned upon the cushion.

G. I am sorry for it, sorry indeed; can you not name the heads of that discourse, and I will endeavour to retain them in my memory.

M. Alas! it is impossible, at least at this time; but when I have leisure and freedom, I will endeavour to recollect and arrange my ideas upon the holy garments, and should I be able to please myself, I will furnish you with a copy.

G. You will oblige me exceedingly; but I am afraid you will forget me.

M. I wish I was as sure of remembering the sermon, as I am of not forgetting you.

This conversation was preserved in my Journal as a memorandum, and it is transcribed as another proof of the folly of procrastination. I delayed to comply with the wish of this warm hearted christian; and now when I am solicited for my views of this symbolic dress, and told by many, that it will greatly enrich my contemplated publication, enfeebled by a weight of years, and still more by infirmities, I have hardly produced the shadow of what once lived in my understanding; but my partial friends, and I presume, few others, *will* peruse these volumes, will accept my ardent *will* instead of more vigorous *deeds*. I have come the nearest to obedience which my imbecility will permit.

SKETCH VI.

Exodus xl. 33, 34, 35.

First, The work was finished. "*It is finished, said the Redeemer of the world.*"

Secondly, Immediately on the completion of the work, the glory of the Lord filled the tabernacle. 1 Kings, viii. 10, "And it came to pass when the priests were come out of the holy place, that the cloud filled the house of the Lord." Chapter xiii. 21, 22, "And the Lord went before them by day in a pillar of a cloud, to lead them the way; and by night in a pillar of fire, to give them light; to go by day and night. He took not away the pillar of the cloud by day, nor the pillar of fire by night from before the people." Ezekiel xliii. 4, 5, "And the glory of the Lord came into the house by the way of the gate whose prospect is toward the east. So the Spirit took me up and brought me into the inner court, and behold the glory of the Lord filled the house."

Thirdly, When the glory of the Lord filled the tabernacle, Moses was not able to enter therein. 1 Kings viii. 11, "So that the priests could not stand to minister because of the cloud: for the glory of the Lord had filled the house of the Lord." 2 Chronicles, v. 13, 14, "It came even to pass, as the trumpeters and singers were as one, to make one sound to be heard in praising and thanking the Lord, and when they lifted up their voice with the trumpets and cymbals and instruments of music, and praised the Lord, saying, For he is good; for his mercy endureth forever: that then the house was filled with a cloud, even the house of the Lord; so that the priests could not stand to minister by reason of the cloud: for the glory of the Lord had filled the house of God."

Either this tabernacle and every thing which appertained thereto was figurative of, and pointed to the dealings of the Creator with mankind in general, or it is of no consequence to any part of the human family, except the select people among whom it was reared. Human nature is, in various parts of sacred writ, said to be the *house of God*, *the building of God*, and the *temple of God*. When the tabernacle was finished, it was filled by the glory of the Lord; when the plans of God are finished, the human building of Jehovah will be filled with his glory. And truly as I live, saith the Lord, the whole earth shall be filled with my glory, and the knowledge of the Lord shall cover the earth as the waters cover the sea. *What earth?* The insensate clod on which we tread, is not susceptible of knowledge. *The sons and daughters of men are the earth* of which God the Lord speaketh. This view of the text, renders it deeply and importantly interesting to every human being; the exposition becomes easy, and the result is glorious.

SKETCH VII.

Leviticus i. 4, 5.

First, The hand of the representative of the people was placed upon the head of the sacrifice, before it could be accepted as an atonement, thus evincing an acknowledgment of guilt, and of the justice of that sentence which pronounceth, the *soul* that *sinneth shall die.*

Secondly, After this transaction, the sacrifice was accepted; and it shall be accepted for him, to make atonement for him. What do the sacred oracles teach respecting the atonement? Daniel ix. 24, " Seventy weeks are determined upon thy people, and upon thy holy city, to finish the transgression, and to make an end of sins, and to make reconciliation for iniquity, and to bring in everlasting righteousness." 2 Corinthians v. 19, " To wit, that God was in Christ reconciling the world unto himself, not imputing their trespasses unto them." Ephesians ii. 7, " That in the ages to come, he might shew the exceeding riches of his grace, in his kindness towards us through Christ Jesus." Colossians i. 14, " In whom we have redemption through his blood, even the forgiveness of sins." 1 John ii. 1, 2, " My little children, these things I write unto you, that ye sin not. And if any man sin, we have an Advocate with the Father, Jesus Christ the righteous: And he is the propitiation for our sins: and not for ours only, but also for the sins of the whole world."

Thirdly, And he shall kill the bullock before the Lord. And the priests, Aaron's sons, shall bring the blood, and shall sprinkle the blood round about upon the altar. Blessed be God, that our expositors are the prophets, the Redeemer of men, and the apostles. Isaiah lii. 13, 14, 15, " Behold, my servant shall deal prudently; he shall be exalted and extolled, and be very high. As many were astonished at thee; his visage was so marred more than any man, and his form more than the sons of men: So shall he sprinkle many nations; the kings shall shut their mouths at him: for that which had not been told them shall they see; and that which they had not heard shall they consider." Hebrews

xii. 24, "And to Jesus the mediator of the new covenant, and to the blood of sprinkling, that speaketh better things than that of Abel." 1 Peter i. 2, " Elect according to the foreknowledge of God the Father, through sanctification of the Spirit, unto obedience and sprinkling of the blood of Jesus Christ: Grace unto you, and peace be multiplied."

It is observable, that the inwards and legs of the sacrifice were to be washed with water. The following scriptures elucidate this regulation. Ephesians ii. 16, "And that he might reconcile both unto God, in one body by the cross, having slain the enmity thereby." 1 Peter ii. 24, " Who, his own self, bare our sins in his own body on the tree, that we, being dead to sins, should live unto righteousness: by whose stripes ye were healed." 1 Corinthians vi. 11, "And such were some of you: but ye are washed, but ye are sanctified, but ye are justified in the name of the LORD Jesus, and by the spirit of our God. Titus iii. 5, 6, " Not by works of righteousness which we have done, but according to his mercy, he saved us by the washing of regeneration, and renewing of the Holy Ghost; which he shed on us abundantly, through Jesus Christ our Saviour." John xiii. 5—10, " After that he poureth water into a bason, and began to wash the disciples' feet, and to wipe them with the towel wherewith he was girded. Then cometh he to Simon Peter; and Peter said unto him, LORD, dost thou wash my feet? Jesus answered and said unto him, What I do thou knowest not now; but thou shalt know hereafter. Peter saith unto him, Thou shalt never wash my feet. Jesus answered him, If I wash thee not, thou hast no part with me. Simon Peter saith unto him, LORD, not my feet only, but also my hands and my head. Jesus saith to him, He that is washed, needeth not save to wash his feet, but is clean every whit." This assertion will not admit a literal acceptation; for it is undeniably true, that as an individual, *my feet* may be perfectly clean, and my hands and my face much soiled. The consistency of this passage is to be found in him, in whom all things consist. Without a figure or parable, Jesus spake not to the people. The human nature, in the aggregate, formed one complete man; the man Christ Jesus, the God-man. Of this illustrious, this comprehensive man, the feet only were defiled, when the *iniquity of my heels compass me about, &c. &c.* In this view, and in this view only, the consistency and propriety of the passage is transcendently beautiful. He that is washed, needeth not save to wash his feet, but is clean every whit. Thus shall Jesus Christ, separated from the *iniquity of his heels, of the human nature,* agreeably to the testimony of the Apostle Paul, Hebrews ix. 28, be manifested *without sin unto salvation.*

The washing or purifying the inwards of the sacrifice, points not only to that purification which we obtain in the Redeemer, who is the heart as well as the head of every man, and who is made of God unto us, sanctification, but also to that individual cleansing with which the family of man shall be cleansed, when he, who is their life, shall appear, when we shall see our Redeemer as he is, and be made like unto him in all things conformable unto our glorious head. The cleansing the feet, as applicable to individuals, may refer to externals; to our adorning the doctrines of God our Saviour. As ye have received the LORD Jesus, so walk ye in him.

SKETCH VIII.

LEVITICUS ii. 12, 13.

First, WHENCE the command, that the first fruits should not be burned upon the altar for a sweet savour? Was not Christ Jesus considered as the first fruits? Undoubtedly he was thus considered in his resurrection. 1 Corinthians xv 20, "But now is Christ risen from the dead, and become the first fruits of them that slept."

Secondly, Israel is considered as the first fruits. Jeremiah ii. 3, "Israel was holiness to the LORD, and the first fruits of his increase."

Thirdly, Believers are spoken of as the first fruits. Romans viii. 23, "And not only they, but ourselves also, which have the first fruits of the Spirit, even we ourselves groan within ourselves, waiting for the adoption, to wit, the redemption of our body." Again xi. 16, "For if the first fruit be holy, the lump is also holy: and if the root be holy, so are the branches." And James i. 18, "Of his own will begat he us with the word of truth, that we should be a kind of first fruits of his creatures." Revelations xiv. 4, "These are they which follow the Lamb whithersoever he goeth. These were redeemed from among men, being the first fruits unto God, and to the Lamb."

Fourthly, What are we to understand by the regulation so solemnly established? And every oblation of thy meat offering shalt thou season with salt, neither shalt thou suffer the salt of the covenant of thy God to be lacking from thy meat offering: with all thine offerings thou shalt offer salt. Salt literally preserves a substance from putrefaction; salt then is the figure of salvation. But we have salvation, eternal salvation, only in Christ Jesus the LORD. This salt is a figure of the divinity of his nature, without which divinity, his humanity would have seen corruption. Our Saviour addressing his disciples, Matthew v. 13, thus speaketh. " Ye are the salt of the earth: but if the salt has lost its savour wherewith shall it be salted? What is this savour? 2 Corinthians ii. 14, 15, "Now thanks be unto God, which always causeth us to triumph in Christ, and maketh manifest the savour of his knowledge by us in every place. For we are unto God a sweet savour of Christ in them that are saved, and in them that perish." Colossians iv. 6, " Let your speech be alway with grace, seasoned with salt, that ye may know how ye ought to answer every man."

Fifthly, This salt is called the salt of the covenant, the salt of the covenant of God which must *never be lacking* from the meat offerings, and with every offering this salt must be offered. What is this salt of the covenant? We have already considered it as the salvation of God, and it is spoken of as an everlasting salvation. Numbers xviii. 19, " All the heave-offerings of the holy things, which the children of Israel offer unto the LORD, have I given thee, and thy sons and thy daughters with thee, by a statute forever: it is a covenant of salt forever before the LORD unto thee, and to thy seed with thee." Isaiah xlii. 6, " I the LORD, have called thee in righteousness, and will hold thine hand, and will keep thee, and give thee for a covenant to the people, for a light of the Gentiles." The thirty-first chapter of Jeremiah, is full to our purpose.

" And they shall teach no more every man his neighbour, and every man his brother, saying, Know the LORD: for they shall all know me from the least of them unto the greatest of them, saith the LORD: for I will forgive their iniquity, and I will remember their sin no more.

SKETCH VIII.

"Thus saith the LORD, which giveth the sun for a light by day, and the ordinances of the moon and of the stars for a light by night, which divideth the sea when the waves thereof roar; the LORD of hosts is his name:

"If those ordinances depart from before me, saith the LORD, then the seed of Israel also shall cease from being a nation before me forever.

"Thus saith the LORD; If heaven above can be measured, and the foundations of the earth searched out beneath, I will also cast off all the seed of Israel for all that they have done, saith the LORD."

But the shades of evening would descend upon us, ere I could detail to my beloved hearers a moiety of those sacred testimonies which describe this *covenant*, this *new* and *everlasting covenant*, in other words, *eternal salvation*. A covenant of salt. Every one, saith the Redeemer, shall be salted with fire, and every sacrifice shall be salted with salt. Matthew, iii. 11, "I indeed baptize you with water unto repentance: but he that cometh after me is mightier than I, whose shoes I am not worthy to bear: he shall baptize you with the Holy Ghost and with fire."

But as for the oblation of the first fruits ye shall offer them unto the LORD, but they *shall not be burnt upon the altar for a sweet savour*. What is this that shall not be burnt upon the altar for a sweet savour? The sacred oracles have designated these first fruits. Jesus the elect precious, the people of Israel, and believers. Perhaps the non consumption of these first fruits by fire may intend the exemption from trial, by which, select characters will be indulged at the final winding up of the great drama. The works of genuine believers are not then to be tried; *they have judged themselves and are not therefore again to be judged;* upon them the caustic flame has done its office, and they have entered into the joy of their LORD.

Reflections upon the SABBATH DAY, *dictated by the author upon the ninth day of June, one thousand eight hundred and eleven, being* LORD'S DAY, *and lacking only nine days of twenty months from the commencement of his melancholy and debilitating confinement.*

MUCH is said in the sacred volume of the number seven. It is a *perfect number.* It takes in the whole of creation of *labour* and of *rest:* for though the Almighty could not, *as a Creator,* be weary, yet it is said that on his finishing the work of creation, and finding it all good, *very good,* not admitting of addition, the faithful Creator *rested* from all his work, and hallowed the *seventh day.* It was an *holy day:* it was a *sign* between God the Creator, and man the created.

It appears to me, that neither Jew nor Gentile have allowed sufficient weight to *this sign.* There is no sign more frequently, nor more solemnly spoken of in the book of God; and the people of God, during their first residence in the possession given to them, and to their children, seemed to be fully sensible of this truth, in the *letter* at least, if not in the *spirit.* Of the *genuine* spirit of this sacred *sign,* they never could be made sensible, without the teaching of that spirit, which exhibits to the understanding, him who is the glorious substance of this expressive figure.

The Sabbath is first mentioned in the book of Exodus, xx. 8—11, " Remember the Sabbath day to keep it holy. Six days shalt thou labour, and do all thy work: But the seventh day is the *Sabbath* of the LORD thy God: in it thou shalt not do any work, thou, nor thy son, nor thy daughter, thy man servant, nor thy maid servant, nor thy cattle, nor thy stranger that is within thy gates: For in six days the LORD made heaven and earth, and rested the seventh day: wherefore the LORD blessed the Sabbath day and hallowed it."

Six days shalt thou labour; this may be a *permission*, or a *command*, perhaps the *former;* but the seventh day is the Sabbath of the Lord thy God. We are told that God blessed the Sabbath day, ordained it a day of blessing to the people, and to himself. It was to be an holy day; but it is observable that on these holy days the people who kept them were to do no work. They did not therefore render the day holy by any work of theirs, nor did the Creator render the work holy by any work of his; for his works were finished, all perfectly finished, all pronounced by the God who made them, good, very good, needing no addition from God nor man. This day then was set apart for rest, and, that God's people may have leisure to contemplate with holy wonder, the finished works of Omnipotence, they are called upon to cease from every thing that could allure them from devout and appropriate contemplation.

But in the sacred book of God, we are frequently reminded that this *Sabbath* was a *sign* between God and his people, and those who are acquainted with this precious book, and with this *sabbatical sign*, will view the holy symbol with devout gratitude and never ending admiration.

Our Apostle was blest with an acquaintance with the sacred oracles of God, and with this *sabbatical sign;* and being led by the grace of God to the substance of this symbol, he was anxious to bring his brethren and his kinsfolks, into the knowledge of the same glorious truth, which so effectually irradiated his own understanding. A recurrence to the fourth chapter of Paul's Epistle to his Hebrew brethren, will furnish a striking illustration of this subject. Thus the man of Tarsus expresses himself, "Let us therefore, fear, lest, a promise being left us of entering into *his rest*, any of you should seem to come short of it. For we which have believed do enter into rest, as he said, as I have sworn in my wrath, *if they shall enter into my rest, although the works were finished from the foundation of the world.* For he spake in a certain place of the *seventh day* on this wise, and God did rest the *seventh day from all his works*. And in this place, again, if they shall enter into my rest. Seeing, therefore, it remaineth that some must enter therein, and they to whom it was first preached entered not in because of unbelief. Again he limiteth a certain day, saying in David, to-day, after so long a time, as it is said, to-day if ye will hear his voice, harden not your hearts; for if Jesus had given them rest, then would he not afterwards have spoken of another day. There remaineth, therefore, a rest to the people of God. *For he that is entered into his rest, he also hath ceased from his own works, as God did from his."*

Such was the use made by this well instructed scribe of this symbol, and indeed every one who is taught of God will see that this grand figure pointed to Jesus. Jesus Christ is that day star, in which his people will, and do rejoice, in which they cease from their labours, as God did from his. Yea, they are exceeding glad therein. Jesus is emphatically the *day of the* LORD; he is the light of the world; he it is who is the *day of salvation.* There is salvation in no other name. 2 Corinthians, vi. 2, " For he saith I have heard thee in a time accepted, and in the day of salvation have I succoured thee: behold, now is the accepted time, behold, now is the day of salvation."

God in the beginning made two great lights, the one to rule the day, and the other to rule the night; he made the stars also. And the holy spirit assures us, these luminaries were made not only for seasons, but for *signs;* and this ruler of the day is truly a very striking, significant sign. This luminous *sign* was manifested on the fourth day of creation; and the transcendent *substance* of this *sign* was manifested on the fourth day of time; for a *thousand years are in the sight of God as one day;* so saith the oracles of truth, and Christ Jesus was born on the *fourth thousand year* of the world. When the orient beams of day break from the chambers of the east, how beautifully glorious is the sign: But when, by an eye of faith, we catch a glimpse of the divine *substance of this sign*, when we behold the sun of righteousness rising with healing under his wings, how do our souls rejoice. How do our spirits magnify the LORD. The day of the LORD is indeed a day of emancipation, a day of rest. We repeat, and we delight to repeat, Christ Jesus is the day star, the star of Bethlehem. It is this splendid day star of which the Apostle Peter speaks, in his second General Epistle, i. 19, " We have also a more sure word of prophecy; whereunto ye do well that ye take heed, as unto a light that shineth in a dark place, until the day dawn, and the day star arise in your hearts."

How unclouded is our holy day, the day of the LORD, the true light that lighteneth every man that cometh into the world. O ye highly favoured children of men, it cannot be matter of wonder that the angels desire to look into this mystery. To those bright inhabitants of the upper world, it must indeed be profoundly mysterious to behold their sovereign, as our Saviour, wrapt in flesh!! Great, astonishingly great, is the mystery of Godliness! God manifested in the flesh! in other words, The true light, dwelling in the darkness, and the darkness comprehending it not, *yet the true light comprehendeth the darkness.*

But they who were sometimes darkness, are now light in the LORD; with strict propriety, therefore, are God's children, the children of light, exhorted to walk in the light; blessed are they who walk in the light, they stumble not as those who walk in the darkness; who have no knowledge of this light of the world, who have never yet put on the LORD Jesus, and who of course cannot walk in him, who cannot *rest* in him, in him who is truly *our rest, which rest is glorious.*

In this state, however, this rest is broken; but in this rest we are destined to enjoy, more than faith can imagine. What though in this dark distempered state, we see through a glass darkly, yet let us keep our eyes steadfastly fixed on this light of life, on this light which is indeed our life, the true light, the unequivocal *sign* of the love of God!

But we hear of *Sabbaths* in the plural; undoubtedly we do, and all those Sabbaths are good, or they would not be given for *signs*. I am peculiarly delighted with the last *sabbatical sign*, the yearly sign. How good is our God to indulge us with weekly signs, with monthly signs, and with yearly signs; that we may never forget his loving kindness. What a soul transporting sound, must the sound of the trumpet, mentioned in Leviticus have been? surely, the most rapturous, the most exhilerating that ever vibrated on the mortal ear; it can only be surpassed by that last trumpet which is destined to raise the dead. I am charmed by the commencement of a hymn, which I have a thousand times repeated.

> "Blow ye the trumpet, blow,
> The glad, the solemn sound,
> Let all the nations know,
> To earth's remotest bound,
> The year of Jubilee is come,
> Return ye ransomed sinners home."

But the trumpet was to sound on the *tenth* day of the *seventh* month. What a divine figure, the *tenth* and the *seventh!* these are both considered as perfect numbers. The kingdom of heaven was likened unto *ten* virgins. Seven days comprized the whole of creation, and rest; the fulness of the Creator, and created Seven and three are ten; what is the three? There are three who bear witness in heaven, the Father, the word, and the spirit. These three complete the ten; thus the divine and the human nature constitute a perfect whole. It was on the day of atonement the trumpet was to sound. It was to sound throughout the *whole land*, proclaiming liberty, divine *liberty* to the whole of Emmanuel's land, and, as the sons of Israel were so well acquainted with the *letter* of this symbolic institution, what strong emotions must have struggled in their enraptured bosoms, when the glorious sound of the emancipating trumpet broke upon their ears. Especially those desolate beings enchained by servitude, and kept out of their hereditary possessions: how did their harassed, woe worn souls, leap for joy: what elevation of spirit, what universal agitation. Is there a heart which is not lifted with divine enthusiasm, is there a bosom which doth not swell with immeasurable transport at beholding the Redeemer enter the synagogue, at seeing him receive the book, at hearing him read? and when we trace his selection to the prophecy of Isaiah lxi. 1, 2, "The spirit of the LORD God is upon me; because the LORD hath anointed me to preach good tidings unto the meek; he hath sent me to bind up the broken hearted, to proclaim liberty to the captive, and the opening of the prison to them that are bound; to proclaim the acceptable year of the LORD and the day of vengeance of our God; to comfort all that mourn." And chapter lxiii. verse 4, " For the day of vengeance is in my heart, and the year of my redeemed is come. Jeremiah, xxxiv 8, 9, " This is the word that came unto Jeremiah from the LORD after that the king Zedekiah had made a covenant with all the people that were at Jerusalem, to proclaim liberty unto them. That every man should let his man servant, and every man his maid servant being an Hebrew, or an Hebrewess, go free; that none should serve himself, to wit, of a Jew his brother." John viii. 35, 36, "And the servant abideth not in the house forever: but the son abideth ever. If the son therefore shall make you free, ye shall be free indeed." Ephesians iii. 14, 15, " For this cause I bow my knees unto the Father of our Lord Jesus Christ, of whom the whole family of heaven and earth is named." In the year of this Jubilee ye shall return, every man to his possession. When the trumpet shall sound, every man shall return to his possession. In my Father's house are many mansions, I go to prepare a place for you. Well, then, I do homage to my God, and I exult that I am a man. Gracious God, my bounding heart swells as it would burst its prison, while the gladdened spirit immeasurably elevated, is mounting to its heavenly home ; my stiffened limbs too seem regaining their elasticity, and I am as if soaring upward to worlds beyond the sky. Well, well, what though it be true, that I am still enchained by cold and comfortless palsy, and oppressed by a combination of lurking foes ; what though I have been nearly twenty months imprisoned in the jaws of death, yet the trumpet will sound, and the year of Jubilee will come. These galling fetters shall be knocked off. I, my best self, shall be emancipated ; *I, even I, the cripple I, shall clap my glad wings and soar away.* But how know I this? How do I know it? Why the Lord Jesus himself hath preached liberty to the captive, and the opening of the prison to them that are bound.

Do you say I have lost sight of my subject? No, by no means; Jesus is *my rest, my eternal Sabbath ;* and whatever points to bliss beyond the sky, to bliss unutterable, points to him.

One remark I cannot forbear repeating; throughout all these Sabbaths and holy times, no *labour was to be performed by the people to whom they were given.* The people in every possible description, were particularly and emphatically enjoined to do no work on the Sabbath day. God determined to perform, and he did perform his own work without their assistance. These seasons, these Sabbath seasons, were seasons of rest, of rejoicing. It is wonderful this is not more generally taken into view. Thou shalt do no manner of work ; such is the commandment of the God whom we adore. The inference is plain ; God does not think so highly of our performances as we ourselves do, yet he is very willing we should be found in the practice of good works, even upon the Sabbath day. The author and finisher of our faith, thus questioned his pious children, who were judging and condemning him as a sinner—Pray is it lawful to do good on the Sabbath day? They did not know, that the inquirer was himself the Lord of the Sabbath ; that it was made for him for whom all things were made, and that it was a constant witness for him to the people.

The Sabbath is a luminous *sign* not only of the salvation of the human family, but of the *nature* of that salvation; that it was by *grace* and not by *works*. "*By grace are ye saved.*" It is a glorious truth, that we are saved, and that it is by grace we are saved. Yes, truly, it is by grace, both in the first instance and in the last; for the top stone will be brought forth with shouting, crying grace, grace unto it.

The believer of these truths ardently longs for his heavenly home. Be not angry, O my friends, if I reiterate my wishes to depart; if I am in haste to be gone. I pray the God of my salvation, to grant me patience to wait quietly for the blessed, the liberating period; but indeed, and in truth, hope deferred maketh the heart sick; and of my connexion with this sluggish body, I am truly sick and very weary.

The twenty-fifth chapter of Leviticus contains many particulars, that are highly worthy observation The august Creator of the universe, considers both the land and its possessors as his own; at all times they are his own, nor is the right to dispose of themselves for wise purposes, delegated to them, a continued right; Its duration is limited. Hath any one sold his possession, any of his kindred may redeem it; or should he have the means in his own hands, he may redeem it himself; but if neither his kindred nor himself be able to redeem it, still it shall not be *finally lost.* In the Jubilee, it shall return to its original owner without money and without price:

> "O Jesus ever blest, thou art our Jubilee,
> Our restoration and our rest,
> Are both, dear Lamb, in thee.
> In thee our souls have found
> Whate'er we lost, and more,
> We see thy grace much more bound,
> Than sin had done before"

Through the whole of these transactions respecting persons, places, and things, the grand reason for the restoration is given in few words. "*The land shall not be sold forever: for the land is mine, saith the* LORD."

But in the year of Jubilee, they were enjoined neither to sow their grounds, nor to gather the grapes in, of their vine undressed. Whence then were they to derive their support? I will take care of that, saith the LORD; I will cause the earth to bring forth abundantly, so that ye shall feed throughout the sabbatic years, and through the year of Jubilee upon its increase; and thus you shall suffer no loss by your obedience to my command; to this, however, they refused credit. How is it possible? What, the earth give her increase without culture? No, it can never be. This, no doubt, they called *reasoning;* they could not see how man should reap what he did not sow; and many were ready to say, let them make the experiment, let them pass the seed time, and see how they will fare in harvest. Well, I will venture, says one; aye, it will do very well for you, says another, it will suit you admirably; you are an indolent fellow. "Ye are idle, ye are idle," said the task masters in Egypt, when the Israelites would have passed into the wilderness to worship the God of their fathers, "ye are idle, and idleness is the source of your devotion;" and the accusation is brought down to this our day. We are saved by grace, says the believer; "*it is not of works, lest any man should boast.*" Ye are idle, cry our task masters, while the moderate man mildly says—"Hazard your hopes of happiness, if you please; make no effort for yourself, but for me; I will cultivate my land, and if, as you say, it will really be more fruitful than usual, it will do me no harm; but if it should not, what will be then your situation? You will come to me for help, but shall I not be justified in saying, he that will not sow, shall not reap. God will help us when we do our duty, but except we do our part, he will not lend us aid." The great Mr. Burket observes, "We *can* do nothing without God, and God *will* do nothing without us." "Upon the whole, neighbour, you had better attend to your plough; work while it is day."

To every thing secular, in every thing terrestrial, this reasoning is indubitably conclusive; we must put our shoulders to the waggon if we would extricate, and again set it upon its wheels; but in the *matter of our justification before God, we are not, we can never be fellow helpers;* our work is not sufficiently *perfect to be presented before God*, and it is, therefore, God commandeth, "*On this sabbatic year, thou shalt do no work.*" "You cannot be right," says the objector, "but your doctrine is sweet to the idle and the worthless." Such was the language of the rebellious Israelites, when Moses addressed them; but their opposition yielded them neither pleasure nor profit. Human nature is not naturally disposed to do good; but the children of men are naturally disposed to doubt the truth of God. The history of God's people, from the commencement to the close, evinces this truth. Never was so bad a people, never was so good a God. Throughout the Israelitish story, the brightest colours are exhibited upon the darkest ground.

But we are not furnished with a rational cause of complaint. To those who wish to work, there is an ample recompense offered; and *except when tendered as payment for the great salvation, good works are beautiful, nay, they are more, they are good and profitable unto man, and in this view, well pleasing unto God.* To these good works, every stimulous is offered; *rewards*, ample *rewards* are tendered, so that the ambitious may find their account in the service of God, without the loss of liberty; for the service of God is perfect freedom. Blessed be God, the Sabbath is the theme of christian professors of every denomination, while both Jews and Gentiles are equally ignorant of the grand design of that God, who gave us the Sabbath as an emblem of grace. I recollect, some years since, walking the street in company with a very religious friend, who was remarking upon the ignorance, and consequent prejudices of christian professors.

Yes, Sir, it is astonishing; I have known many instances of absurd prejudices obtaining in the minds, even of rational professors. For example; I am acquainted with a serious, sensible man, who is a regular attendant on public worship; I have seen him in the act of his devotional exercises, and when the minister approached the altar and repeated the commandments, this worthy, serious, sensible man, with great sincerity followed the responses, and upon the repetition of the fourth commandment, *Remember thou keep holy the Sabbath day; six days shalt thou labour, and do all that thou hast to do; but the seventh day is the Sabbath of the* LORD *thy God, in it thou shalt do no manner of work*, &c. &c. This honest, sincere man, year after year, never failed to repeat in his responses, "the LORD have mercy upon me, and incline my heart to keep this law." This commandment is written in letters of gold before his eyes; he cannot approach the altar without observing it, and yet this man never did, nor never intended to keep this law. He knew it was on the *first day* of the week he worshipped; he knew it was the *seventh day* of the week which God had hallowed, and yet, year after year, he passed on without recurring to this fact, still repeating, "LORD have mercy upon me, and incline my heart to keep this law."

"Well, this is really surprising; but thus the world goes on."

Yes, it is very suprising; and you will be still more surprised when I say, "Thou art the man."——He started, he paused—

"I am really astonished; I never before reflected upon this, and yet it is a truth."

Aye, you see, my dear Sir,

"We to, ourselves, most partial judges be;
The faults of others, not our own own we see."

"Sir, I both see and feel this truth. But what are we to do in this case? Why do christians keep this day?"

The ancient christians preferred the day of resurrection to the day of rest. But neither ancient nor modern christians, possessed any right to change the ordinances of God.

"I have been told, the Apostles observed the first day of the week."

They met together upon the first day of every week, to make collections for their poor, and to attend to their secular concerns; to which business, it was unlawful for them to attend on the *Sabbath day*. The Jews do thus, in every place, upon the first day of the week.

"But did not our Saviour command us to keep the first day of the week?"

He commanded his disciples to keep the seventh day as the Sabbath.

"I have heard it observed, that the seventh part of time was all that was intended. Will not this answer as well?"

By the same rule, it might be as well to observe Monday or Tuesday.

"Why, yes, it might be as beneficial to the Redeemer; but it is the act of obedience which is of importance."

Yet the law is broken, and to break the law constitutes sin; sin is a transgression of the law, and where then is our obedience?

"But what do you yourself do in this case?"

Why, almost as you do; I do not indeed pray, that God would incline my heart to keep this law; I am a professed christian; I do not reckon myself under the law, but under grace, I consider that Jesus Christ is the end of the law, and the LORD *of the Sabbath*. But our rulers have consecrated the first day of the week for the purposes of religious worship, and I, as a subject, hold myself bound to obey the ordinances of man, for God's sake.

"Then you observe this day as an ordinance of man?"

Undoubtedly; and I am very grateful for the institution. But if I considered myself under the law, and not under grace, I should be persuaded I was as much a law breaker in violating the Sabbath, appointed by God, as in breaking the sixth or any other commandment. I bless God for Jesus Christ, as the end of the law for righteousness. But, my dear Sir, I do not mean to censure or condemn any one, for their modes or forms. Let every one be persuaded in his own mind, *some men esteem one day above another, and some esteem every day alike.*

At the crucifixion of our Redeemer, which astonishing event terminated the Jewish dispensation, the Jewish ceremonies became a subject of contest. Many Jews believed, who were still zealous for the law of ceremonies. It is difficult to surmount the force of habit, and the Jews were accustomed to the observation of days.

The Apostles were diligently employed in the cultivation of good morals, yet they laboured to destroy that attachment which their adherents manifested to ceremonies. Galatians iv. 9, 10, 11, "But now, after that ye have known God, *or rather, are known of God,* how turn ye again to the weak and beggarly elements, whereunto ye desire again to be in bondage? *Ye observe days, and months, and times, and years.* I am afraid of you, lest I have bestowed upon you labour in vain." Colossians ii. 16, 17, "Let no man, therefore, judge you in meat, or in drink, or in respect of an holy day, or of the new moon, or of the Sabbath days: Which are a *shadow of things to come, but the body is of Christ.*" Here we are led to believe that the *Sabbath* is a *shadow of the body, which body is Christ.* Let no man judge you with respect to meat or drink, or of the new moon, or of the Sabbath. It is observable, *days* were not in the original, the word is printed in italics. The Apostle in his Epistle to the Galatians speaks very fully, and feelingly upon this subject, iii. 22, "But the scripture hath concluded all under sin, that the promise by faith of Jesus Christ might be given to them that believe." Thus we learn, that God concluded all under sin. For what purpose? that the promise by *faith of Jesus Christ* might be given to them that believe. So that the promise, or the grace it contained, came not on them by their own *personal faith, but by the faith of Christ.* There are who are shocked when we speak of the *faith of Christ*, although all the promises were made to the Redeemer, and it is said, *he endured the cross for the joy that was set before him.* Yet such individuals will not admit that our Saviour *believed those promises.* But the christian is a believer in Christ. He believes in Christ, that he may be justified *by the faith of Christ.* Jesus Christ was indeed raised from the dead for our justification, whether we believe it or not, and hence the Apostle says, if Christ be not risen, our preaching is vain; your faith is vain; ye are yet in your sins. If the change in the creature were in any sort the salvation of the sinner, that change would have remained the same, whether the Saviour had burst the barriers of the tomb, or whether he had not. But Christ Jesus having suffered death for sin, for our sin, because the wages of sin was death, he appears, in his resurrection, the second time *without sin*, and consequently unto salvation. Hence, saith the Apostle, we are begotten again unto a lively hope, by the resurrection of Christ Jesus from the dead.

Peter adverts to this sacred testimony in his first General Epistle, i. 3, "Blessed be the God and Father of our Lord Jesus Christ, which according to his abundant mercy hath begotten us again unto a lively hope, by the resurrection of Jesus Christ from the dead."

But these divinely instructed scribes were taught by the spirit of God to know, that in the birth, in the life, in the death, and in the resurrection of Jesus Christ, it pleased the Father that all fulness should dwell.

Yet there is one most essential and highly glorious consideration, which will ever render this day, this Lord's day, truly precious to the soul of the christian man. We have reason to suppose it is the day on which the Saviour burst the barriers of the tomb: on which he arose greatly triumphant over death and hell, leading captivity captive, and bestowing gifts unto men. This is sufficient; we ask no commandment to enroll this day among the dearest of our treasures; it comes forward with a most benign aspect; we embrace it as the first of blessings; it seems another word for whatsoever things are lovely, whatsoever things are virtuous, whatsoever things are of good report; and we would adopt the sentiments of a respectable clergyman, once of high standing in this town, but now, we believe, gathered into the garner of his God; who, upon being asked which he thought ought to be observed, Saturday or Sunday evening? pertinently and piously replied, I would treat the LORD's *day* as a *very dear friend;* and when I expected this *very dear friend*, I would choose to array myself in my best apparel, and go forth to meet this friend; I would certainly commence my journey on Saturday afternoon. And when a friend so very dear, was departing from me, I would certainly accompany him on his way; I should not wish to return again, until Monday morning, nor then except commanded by imperious necessity.

Thus do we, with every faculty of our souls, accept this splendid day, as the *christian Sabbath;* and while I can open my eyes upon the things of time, I will continue to call it blessed, to hail its return, and to regard it as a dear memorial of many rich, of many sweet enjoyments. What though they are gone past, they still live in my recollection, and they will ever be held by me in merited, in high, in sacred estimation.

SKETCH. IX.

NUMBERS, ii. 3.

And on the east side toward the rising of the sun, shall they of the standard of the camp of Judah pitch, throughout their armies: and Nahshon, the son of Amminadab, shall be captain of the children of Judah.

First, JUDAH is the first standard. Of whom was Judah a figure? A recurrence to the signification of the name Judah, will facilitate our ideas upon this question.

Judah in the Hebrew tongue signifies literally the praise of the LORD. But in Genesis xlix. 8—12, we have a luminous answer to this important, and highly interesting question "Judah thou art he whom thy brethren shall praise: thy hand shall be in the neck of thine enemies; thy father's children shall bow down before thee. Judah is a lion's whelp: from the prey my son thou art gone up: he stooped down, he couched as a lion; and as an old lion; who shall rouse him up? The sceptre shall not depart from Judah, nor a lawgiver from between his feet, until Shiloh come; and unto him shall the gathering of the people be. Binding his foal unto the vine, and his ass's colt unto the choice vine; he washed his garments in wine, and his clothes in the blood of grapes: His eyes shall be red with wine, and his teeth wet with milk." From this passage it becomes evident that Judah was a type of the Redeemer.

Secondly, The standard of Judah was by the direction of God reared on the east side of the camp, toward the rising of the sun. Thus, the character of Judah or Jesus is supported. John i. 1, "In the beginning was the word, and the word was with God, and the word was God." Revelations i. 8, "I am Alpha and Omega, the beginning and the ending, saith the Lord, which is, and which was, and which is to come, the Almighty." Isaiah lx. 3, "And the Gentiles shall come to thy light, and kings to the brightness of thy rising." And again, Isaiah lix. 19, "So shall they fear the name of the Lord from the west, and his glory from the rising of the sun. When the enemy shall come in like a flood, the spirit of the Lord shall lift up a standard against him." Malachi i. 11, "For from the rising of the sun even unto the going down of the same, my name shall be great among the Gentiles; and in every place incense shall be offered unto my name, and a pure offering: for my name shall be great among the heathen, saith the Lord of hosts."

Thirdly, The literal idea conveyed by the word or name Nahshon is a divine, one who predicts events yet hidden in the womb of time. The business of a captain is to foresee difficulties, and to guard against every possible emergency. A captain is properly a leader. The spirit of truth is a leader. The spirit prophesying testifieth of Jesus. Revelations xix. 10, "And I fell at his feet to worship him. And he said unto me see thou do it not: I am thy fellow servant and of thy brethren that have the testimony of Jesus: worship God: for the testimony of Jesus is the spirit of prophecy." The spirit led Judah or Jesus into the wilderness. The spirit takes of the things of Jesus and exhibits them to the understanding. May this blessed spirit guide us into all truth.

SKETCH X.

NUMBERS vi. 22—27.

"And the LORD spake unto Moses, saying, Speak unto Aaron and unto his sons, saying, on this wise ye shall bless the children of Israel, saying unto them, The LORD bless thee and keep thee. The LORD make his face to shine upon thee, and be gracious unto thee; The LORD lift up his countenance upon thee, and give thee peace. And they shall put my name upon the children of Israel and I will bless them."

First, Moses is commanded to direct Aaron and his sons to bless the children of Israel. This commandment of God is perfectly conformable to all the dealings of the divine nature with the human being. The plans of Jehovah are full of grace and truth. In the same moment that the spirit gives us an account of the formation of our nature, we are furnished with multiplied instances of the goodness of our Creator. Genesis i. 28, 29, "And God blessed them, and God said unto them, be fruitful and multiply, and replenish the earth, and subdue it; and have dominion over the fish of the sea, and over the fowl of the air, and over every living thing that moveth upon the earth. And God said, behold I have given you every herb bearing seed which is upon the face of all the earth, and every tree, in the which is the fruit of a tree yielding seed; to you it shall be for meat."

How rich, how various the catalogue of blessings! But where is the page, chapter or text, which records the *revocation* of those blessings? God sendeth his rain upon the just and the unjust. Summer and Winter, day and night, sunshine and storms, seed time and harvest, succeed alike to all. No, assuredly, God doth not revoke his blessings. The Almighty in the garden of Eden was not heard to curse the human pair.

The first syllable which is uttered of cursing is in Genesis iii 14, "And the LORD God said unto the serpent, because thou hast done this, thou art cursed above all cattle, and above every beast of the field; upon thy belly shalt thou go, and dust shalt thou eat all the days of thy life." In the seventeenth verse we again hear of cursing. "And unto Adam he said, because thou hast hearkened unto the voice of thy wife, and hast eaten of the tree, of which I commanded thee, saying thou shalt not eat of it: *cursed is the ground for thy sake ;* in sorrow shalt thou eat of it all the days of thy life."

Should it be urged that God spake all the words of the law, in which there are a variety of curses denounced upon offenders, we answer, that as it was the original design of God to appear in our nature under the law, to redeem them that were under the law, we cannot see that the curses of the law are contradictory to the blessings or the promises which contain those blessings. God forbid that they should be thus considered. Nay, although it was through the instrumentality of Moses and of Aaron, that the law was given, yet even Aaron and his sons are commanded to bless the people.

Secondly, What are we to understand by the blessing pronounced upon the people? Various descriptions of blessings are pointed out, but we shall at present confine ourselves to two particular instances. The first is recorded in the Acts of the Apostles, iii. 26, "God having raised up his son Jesus, sent him to bless you, in turning away every one of you from his iniquities." Here the Apostle Peter delineates the nature and extent of the blessing. *It is to turn every one of you from his iniquities.* The second particular instance which indeed includes every thing that can lay claim to durable importance is recorded in Ephesians i. 3, "Blessed be the God and Father of our Lord Jesus Christ, who hath blessed us with all spiritual blessings in heavenly places in Christ." Here the divine nature is represented as blessing the human nature with spiritual blessings, with all spiritual blessings, not temporal blessings in earthly places, but with all spiritual blessings in heavenly places; and to show that these blessings can never be lost, God hath given them to us in Christ Jesus. Again, it is not a promise that he will bless us in *future*, but God *hath* blessed us with all spiritual blessings in heavenly places in Christ.

Thirdly, The second clause in the blessing with which the people were to be blest, refers to their preservation. *The Lord bless thee and keep thee.* It is frequently observed, they must be well kept whom God keeps; therefore it is with strict propriety, that David saith in the hundredth and twenty-first Psalm, "He will not suffer thy foot to be moved. Behold he that keepeth Israel, shall neither slumber nor sleep. The Lord is thy keeper: the Lord is thy shade upon thy right hand. The sun shall not smite thee by day, nor the moon by night. The Lord shall preserve thee from all evil; he shall preserve thy soul." Again, the Apostle Peter, in his first Epistle, in the genuine spirit of inspiration, thus expresseth himself: "Blessed be the God and Father of our Lord Jesus Christ, which according to his abundant mercy hath begotten us again unto a lively hope, by the resurrection of Jesus Christ from the dead. To an inheritance incorruptible and undefiled, and that fadeth not away, reserved in heaven for you."

From these testimonies it is evident, that it is the soul that is especially kept, the soul that is preserved, and that God, in his abundant mercy, hath already begotten us again. When we were first conceived, it was in sin, and subjected by law to death; but God hath begotten us again unto a lively hope, by the resurrection of Jesus Christ from the dead. As Jesus, when lifted up from the earth, drew all men unto him, as Jew and Gentile were reconciled in one body on the cross, as the fulness of Jew and Gentile constituted the fulness of the body of our second Adam, in his death, his burial, and his resurrection, the royal Psalmist, in the seventh and eight verses of the second Psalm, speaking in the character of him that sitteth in the heavens, emphatically says, "I will declare the decree: the Lord hath said unto me, Thou art my Son; this day have I begotten thee. Ask of me, and I will give thee the heathen for thine inheritance, and the uttermost parts of the earth for thy possession." The Apostle, directed by the spirit of truth, thus expresseth himself. "And we declare unto you glad tidings, how that the promise which was made unto the fathers, God hath fulfilled unto us their children, in that he hath raised up Jesus again;" as it is also written in the second Psalm, Thou art my Son; this day have I begotten thee.

It was to Jesus Christ, in his public character, the divine Nature said on his resurrection from the dead, This is my Son, my beloved Son; this day have I begotten thee. Therefore the Spirit of God directeth the Apostle Peter to say, He hath begotten us again unto a lively hope, which hope is full of immortality by the resurrection of Jesus Christ. But this is not all—Peter is constrained to tell us what we are begotten unto. It is to an incorruptible inheritance. He who died to purchase a lost race, must not, cannot be defeated ; and hence *we are kept by the power of God*, through faith, unto full salvation, ready to be revealed in the last time.

If we would know what this salvation, ready to be revealed in the last time intends, we have only to turn to Revelations xi. 15, " And the seventh angel sounded ; and there were great voices in heaven saying, The *kingdoms* of this world are become the kingdoms of our Lord, and of his Christ; and he shall reign forever and ever." Again xii. 10, " And I heard a loud voice saying in heaven, Now is come salvation, and strength, and the kingdom of our God, and the power of his Christ : for the accuser of our brethren is cast down, which accused them before our God day and night." But if we be desirous of becoming still better acquainted with that salvation which is to be revealed in the last times, let us listen to the Apostle Peter, " And he shall send Jesus Christ, which before was preached unto you. Whom the heavens must receive until the time of the restitution of all things, which God hath spoken by the mouth of all his holy prophets since the world began."

But pursuing our inquiries relative to the nature and extent of the salvation, to be revealed in the last times, we cannot pass by Revelations xiii. 5, "And every creature which is in heaven, and on the earth, and under the earth, and such as are in the sea, and all that are in them heard I saying, Blessing, and honour, and glory, and power, be unto him that sitteth on the throne, and unto the Lamb forever and ever."

Thus the *blessed* are to be kept by the *power of God*, for the enjoyment of the inheritance *reserved in heaven for the saved of the Lord*, and to be revealed in the last times, which salvation is a salvation from sin, from its cause and effect, consequent on the destruction of the devil and his works.

But *who* are they, that by the *power of God* are to be thus kept ? To this question, the following scriptures furnish a full answer. The thief cometh not, but for to steal, and to kill, and to destroy ; I am come, that they might have life, and that they might have it more abundantly. I am the good Shepherd : the good shepherd giveth his life for the sheep. And other sheep I have, which are not of this fold : them also I must bring ; and they shall hear my voice ; and there shall be one fold and one shepherd. And I give unto them eternal life ; and they shall never perish, neither shall any man pluck them out of my hand. My Father, who gave them me, is greater than all, and no man is able to pluck them out of my Father's hand I and my Father are one.

They who by the *power of God* are kept unto this salvation, are all that the Father gave unto the Son. But who did the Father give unto the Son? Our blessed Master, John iii. 35, declares, " The Father loveth the Son, and hath given *all things* into his hand." Again, John xiii. 3, "Jesus knowing that the Father had given all things into his hands, and that he was come from God and went to God." Again, He who said I am the truth declares, John xvi. 15, "All things that the Father hath are mine, and therefore, said I, he shall take of mine and show it unto you" God the Creator, saith Ezekiel xviii. 4, "Behold all souls are mine; as the soul of the Father, so also the soul of the Son is mine."

If then *all* souls belonged unto the Father, and *all* that the Father had he gave unto the Son, *as heir of all things, for whom all things were made, and if all souls* belonged unto the divine Nature, and were put into the hands of the Son, who is the head of every man, and if none can pluck them out of his hand, then assuredly they who are *kept by the power of God unto salvation*, unto that salvation which is to be revealed in the last times, must be *every individual of mankind;* every individual must constitute the fulness of Jew and Gentile, the *every man* for whom Jesus, by the grace of God, tasted death. Blessed be God for thus manifesting to our understandings, that this division of the blessing, *and keep thee,* is by the grace of God the portion of the whole human race. Not now as heretofore confined to the Jews. For the middle wall of partition being broken down, Jew and Gentile are considered as one Israel redeemed by the Lord, and blessed with all spiritual blessings in Christ Jesus.

SKETCH XI.

We are now to proceed in our subject.

Fourthly, The next division of this memorable blessing, is thus most beautifully expressed. The Lord make his face to shine upon thee, and be gracious unto thee. The ambassadors of the Most High are truly privileged ; they are sent forth with a commission *to bless ; curses should never be found in their mouths.* Go ye into all the world and preach my gospel to every creature, this is the matter of the embassy, the consequences are the effect, and make no part of their declaration. The gospel is glad tidings. How beautiful upon the mountains are the feet of him that bringeth good tidings, that publisheth peace, that bringeth good tidings of good, that publisheth salvation, that saith unto Zion, thy God reigneth! Surely the Lord is gracious unto such individuals, unto such messengers of peace ; surely the Lord maketh his face to shine upon them.

The countenance or face is an index to the mind. Men discover their good or evil disposition toward each other by their countenances. Thus Jacob said unto his wives Rachel and Leah, " I see your Father's countenance that it is not toward me as before, although I have served him so long, and although he has changed my wages so many times," and from the appearance of his countenance he concluded he was not his friend.

We read in the countenance the disposition of the man toward us. The Psalmist prays, " Behold, O God, our shield and look upon the face of thine anointed." The glory of God is conspicuous in the face of Jesus, the glory of God is the fulness of grace and truth, and this grace and truth is beheld in the *shining*, which is the light of God's countenance. The sweet singer of Israel impressively says and devoutly supplicates, " There be many that say, Who will shew us any good? Lord, lift thou up the light of thy countenance upon us," as though he had said in the light of thy countenance we shall discern every felicity. " Make thy face to shine upon thy servant : save me for thy mercy's sake, God be merciful unto us and bless us ; and cause his face to shine upon us. Selah."

From the creation of Adam until the present moment every child of God hath deprecated the hiding of God's face as the greatest possible calamity.

"How long wilt thou forget me, O Lord? Forever? How long wilt thou hide thy face from me ; hide not thy face far from me ; put not thy servant away in anger ; thou hast been my help, leave me not, neither forsake me, O God of my salvation." The prophet Isaiah declares he will wait upon the Lord that hideth his face from the house of Jacob, and that he will look for him. Again,

"And there is none that calleth upon thy name, that stirreth up himself to take hold of thee : for thou hast hid thy face from us, and hast consumed us because of our iniquities." The testimony of Ezekiel corresponds with that of Isaiah. "According to their uncleanness and according to their transgressions have I done unto them, and hid my face from them. Yet God saith, Neither will I hide my face any more from them : for I have poured out my spirit upon the house of Israel, saith the LORD God"

Daniel evinceth the just estimation in which he held the light of God's countenance, when he saith, "Now, therefore, O our God, hear the prayer of thy servant, and his supplications, and cause thy face to shine upon thy sanctuary that is desolate, for the LORD's sake."

The Psalmist supplicates, "Turn us again, O God, and cause thy face to shine; and we shall be saved."

The shining of God's countenance is a reviving testimony of his favour, of the favour of the Most High. We have seen what melancholy ideas filled the minds of the children of God, when the Creator hid his face from them. Thou hidest thy face and I am troubled. Thus when the face of the LORD shineth upon the children of men, he is indeed gracious unto them, and this is truly a very essential part of the blessing pronounced by the ministers of God, upon his people. *The LORD make his face to shine upon thee, and be gracious unto thee.*

Fifthly, The LORD lift up the light of his countenance upon thee.

What are we to understand by the lifting up of the countenance upon God's inheritance. We are told that when Cain was very wroth with his brother, his countenance fell. But the reverse of every thing vindictive, and every thing unpleasant, is indicated by the lifting up of the countenance. It should seem it is no more than repeating, in other words, the last division in the blessing. "The LORD make his face to shine upon thee. For thou hast made him most blessed forever: thou hast made him exceeding glad with thy countenance." The countenance of God is strikingly characterized as lending aid. "Why art thou cast down, O my soul? and why art thou disquieted in me? Hope thou in God: for I shall yet praise him for the help of his countenance."

Hope in God is cherished, who is piously styled the health of the countenance; and salvation is pertinently ascribed to the lifting up, to the light of God's countenance; for they got not the land in possession by their own sword, neither did their own arm save them: but thy right hand, and thine arm, and the *light of thy countenance* because thou hadst a favour unto them. In the eighty-ninth Psalm, the privileges of those on whom God vouchsafeth to lift up the light of his countenance are expatiated upon with a kind of holy rapture.

"Justice and judgment are the habitation of thy throne; mercy and truth shall go before thy face.

"Blessed are the people that know the joyful sound: they shall walk, O LORD, in the *light of thy countenance*, &c. &c.

These are some of the privileges enjoyed by those on whom the countenance of God is lifted up. The wise man informs us that in the light of the King's countenance, is life, and that his favour is as a cloud of the latter rain. The countenance of God is described as bestowing a fulness of joy. "Thou hast made known to me the ways of life; thou shalt make me full of joy with thy countenance! The countenance of our Redeemer is like lightening." Contrast this with the countenance of the hypocrites, as pourtrayed by our Saviour. "Their countenance is sad, for they disfigure their faces that they may appear unto men to fast."

It is written Revelations i. 16, "And he had in his right hand seven stars, and out of his mouth went a sharp two edged sword: and his countenance as the sun shineth in his strength." The succeeding verse informs us that this was he who liveth, who was dead, and who is alive forever more. "Who is the Redeemer of the world, who hath the key of hell and death, and who says, Fear not?" But why should we not fear? Let the lip of truth give us an answer, "Because I, your elder Brother, your Creator, your everlasting Father, your Almighty friend, your Redeemer, your husband, bone of your bone, flesh of your flesh, the head of every man. Because I am the first and the last. What though this two edged sword proceedeth out of my mouth; what though with it I slay the nation.

"Yet will their death be no other, than that which happened to the Apostle Paul, when the commandment slew him, and he died." The God that killeth, can also make alive; he hath the keys of hell and death, all power is committed unto him, and we cannot be afraid of him, who died for us, and who liveth forever more, that we may never die, who liveth to protect, who commanded his ministers, Aaron and his sons to bless the people, to say unto them, "The LORD bless thee, and keep thee: The LORD make his face shine upon thee, and be gracious unto thee: The LORD lift up his countenance upon thee, and give the peace." Is there a blessing not included in this rich catalogue, how ample is the charter of our privileges. How vast is the debt we owe to the LORD of all worlds, and shall the liberality and forbearance of our august Creditor, teach us supine indifference, or worse still, criminal indulgence? Shall we continue in sin, that grace may abound? God forbid. I pity the mind that is so much under the dominion of the infernal fiend, as to be able to harbour, or even to conceive such a diabolical idea. Yet if there are such human beings, we know who hath said, "If my children forsake my law, and walk not in my judgments; If they break my statutes and keep not my commandments, then will I visit their transgressions with the rod, and their iniquities with stripes. Nevertheless, my loving kindness will I not utterly take from him, nor suffer my faithfulness to fail." The last clause in the twenty-sixth verse remains to be considered, "And give thee peace." Should we be indulged with a future opportunity we will, with ineffable pleasure resume our subject, and, in the interim, may you be with every blessing blest.

SKETCH XII.

NUMBERS, vi. 26.

Sixthly, "AND give thee peace."

Man as fallen and wicked, is not, cannot be in peace with his God. We are by nature, enmity toward God, and haters of each other. Titus, iii. 3, "For we ourselves also, were sometimes foolish, disobedient, deceived, serving divers lusts and pleasures, living in malice and envy, hateful, and hating one another."

Peace is not so natural to fallen man, as *war, one with another.* There is no greater blessing than peace, personal, domestic, social and civil. But however great this blessing, we have no reason to expect it in the present state of things. But what are we to understand by the peace here spoken of? certainly not such a peace as the world giveth. We are told that in this world we shall have tribulation. Let us listen to our blessed Saviour, John, xvi. 33.

" These things have I spoken unto you, that in *me ye might have peace*. In the world ye shall have tribulation : but be of good cheer ; I have overcome the world." But this peace, is the peace of God between him and his offending people. " We know who is our peace," Ephesians, ii. 14, 15, " For he is our peace, who hath made both one, and hath broken down the middle wall of partition between us ; Having abolished in his flesh the enmity, even the law of commandments contained in ordinances for to make in himself of twain one new man, so making peace."

Yet, we repeat, in the dispensation finished by the sufferings and death of the Redeemer ; the Saviour came not to send peace on earth. Luke, xii. 51, " Suppose ye that I am come to give peace on earth ? I tell you nay, but rather division."

Peace in this world, is not the lot of humanity. " *But in me you shall have peace.*"

First, The blessing of God is peace. Peace between the offended and offending natures.

Secondly, It is found in the conscience of the blessed.

Thirdly, With one another.

First, Between the offended and offending natures. This must be done by removing the cause of hostilities. Isaiah, lix. 2, "Your iniquities separate between you, and your God, and your sins have hid his face from you, that he will not hear." These must be put away, But are they put away ? Ask the author of the Epistle to the Hebrews, ix. 26.

" For then must he often have suffered since the foundation of the world : but now, once in the end of the world hath he appeared to put away sin, by the sacrifice of himself."

Inquire of John, the Evangelist, i. 29.

" The next day John seeth Jesus coming unto him, and saith, Behold the Lamb of God, which taketh away the sin of the world." And this same evangelist in his first Epistle, i. 7, informs us, " But if we walk in the light, as he is in the light, we have fellowship one with another, and the blood of Jesus Christ, his Son, cleanseth us from all sin." First, sin is put away; secondly, we are told whose sin is put away; the sin of the world; thirdly, it is confirmed; he cleanseth from all sin. But this is not all, there must be *righteousness*, or there can be no *peace*, for there is no peace to the wicked. Isaiah, xxxii 16, " Then judgment shall dwell in the wilderness, and righteousness remain in the fruitful field." And again lx. 21, " Thy people also shall be all righteous: they shall inherit the land forever, the branch of my planting, the work of my hands that I may be glorified."

Consequent on this grand consummation there is peace, and the blessing is confirmed. Ephesians, ii. 14, " For he is our peace, who hath made both one, and hath broken down the middle wall of partition between us." The countenances of my beloved hearers assure me the tidings of salvation cannot too often resound in their ears; with ineffable delight, therefore, I proceed in this important, and very interesting investigation. In Psalms, xxix. 11, It is recorded,

"The Lord will give strength unto his people, the Lord will bless his people with peace." And lxxii. 7, " In his days shall the righteous flourish; and abundance of peace so long as the moon endureth." Philippians, iv. 7, This peace is called the peace of God. " And the peace of God, which passeth all understanding, shall keep your hearts and minds through Christ Jesus." Hence, God is called, Romans, xv. 33, " The God of peace." And xvi. 20, " And the God of peace shall bruise satan under your feet shortly." And 2 Corinthians, xiii. 11, " Finally, brethren, farewell; be perfect, be of good comfort, be of one mind, live in peace, and the God of love and peace shall be with you." 1 Thessalonians, v. 23, God is styled the very God of peace. " And the very God of peace sanctify you wholly." And this, because he is the author, the finisher, and the giver of this peace.

First, The author, Zechariah, vi. 13, " Even he shall build the temple of the Lord; and he shall bear the glory, and shall sit and rule upon his throne; and he shall be a priest upon his throne: and the council of peace shall be between them both."

Jeremiah, xxix. 11, " For I know the thoughts that I think toward you, saith the Lord, are thoughts of peace, and not of evil to give you an expected end." The covenant of God, is a covenant of peace. Ezekiel, xxxvii. 26, " Moreover, I will make a covenant of peace with them; it shall be an everlasting covenant with them: and I will place them, and multiply them, and will set my sanctuary in the midst of them, forevermore."

Secondly, The finisher of peace. Colossians, i. 20, "And having made peace by the blood of the cross, by him to reconcile all things unto himself, by him, I say, whether they be things on earth or things in heaven."

Thirdly, He is the giver of this peace. John, xiv. 7, " Peace I leave with you, my peace I give unto you: not as the world giveth, give I unto you. Let not your heart be troubled, neither let it be afraid."

Secondly, This blessing contains peace of conscience. The conscience sitteth in judgment upon the mind taught by the spirit of God, and it is only in this peace given by our God, that we can have a conscience *not guilty.* Hebrews x. " For the law having a shadow of good things to come, and not the very image of the things, can never with those sacrifices which they offered year by year continually, make the comers thereunto perfect. For then would they not have ceased to be offered? Because that the worshippers once purged should have had no more conscience of sins. But in those sacrifices there is a remembrance again made of sin every year. For it is not possible that the blood of bulls and of goats should take away sins. Wherefore, when he cometh into the world, he saith, sacrifice and offering thou wouldst not, but a body hast thou prepared me. In burnt offerings and sacrifices for sins thou hast had no pleasure. Then, said I, Lo I come, (in the volume of the book it is written of me) to do thy will, O God. Above, when he said, sacrifices and offering, and burnt offerings, and offering for sin thou wouldst not, neither hadst pleasure therein, which are offered by the law; Then, said he, Lo I come, to do thy will, O God. He taketh away the first that he may establish the second. By the which will we are sanctified through the offering of the body of Jesus Christ once for all." Peter in his First Epistle, iii. 21, thus expresses himself, " The like figure whereunto even baptism doth also now save us, (not the putting away the filth of the flesh but the answer of a good conscience toward God) by the resurrection of Jesus Christ." " Therefore," says the Apostle Paul, Romans v. 1, " being justified, by faith we have peace with God through our Lord Jesus Christ." Isaiah assures us, xxvi. 3, " That God will keep them in perfect peace, whose mind is stayed on him." And Paul supplicates, Romans xv. 13, " Now the God of hope fill you with all joy, and peace in believing, that ye may abound in hope through the power of the Holy Ghost."

Thirdly, and lastly, This blessing includes peace with each other. 1 Corinthians vii. 15, " God hath called us to peace." In him the brethren dwell together in peace. Isaiah xxvi. 12, " Lord, thou wilt ordain peace for us : for thou also hast wrought all our works in us." And lvii. 19, " I create the fruit of the lips; peace, peace to him that is far off and to him that is near, saith the Lord, and I will heal him." And the Lord saith by the prophet Micah, v. 5, "And this man shall be our peace when the Assyrian shall come into our land." We are told by the prophet Habakkuk, ii. 14, " For the earth shall be filled with the knowledge of the glory of the Lord, as the waters cover the sea." " Our God" saith, Isaiah ii. 2, "And it shall come to pass in the last days, that the mountain of the Lord's house shall be established in the top of the mountains, and shall be axalted above the hills and all nations shall flow unto it." And again, xxv. 6—9, " And in this mountain shall the Lord of hosts make unto all people a feast of fat things, a feast of wines on the lees, of fat things full of marrow, of wines on the lees well refined. And he will destroy in this mountain the face of the covering, cast over all people ; and the veil that is spread over all nations. He will swallow up death in victory ; and the Lord God will wipe away tears from off all faces ; and the rebuke of his people shall he take away from off all the earth: for the Lord hath spoken it. And it shall be said in that day, Lo this is our God ; we have waited for him and he will save us ; this is the Lord , we have waited for him, we will be glad, and rejoice in his salvation."

Let us, my beloved hearers, hearken unto the Lord our God speaking by the prophet Micah, " But in the last days it shall come to pass, that the mountain of the house of the Lord shall be established in the top of the mountains, and it shall be exalted above the hills; and people shall flow unto it. And many nations shall come, and say, come and let us go up to the house of the Lord, and to the house of the God of Jacob ; and he will teach us of his ways, and we will walk in his paths ; for the law shall go forth of Zion, and the word of the Lord from Jerusalem And he shall judge among many people, and rebuke strong nations afar off; and they shall beat their swords into ploughshares, and their spears into pruning hooks: nation shall not lift up a sword against nation, neither shall they learn war any more. But they shall set every man under his own vine, and under his own fig tree, and none shall make them afraid: for the mouth of the Lord of hosts hath spoken it. For all people will walk every one in the name of his God, and we will walk in the name of the Lord our God forever and ever. In that day, saith the Lord, will I assemble her that halteth, and I will gather her that is driven out, and her that is afflicted."

This is indeed wonderful, very wonderful. But it is the doings of our God, and justly marvellous in our eyes. That this blessing includes *peace with each other*, we produce from the rich treasury of our God; one more proof, 1 Thessalonians v. 9, 10, " For God hath not appointed us to wrath, but to obtain salvation by our Lord Jesus Christ; Who died for us, that whether we wake or sleep, we should live *together* with him."

Whenever we are thus collected, we shall not only go out no more, but we shall never more be at variance " *See that ye fall not out by the way,*" said Joseph. Blessed be God, it is only *by the way, that we can fall out* As no whisperer, nor any thing that defileth can enter into our Father's house, his family assembled in his presence, will *together* enjoy uninterrupted peace, worlds without end.

Seventhly, "And they shall put my name upon the children of Israel, and I will bless them " This is the top stone of the building, the climax of our privileges This is the name, says the prophet Jeremiah, xxiii. 6, " This is the name whereby *he shall be called, the* Lord *our righteousness*." Who shall be called the Lord our righteousness? The Prophet informs us. " Behold the days come, saith the Lord, that I will raise unto David a righteous branch; and a king shall reign and prosper, and shall execute judgment and justice upon the earth. In his days Judah shall be saved, and Israel shall dwell safely: and this is the name whereby *he* shall be called, *the* Lord *our righteousness*." Thus it is he, Jesus, the righteous branch; the king who reigneth and prospereth, and who executeth judgment and justice in the earth, who shall *be called the* Lord *our righteousness*. And this same prophet Jeremiah informs us, xxxiii. 15, 16, "That in those days, and at that time, God will cause the branch of righteousness to grow up unto David, and that he shall execute judgment and righteousness in the land. In those days shall Judah be saved, and Jerusalem shall dwell safely; and this is the name wherewith *she* shall be called, the LORD our righteousness."

Thus did the Almighty, all gracious God, command his ministers to put his name upon the people, and they shall be my people, saith God. The propriety of this name being named upon our nature, is strikingly apparent—" *Thy Maker is thy husband,*" says the Spirit of truth, "the LORD of the whole earth shall he be called." Why should she not bear the name of her husband? I will give them my *own name, saith the* LORD.

Blessed, ever blessed God, shall we who by nature and by practice are children of wrath, slaves of sin, and bound by its chains; shall we be made the partners of his throne, adorned with an everlasting crown, and distinguished by his name? Yea, verily; and it is added, *I will bless them!* Amazing grace, stupendous love! Our name and nature became a *curse* unto him. His name and nature is a *blessing* unto us! O, may a spark from the sacred altar of gratitude, enkindle in our bosoms an unextinguishable flame; and may we henceforward studiously adorn our profession. May we live to the honour and glory of that name which is named upon us.

SKETCH XIII.

NUMBERS vi. 27.

"AND they shall put my name upon the children of Israel, and I will bless them."

First, What is the name of the LORD? Exodus iii. 14, 15, " And God said unto Moses, I AM THAT I AM: and he said, Thus shalt thou say unto the children of Israel, I AM hath sent me unto you. And God said moreover unto Moses, Thus shalt thou say unto the children of Israel, The LORD God of your fathers, the God of Abraham, the God of Isaac, and the God of Jacob, hath sent me unto you: this is my name forever, and this is my memorial unto all generations." Hosea xii. 9, "And I that am the Lord thy God from the land of Egypt, will yet make thee to dwell in tabernacles, as in the days of the solemn feasts." Revelations i. 4—8, " John to the seven churches which are in Asia: Grace be unto you, and peace, from him which is, and which was, and which is to come; and from Jesus Christ who is the faithful witness, and the first begotten of the dead. I am Alpha and Omega, the first and the last." Hebrews xiii. 8, "Jesus Christ the same yesterday, to day, and forever." That is, from everlasting to everlasting, the only wise God, the Almighty God, the Redeemer of the world. Exodus vi. 3, " And I appeared unto Abraham, unto Isaac, and unto Jacob, by the name of God Almighty; but by my name Jehovah was I not known to them." Isaiah ix. 6, "And his name shall be called Wonderful, Counsellor, The might God, The everlasting Father, the Prince of peace." Revelations xix. 13, " And his name is called the Word of God." John i. 1, " In the beginning was the word, and the word was with God, and the word was God."

Secondly, And they shall put my name upon the children of Israel. Jeremiah xxiii. 6, " And this is his name whereby HE shall be called, the Lord our righteousness." Chapter xxxiii. verse 16, "And this is the name wherewith SHE shall be called, the Lord our righteousness." Psalm xcix. 3, " Let them praise thy great and terrible name: for it is holy." Isaiah lxii. 2, " And thou shalt be called by a new name, which the mouth of the Lord shall name." Chapter lxv. verses 15—20, "*And ye shall leave* your name for a *curse unto my chosen:* for the Lord God shall slay thee, and call his servant by another name; that he who blesseth himself in the earth, shall bless himself in the God of truth; and he that sweareth in the earth, shall swear by the God of truth; because the former troubles are forgotten, and because they are hid from mine eyes. For, behold, I create new heavens and a new earth: and the former shall not be remembered, nor come into mind. But be ye glad and rejoice forever in that which I create: for, behold, I create Jerusalem a rejoicing, and her people a joy. And I will rejoice in Jerusalem, and joy in my people: and the voice of weeping shall be no more heard in her, nor the voice of crying. There shall be no more thence an infant of days, nor an old man that hath not filled his days: for the child shall die an hundred years old; but the sinner, being an hundred years old, shall be accursed." Verses 24, 25, "And it shall come to pass, that before they call, I will answer; and while they are yet speaking, I will hear. The wolf and the lamb shall feed together, and the lion shall eat straw like the bullock: and dust shall be the serpent's meat. They shall not hurt nor destroy in all my holy mountain, saith the LORD." Chapter xxix. 19, "The meek also shall increase their joy in the LORD, and the poor among men shall rejoice in the Holy One of Israel." Chapter xxxi. 1, "But they look not unto the Holy One of Israel." But who is the Holy One of Israel? Isaiah xli. 14, "I will help thee, saith the LORD, and thy Redeemer, the Holy One of Israel." Chapter xliii. 14, "Thus saith the LORD, your Redeemer, the Holy One of Israel." Chapter xlv. 11, "Thus saith the LORD, the Holy One of Israel, and his Maker." Chapter xli. 20, "That they may see, and know, and consider, and understand together, that the hand of the LORD hath done this, and the Holy One of Israel hath created it." Chapter liv. 7, "For thy Maker is thine husband; the LORD of hosts is his name; and thy Redeemer, the Holy One of Israel: The God of the whole earth shall he be called."

Fourthly, This Creator, this Preserver, this Husband of human nature, this *Holy One* of Israel, hath put his name upon us, hath blessed us; yea, and we shall be blessed.

SKETCH XIV.

NUMBERS vii.

First, IMMEDIATELY after the blessing an account of which closed the sixth section the voluntary offerings of the people were liberal and splendid.

Secondly, Judah takes the lead. Judah so eminently typical of the world's Saviour. ii. 3, "And on the east side toward the rising of the sun shall they of the standard of the camp of Judah pitch throughout their armies, and Nahshon the son of Aminidab shall be captain of the children of Judah."

Thirdly, There is no difference in the quantity or quality of the offerings.

Fourthly, Naphtali is the last who offers. Deuteronomy xxxiii. 23, "And of Naphtali he said, O Naphtali, satisfied with favour, and full with the blessings of the Lord possess thou the west and the south." This is said to Naphtali the last who offered.

Fifthly, The Lord spake to Moses. From whence did the Lord speak to this faithful servant?

Sixthly, and lastly, From the mercy seat that was upon the ark of testimony between the two Cherubims.

SKETCH XV.

Numbers viii. 1—4.

"And the Lord spake unto Moses, Saying, speak unto Aaron and say unto him, when thou lightest the lamps, the seven lamps shall give light over against the candlestick. And Aaron did so; he lighted the lamps thereof over against the candlestick, as the Lord commanded Moses. And this work of the candlestick was of beaten gold, unto the shaft thereof, unto the flowers thereof was beaten work: according unto the pattern which the Lord had shewed Moses, so he made the candlesticks."

First, The Lord spake unto Moses. The condescending God spake unto many of his chosen servants. Genesis xxxii. 30, "And Jacob called the name of the place, Peniel; for I have seen God face to face, and my life is preserved." Exodus xxxiii. 11, "And the Lord spake unto Moses face to face, as a man speaketh unto his friend;" Yet it is said, John i. 18, "No man hath seen God at any time." Let us *attempt* to reconcile these passages. We are directed to search the scriptures, and the effort to prove the divinity of scripture, by their consistency, is a praise worthy effort. In fact, it is morally impossible that the scriptures should in *reality* be inconsistent. Yet we sometimes meet with sacred testimonies *apparently* contradictory; and I confess that the circumstance of God's conversing face to face with several individuals of the human family, as recorded in the books of Moses, seems to clash with the Evangelist i.18, "No man hath seen God at any time." Nay, God himself speaking unto his servant Moses, saith, "Thou canst not see my face and live:" for there shall no man see me and live. God is a spirit, and a spirit is not clothed in flesh. But God is supplicated to lift up the light of his countenance; and it is frequently said, he doth lift up the light of his countenance upon individuals. When one friend averteth his face from another, he gives evidence of an unfriendly disposition. The mode of expression in holy writ is often accommodated to our understandings, it is generally figurative; when therefore a servant of God is said to have seen the face of God, when the everlasting Father is said to have conversed with his children, as one friend converseth with another, what is it but an evidence of affection and approbation. Thou hidest thy face, and I was troubled, said one. No man hath seen God at any time—Ye cannot see my face and live. Well, these testimonies are perfectly in unison. We can behold God manifest in the flesh, in the person of Christ Jesus, in the angel of the covenant, which angel of the covenant hath on various occasions conversed face to face with the children of men. But no man hath at any time seen God, the pure essence of all intelligence, the self existent source of being. We cannot see the wind which bloweth, the atmosphere in which we live, the fire which warmeth or consumeth, but the effects produced by those elements are visible to our understanding. No man hath seen God at any time. God the divine nature, is like the soul in the body, which is the figure of the divine nature. Who hath at any time seen the soul? The soul cannot be seen; it is invisible. Neither can any man at any time, see God, the divine nature. Show us the Father, said Philip, and it sufficeth us. Have I been so long with thee, Philip, and thou hast not known me? To men and angels, out of Christ, Jehovah is unknown. Thus, it is apparent, our souls would be forever unknown (for our souls are the breath of God) if they had never been embodied; but we were made in the image of God. No man, then, hath at any time seen the divine nature: but the human nature, the head of every man, was the clothing of Deity. Yet, when God graciously shows favour to his children, he lifts up upon them the light of his countenance, and then they are said to see his face.

Secondly, Our subject. The candlestick and the lamps. First, The candlestick. This candlestick is described, Exodus xxv. And it is spoken of in the singular character; but there is a shaft, and there are branches described; three on one side, and three on the other; and these branches were all to *proceed out of the candlestick, and altogether* were to be made of *pure gold*, of beaten work, of *one piece*. It is remarkable that for these candlesticks, seven lamps were made.

Thirdly, What are we to understand by the lamps. These were first *of the candlesticks;* Secondly, they were to be placed *over against* the candlesticks: Thirdly, they must burn in them pure olive oil: Fourthly, they must burn continually.

Fourthly, We will diligently inquire, if peradventure we may catch a glimpse of the grand design of the Omnipotent architect, in this *circumstantial delineation*. We know that the candlesticks are emblematic of the churches. Revelations i. 20, " The mystery of the seven stars which thou sawest in my right hand, and the seven golden candlesticks. The seven stars are the angel of the seven churches: and the seven candlesticks which thou sawest, are the seven churches." The shaft and the branches were of one piece. Hebrews ii. 11, " For both he that sanctifieth, and they who are sanctified, are all of one; for which cause he is not ashamed to call them brethren." The candlesticks were to be of pure gold. Isaiah xiii 12, " I will make a man more precious than fine gold: even a man than the golden wedge of Ophir."

The branches proceeded *out of the candlestick, and are in the candlestick*. John xvii 23, " I in them, and thou in me, that they may be made perfect in one." John xv. 5, " I am the vine, ye are the branches." Ephesians ii. 15, 16, " Having abolished in his flesh the enmity, even the law of commandments, contained in ordinances, for to make in himself of twain one new man, so making peace; And that he might reconcile both unto God in one body by the cross, having slain the enmity thereby," The human nature of Christ, and the human nature of the sons and daughters of Adam, have but one origin in birth, in life, in death, in resurrection. Galatians iii. 28, " There is neither Jew nor Greek, there is neither bond nor free, there is neither male nor female; for ye are all one in Christ Jesus."

Thirdly, We are to inquire the design of the spirit of truth in the figure of the lamps. But this investigation must be reserved till we are indulged with the privilege of again assembling together in this place.

QUESTION PROPOSED.

Genesis vi. 6 7.

"And it repented the Lord that he had made man on the earth, and it grieved him at the heart. It repenteth me that I have made them." Exodus xxxii. 14, "And the Lord repented of the evil which he thought to do unto his people." Judges ii. 18, "For it repented the Lord because of their groanings." 1 Samuel xv. 35, "And the Lord repented that he made Saul king over Israel." 2 Samuel xxiv. 16, "The Lord repented him of the evil, and said to the angel that destroyed the people, it is enough." 1 Chronicles xxi. 15, "And God sent an angel unto Jerusalem, to destroy it; and as he was destroying, the Lord beheld, and he repented him of the evil." Jeremiah xxvi. 19, "And the Lord repented him of the evil which he had pronounced against him." Psalm cvi. 45, "And the Lord repented according to the multitude of his mercies." Amos vii. 3, "The Lord repented for this; It shall not be, saith the Lord." Jonah iii. 10, "And God repented of the evil that he had said that he would do unto them, and did it not."

CONTRAST.

Numbers xx. 19, "God is not a man, that he should lie; neither the Son of man, that he should repent: Hath he said, and shall he not do it? Or hath he spoken, and shall he not make it good?" 1 Samuel xv. 29, "And also the strength of Israel will not lie nor repent: for he is not a man, that he should repent." Psalm cx. 4, "The Lord hath sworn and will not repent." Jeremiah iv. 28, "I have spoken it, I have purposed it, and will not repent, neither will I turn back from it." Ezekiel xxiv. 14, "I the Lord have spoken it; it shall come to pass, and I will do it;

I will not go back, neither will I spare, neither will I repent." Hosea xiii. 14, "Repentance shall be hid from mine eyes." Zechariah viii. 14, "For thus saith the LORD God of hosts, As I thought to punish you, when your fathers provoked me to wrath, saith the LORD of hosts, and I repented not." Romans xi. 29, "For the gifts and callings of God are without repentance." Can these opposite testimonies be reconciled?

ANSWER ATTEMPTED.

Two particulars must be acknowledged indisputable, by every individual who admits the prescience and omnipotence of Deity. Grant to the great first cause these two attributes, and we must pronounce positively, he never could *repent* agreeably *to our* acceptation of the word repentance. Invested with prescience, the events of time and eternity must have been disclosed to his view. Invested with omnipotence, he could direct every event according to his own good pleasure. If by repentance we understand nothing more than a change of measures, we acknowledge the dispensations of heaven to be various, and they were no doubt designed so to be.

It is undeniably true, testimonies diametrically contradictory, cannot consist; and yet, perhaps, the divinity of revelation resteth, in a great measure, upon its consistency. Scripture testimonies *may appear* contradictory, but I hesitate not to affirm decisively, that it is only in *appearance* that scripture testimonies can contradict each other. Although I may not always be able to point out the consistency of scripture, yet I do verily believe, that it always does consist both with itself, and with the honour of God.

But how are we to manage, when, as in the present case, the contradiction is so apparent? Shall we say the translator is in an error? This *may* be the case; and in many instances translators have, no doubt, given a false and a mutilated translation. The Bible was translated by *fallible* men. These men had, no doubt, ideas and a system of their own, and they could scarcely forbear a bias in favour of their *own sentiments;* and by the way, as I do not know that the Bible was ever translated by a *Universalist*, it appears to me wonderful, that a number of passages which so strikingly declare this God honouring truth, should be continued, and that too in an unmutilated state. I think a result so happy for the believer, must have been effectuated by the interposition of the overruling spirit of truth. In fact, this circumstance appears to me as great a miracle as any which the sacred volume records.

I am not, however, fond of imputing errors to translators. Were we, upon every occasion when the text did not suit our purpose, to question the accuracy of the translation, it would lead us *too far;* it would ultimately *destroy our standard;* and persons would consider themselves justified in giving such a sense to scripture, as might best correspond with a wildered and distempered imagination. I cannot be satisfied with asserting, that the sacred oracles do not *mean* as they *speak,* for this would end in countless and *cureless* evils. "But, what then can we do when the contradiction is so palpable?" Do? Why I would do any thing rather than make God a liar.

Were I to receive a letter from a respectable friend, which letter contained some ideas or expressions, that did not correspond with the opinion I had formed of his general character, I would recur to former letters, and endeavour to collect something explanatory of the present embarrassment; but if former letters would not elucidate, I would call to mind the well-known, the well-established character of my respectable friend, and if this recollection would not extricate me from the perplexity in which I was involved, if the mystery still continued, I would attribute it either to *my want of understanding, or to some misconception.*

From every manifestation of my almighty Father, and from all I ever heard or saw of the God who made me, it is evident to my comprehension, that he is infinitely *wise* and infinitely *good.* But what ideas does the word repentance convey? Repentance has its origin in a conviction of error or of sin. It furnishes regret for the want of that capacity which has precipitated us into folly, or it is sorrow for that degree of turpitude which has involved us in guilt. But neither of these sources of repentance can be considered as proper to the *infinitely wise,* the *infinitely good God.*

It hath been observed, that the Creator communes with the creature he hath fashioned, in his own language, that he may the more readily be comprehended. Thus spake he to his disciples respecting the death of Lazarus. But this idea will not aid us in the present instance, for we are told it repented God, that he had made man! But why did he repent? Was the result such as he had not calculated? Was not every event present to his view before the foundation of the world? Could an *all-wise God* be mistaken in his calculation? Was he to whom one eternal now was ever present, disappointed in his expectation? Could not an omnipotent Being *control* events according to his own purpose? Must not an *all-wise*, an *all-good*, an omnipotent Being, be necessarily an *unchanging Being?* And is not our God said to be an *unchanging* God? Should any passage in the sacred writings assert, that God *was not good*, ought I to consider such testimony as *stamped by divine authority?* Ought I not rather unhesitatingly to pronounce that *error, gross error, existed somewhere*, and that the text was *impiously* deformed? It is really astonishing, when we take every circumstance into view, that so few errors are to be found in the translations of scripture which are now extant.

For myself, whenever insuperable difficulties occur, I am neither afraid nor ashamed to acknowledge that they are so. If declarations are confessedly diametrically opposed, I dare affirm, they cannot both be *literally* true; and thus circumstanced, I will accept that testimony as *literal*, which most comports with reason and with the attributes of the Almighty. Of one thing I am at all times positive, that *God is true*. Something must remain to be elucidated in that state upon which we verge, and we shall ultimately confess, from conviction confess, *that all things are right*.

I say then, and it appears to me I cannot too often say, that the infinitely *wise* God must know, and the infinitely *good* God must *do* all things well. I reverence the Bible; it is the Book of God. There is no *yea* and *nay* in the Bible. But it may contain passages beyond my comprehension. Yet I can find enough in it, that I can understand; and it is, and I trust it will continue unto me an abiding source of consolation.

SKETCH XVI.

Numbers ix. 1—14.

First, WHAT was the origin of the passover? In the book of Exodus, chapter twelfth, Moses gives us an answer to this question. "And the Lord spake unto Moses and Aaron, in the land of Egypt, saying, This month shall be unto you the beginning of months; it shall be the first month of the year to you. Speak ye unto all the congregation of Israel, saying, In the tenth day of this month, they shall take to them every man a lamb, according to the house of their fathers, a lamb for an house. And if the household be too little for the lamb, let him and his neighbour next unto his house, take it according to the number of the souls; every man according to his eating shall make your count for the lamb. Your lamb shall be without blemish, a male of the first year; ye shall take it out from the sheep, or from the goats: and ye shall keep it up until the fourteenth day of the same month; and the whole assembly of the congregation of Israel shall kill it in the evening. And they shall take of the blood, and strike it on the two side-posts, and on the upper door-post of the houses, wherein they shall eat it. And they shall eat the flesh in that night, roast with fire, and unleavened bread; and with bitter herbs shall they eat it. Eat not of it raw, nor sodden at all with water, but roast with fire; and ye shall let nothing of it remain until the morning. And thus shall ye eat it; with your loins girded, your shoes on your feet, and your staff in your hand; and ye shall eat it in haste: it is the LORD's passover. For I will pass through the land of Egypt this night, and will smite all the first-born in the land of Egypt, both man and beast; and against all the gods of Egypt I will execute judgment: I am the LORD. And the blood shall be to you for a token upon the houses where ye are: and when I see the blood, I will pass over you, and the plague shall not be upon you to destroy you, when I smite the land of Egypt. And this day shall be unto you for a memorial; and ye shall keep it a feast to the LORD throughout your generations: ye shall keep it a feast by an ordinance forever."

Secondly, The time when this passover was kept, requires our marked and pious attention. It was on the evening immediately preceding the deliverance of the children of Israel.

Thirdly, Of what was the passover typical? 1 Corinthians, v. 7, 8, "Purge out therefore the old leaven, that ye may be a new lump, as ye are unleavened. For even Christ our passover is sacrificed for us. Therefore let us keep the feast, not with old leaven, neither with the leaven of malice and wickedness; but with the unleavened bread of sincerity and truth." As the destroying angel injured none on whose door the blood of the passover was sprinkled so divine justice is completely satisfied for all those for whom the blood of Christ was shed: purchased by the blood-shedding of the Redeemer, justice passes over them, without an accusation.

Fourthly, As the lamb was slain, and the blood sprinkled, before the deliverance of the people : so it was necessary that Christ Jesus should suffer death, for the lost family of man, before it could be redeemed from the ruin into which it had been precipitated. John, xi. 50, 51, 52, " Nor consider that it is expedient for us, that one man should die for the people, and that the whole nation perish not. And this spake he not of himself: but being high Priest that year, he prophesied that Jesus should die for that nation. And not for that nation only, but also that he should gather together in one the children of God that were scattered abroad." Isaiah, liii. 5, " But he was wounded for our transgressions, he was bruised for our iniquities: the chastisement of our peace was upon him; and with his stripes we are healed." Daniel, ix. 24, 26, " Seventy weeks are determined upon thy people, and upon thy holy city, to finish the transgression, and to make an end of sins, and to make reconciliation for iniquity, and to bring in everlasting righteousness, and to seal up the vision and prophecy, and to anoint the Most Holy. And after three score and two weeks shall Messiah be cut off: but not for himself." Hosea, vi. 2, " After two days will he revive us: in the third day he will raise us up, and we shall live in his sight." Luke, xxiv. 25, 26, 27, " Then he said unto them, O fools, and slow of heart to believe all that the prophets have spoken. Ought not Christ to have suffered these things, and to enter into his glory? And beginning at Moses and all the prophets, he expounded unto them in all the scriptures, the things concerning himself." Acts, xxvi. 22, 23, " Having therefore obtained help of God, I continue unto this day, witnessing both to small and great, saying none other things than those which the prophets and Moses did say should come. That Christ should suffer, and that he should be the first that should rise from the dead, and should shew light unto the people, and to the Gentiles."

Fifthly, As the passover was kept and the lamb slain before the law was given by Moses, or the ceremonies performed, it teaches that our salvation resteth not upon the law, nor upon the instituted ceremonies, but upon the Lamb slain from the foundation of the world. Revelations, xiii. 8, " And all that dwell upon the earth, shall worship him, *whose names are not written in the book of life,* of the Lamb slain from the foundation of the world.* Romans, iii. 25, "Whom God hath set forth to be a propiuation through faith in his blood, to declare his righteousness for the remission of sins that are past, through the forbearance of God." Hebrews, ix 17, " How much more shall the blood of Christ, who, through the eternal spirit offered himself without spot to God, purge your concience from dead works to serve the living God ?"

Sixthly, The passover was slain in the first month in the year, in which month was Christ, our passover sacrificed for us.

Seventhly, The passover was put to death in the evening, to intimate the Redeemer should suffer in the last dispensation, and indeed in the evening of the day. Hebrews, ix. 26, " For then must he often have suffered since the foundation of the world : but now once in the end of the world hath he appeared to put away sin by the sacrifice of himself."

Eighthly, The passover was to be roasted with fire, not only to indicate the agonies which were to attend the suffering Saviour, but to exhibit, by this striking type, the purpose of God respecting *our passover*, Christ Jesus, who thus dwelt with everlasting burnings, when the day of the Lord's vengeance burned as an oven. Isaiah, xxxiii. 14, 15, " The sinners in Zion are afraid; fearfulness hath surprised the hypocrites. Who among us shall dwell with the devouring fire? Who among us shall dwell with everlasting burnings ? He that walketh righteously, and speaketh uprightly ; he that despiseth the gain of oppressions, that shaketh his hands from holding of bribes, that stoppeth his ears from hearing of blood, and shutteth his eyes from seeing evil " Malachi, iv. 1, " For, behold, the day cometh, that shall burn as an oven ; and all the proud, yea, and all that do wickedly, shall be stubble ; and the day that cometh shall burn them up, saith the Lord of hosts, that it shall leave them neither root nor branch." John, xii. 32, 33, " And I, if I

---

* Those who had a lodging in the breast of the man who dwelt among the tombs, with those legions of spirits that work in the hearts of the children of disobedience, and who will continue to dwell upon the earth. until the time of the restitution of all things, never had their names written in the Lamb's book of life.

be lifted up from the earth, will draw all men unto me. This he said, signifying what death he should die."

Ninthly, The Lamb was to be eaten with bitter herbs. Bitter is a word expressive of sore affliction. Isaiah, xxxviii. 17, " Behold, for peace I had great bitterness : but thou hast in love to my soul delivered it from the pit of corruption : for thou hast cast all my sins behind thy back." Eating the passover with bitter herbs, is not only descriptive of the depth of misery from which they were delivered, but it also points to the agonies suffered by our great passover, while extended upon the cross for us men, and for our salvation. It is observable that in the midst of those agonies, when the Redeemer cried, I thirst, they gave him vinegar to drink, mingled with *gall !*

Tenthly, A bone of the paschal Lamb was not to be broken. *Thus the union between the head and members remained indissoluble.* The soldiers were under the influence of the over-ruling spirit of truth. John, xix. 32—37, " Then came the soldiers, and brake the legs of the first, and of the other which was crucified with him. But when they came to Jesus, and saw that he was dead already, they brake not his legs. But one of the soldiers with a spear, pierced his side, and forthwith came there out blood and water. And he that saw it bare record, and his record is true; and he knoweth that he saith true, that ye might believe. For these things were done, that the scripture should be fulfilled, A bone of him shall not be broken. And again, another scripture saith, They shall look on him whom they pierced."

Eleventhly, The passover must be eaten with unleavened bread. Matthew, xvi. 6, " Then Jesus said unto them, take heed and beware of the leaven, of the Pharisees and of the Sadducees." 1 Corinthians, v. 7, 8, " Purge out therefore the old leaven, that ye may be a new lump, as ye are unleavened. For even Christ our passover is sacrificed for us : therefore, let us keep the fast not with old leaven, neither with the leaven of malice and wickedness ; but with the unleavened bread of sincerity and truth."

Twelfthly, and lastly, *The men who were defiled were nevertheless enjoined to keep the passover.* The stranger also was permitted to keep the passover. " Ye shall have one ordinance, both for the stranger, and for him that was born in the land."

As the communion is the superstructure of this institution, we shall derive both instruction and consolation, from a regular, serious, pious and faithful observance of this sacrament.

SKETCH XVII.

NUMBERS, ix. 15—23.

First, The tabernacle. Moses gives us a copious description of this tabernacle. Exodus, chapters xxv. xxvi. xxvii. And that the tabernacle was typical of the human Nature of Jesus Christ, is abundantly apparent from Hebrews, viii. 2, 5, " A minister of the sanctuary, and of the true tabernacle, which the LORD pitched, and not man. Who serve unto the shadow and example of heavenly things, as Moses was admonished of God when he was about to make the tabernacle; for, see, saith he, that thou make all things according to the pattern shewed thee in the mount."

Secondly, The cloud. What are we to understand by the cloud? and by its resting on the tabernacle? Exodus, xiii. 21, 22, " And the LORD went before them by day in a pillar of a cloud to lead them the way: and by night in a pillar of fire, to give them light; to go by day and night. He took not away the pillar of the cloud by day, nor the pillar of fire by night, from before the people." The cloud was in the form of a pillar. The base broad, the top pointed; the base resting on the tabernacle, the top pointing to the heavens, like Jacob's ladder, the foot of which rested upon the earth, while its top reached to heaven, upon which ladder the angels of God ascended and descended. But this cloudy pillar answered a double purpose. It sheltered them from the heat of the day, which in the desert, was intense, and by the luminous light of that fire with which it was irradiated, it guided them through the night. It was the same cloud which, if I may so express myself, took the Hebrews under its direction, and protection, from their leaving Egypt, even until the elevation of the tabernacle.

This cloudy pillar, we are instructed by the sacred oracles, to consider as a figure of the divine nature, resting on the humanity. The divine nature is frequently described to us under the figure of fire. Hebrews, xii. 29, " For our God is a consuming fire."

This fire was in the cloud, thus God dwelleth in the thick darkness. Psalm, xviii. 11, " He made darkness his secret place; his pavilion round about him were dark waters and thick clouds of the skies." Psalm, xcvii. 2, " Clouds and darkness are round about him: righteousness and judgment are the habitation of his throne." 2 Samuel, xxii. 10, 12, " He bowed the heavens also, and came down: and darkness was under his feet. And he made darkness pavilions round about him, dark waters and thick clouds of the skies."

Thirdly, What do we learn from the moving of the cloud. The cloud moved for the direction of the people, and that in all their journeyings the presence of God might still abide with them. Moses built his every hope of prosperity and happiness, upon the presence of his God. Exodus, xxxiii 14, 15, 16, " And he said, my presence shall go with thee, and I will give thee rest. And he said unto him, if thy presence go not with me, carry us not up hence. For wherein shall it be known here, that I and thy people have found grace in thy sight? Is it not in that thou goest with us? So shall we be separated, I, and thy people, from all the people that are upon the face of the earth." Psalm, xxxi. 20, " Thou shalt hide them in the secret of thy presence from the pride of man: thou shalt keep them secretly in a pavilion from the strife of tongues." Ezekiel, x. 3, 4, " Now the cherubims stood on the right side of the house, when the man went in; and the cloud filled the inner court. Then the glory of the Lord went up from the cherub, and stood over the threshold of the house, and the house was filled with the cloud, and the court was full of the brightness of the Lord's glory."

Fourthly, The Lord commanded the people to continue stationary, until he, by his appearance in the cloud, gave them direction to proceed, and that the people submitted to this command, is apparent from the conclusion of this chapter.

Fifthly, The ultimate purpose of these regulations is given in the two last verses of the tenth chapter of this book of Numbers. "And it came to pass, when the ark set forward, that Moses said, rise up, Lord, and let thine enemies be scattered, and let them that hate thee flee before thee. And when it rested, he said, return, O Lord, unto the many thousands of Israel."

Sixthly, In the thirty-third verse, we are told, that the children of Israel departed from the mount of the Lord three days' journey. We shall determine what mountain this mount of the LORD was, by consulting Exodus iii. "Now Moses kept the flock of Jethro his father-in-law, the priest of Midian: and he led the flock to the back side of the desert, and came to the mountain of God even to Horeb. And the angel of the LORD appeared unto him in a flame of fire out of the midst of a bush: and he looked, and, behold, the bush burned with fire, and the bush was not consumed. And Moses said, I will now turn aside, and see this great sight, why the bush is not burnt. And when the LORD saw that he turned aside to see, God called unto him out of the midst of the bush." God informed Moses by what name he would choose to be designated among the Hebrews, and he said, "Thus shalt thou say unto the children of Israel, I AM hath sent me unto thee." John viii. 58, "Jesus said unto them, verily, verily, I say unto you, before Abraham was, I AM."

Seventhly, When the ark of the LORD went forward "Moses said, let thine enemies be scattered, and let those who hate thee flee before thee." Psalm lxviii. "Let God arise, let his enemies be scattered: let them also that hate him flee before him. As smoke is driven away, so drive them away: as wax melteth before the fire, so let the wicked perish at the presence of God." Revelations xii. 9, 10, "And the great dragon was cast out, that old serpent, called the devil and satan, which deceiveth the whole world: he was cast out into the earth, and his angels were cast out with him. And I heard a loud voice saying in heaven, now is come salvation, and strength, and the kingdom of our God, and the power of his Christ: for the accuser of our brethren is cast down, which accused them before our God day and night." This transaction is circumstantially delineated, in the close of the twenty-fifth chapter of Matthew. When, consequent upon the casting out of this deceiver, and his angels, who had occupied dwellings in the human earth, the righteous shine forth as the sun and enter into life eternal.

Eighthly, When the tabernacle and the cloud rested, then said Moses, "Return, O LORD, to the many thousands of Israel" Thus saith the holy spirit, Acts xv. 15—17, "And to this agree the words of the prophets, as it is written; After this I will return, and will build again the tabernacle of David, which is fallen down; and I will build again the ruins thereof, and I will set it up: That the residue of men might seek after the LORD, and all the Gentiles upon whom my name is called, saith the LORD, who doeth all these things." Zechariah i. 16, 17, " Therefore, thus saith the Lord, I am returned to Jerusalem with mercies: my house shall be built in it, saith the Lord of hosts; and a line shall be stretched forth upon Jerusalem. Cry yet, saying, thus saith the Lord of hosts; my cities through prosperity shall yet be spread abroad; and the Lord shall yet comfort Zion, and shall yet choose Jerusalem." Romans xi. 26, "And so all Israel shall be saved; as it is written, there shall come out of Zion the deliverer, and shall turn away ungodliness from Jacob." Isaiah gloriously confirms and amplifies this blessed truth, xi. 10—12, "And in that day there shall be a root of Jesse, which shall stand for an ensign of the people; to it shall the Gentiles seek; and his rest shall be glorious. And it shall come to pass in that day, that the Lord shall set his hand again the second time to recover the remnant of his people, which shall be left from Assyria, and from Egypt, and from Pathros, and from Cush, and from Elam, and from Shinar, and from Hamath, and from the islands of the sea. And he shall set up an ensign for the nations, and shall assemble the out casts of Israel, and gather together the the dispersed of Judah, from the four corners of the earth." Micah vii. 19, 20, " He will turn again, he will have compassion upon us; he will subdue our iniquities; and thou wilt cast all their sins into the depths of the sea. Thou wilt perform the truth to Jacob, and the mercy to Abraham, which thou hast sworn unto our fathers from the days of old." What is the truth which the spirit assures us will be performed to Jacob? Genesis xxviii. 14, " And thy seed shall be as the dust of the earth, and thou shalt spread abroad to the west, and to the east, and to the north, and to the south; and in thee, and in thy seed shall all the families of the earth be blessed." What was the mercy sworn unto Abraham? Genesis xxii. 16—18, " By myself have I sworn, saith the Lord, for because thou hast done this thing, and hast not withheld thy son, thine only son: that in blessing I will bless thee, and in multiplying I will multiply thy seed, as the stars of the heaven: and as the sand which is upon the sea shore; and thy seed shall possess the gates of his enemies. And in thy seed shall all the nations of the earth be blessed."

An oath, saith the Apostle, is amongst men an end of all strife. How is it that the oath of Jehovah is the source of strife between those who believe his words, and those who do not.

SKETCH XVIII.

Numbers xxvii. 16, 17.

First, God is the God of the spirits of all flesh. Chapter xvi. 22, "And they fell upon their faces, and said, O God, the God of the spirits of all flesh, shall one man sin, and wilt thou be wroth with all the congregation?" Hebrews ii. 9, "But we see Jesus who was made a little lower than the angels, for the suffering of death, crowned with glory and honour, that he, by the grace of God, should taste death for every man."

Secondly, But as God is the God of the spirits of *all flesh*, so doth *all flesh*, in *the aggregate, constitute his body*. Ephesians iv. 4, "There is one body and one spirit, even as ye are called in one hope of your calling." Hebrews x. 5, "Wherefore when he cometh into the world, he saith, Sacrifices and offerings thou wouldest not, but a *body* hast thou prepared me."

Thirdly, What is this body? Ephesians ii. 16, "And that he might reconcile both unto God in one body on the cross, having slain the enmity thereby." 1 Corinthians, xii. 12, "For as the body is one, and hath many members, and all the members of that one body, being many, are one body ; so also is Christ." John xii. 33, "This he said, signifying what death he should die."

Fourthly, What are we to understand by going in and going out before the people ? The following scriptures furnish an answer. Deuteronomy xxxi. 2, "And he said unto them, I am an hundred and twenty years old this day ; I can no more go out and come in: also the Lord hath said unto me, Thou shalt not go over this Jordan." 1 Kings iii. 7, "And now, O Lord my God, thou hast made thy servant king instead of David my father; and I am but a little child : I know not how to go out or come in." John x. 3, 4, 5, "To him the porter openeth ; and the sheep hear his voice: and he calleth his own sheep by name, and leadeth them out. And when he putteth forth his own sheep, he goeth before them, and the sheep follow him : for they know his voice. And a stranger will they not follow, but will flee from him : for they know not the voice of strangers." 1 Peter ii. 9, "But ye are a chosen generation, a royal priesthood, an holy nation, a peculiar people; that ye should shew forth the praises of him who hath called you out of darkness into his marvellous light."

Fifthly, What are the sheep? And what is the shepherd?

Sixthly, and lastly, What is intended by the clause in the text, which represents the people as sheep having no shepherd?

We turn, as usual, to the volume of inspiration for answers to to these queries.

Zechariah x. 3, "Mine anger was kindled against the shepherds, and I punished the *goats:* for the Lord of hosts hath visited his flock the house of Judah, and hath made them as his goodly horse in the battle." Matthew ix. 36, 37, 38, "But when he saw the multitudes, he was moved with compassion on them, because they fainted, and were scattered abroad, as sheep having no shepherd. Then saith he unto his disciples, The harvest truly is plenteous, but the labourers are few; pray ye therefore the Lord of the harvest, that he will send forth labourers into his harvest." John x. 10—16, "The thief cometh not but for to steal, and to kill, and to destroy: I am come that they might have life, and that they might have it more abundantly. I am the good Shepherd: the good shepherd giveth his life for the sheep. I am the good Shepherd, and know my sheep, and am known of mine. As the Father knoweth me, even so know I the Father: and I lay down my life for the sheep. And other sheep I have, which are not of this fold: them also I must bring, and they shall hear my voice; and there shall be one fold, and one shepherd."

SKETCH XIX.

Numbers xxix. 1.

First, What are we to understand by the seventh month? It is a Sabbath of rest unto you. Leviticus xxiii. 3, 24, "Six days shall work be done; but the seventh day is the Sabbath of rest, an holy convocation, ye shall do no work therein: it is the Sabbath of the Lord in all your dwellings. Speak unto the children of Israel, saying, In the seventh month, in the first day of the month, shall ye have a Sabbath, a memorial of blowing of trumpets, an holy convocation."

Secondly, This portion of time is termed a *holy convocation.*

Thirdly, No servile work must be performed thereon.

Fourthly, and lastly, It is a day of blowing the trumpets. Leviticus xxiii. 24, " Speak unto the children of Israel, saying, In the seventh month, in the first day of the month, shall ye have a Sabbath, a memorial of blowing of trumpets, an holy convocation." To what does this sabbatic month, this blowing of trumpets spiritually point? 1Corinthians xv. 52, " In a moment, in the twinkling of an eye, at the last trump: for the trumpet shall sound, and the dead shall be raised incorruptible, and we shall be changed." Zechariah ix. 14, " And the Lord shall be seen over them, and his arrow shall go forth as the lightening, and the Lord God shall blow the trumpet, and shall go with whirlwinds of the south " Isaiah xxvii. 13, " And it shall come to pass in that day, that the great trumpet shall be blown, and they shall come who were ready to perish in the land of Assyria, and the out-casts in the land of Egypt, and shall worship the Lord in the holy mount at Jerusalem." John v. 25, " Verily, verily, I say unto you, The hour is coming, and now is, when the dead shall hear the voice of the Son of God: and they that hear shall live." 1 Thessalonians, vi. 16, 17, 18, " For the Lord himself shall descend from heaven with a shout, with the voice of the archangel, and with the trump of God: and the dead in Christ shall rise first: then we which are alive and remain, shall be caught up together with them in the clouds, to meet the Lord in the air: and so shall we ever be with the Lord. Wherefore, comfort one another with these words."

SKETCH XX.

Numbers xxxv. 32.

First, The city of refuge. What was it? A sanctuary for individuals, whose lives were forfeited.

Secondly, What did God design by this establishment? Undoubtedly an exhibition of himself in his character of a hiding place from the storm. This is not *fancy*, but *fact.* I produce my vouchers. Deuteronomy xxxiii. 27, "The eternal God is thy refuge, and underneath are the everlasting arms: and he shall thrust out the enemy from before thee; and shall say, Destroy them." 2 Samuel xxii. 3, "The God of my rock, in him will I trust: he is my shield, and the horn of my salvation, my high tower, and my refuge, my Saviour; thou savest me from violence." Psalm ix. 9, "The LORD also will be a refuge for the oppressed, a refuge in times of trouble." Psalm xiv. 6, "Ye have shamed the counsel of the poor, because the LORD is his refuge." Psalm xlvi. 1, "God is our refuge and strength, a very present help in trouble." Psalm lxii. 7, 8, "In God is my salvation and my glory: the rock of my strength, and my refuge is in God. Trust in him at all times, ye people; pour out your heart before him: God is a refuge for us. Selah. Psalm xci. 2, 9, "I will say of the LORD, He is my refuge and my fortress: my God; in him will I trust. Because thou hast made the LORD which is my refuge, even the Most High, thy habitation." Psalm xciv. 22, "But the LORD is my defence; and my God is the rock of my refuge." Psalm cxlii. 5, "I cried unto the LORD; I said, Thou art my refuge, and my portion in the land of the living." Isaiah iv. 6, "And there shall be a tabernacle for a shadow in the daytime from the heat, and for a place of refuge, and for a covert from storm and from rain." Chapter xxv. 4, "For thou hast been a strength to the poor, a strength to the needy in his distresses, a refuge from the storm, a shadow from the heat, when the blast of the terrible ones is as a storm against the wall." Jeremiah xvi. 19, "O LORD, my strength, and my fortress, and my refuge in the day of affliction, the Gentiles shall come unto thee from the ends of the earth, and shall say, Surely our fathers have inherited lies, vanity, and things wherein there is no profit." Hebrews vi. 18, "That by two immutable things, in which it was impossible for God to lie, we might have a strong consolation, who have fled for refuge, to lay hold on the hope set before us."

SKETCH XXI.

Deuteronomy, iv. 5, 6.

First, Moses taught no statutes nor judgments but such as the Lord commanded him. A prophet shall the Lord your God raise up unto you like unto me. John, xiv 24, " He that loveth me not, keepeth not my sayings: and the word which ye hear is not mine, but the father's which sent me. xvii. 8, " For I have given unto them the words which thou gavest me, and they have received them, and have known surely that I came out from thee, and they have believed that thou didst send me."

Secondly, " The people keeping those statutes thus evinced their wisdom. To this truth Job beareth witness, chapter xxviii. 28, " And unto man he said, Behold, the fear of the Lord, that is wisdom; and to depart from evil is understanding." Psalm, xix. 7, " The law of the Lord is perfect, converting the soul: the testimony of the Lord is sure, making wise the simple." Psalm cxi. 10, " The fear of the Lord is the beginning of wisdom: a good understanding have all they that do his commandments: his praise endureth forever." Psalm, cxix. 98, 99, " Thou through thy commandments hast made me wiser than mine enemies: for they are ever with me. I have more understanding than all my teachers: for thy testimonies are my meditation." 2 Timothy, iii. 15, " And that from a child thou hast known the holy scriptures, which are able to make thee wise unto salvation, through faith which is in Christ Jesus."

Thirdly, Did ever any human being keep these statutes and judgments in his own person? Let the oracles of God decide. Psalm, xiv. 2, " The Lord looked down from heaven upon the children of men, to see if there were any that did understand, and seek God." Romans, iii. 10, " As it is written, there is none righteous, no, not one." The framers of the assembly's Catechism avow sentiments in union with the foregoing testimonies. No mere man, say they, since the fall, is able to keep these commandments, but daily doth break them in thought, word and deed.

Fourthly, Is it possible to obtain life in any other way than by keeping the commandments? Matthew, xix. 17, " And he said unto him, why callest thou me good? There is none good but one, that is God: but if thou wilt enter into life keep the commandments." No, it is not possible to enter into life in any other way, for the soul that sinneth shall die.

Fifthly, How then can any sinner be saved? By keeping the whole law with a *perfect heart, in his perfect head!* Jesus, who is the head of every *man, was made under the law.* Galatians, iii. 13, " Christ hath redeemed us from the curse of the law, being made a curse for us: for it is written, Cursed is every one that hangeth on a tree." Verse 23, " But before faith came, we were kept under the law, shut up unto the faith which should afterwords be revealed." Galatians, iv. 5, " To redeem them that were under the law, that we might receive the adoption of sons."

Sixthly, and lastly, *Did* Jesus keep the law? I came not, said he, to destroy the law, but to fulfil it. *Did* Jesus keep the law *with his whole heart?* Thy law is in my heart, said the Redeemer. Is he in consequence of keeping the law the life of the world? Is he consequently the wisdom, the righteousness, and sanctification of sinners? 1 Corinthians, i. 30, 31, " But of him are ye in Christ Jesus, *who of God is made unto us wisdom, and righteousness, and sanctification, and redemption. That according as it is written, He that glorieth, let him glory in the* LORD.

―――

SKETCH XXII.

DEUTERONOMY, viii. 31, 32.

First, GOD the LORD was indeed the God of the Hebrews, and addressing this people, Exodus, xix. 4, He saith, " Ye have seen what I did unto the Egyptians, and how I bear you on eagle's wings and brought you to myself. Deuteronomy, xxxii. 9—12, " For the LORD's *portion* is his people; Jacob is the lot of his inheritance. He found him in a desert land, and in the waste howling wilderness; he led him about, he instructed him, he kept him as the apple of his eye. As an eagle stirreth up her nest, fluttereth over her young, spreadeth abroad her wings, taketh them, beareth them on her wings: So the LORD alone did lead him." Hosea, xi. 3, 4, " I taught Ephraim also to go, taking them by their arms; but they knew not that I healed them. I drew them with cords of a man, with bands of love: and I was to them as they that take off the yoke on their jaws, and I laid meat unto them."

Secondly, Yet these people were not believers! Psalm, lxxviii. 22, " Because they believed not in God, and trusted not in his salvation." Hebrews, iii. 1, 2, " Wherefore, holy brethren, partakers of the heavenly calling, consider the apostle, and high Priest of our profession, Christ Jesus; Who was faithful to him that appointed him, as also Moses was faithful in all his house." And to whom sware he that they should not enter into his rest, but to them that *believed not* ? So we see that they could not enter in, because of unbelief. Jude 5, " I will therefore put you in remembrance, though ye once knew this, how that the LORD having saved the people out of the land of Egypt, afterwards destroyed them that believed not." Yes, the people were destroyed in the wilderness, even Moses died short of the promised land. *Yet God himself declared he had pardoned those very people;* and a day shall come when these *dead men shall hear the voice of the Son of God and live;* members of the body of Christ, they shall assuredly arise. Because of unbelief they were cut off, *but God hath concluded all in unbelief, that he might have mercy upon all,* that the accusation of partiality might not rest upon his arrangements. The *unbeliever will doubtless be destroyed; but the believer will supply his place,* for they shall all be taught of God, from the least to the greatest, and *thus taught,* it will be *impossible* to find an unbeliever, for the Redeemer will come from Zion, and will turn away ungodliness from Jacob And so all Israel will be saved.

SKETCH XXIII.

Deuteronomy xviii. 15—22.

First, THE LORD thy God will raise up unto thee a prophet from the midst of thee. Acts iii. 22, "For Moses truly said unto the fathers, a prophet shall the LORD your God raise up unto you of your brethren, like unto me: him shall ye hear in all things whatsoever he shall say unto you."

Secondly, This prophet, thus raised up, is of our brethren. Hebrews ii. 17, "Wherefore, in all things it behoved him to be made like unto his brethren, that he might be a merciful and faithful high Priest in things pertaining to God, to make reconciliation for the sins of the people." But he was not only in his birth the first born of many brethren, but in his resurrection also. John xx. 17, " Jesus saith unto her, Touch me not; for I am not yet ascended unto my Father, and your Father; unto my God, and your God. Do you say he was only the elder brother of believers? John the Evangelist bears a different testimony, chapter vii. verse 5. of his gospel, "*For neither did his brethren believe in him.*"

Thirdly, Moses informed the people the future prophet should be like unto him. In what particular did Jesus Christ resemble Moses? Like Moses he was a mediator, but although the resemblance is striking, the superiority is incontrovertible, the one was man, the other God, the *God man*, the son that abode in the house forever, who gave himself a ransom for all.

Fourthly, Unto him ye shall hearken. Matthew xvii. 5, "While he yet spake, behold, a bright cloud overshadowed them; and behold a voice out of the cloud, which said, this is my beloved son, in whom I am well pleased; hear ye him."

Fifthly, What did the people require of the LORD? Go *thou* near, and hear all that the LORD our God shall say, and speak *thou* unto us, all that the LORD our God shall speak unto thee, and we will hear it and do it.

Sixthly, Christ Jesus was the prophet here pointed out. Acts vii. 37, " This is that Moses which said unto the children of

Israel a prophet shall the LORD your God raise up unto you of your brethren, like unto me, him shall ye hear."

Seventhly, The words of the divine lawgiver were put into his mouth. John xii. 49, "For I have not spoken of myself, but the Father which sent me; he gave me a commandment, what I should say, and what I should speak."

Eighthly, It shall come to pass that whosoever will not hearken unto my words which he shall speak in my name, I will require it of him. The prophet Isaiah beareth witness to this grand truth, liii. 6, "All we like sheep have gone astray; we have turned every one to his own way; and the LORD hath laid on him the iniquities of us all." The apostle Paul unites his suffrage, Romans iv. 25, "Who was delivered for our offences, and raised again for our justification." 2 Corinthians v. 21, "For he hath made him to be sin for us who knew no sin, that we might be made the righteousness of God in him." Hebrews vii. 22, "By so much was Jesus made the surety of a better testament." Chapter viii. 6, "But now hath he obtained a more excellent ministry, by how much also he is the mediator of a better covenant, which was established upon better promises." Chapter ix. 15, "And for this cause he is the mediator of the New Testament, that by means of death, for the redemption of the transgressions that were under the first testament, they which are called might receive the promise of eternal inheritance." Chapter xii. 24, "And to Jesus the Mediator of the new covenant, and to the blood of sprinkling that speaketh better things than that of Abel."

Ninthly, What are the marks of the false prophet? First, he is presumptuous; Secondly, he speaks in the name of the LORD, what the LORD did not command him to speak; Thirdly, He speaks in the name of other gods. Jeremiah xxvii. 15, "For I have not sent them, saith the LORD, yet they prophesy a lie in my name; that I might drive you out, and that ye might perish, and the prophets that prophesy unto you." Jeremiah xxiii. 21, "I have not sent these prophets yet they ran; I have not spoken to them yet they prophesied." Isaiah lix. 1—8, "Behold the LORD's hand is not shortened that it cannot save, neither his ear heavy that it cannot hear; But your iniquities have separated between you and your God, and your sins have hid his face from you, that he will not hear. For your hands are defiled with blood, and your fingers with iniquity; your lips have spoken lies, your tongue hath muttered perverseness. None calleth for justice, nor any pleadeth for truth: they trust in vanity, and speak lies: they conceive mischief, and bring forth iniquity. They hatch cockatrice's eggs, and weave the spider's web: he that eateth of their eggs dieth, and that which is crushed breaketh out into a viper. Their webs shall not become garments, neither shall they cover themselves with their works: their works are works of iniquity, and the act of violence is in their hands. Their feet run to evil, and they make haste to shed innocent blood; their thoughts are thoughts of iniquity; wasting and destruction are in their paths. The way of peace they know not; and there is no judgment in their goings; they have made them crooked paths; whosoever goeth therein shall not know peace."

Jeremiah xxix. 8—14, "For thus saith the LORD of hosts, the God of Israel; Let not your prophets and your diviners, that be in the midst of you, deceive you, neither hearken to your dreams which you cause to be dreamed. For they prophesy falsely unto you in my name: I have not sent them, saith the LORD. For thus saith the LORD, That after seventy years be accomplished at Babylon, I will visit you, and perform my good word toward you, in causing you to return to this place. For I know the thoughts that I think toward you, saith the LORD, thoughts of peace and not of evil, to give you an expected end. Then shall ye call upon me, and ye shall go and pray unto me, and I will hearken unto you. And ye shall seek me and find me, when ye shall search for me with all your heart. And I will be found of you, saith the LORD: and I will turn away your captivity, and I will gather you from all the nations, and from all the places whither I have driven you, saith the LORD; and I will bring you again into the place whence I caused you to be carried away captive."

Tenthly, and lastly, Of the prophet who speaketh what is not true, that is, what never came to pass, thou shalt not be afraid. Psalm cxii. 7, "He shall not be afraid of evil tidings: his heart is fixed, trusting in the LORD." Isaiah xxxi. 4, "For thus hath the LORD spoken unto me like as the lion and the young lion roaring on his prey, when a multitude of shepherds is called forth against him, he will not be afraid of their voice, nor abase himself for the noise of them; so shall the Lord of hosts come down to fight for mount Zion, and for the hill thereof." Ezekiel ii. 6, "And thou, son of man, be not afraid of them, neither be afraid of their words, though briars and thorns be with thee, and thou dost dwell among scorpions: be not afraid of their words, nor be dismayed at their looks, though they be a rebellious house." Acts xviii. 9, " Then spake the Lord to Paul in the night by a vision. Be not afraid, but speak, and hold not thy peace."

SKETCH XXIV.

Deuteronomy xxi. 22. 23.

First, There were some sins not worthy of death. Deuteronomy xix. 6, " Lest the avenger of blood pursue the slayer, while his heart is hot, and overtake him, because the way is long, and slay him; whereas he was not worthy of death, inasmuch as he hated him not in time past." 1 John v. 16, " If any man see his brother sin a sin which is not unto death, he shall ask, and he shall give him life for them that sin not unto death. There is a sin unto death: I do not say that he shall pray for it."

Secondly, But if the sin be worthy of death and thou hang him on a tree; His body shall not remain all night upon the tree. It was considered a very great calamity to remain unburied. Jeremiah xvi. 4, " They shall die of grievous deaths; they shall not be lamented, neither shall they be buried." But the spirit of God directs this degree of mitigation to the sufferings of the malefactor, his body shall not remain unburied.

Thirdly, When the offender was buried, the defilement of the land, given by the Lord God as an inheritance, was removed. This scripture points to the character and sufferings of Jesus Christ, the Saviour of the world, and to the glory which should follow. Galatians iii. 13, " Christ has redeemed us from the curse of the law, being made a curse for us; for it is written, cursed is every one that hangeth on a tree." 2 Corinthians, v. 21, " For he hath made him to be sin for us who knew no sin; that we may be made the righteousness of God in him."

SKETCH XXV.

Deuteronomy xxii. 1—4.

First, Who is our brother? Undoubtedly every son and daughter of Adam, without distinction. Yea, even those who hate us with the most bitter and virulent hatred. One is our Creator, one our origin, and one our Redeemer. In one way we enter into life, and by death we all make our exit.

Secondly, Jesus Christ, the Redeemer, the Saviour of the world, was made under this law. Ezekiel xxxiv. 4, 16, " The diseased have ye not strengthened, neither have ye healed that which was sick, neither have ye bound up that which was broken, neither have ye brought again that which was driven away, neither have ye sought that which was lost, but with force and with cruelty have ye ruled them." Observe now the contrast. " I will seek that which was lost, and bring again that which was driven away, and will bind up that which was broken, and will strengthen that which was sick: but I will destroy the fat, and the strong; I will feed them with judgment." 1 Peter, ii. 25, " For ye were as sheep going astray; but are now returned to the Shepherd and Bishop of your souls." James v. 19, 20, " Brethren, if any of you do err from the truth, and one convert him, let him know, that he which converteth the sinner from the error of *his way* shall save a soul from death, and shall hide a multitude of sins."

SKETCH XXVI.

Deuteronomy xxii. 9—11.

First, What are we to understand by the vineyard? Isaiah v. 7, " For the vineyard of the Lord of hosts is the house of Israel, and the men of Judah his pleasant plants: and he looked for judgment, and behold oppression; for righteousness, but behold a cry." Jeremiah xii. 10, " Many pastors have destroyed my vineyard, they have trodden my portion under foot, they have made my pleasant portion a desolate wilderness."

Secondly, They were not permitted to yoke the ox and the ass in the plough, while labouring in this vineyard. What did this prohibition intend? The ox was figurative of the great sacrifice offered up for us; the ass a figure of human nature. Job xi. 12, " For vain man would be wise, although man be born like the wild ass's colt." Jeremiah ii. 24, " Thou art a wild ass, used to the wilderness, that snuffeth up the wind at her pleasure." These two natures must not be *united in their efforts;* the work of the Redeemer was *finished by himself;* his *own* arm obtained for him the victory. But although these two natures were not united in the plough, we are presented with a striking and most glorious figure of their union, in Genesis xlix. 10, 11, " The sceptre shall not depart from Judah, nor a lawgiver from between his feet, until Shiloh come; and *unto him shall the gathering of the people be.* Binding his foal unto the vine, and his *ass's colt unto* the *choice vine;* he washed his garments in wine, and his clothes in the blood of grapes."

Thirdly, Of what is linen figurative? Revelations xix. 8, " And to her was granted, that she should be arrayed in fine linen, clean and white: for the fine linen is the righteousness of the saints." What is the woollen? *It is the covering growing upon the sheep.* This linen and this woollen the house of Israel were forbidden to *unite;* they should wear no garment thus constructed. The Apostle Paul prayed earnestly, that he may be found clothed in none other than the *linen garment.* Philippians iii. 9, " And be found in him, not having mine own righteousness, which is of the law, but that which is through the faith of Christ, the righteousness which is of God by faith. Thus these three beautiful figures point to one evangelical truth; and the commandment which forbids the sowing the field with divers seeds, the yoking the ox and the ass, and the wearing the garment of linen and woollen, is, in other words, directing the people to *assume the robe of righteousness, wrought out for them by the Redeemer, without any addition of their own imperfect efforts as the plea of their justification before that God, in whose sight the very heavens are impure.*

SKETCH XXVII.

Deuteronomy xxxii. 1, 2, 3, 4.

Deuteronomy xxxii. 1, 2, 3, 4, "Give ear, O ye heavens, and I will speak; and hear, O earth, the words of my mouth. My doctrine shall drop as the rain, my speech shall distil as the dew; as the small rain upon the tender herb, and as the showers upon the grass: because I will publish the name of the Lord; ascribe ye greatness unto our God. He is the rock; his work is perfect; for all his ways are judgment: a God of truth, and without iniquity, just and right is he."

First, The audience, heaven and earth, this audience is indeed august, *angels* and *men*. May it not be said to comprise the universe? Every intelligent being is called upon to hear; nor should this be considered as matter of wonder, when God Omnipotent is himself the preacher."

Secondly, What doctrine doth this almighty Teacher inculcate? There are three descriptions of doctrines. 1st. The doctrine of men. Colossians ii. 22, "(Which all are to perish with the using) after the commandments and doctrines of men. 2dly, The doctrine of devils. 1 Timothy, iv. 1, "Now the Spirit speaketh expressly, that in the latter times some should depart from the faith, giving heed to seducing spirits, and doctrines of devils." And 3dly, The doctrine in our text; the doctrine inculcated by this almighty Teacher, which is, with beautiful propriety, called the doctrine of God our Saviour." Titus ii. 10, "Not purloining, but shewing all good fidelity; that they may adorn the doctrine of God our Saviour in all things" 1 Timothy, iv. 6, "If thou put the brethren in remembrance of these things, thou shalt be a good minister of Jesus Christ, nourished up in the words of faith and of good doctrine." But what is this doctrine? The descriptions given in scripture of this doctrine are so luminous and so frequent, that we are at a loss where to make our selection. Paul's second Epistle to Timothy i. 9, 10, first presents: "Who hath saved us, and called us with an holy calling, not according to our works, but according to his own purpose and grace, which was given us in Christ Jesus before the world began. But is now made manifest by the appearing of our Saviour Jesus Christ, who hath abolished death, and hath brought life and immortality to light by the gospel." It is this gospel doctrine of God our Saviour, which the divine preacher in our text declares shall drop as the rain.

Thirdly, My speech shall distil as the dew, as the small rain upon the tender herb, and as the showers upon the grass.

Fourthly, Why is this? Because I will publish the name of the Lord.

Fifthly, An exhortation. Ascribe ye greatness unto our God. Wherefore? Because he is a rock, and his work is perfect. How does this appear? All his ways are judgment. He is a God of truth; he is without iniquity; he is just and doeth righteously.

SKETCH XXVIII.

Deuteronomy xxxiii. 1, 2, 3, 4, 5.

First, Moses, the man of God, blessed the children of Israel before his death. Bring me savoury meat, said Isaac, that my soul may bless thee before I die.

Secondly, To prove the right of the people to this blessing. The Lord came from Sinai. Exodus xix. 18, "And mount Sinai was altogether on a smoke, because the Lord descended upon it in fire: and the smoke thereof ascended as the smoke of a furnace, and the whole mount quaked greatly." Habakkuk iii. 3, "God came from Teman, and the holy One from mount Paran. Selah. His glory covered the heavens, and the earth was full of his praise."

Thirdly, The Lord rose up from Seir unto them. Chapter ii. 4, "And command thou the people, saying, Ye are to pass through the coast of the children of Esau, which dwell in Seir; and they shall be afraid of you: take ye good heed unto yourselves therefore."

Fourthly, He shined forth from mount Paran. Genesis xxi. 21, "And he dwelt in the wilderness of Paran: and his mother took him a wife out of the land of Egypt." The LORD came with ten thousand of his saints.

Fifthly, From his right hand went a fiery law, and this law *was for them.*

Sixthly, God loved the people. Exodus xix. 5, "Now, therefore, if ye will obey my voice indeed, and keep my covenant, then ye shall be a peculiar treasure unto me, above all people, for all the earth is mine: all his saints are in thy hand." John x. 28, 29, "And I give unto them eternal life; and they shall never perish, neither shall any man pluck them out of my hand. My Father, which gave them to me, is greater than all: and no man is able to pluck them out of my Father's hand."

Seventhly, They sat down at thy feet. Acts xxii. 3, "I am, verily, a man which am a Jew, born in Tarsus, a city in Cilicia, yet brought up in this city at the feet of Gamaliel, and taught according to the perfect manner of the law of the fathers, and was zealous toward God, as ye all are this day." Every one shall receive of thy words. Proverbs ii. 1, "My son, if thou wilt receive my words, and hide my commandments with thee."

Eighthly, The law is the inheritance of the congregation of Jacob. Psalm cxix. 111, "Thy testimonies have I taken as an heritage forever: for they are the rejoicing of my heart."

REMARKS.

First, Moses blessed the people as his last act. Secondly, The law is not against the promises. Thirdly, If God loved the children of Israel, he will continue to love them, for he changeth not. Fourthly, Yea, verily, they shall all receive of his words, for they shall be all taught of God. Fifthly, The people are saints, or sanctified in Christ Jesus, in whom they are blessed with all spiritual blessings. Lastly, Let us rejoice in our inheritance, the law. Psalm xix. 7, "The law of the LORD is perfect, converting the soul: the testimony of the LORD is sure, making wise the simple."

SKETCH XXIX.
Deuteronomy xxxiii. 6, 7.

First, Reuben was the first born; he shall live and not die. Genesis xlix. 3, " Reuben thou art my first born, my might, and the beginning of my strength, the excellency of dignity, and the excellency of power."

Secondly, This is the blessing of Judah. Genesis xlix. 8—12, "Judah, thou art he whom thy brethren shall praise: thy hand shall be in the neck of thine enemies; thy father's children shall bow down before thee. Judah is a lion's whelp: from the prey, my son, thou art gone up: he stooped down, he couched as a lion, and as an old lion; who shall rouse him? The sceptre shall not depart from Judah, nor a lawgiver from between his feet, until Shiloh come; and unto him shall the gathering of the people be: binding his foal unto the vine, and his ass's colt unto the choice vine; he washed his garments in wine, and his clothes in the blood of grapes: his eyes shall be red with wine, and his teeth white with milk." And he said, hear Lord, the voice of Judah.

Thirdly, And bring him to his people. Zechariah ii 12, "And the Lord shall inherit Judah his portion in the holy land, and shall choose Jerusalem again."

Fourthly, Let his hands be sufficient for him, and thy hand shall be in the neck of thine enemies

Fifthly, And be thou a help to him from his enemies. Judah could have but two descriptions of enemies; Jews and Gentiles. The Redeemer can have but two descriptions of enemies; men and angels, fallen men and fallen angels.

Remarks.

First, We cannot read the sacred volume with advantage, except we understand it. A single eye fixed upon the Saviour of the world, should be ever open. Secondly, But except we are under the influence of that blessed Spirit, by whose direction the oracles of truth were penned, the veil is upon our hearts, and we cannot discern the things that make for our peace. Thirdly, The holy Spirit teacheth the soul, that every scripture testimony leadeth either directly or indirectly to Christ Jesus. Fourthly, When we behold Christ Jesus, we behold ourselves, for he is the head of every man. In him dwelleth all fulness. In Christ Jesus, both Jew and Gentile constitute one new man. In one word, it is in Christ Jesus, that all things are made new.

SKETCH XXX.

Deuteronomy xxxiii. 8—11.

First, And of Levi he said, Let thy Thummim and thy Urim be with thy holy one, with whom thou didst strive at the waters of Meribah. Many pages have been written by way of explaining what this Urim and Thummim mean ; but, it appears to me, an attention to our text and its references, will indubitably establish the opinion of those who assert, that the Urim and Thummim designate light and perfection. Let thy Thummim and thy Urim be with thy holy one, with whom thou didst strive at the waters of Meribah. With whom did the children of Israel strive at the waters of Meribah? Numbers xx. 13, "This is the water of Meribah; because the children of Israel strove with the Lord." The direction of Moses then, to the tribe of Levi, is simply this, Let thy light and perfection, let the manifestation of truth remain with thy God, and be content to receive from the Holy One of Israel, as from the hands of the bountiful.

Secondly, Who said to his father and to his mother, I have not seen him. Exodus xxxii. 26, "Then Moses stood in the gate of his camp, and said, Who is on the Lord's side? let him come unto me. And all the sons of Levi gathered themselves unto him."

Thirdly, They shall teach Jacob thy judgments and Israel thy laws. Deuteronomy xvii. 9, 11, "And thou shalt come unto the priests, the Levites, and unto the judge, that shall be in those days, and inquire; and they shall shew thee the sentence of judgment. According to the sentence of the law, which they shall teach thee, and according to the judgment which they shall tell thee, thou shalt do: thou shalt not decline from the sentence which they shall shew thee, to the right hand nor to the left." Ezekiel xliv. 23, " And they shall teach my people the difference between the holy and the profane, and cause them to discern between the unclean and the clean." Malachi ii 7, " For the priest's lips should keep knowledge, and they should seek the law at his mouth: for he is the messenger of the LORD of hosts."

Fourthly, They shall put incense before thee, and whole burnt sacrifices upon thine altar. Ezekiel xliii. 27, " And when those days are expired, it shall be, that upon the eighth day, and so forward, the priests shall make your burnt offerings upon the altar, and your peace offerings: and I will accept you, saith the LORD God."

Fifthly, Bless LORD his substance, and accept the work of his hands. Ephesians i. 6, " To the praise of the glory of his grace wherein he hath made us accepted in the beloved.

Sixthly, Smite through the loins of them that rise against him, and of them that hate him, that they rise not again.

REMARKS.

First, It is manifest that the Priesthood is pointed out by Moses in this passage. And secondly, That Jesus Christ is intended, who is a Priest forever after the order of Melchisedec. Thirdly, This Priest will teach the people; for it is written they shall be all taught of God. Fourthly, His substance shall indeed be blessed. Fifthly, The work of his hands shall be blessed. What is the work of his hands? It is God who hath made us, we are the work of his hands, and in him every individual shall be blessed. Sixthly, Them that hate him shall fall to rise no more. Babylon, the mother of harlots and abominations of the earth, is fallen, to rise no more forever.

SKETCH XXXI.

Deuteronomy xxxiii. 12—17.

First, And of Benjamin he said, the beloved of the Lord shall dwell in safety by him. This, it is said, was literally accomplished. The temple of Jerusalem, the place where the divine majesty especially resided, being in the tribe of Benjamin.

Secondly, The Lord shall cover him all the day long, and he shall dwell between his shoulders. Psalm, xci 1, " He that dwelleth in the secret place of the Most High, shall abide under the shadow of the Almighty."

Thirdly, And of Joseph he said, Genesis xlix. 26, "The blessings of thy father have prevailed above the blessings of my progenitors, unto the utmost bound of the everlasting hills; they shall be on the head of Joseph, and on the crown of the head of him that was separate from his brethren." Psalm xxiv. 1, " The earth is the Lord's, and the fulness thereof; the world, and they that dwell therein." Blessed of the Lord be his land.

Fourthly, For the precious things of heaven, &c. &c. &c.

Fifthly, For the good will of him that dwelt in the bush.

Sixthly, His glory is like the firstlings of his bullock, &c. &c. &c. Numbers, xxiii. 22, " God brought them out of Egypt, he hath, as it were, the strength of an unicorn." Psalm xliv. 5, " Through thee will we push down our enemies."

Remarks.

First, Joseph also is a type of the Redeemer. In many particulars of his eventful life he is, undoubtedly, a luminous type. As the earth is the Lord's, and the fulness thereof. Secondly, His land shall be blessed with every thing precious. Thirdly, With the good will of him that dwelt in the bush. Fourthly, His glory, the firstling of the bullock. He shall, with his horn, push the people together to the ends of the earth. Divide and conquer saith the adversary. Unto him shall the gathering of the people be, saith that Omnipotent God, who can neither err, nor be defeated in any of his purposes.

SKETCH XXXII.

Joshua ii. 9—13.

First, Rahab makes confession of her faith.

Secondly, She renders a reason for the hope that is in her, she knew the Lord had given them the land, because his terrors had fallen on the inhabitants. Psalm ix. 16, " The Lord is known by the judgment which he executeth: the wicked is snared in the work of his own hands. Higgaion. Selah." Genesis xxxv. 5, " And they journeyed: and the terror of God was upon the cities that were round about them, and they did not pursue after the sons of Jacob." Deuteronomy xi. 25, " There shall be no man able to stand before you: for the Lord your God shall lay the fear of you and the dread of you upon all the land that ye shall tread upon, as he hath said unto you."

Thirdly, Rahab had heared of the wonderful works of Jehovah in dividing the sea, for the safety of the Israelites, and in the returning of the waves to the o'erwhelming the pursuing enemy: from all which she rationally concluded, that the Lord God, their God, was God in heaven above, and earth beneath.

Fourthly, Rahab solicitous for the preservation of her family, requires an oath of the spies, that both herself, and her father's house, should be exempted from the general destruction: 1 Timothy, v. 8, " But if any provide not for his own, and specially for those of his own house, he hath denied the faith, and is worse than an infidel."

Remarks.

First, Rahab's faith was not fancy, it was founded on facts. Secondly, She rendered a reason for her faith. Thirdly, Her faith came by hearing. We have heard &c. &c. Fourthly, She was thus convinced there was no God in heaven, or earth, save the God of Israel. Fifthly, Thus believing she required of the spies an oath for the security of her kindred. Sixthly, She solicits for a token that her father, mother, brethren and sisters, and all that they have, shall be delivered from death. Seventhly, It is worthy of observation, that not one of these characters had any thing to do in this business.

SKETCH XXXIII.

Joshua ii. 14—24.

First, The men, the spies commissioned by Joshua, declare their lives should be forfeited if the demands of Rahab were not answered, on this one condition, that she should make no disclosure of the business transacted between them.

Secondly, They engage when they come into possession of the land, that they will deal kindly and truly with her.

Thirdly, Consequent upon this assurance, she conveyed the spies by the assistance of a cord out of her window, and this was the more easily effectuated as she dwelt upon the town wall.

Fourthly, On parting with these men of Israel, she counselled them to flee to the mountains, to shelter there for three days, until the ardour of the pursuit was expired; when they might securely return.

Fifthly, The men of Israel requested Rahab to bind a line of scarlet thread in the window through which they escaped. They requested her to gather into her house the family she loved, for should any of her kindred be out of the house, they could not be responsible for their safety.

Sixthly, Should she utter a syllable of the business, they would consider themselves as exonerated from the oath which she had made them swear.

Seventhly, She pledged herself to a punctual observance of the condition, and delayed not to bind the scarlet line in her window.

Eighthly, They abode three days in the mountains until the pursuit was no more, when they returned to Joshua, and told him all that had befel them.

Remarks.

First, These men were faithful to Joshua, and discharged most judiciously the duties confided to them. Secondly, Thus the ministers of Jesus, wherever they may wander, or wherever they may be stationary, will never lose sight of the grand object of their mission : but while they are *harmless* as doves, they are wise as serpents, and they will be upon their guard before all those with whom they chance to be connected. Thirdly, Yet they do not pause for a character of their hearers, that they may govern themselves accordingly, but unto whatsoever house they enter, their salutation is a salutation of peace. Fourthly, Their utmost efforts are embodied to convince all those who come within the sound of their voice, that it is equally their interest, and their duty, to receive and to adorn the doctrines of God, our Saviour, in all things. Fifthly, Their steps will always be steps of caution, for well they know, it is easy to be deceived. Sixthly, In every danger their hiding place is the munition of rocks, they take refuge under the wing of their almighty Friend, until the storm be over and past. Seventhly, They delight to commune with their Saviour, the Captain of their salvation, and to tell him all things that hath befallen them.

SKETCH XXXIV.

Joshua iii. 1—8.

First, Joshua leads the people from Shittim to Jordan, where all the children of Israel were lodged.

Secondly, After three days the officers passed through the hosts of Israel to regulate and direct the people.

Thirdly, They were commanded to regulate their movements by those of the ark of the covenant of the Lord their God; which was to be borne before them.

Fourthly, Joshua commanded the people to sanctify themselves, for upon the ensuing day the Lord would do wonders among them.

Fifthly, Joshua ordered the Priests to take up the ark of the covenant and to proceed before the people.

Sixthly, The Lord said unto Joshua, This day will I begin to magnify thee in the sight of all Israel, that they may know, that as I was with Moses, so I will be with thee. Joshua i. 5, " There shall not any man be able to stand before thee all the days of thy life. As I was with Moses, so I will be with thee: I will not fail thee, nor forsake thee."

Seventhly, And thou shalt command the Priests that bear the ark of the covenant, saying, When ye are come to the brink of the water of Jordan, ye shall stand still in Jordan.

Remarks.

First, Joshua rose early in the morning after the third day, and brought all the people of Israel with him. Secondly, The ark of the covenant was their precursor every step of the way. Thirdly, The people were commanded to sanctify themselves because the Lord would do wonders among them. Fourthly, Joshua commanded the Priests to take up the ark of the covenant and advance before the people. Fifthly, God magnified Joshua in the sight of all Israel, thus evincing that he was as much with the *Saviour*, as he was with the lawgiver. Joshua i. 7, 8, 9, " Only be thou strong, and very courageous, that thou mayest observe to do according to all the law which Moses my servant commanded thee : turn not from it to the right hand or to the left, that thou mayest prosper whithersoever thou goest. This book of the law shall not depart out of thy mouth ; but thou shalt meditate therein day and night, that thou mayest observe to do according to all that is written therein : for then thou shalt make thy way prosperous, and thou shalt have good success. Have not I commanded thee ; Be strong and of good courage ; be not afraid, neither be thou dismayed ? for the Lord thy God is with thee whithersoever thou goest." How eminently did the omnipotent Antitype of this illustrious type perform all these requisitions. Sixthly, Joshua was directed to command the Priests to bear the ark to the brink of the river Jordan, and there standing still, to behold the salvation of God. The minister of the New Testament, well instructed in the things of the kingdom, will find great delight in filling up these general heads.

SKETCH XXXV.

Joshua iii. 9, 10, 11.

First, "And Joshua said unto the children of Israel, come hither, and hear the words of the Lord your God."

Secondly, He instructs the Hebrews how they are to determine, when the living God was amongst them. That he would without fail drive out from before them all their enemies, all those who opposed their entrance into the promised inheritance. Joshua, however, did not direct them to *look unto themselves* for marks, evidences, or signs; Psalm xliv. 3, " For they got not the land in possession by their *own sword*, neither did their *own arm save them:* but thy right hand, and thine arm, and the light of thy countenance, because thou hadst a favour unto them."

Thirdly, The Hebrews were assured that the living God was among them because the ark of the covenant of the Lord of all the earth passed over before them unto the river Jordan. This was to these wanderers, an indubitable proof, that he would do all that they had been taught to expect he would do. Behold the ark of the covenant of the Lord, of all the earth, passeth over before them into Jordan. What is this ark of the covenant? Let us inquire at the lively oracles of God. Isaiah xlii. 6, " I the Lord have called thee in righteousness, and will hold thine hand, and will keep thee, and give thee for a covenant of the people, for a light of the Gentiles." Isaiah xlix. 8, " Thus saith the Lord, in an acceptable time have I heard thee : and in a day of salvation have I helped thee: and I will preserve thee, and give thee for a covenant of the people, to establish the earth, to cause to inherit the desolate heritages."

But this ark of the covenant is the ark of the covenant of the Lord of all the earth. Psalm xlvii. 2, " For the Lord most high is terrible ; he is a great king over all the earth." Psalm cv. 7, " He is the Lord our God, his judgments are in all the earth." Psalm xcvi. " O sing unto the Lord a new song; sing unto the Lord, all the earth. Sing unto the Lord, bless his name; shew forth his salvation from day to day. Declare his glory among the heathen, his wonders among all people. For the Lord is great, and greatly to be praised: he is to be feared above all gods. For all the gods of the nations are idols: but the Lord made the heavens. Honour and majesty are before him: strength and beauty are in his sanctuary. Give unto the Lord, O ye kindreds of the people, give unto the Lord, glory and strength." Psalm xcviii. 4, " Make a joyful noise unto the Lord; all the earth make a loud noise, and rejoice, and sing praise. Because God is the God of the whole earth, therefore the whole earth shall worship him." Psalm lxvi, 4, " All the earth shall worship thee, and shall sing unto thee, they shall sing to thy name. Selah." Isaiah xii. 6, " Cry out and shout, thou inhabitants of Zion: for great is the Holy One of Israel in the midst of thee."

Remarks.

First, Blessed are the people who know the joyful sound. Secondly, God himself hath given a sign, and an evidence. A virgin shall conceive. There shall no sign be given you, but the sign of the prophet Jonah. The birth, death and resurrection of Jesus Christ are infallible signs of the love of God, and of the consequent salvation of man. Thirdly, After such signs as these, to ask after a sign, by which I may know whether I myself, or every individual of the human family shall be saved from sin and death, from sorrow and pain, is an unquestionable sign of a wicked and an adulterous heart.

SKETCH XXXVI.

Joshua iii. 12—17.

First, Joshua commanded that a man should be chosen from every tribe; twelve men were to be chosen—and for what purpose they were chosen, we shall learn in our progress through the next chapter of this book.

Secondly, And it shall come to pass as soon as the soles of the feet of the priests that bear the ark of the Lord, the Lord of all the earth, shall rest in the waters of Jordan; that the waters of Jordan shall be cut off from the waters that come down from above; and they shall stand upon an heap. Exodus xv. 8, "And with the blast of thy nostrils the waters were gathered together, the floods stood upright as an heap, and the depths were congealed in the heart of the sea." Psalm cxiv. 3, "The sea saw it and fled: Jordan was driven back." Jeremiah xlix. 19, "Behold he shall come up like a lion from the swelling of Jordan to the habitation of the strong: but I will suddenly make him run away from her: and who is a chosen man that I may appoint over her? For who is like me? And who will appoint me the time? And who is that shepherd that will stand before me?"

Thirdly, And the priests that bear the ark of the covenant of the LORD stood firm on dry ground in the midst of Jordan. Exodus xiv. 29, "But the children of Israel walked upon dry land in the midst of the sea; and the waters were a wall unto them on their right hand, and on their left."

Fourthly, The priests continued in Jordan until all the people passed over.

REMARKS.

First, The priests are the first who enter into Jordan, and the last who quit it. Secondly, It is remarkable that the miracle of dividing the sea, was wrought immediately after the deliverance from Egyptian bondage, and that of dividing the river, immediately preceding their entrance into the promised land; to neither of which astonishing events, were the people either *directly* or *indirectly instrumental*. Thirdly, Nothing more was expected of the priests, than merely to advance before the people, bearing the ark of the covenant of the LORD of the whole earth. The business of the gospel minister is only to point his hearers to Jesus Christ, the true ark of the covenant. Fourthly, In leaving Egypt, the people *fled from their pursuers*, who were their enemies. But in entering upon the promised land, *their enemies flee before them*. So immeasurable is the difference between *Moses* and *Christ Jesus*, between the *law* and that grace and truth which came to light by the *gospel*, between *death* and *life*, between the two dispensations

VOL. III.   17

SKETCH XXXVII.

Joshua iv. 1—9.

First, "And it came to pass when all the people were clean passed over Jordan, that the Lord spake unto Joshua, saying, take you twelve men out of the people, out of every tribe a man.

Secondly, "And command you them, saying, take ye hence out of the midst of Jordan, out of the place where the priest's feet stood firm, twelve stones; and ye shall carry them over with you, and leave them in the lodging place, where ye shall lodge this night.

Thirdly, " Then Joshua called the twelve men whom he had prepared of the children of Israel, out of every tribe a man. And Joshua said unto them, pass over before the ark of the covenant of the Lord your God into the midst of Jordan, and take ye up every man of you a stone upon his shoulder, that this may be a sign among you when your children shall in future ask what mean ye by these stones."

Fourthly, The answer to this question. The waters of Jordan were cut off before the ark of the covenant of the Lord; when it passed over Jordan, and these stones are for a memorial of this miraculous event. Psalm ciii. 2, "Bless the Lord, O my soul, and forget not all his benefits."

Fifthly, And Joshua set up twelve stones in the midst of Jordan, in the place where the feet of the priests which bear the ark of the covenant stood; and they are there unto this day.

Remarks.

First, God directs Joshua to take twelve men; not twelve men from one tribe, but one from each tribe. If Joshua was a *figure of Jesus Christ*, are not these twelve men figures of the apostles? Secondly, These stones were to continue under the law. Did not the apostles upon every occasion appeal to the law, and to the testimony? Thirdly, These monumental stones were to remain as witnesses, to succeeding generations, of what the Lord had done for the children of Israel. Fourthly, As the waters of Jordan would have been the death of the people, had they closed upon them; they are to continue as evidences of their miraculous salvation. Fifthly, the children of Abraham are those individuals in the human family who are witnesses to the truth which Abraham believed, respecting the great salvation. These stones were for witnesses; and, saith John the Baptist, God is able of these stones to raise up children unto Abraham. If by this allusion the baptist intended the Gentiles, or any of those who listened to his ministration, he must have designed to show that they were but as these stones, which took any impression that the artist imprinted or engraved upon them; and indeed we know that believers are called living stones, built upon the foundation of the prophets and the apostles, Jesus Christ himself being the corner stone, and their builder is God; and to show that they were not fashioned by the art of man, there was no tool to lift upon them.

SKETCH XXXVIII.

Joshua v. 10—15.

First, And the children of Israel encamped at Gilgal, at which place the reproach of Egypt was rolled away from the people. Ezekiel xx. 7, "Then said I unto them, Cast ye away every man the abominations of his eyes, and defile not yourself with the idols of Egypt: I am the Lord your God."

Secondly, There they kept the passover on the fourteenth day of the month at even. Exodus xii. 26, 27, "And it shall come to pass when your children shall say unto you, What mean ye by this service? that ye shall say, It is the sacrifice of the Lord's passover, who passed over the houses of the children of Israel in Egypt, when he smote the Egyptians, and delivered our houses And the people bowed the head and worshipped."

Thirdly, And the manna ceased on the morrow after they had eaten of the old corn of the land.

Fourthly, "And it came to pass when Joshua was by Jericho, that he lifted up his eyes and looked, and, behold, there stood a man over against him with his sword drawn in his hand: and Joshua went unto him, and said unto him, Art thou for us, or for our adversaries? And he said, Nay; but as captain of the host of the Lord am I now come." Revelations xix.11,13,15, "And I saw heaven opened, and behold a white horse; and he that sat upon him was called Faithful and True, and in righteousness he doth judge and make war. And he was clothed in a vesture dipped in blood: and his name is called, The word of God. And out of his mouth goeth a sharp sword, that with it he should smite the nations: and he shall rule them with a rod of iron: and he treadeth the winepress of the fierceness and wrath of Almighty God." Exodus xxiii. 20, "Behold, I send an angel before thee, to keep thee in the way, and to bring thee into the place which I have prepared."

Fifthly, That Joshua may be at no loss respecting the character before whom he stood, the Captain of the Lord's host said unto him, Loose thy shoe from off thy foot; for the place where thou standest is holy." Exodus iii. 5, "And he said, Draw not nigh hither: put off thy shoes from off thy feet, for the place where thou standest is holy ground." 2 Peter, i. 18, "And this voice which came from heaven we heard, when we were with him in the holy mount."

Remarks.

First, After they began to eat of the fruits of the earth, there was no more manna! The food of angels must not be mixed with the food of mortals. Secondly, Our Saviour assumes his proper character, when he appears as Captain of salvation; and that this horseman could be none other than the Lord Jesus, is abundantly manifest from the following considerations.—First, Captain of the Lord's host, is an appellation by which God is known. Isaiah xiii. 4, "The noise of a multitude in the mountains, like as of a great people, a tumultuous noise of the kingdoms of nations gathered together: the Lord of hosts mustereth the host of the battle." Secondly, Joshua calleth him Lord or Jehovah, a name which Joshua would not have given nor he accepted, had he been nothing more than a messenger of the Most High. Thirdly, Joshua fell down and worshipped him, which he durst not have done, since he knew that God, and God only was the proper object of worship. Revelations xxii. 9, "Then said he unto him, See thou do it not: for I am thy fellow servant, and of thy brethren the prophets, and of them which keep the sayings of this book; worship God." Fourthly, The direction to Joshua to take off his shoes, which direction was only given to those in the divine presence. Fifthly, As God appeared unto Moses when he sent him to bring the children of Israel out of Egypt or bondage, so he manifests himself to Joshua, when he is on the point of bringing them into the promised land. Thus he is the first and the last; the Alpha and Omega.

SKETCH XXXIX.

Joshua vi. 1—16.

First, Jericho was straitly shut up, because of the children of Israel: none went out, and none came in.

Secondly, And the Lord said unto Joshua, See, I have given into thine hand Jericho. This is the same God to whom we have done homage, in the thirteenth verse of the foregoing chapter. God hath a right to dispose of kings and kingdoms. The prophet Daniel ii. 20, 21, devoutly saith, "Blessed be the name of God forever and ever: for wisdom and might are his. And he changeth the times and the seasons: he removeth kings, and sitteth up kings: he giveth wisdom unto the wise, and knowledge to them that know understanding."

Thirdly, That it might be made manifest to the whole earth, that the conquest of Canaan was to be ascribed solely to the omnipotent power of God, Joshua is instructed to besiege this first walled city, Jericho, and the operations of the siege are apparently most inadequate to the desired purpose. They were to go round about the city once every day for six successive days, and seven priests were to bear the ark of the Lord, blowing with seven trumpets of ram's horns, when, at an appointed time, the walls of the city were to fall flat down. This was a repetition of the miracle wrought at the river Jordan, by instruments the most contemptible. 2 Corinthians iv. 7, "We have this treasure in earthen vessels, that the excellency of the power may be of God, and not of us." 1 Corinthians i. 25, " Because the foolishness of God is wiser than men; and the weakness of God is stronger than men." Thus the priests were only to precede the ark of the Lord, blowing with ram's horns.

Fourthly, And it shall come to pass, that when they make a long blast with the ram's horns, and when ye hear the sound of the trumpet, all the people shall shout with a great shout; and the wall of the city shall fall down flat, and the people shall ascend up every man straight before him. 2 Kings v. 10, " And Elisha sent a messenger unto him, saying, Go and wash in Jordan seven times, and thy flesh shalt come again unto thee, and thou shalt be clean." By faith, says the Apostle Paul, Hebrews xii. 30, " By faith, the walls of Jericho fell down, after they were compassed about seven days." But this faith must have been *the faith of Joshua*, since it was to him only the promises were made.

Fifthly, The seven priests bearing the seven trumpets of ram's horns, passed on before the Lord, and blew with the trumpets, and the ark of the covenant of the Lord followed them.

Sixthly, And it came to pass at the seventh time, when the priests blew with the trumpets, Joshua said unto the people Shout: for the Lord hath given you the city.

Remarks.

Verily, Joshua was an eminent *type of the Redeemer*, and hence it is worthy of observation—First, That all things were given into his hands. Secondly, That all things were given into his hands for the people. And thirdly, A striking idea presses upon the mind taught of God. Through this whole transaction, the priests uttered not a syllable; they only blew with the ram's horns. The ram was caught in the thicket by his horns, Genesis xxii. 13. The horns are the emblems of power; even the breath of these was sufficient to destroy the strong walls of Jericho. But, upon this occasion, we should, I had almost said, be impious, were we to stop short of the figure; the substance of this figure is exhibited 2 Thessalonians, ii. 8, "And then shall that wicked be revealed, whom the Lord shall consume with the spirit of his mouth, and destroy with the brightness of his coming." Isaiah xi. 4, " And he shall smite the earth with the rod of his mouth, and with the breath of his lips shall he slay the wicked." Fourthly, Upon the performance of the promise, the people shouted. Psalm xlvii. 1,

"O clap your hands, all ye people, shout unto God with the voice of triumph." Isaiah xlii. 11, "Let the inhabitants of the rock sing, let them shout from the top of the mountains." Shout ye lower parts of the earth, break forth into singing. Shout, O Israel, be glad with all the heart. Zephaniah iii. 14, "Sing, O daughter of Zion; shout, O Israel; be glad and rejoice with all the heart, O daughter of Jerusalem." Ezra iii. 2, "When they praised the LORD, then they shouted." Zechariah iv. 6; 7, "Not by might, nor by power, but by my spirit, saith the LORD of hosts. And he shall bring forth the head stone thereof with shoutings, crying Grace, Grace unto it."

SKETCH XL.

JOSHUA vi. 17—27.

AND the city shall be accursed.

First, What are we to understand by this curse? The next verse informs us. "And you, in any wise, keep yourselves from the accursed thing, lest ye make yourselves accursed, when ye take of the accursed thing, and make the camp of Israel a curse, and trouble it." Jericho was devoted, the treasures consecrated to the LORD and the city to destruction. On this subject we have frequently reflected, but not daring to hazard a conjecture of our own, agreeably to our usual custom, we turn to the law and to the testimony. To curse, signifies to call down mischief upon, or to wish evil to persons or things. Curses are denounced by the following characters:—First, By God himself. Secondly, By his servants. And thirdly, By the servants of the devil. Curses are denounced upon persons, places, and things. We first hear of cursing in Genesis iii. 14, " And the LORD God said unto the serpent, Because thou hast done this thou art cursed." Again, in Genesis iv. 11, " And now art thou cursed from the earth." Again, Genesis ix. 25, "And Noah said, Cursed be Canaan; a servant of servants shall he be." These are the curses of the law; and the fulness of these curses are collected, complicated, and concentrated, Deuteronomy twenty-eighth, " But there is a curse of the law, which leadeth unto another death, even to the death of the soul." Ezekiel xviii 4, "Behold all souls are mine; as the soul of the father, so also the soul of the son is mine: the soul that sinneth, it shall die." This is the greatest malediction which is denounced by the law of God, but this malediction cannot fall upon any mere man among the children of men, and the reason is given Romans v. 6, "For when we were yet without strength, in due time Christ died for the ungodly." Again, 2 Corinthians v. 14, 15, "For the love of Christ constraineth us; because we thus judge, that if one died for all, then were all dead. And that he died for all, that they who live should not henceforth live unto themselves, but unto him who died for them, and rose again." Hebrews ii. 9, "We see Jesus crowned with glory and honour; that he by the grace of God should taste death for every man." But, in one word, whatever curse is denounced by the law of God must have an end; for in Revelations xxii. 2, 3, "We hear one of the seven angels declare, *There shall be no more curse.*"

The curse denounced upon Jericho was of a three fold nature. It was denounced upon the people, upon their property, and upon their city. The people, all but the family of Rahab, were condemned to death. The property was appropriated to the Lord of the whole earth, and the city was devoted to the flames.

Secondly, It is observable, that a curse was denounced on the person who should have the temerity to rebuild the city Jericho; and this curse was executed in its fulness. 1 Kings xvi. 34, "In his days did Hiel the Bethelite build Jericho; he laid the foundation thereof in Abiram his first born, and set up the gates thereof in his youngest son Segub, according to the word of the Lord, which he spake by Joshua the son of Nun." *And here the matter ended*

Remarks.

First, In handling the word of the Lord, the utmost caution is requisite. Secondly, The scribe instructed in the kingdom of God, will rightly divide the word of truth. Thirdly, In the midst of wrath God remembers mercy, as is manifest in the deliverance of Rahab and her family. Fourthly, God *can* be a *just* God and a *Saviour.* Mercy and truth *may* meet together. Righteousness and peace *may* embrace each other. Fifthly, We are redeemed from the law, in consequence of Jesus being made a curse for us, or devoted to that death to which our sin subjected us. Sixthly, We are therefore bound to live unto him who died for us, and to glorify him in our bodies and our spirits which are his.

SKETCH XLI.

Joshua vii.

First, The children of Israel committed a trespass respecting the accursed thing. Joshua xxii. 20, " Did not Achan the son of Zerah commit a trespass in the accursed thing, and wrath fell on all the congregation of Israel? and that man perished not alone in his iniquity."

Secondly, The anger of the Lord was kindled against the children of Israel.

Thirdly, The consequence. They fly before their enemies.

Fourthly, *Joshua appears in the character of a Mediator.*

Fifthly, The answer of Jehovah to the remonstrance of Joshua. Israel hath sinned; they have transgressed my covenant, and it is, therefore, they could not stand before their enemies.

Sixthly, God declares he will no more be with the children of Israel, except they destroy the accursed from among them.

Seventhly, Joshua is commanded to sanctify the people; and he is directed to say unto the people, Sanctify yourselves: for thus saith the Lord God of Israel, there is an accursed thing in the midst of thee, O Israel: thou canst not stand before thine enemies, until ye take away the accursed thing from among you.

Eighthly, Joshua immediately attends to the divine injunction. Psalm ci. 8, " I will early destroy all the wicked of the land, that I may cut off all wicked doers from the city of the Lord."

Ninthly, Joshua's address to Achan. My son, give, I pray thee, glory to the Lord God of Israel.

Tenthly, Achan's confession.

Eleventhly, Achan's execution.

Twelfthly, The consequences. So the Lord turned from the fierceness of his anger. Wherefore the name of that place was called the valley of Achor unto this day. Hosea ii. 15,

"And I will give her, her vineyards from thence, and the valley of Achor for a door of hope: and she shall sing there, as in the days of her youth, and as in the day when she came up out of the land of Egypt."

REMARKS.

First, The sin of Achan was charged upon the children of Israel. Secondly, The consequences of sin. Thirdly, Repentance and confession will not exempt from the punishment denounced by the law. Fourthly, When the cause of God's anger is removed, his anger ceases. Fifthly, God was in Christ reconciling the world unto himself.

SKETCH XLII.

JOSHUA viii.

First, GOD encourages Joshua. "And the LORD said unto Joshua, Fear not, neither be thou dismayed; take all the people of war with thee, and arise, go up to Ai, see I have given into thy hand the king of Ai, and his people, and his city, and his land."

Secondly, The business is accomplished by stratagem.

Thirdly, The execution of the king, with the disposal of his body.

Fourthly, Then Joshua built an altar unto the LORD God of Israel in mount Ebal. Deuteronomy xi. 29, "And it shall come to pass, when the LORD thy God hath brought thee in unto the land whither thou goest to possess it, that thou shalt put the blessing upon mount Gerizem, and the curse upon mount Ebal." And Chapter xxvii. 6, "Thou shalt build the altar of the LORD thy God of whole stones: thou shalt not lift up any iron tool upon them, and thou shalt offer burnt offerings thereon unto the LORD thy God."

Fifthly, And upon this altar the law is written with all the blessings and all the curses contained therein.

SKETCH XLII.

Sixthly, All these laws and all these blessings and curses Joshua read in the presence of all the congregation of Israel, the women, the children, and the strangers with whom they were conversant, not excepted.

Remarks.

First, All the promises are made to Jesus Christ. Galatians, iii. 16, " Now to Abraham and his seed were the promises made. He saith not, and to seeds, as of many ; but as of one, and to thy seed, which is Christ." All the promises of God are *Yea and Amen in Christ Jesus.* Secondly, The altar is a very striking figure of our Saviour. We have an altar, whereof they have no right to eat which serve the tabernacle. Thirdly, Upon this altar were all the laws with its blessings consequent upon obedience, and its curses consequent upon disobedience written Galatians, iii. 13, " Christ hath redeemed us from the curse of the law, being made a curse for us." And Chapter iv. 4, 5, " But when the fulness of the time was come, God sent forth his Son, made of a woman, made under the law, To redeem them that were under the law, that we might receive the adoption of sons." Fourthly, The strangers were present upon reading this law; Deuteronomy xxxi 12, " Gather the people together, men, and women, and children, and thy stranger that is within thy gates, that they may hear, and that they may learn, and fear the Lord your God, and observe to do all the words of this law." Galatians iii. 14, " That the blessing of Abraham might come on the Gentiles through Jesus Christ; that we might receive the promise of the Spirit through faith." Jesus Christ was the blessing of Abraham, in thy seed all the families of the earth shall be blessed. Lastly, The punishments on the Israelites, or upon their enemies, according to the law of God, did not make void the promises. Galatians, iii. 21, " *Is the law then against the promises of God ? God* forbid *:* for if there had been a law given which could have given life, verily righteousness should have been by the law."

SKETCH XLIII.

Joshua xv. 1—12.

First, The land is divided by lot. Numbers xxvi. 55, "Notwithstanding, the land shall be divided by lot: according to the names of the tribes of their fathers they shall inherit." Joshua xiv. 2, "By lot was their inheritance as the Lord commanded by the hand of Moses." Proverbs xvi. 33, "The lot is cast into the lap; but the whole disposing thereof is of the Lord." And it was therefore that,

Secondly, The first lot that came up was for Judah. This was a wonderful instance of the wisdom of God respecting Judah. It was the fulfilment of the prophecy in Genesis xlix. 8, "Judah, thou art he whom thy brethren shall praise. Thy father's children shall bow down before thee." And the fulfilment of this prophecy began where Abraham defeated the kings and rescued his kinsman Lot. Genesis xiv. 14, "And when Abraham heard that his brother was taken captive, he armed his trained servants, born in his own house, three hundred and eighteen, and pursued them unto Dan."

Thirdly, In the lot of Judah we find the valley of Achor, Chapter vii. 2, 6, "Wherefore the name of this place was called the valley of Achor unto this day."

Fourthly, Enrogal, that is the fountain of the fuller, was in this lot. Malachi iii. 2, "But who may abide the day of his coming? and who shall stand when he appeareth? For he is like a refiner's fire, and like fuller's soap."

Fifthly, And the border went up by the valley of the son of Hinnom. 2 Kings xxiii. 10, 13, "And he defiled Tophet, which is in the valley of the children of Hinnom, that no man might make his son or his daughter to pass through the fire to Molech. And the high places that were before Jerusalem, which were on the right hand of the mount of corruption." Jeremiah vii 31, "And they have built the high places of Tophet, which is in the valley of the son of Hinnom, to burn their sons and their daughters in the fire; which I commanded them not, neither came it into my heart."

Sixthly, And the border of this lot reached unto the south side of the Jebusite, or Jerusalem, where was mount Zion, on which the temple was afterward erected. This mount was between Judah and Joseph, and in this arrangement the wonderful wisdom of divine providence is abundantly conspicuous; it was the completion of the prophecy, in Deuteronomy xxxiii. 12, "And of Benjamin he said, the beloved of the Lord shall dwell in safety by him, and the Lord shall cover him all the day long, and he shall dwell between his shoulders."

Seventhly, In the lot of Judah was the mount of olives, which in 2 Kings xxiii. 13, " Is called the mount of corruption." Nehemiah alludes to this mount, Chapter xiii. 26, " Did not Solomon, the king of Israel sin by these things? Yet among many nations was there no king like him, who was beloved of his God." *Did Solomon, king of Israel sin, and was he however beloved by his God?*

Remarks.

First, It is observable that the Lord fixeth the bounds of our habitation. Secondly, The fulfilment of divine predictions is an abundant confirmation of our faith. Thirdly, It is to the humble man (and every sinner who is convinced of sin is humble), a never failing source of consolation, to know that Christ Jesus is the Saviour of sinners. Fourthly, It is a soothing, and a sublime reflection, that from the greatest apparent evil, the Omnipotent power, the Omnipotent grace of God, is constantly educing the greatest good.

SKETCH XLIV.

Joshua xviii. 1—8.

First, And the whole congregation of the children of Israel assembled together at *Shiloh*. The learned Cruden informs us that all christian commentators agree, that this word ought to be understood of the Messiah, that it is one of the glorious names of Jesus Christ, denoting him to be the only procurer of our happiness, and our only peace maker with God, and, he adds that the *word importeth a Saviour*.

Secondly, And the tabernacle of the congregation was set up at Shiloh, where it remained until the death of Eli, a term comprising no less than three hundred and forty-nine years. This tabernacle is one of the proudest themes upon which Moses expatiates. It was here that God promised to meet with him, Exodus xxv. 22, " And there I will meet with thee, and I will commune with thee, from above the mercy seat, from between the two cherubims, which are upon the ark of the testimony, of all things which I will give thee in commandment unto the children of Israel."

Thirdly, Joshua upbraideth the people on account of their indifference respecting their entrance into possession of the land which the LORD God of their fathers had given them. Judges xviii. 19, "And they said unto him, hold thy peace, lay thy hand upon thy mouth, and go with us, and be to us a father, and a priest : Is it better for thee to be a priest unto the house of one man, or that thou be a priest unto a tribe or a family in Israel?" Proverbs xv 19, " The way of the slothful man is as an hedge of thorns : but the way of the righteous is made plain."

Fourthly, Joshua directs that three men should be selected from every tribe, that they should proceed to survey the land, and afterwards return to him at Shiloh, that he may submit the lot of every tribe to the inspection of Deity.

Fifthly, The Levites have no part or lot with the people, and, for this reason, the LORD is their inheritance. Deuteronomy x. 9, " Wherefore, Levi hath no part nor inheritance with his brethren; the LORD is his inheritance, according as the LORD thy God promised him. Lamentations iii. 24, " The LORD is my portion, saith my soul ; therefore will I hope in him "

Sixthly, Verse tenth. "And Joshua cast lots for them in Shiloh, before the LORD ; and there Joshua divided the land unto the children of Israel, according to their division."

REMARKS

First, The people are brought together in Shiloh. Shiloh, to whom the gathering of the people should be. Secondly, The tabernacle is in Shiloh. Hebrews viii. 2, " A minister of the sanctuary, and of the true tabernacle, which the LORD pitched and not man." Thirdly, Though the blessed antitype of Joshua has given us to know that all the promises respecting spiritual blessings, are secure in him, yet they cannot enjoy this assurance until they enter into rest by believing; and as believing is the result of knowledge, for we certainly believe as much as we know, Joshua exhorts the people to appoint certain persons to make discoveries which may confirm their faith. Fourthly, It is Jesus, in the kingdom of his peace, who divides the inheritance, and that not according to personal excellence, but according to their divisions.

SKETCH XLV.

JOSHUA XX.

First, THE LORD also spake unto Joshua, saying, speak to the children of Israel, saying, appoint out to you cities of refuge, whereof I spake unto you by Moses. Numbers xxxv. 13, "And of these cities which ye shall give, six cities shall ye have for refuge."

Secondly, These cities were appointed not for the Israelites only, but also for strangers.

Thirdly, Whatever those cities were literally to the Hebrews, and to strangers, God is spiritually, both to Jews and Gentiles. Thus Moses taught the people; Deuteronomy xxxiii. 27, " The eternal God is thy refuge, and underneath are the everlasting arms." Psalm ix. 9, 10, " The LORD also will be a refuge for the oppressed, a refuge in time of trouble. And they that know thy name will trust in thee." Psalm xlvi. 1, "God is our refuge and strength, a very present help in trouble." Psalm xlviii. 3, " God is known as a refuge in her palaces." Psalm lvii. 1, "Yea, in the shadow of thy wings will I make my refuge, until these calamities be overpast." Psalm lix. 16, " Thou hast been my defence and refuge in the day of my trouble." Psalm lxii. 8, " God is a refuge for us. Selah." Psalm cxlii. 5, " Thou art my refuge and my portion in the land of the living." Isaiah iv. 6, "And there shall be a tabernacle for a shadow in the day time from the heat, and for a place of refuge, and for a covert from storm, and from rain." Jeremiah xvi. 19, "O Lord, my strength, and my fortress, and my refuge in the day of affliction; the Gentiles shall come unto thee from the ends of the earth."

Fifthly, Christ is the christian's refuge, Hebrews vi. 18, " That by two immutable things, in which it was impossible for God to lie, we might have strong consolation, who have fled for refuge to lay hold upon the hope set before us."

Remarks.

First, God directs Joshua to speak to the people, and remind them of what Moses directed them. Thus did his divine antitype upon every occasion—The words I speak I received of my Father. Secondly, The people were directed to appoint those cities of refuge, long before the necessity for such asylums existed. Thus was grace given us in Christ Jesus, before the world began. Thirdly, *Personal* and *present* safety depended upon their *fleeing to, and entering into those cities of refuge;* and their peace and security depended upon their *continuance* in those cities. Thus the christian must not only *lay hold on the hope set before him*, but he must *continue* in faith, holding fast the profession of his faith without wavering; and his *sense* of salvation, and consequent happiness, is only attained by *believing*.

SKETCH XLVI.

Joshua xxi. 1—8.

First, "Then came near the heads of the fathers of the Levites unto Eleazer the priest, and unto Joshua the son of Nun, and to the heads of the fathers of the tribes of the children of Israel; And they spake unto them at Shiloh in the land of Canaan, saying, the Lord commanded, by the hand of Moses, to give us cities to dwell in, with the suburbs thereof for our cattle."

Let us inquire what were the commands of God to Moses? Numbers xxxiv. 17, " These are the names of the men which shall divide the land unto you, Eleazer, the priest, and Joshua, the son of Nun." And chapter xxxv. 2, " Command the children of Israel, that they give unto the Levites of the inheritance of their possessions, cities to dwell in; and ye shall give unto the Levites, suburbs for the cities, round about them."

Secondly, The children of Israel while under the influence of the divine spirit, hasten to obey the command of the Lord communicated to them by his servant Moses

Thirdly, The first lot came out for the children of Aaron, and the first division of their lot was from the tribe of Judah; and the rest in their order according to their lots.

Fourthly, And the children of Israel gave by lot these cities with their suburbs unto the Levites, as the Lord commanded Moses. Numbers xxxv. 4, "And the suburbs of the cities, which ye shall give unto the Levites, shall reach from the wall of the city, and outward, a thousand cubits round about."

Fifthly, Verse 43, "And God gave unto Israel all the land which he sware to give unto their fathers, and they possessed it, and dwelt therein." Luke xxi. 33, " Heaven and earth shall pass away; but my words shall not pass away." Titus i. 2, " In hope of eternal life, which God, that cannot lie, promised before the world began."

Sixthly, Verse 45, " There failed not ought of any good thing which the Lord had spoken unto the house of Israel; all came to pass." Chapter xxiii. 14—16, "And, behold, this day I am going the way of all the earth; and ye know in all your hearts, and in all your souls, that not one thing hath failed of all the good things which the Lord your God spake concerning you; and all are come to pass unto you, and not one thing hath failed thereof. Therefore, it shall come to pass, that as all good things are come upon you, which the Lord your God promised you; so shall the Lord bring upon you all evil things until he have destroyed you from off this good land which the Lord your God hath given you. When ye have transgressed the covenant of the Lord your God, which he commanded you, and have gone and served other gods, and bowed yourselves to them; then shall the anger of the Lord be kindled against you, and ye shall perish quickly from off the good land which he hath given unto you."

Remarks

First, God taketh care of his servants. Matthew x. 10, " Take no scrip for your journey, neither two coats, neither shoes nor yet staves; for the workman is worthy of his meat." 1 Timothy, v. 17, " Let the elders that rule well be counted worthy of double honour, especially they who labour in word and doctrine." 1 Corinthians, ix. 10, " Or saith he it altogether for our sakes? For our sakes, no doubt, this is written: that he that plougheth should plough in hope; and he that thresheth in hope should be partaker of his hope." Secondly, God is a promise performing God. Thirdly, He that believeth must not make haste. It is good that we both hope and quietly wait for the salvation of God. Fourthly, It is for the called of God, as was Aaron, that God engageth to provide. Fifthly, This provision is made through the instrumentality of his people, whose hearts he disposes to act as his almoners. Lastly, God will perform all the good words which he hath spoken.

SKETCH XLVII.

Joshua xxii.

First, Joshua sendeth away the two tribes and a half tribe with a blessing; and he said unto them, ye have kept all that Moses the servant of the Lord commanded you to keep, and have obeyed my voice in all that I commanded you. This declaration, made by Joshua, would seem incredible, did not the scriptures guide us in our inquiries. Numbers xxxii. 20—22, "And Moses said unto them, if ye will do this thing, if ye will go armed before the Lord to war, and go all of you armed over Jordan until he hath driven out his enemies from before him; and the land be subdued before the Lord; then, afterwards, ye shall return and be guiltless before the Lord."

Secondly, And when they came unto the borders of Jordan, that are in the land of Canaan, the children of Reuben, and the children of Gad, and the half tribe of Manasseh, built there an altar by Jordan, a great altar to see to.

Thirdly, When this came to the knowledge of the children of Israel, they were grievously offended. But why were they offended? We read an answer to this question, Deuteronomy xiii. 13—15, "Certain men, the children of Belial, are gone out from among you, and have withdrawn the inhabitants of their city, saying, Let us go and serve other gods which ye have not known; then shalt thou inquire, and make search, and ask diligently; and behold, if it be truth, and the thing certain, that such abomination is wrought among you; thou shalt surely smite the inhabitants of that city with the edge of the sword, destroying it utterly, and all that is therein." In conformity to this divine injunction the Hebrews proceeded to punish these revolters.

Fourthly, And the congregation of the LORD questioned these supposed delinquents. What trespass is this that ye have committed against the God of Israel, to turn away this day from following the LORD, in that ye have builded you an altar, that ye might rebel this day against the LORD. Is the iniquity of Peor too little for us, from which we are not cleansed until this day, although there was a plague in the congregation of the LORD? Notwithstanding, if the land of your possession be unclean, then pass ye over unto the land of the possession of the LORD wherein the LORD's tabernacle dwelleth, and take possession among us; but rebel not against the LORD, nor rebel against us, in building you an altar beside the altar of the LORD our God. Did not Achan, the son of Zerah, commit a trespass in the accursed thing, and wrath fell on all the congregation of Israel? And that man perished not alone in his iniquity.

Fifthly, The supposed offenders, however, ably vindicated their conduct and their innocence, and integrity; their piety, and their devotion to the God of their fathers, became incontestible. Proverbs xviii. 13, "He that answereth a matter before he heareth it, it is folly and shame unto him." 1 Peter, iii. 15, "But sanctify the LORD God in your hearts: and be ready always to give an answer to every man that asketh you a reason of the hope that is in you, with meekness and fear." The accused, while declaring their contemplated purpose, appeal to the God of Gods as a voucher of the sincerity of their intentions, and the priests, the princes, and the heads of the people, were completely satisfied. We have but one remark to make, and this respects the altar. Hebrews vii. 13, "For he of whom those things are spoken pertaineth to another tribe, of which no man gave attendance at the altar." Chapter xiii. 10, "We have an altar, whereof they have no right to eat which serve the tabernacle." Christ Jesus is God's altar, beware of false Christs. The true christian has but one altar, but one Christ.

SKETCH XLVIII.

Joshua xxiii.

First, The affection of Joshua to the people is extended to the last moment of his illustrious career; he had numbered one hundred and ten years, and yet his bosom glowed with all the ardour of new born zeal. He calls upon them with sacred devotion of soul, to be very courageous; and he piously commands them to keep and do all that is written in the book of the law of Moses, to turn not aside therefrom, either to the right hand, or to the left; but to cleave constantly unto the Lord their God, and to attend unceasingly to the things which made for their peace. Thus did the Patriarch Jacob, thus did Moses the servant of the Lord, close their eventful lives.

Secondly, Joshua conjures the people to remember what the Lord their God had done for them. Psalm xliii. 2, "For thou art the God of my strength."

Thirdly, The Hebrews are reminded of what had been effectuated in their favour. "And ye have seen all that the Lord your God hath done unto all these nations because of you: for the Lord your God is he that hath fought for you." And of what was still to be accomplished for their complete establishment, "And the Lord your God, he shall expel them from before you, and drive them from out of your sight: and ye shall possess their land, as the Lord your God hath promised unto you."

Fourthly, Joshua exhorts the Hebrews to have no connexion with the people of the land. Ephesians v. 11, "And have no fellowship with the unfruitful works of darkness, but rather reprove them." 2Corinthians vi. 14, "Be ye not unequally yoked together with unbelievers: for what fellowship has righteousness with unrighteousness? and what communion hath light with darkness?"

Fifthly, But if ye will not obey the voice of Jehovah your God, if ye do, in any wise, go back and cleave unto the remnant of these nations, even these, that remain among you, and shall make marriages with them, and go in unto them, and they to you, know for a certainty, that the Lord your God will no more drive out any of these nations from before you; but they shall be snares and traps unto you, and scourges in your sides, and thorns in your eyes, until ye perish from off this good land which the Lord your God hath given you.

Sixthly, Joshua stimulates the people to obey the God of their salvation, from a consideration of his faithfulness. And, behold, this day I am going the way of all the earth: and ye know in all your hearts and in all your souls, that not one thing hath failed of all the good things that the Lord your God spake concerning you, all are come to pass unto you, and not one thing hath failed thereof.

Seventhly, If they will not hear and obey, they must assuredly reap the consequence; expulsion from the land.

Remarks.

First, If God's faithful servants conceive so strong an affection for the people, how much more will they interest that omnipotent Being, who commanded them into existence? Secondly, We are called upon to observe the danger of associating with unbelievers. Thirdly, The whole of this exhortation is calculated to promote the worship of the true God, and the observance of his covenant. Fourthly, The punishment consequent upon disobedience, extends no further than the present life, than the loss of the good land which the Lord their God had given them.

SKETCH XLIX.

Joshua xxiv. 1—16.

First, THE tribes of Israel are gathered by Joshua to Shechem, to hearken to the words of Jehovah.

Secondly, They are reminded of what the LORD their God had done for their fathers; that he had taken Abraham from the land of idolaters, that he had multiplied his seed, that he had brought his posterity from the house of bondage, and by multiplied miracles through the red sea, that he had bent his ear to the voice of their supplication, that he hearkened not unto Balaam, but blessed them still that he had brought them through the midst of Jordan, dividing the river before them, that he had sent the hornet before them, scattering their enemies without the assistance of *their* sword or *their* bow, and giving them a land for which they did not labour, and cities which they built not, and ultimately giving them to eat of the vineyards and olive yards which they planted not, consequent upon all which,

Thirdly, Joshua exhorts them. "Now, therefore, fear the LORD and serve him in sincerity and truth: and put away the gods which your fathers served on the other side of the flood, and in Egypt, and serve ye the LORD." For myself, the display of divine goodness is sufficiently magnificent to fix my determination; and hence I declare unto you this day, "that as for me and my house, we will serve the LORD." The determination of the Apostle Peter was equally correct. Matthew xxvi. 33, 35, " Peter answered and said unto him, Though all men should be offended because of thee, yet will I never be offended. Peter said unto him, Though I should die with thee, yet will I not deny thee." John vi. 68, " Then Simon Peter answered him, LORD, to whom shall we go? Thou hast the words of eternal life."

REMARKS.

Such are the dealings of God with the children of men. First, He humbles them by a consideration of their origin, and upon this dark ground, he Secondly, displays himself and the nature and magnitude of his grace. Thirdly, From this consideration, he excites the gratitude of his people, and thus they are stimulated to serve him, whose service is perfect freedom. Fourthly, If Joshua be, as we believe he is, a type of Christ, and if the people are his house, whose house we are, Hebrews iii. 6, it follows that the omnipotent Antitype is the master of the house ; and if he be the master of the house, and the *people*, agreeably to scripture testimony, are *the house*, the consequences are obvious ; this house and its master will serve the Lord. Daniel vii. 14, "And there was given him dominion, and glory, and a kingdom, that all people, nations, and languages, should serve him: his dominion is an everlasting dominion which shall not pass away, and his kingdom that which shall not be destroyed." Philippians ii. 9, "Wherefore God also hath highly exalted him, and given him a name which is above every name." Fifthly, Faith points to this state of things. Here, while sinners, we are the servants of sin. But, says the lip of truth, ye cannot serve two masters: and in the state which faith gives us to anticipate, we shall serve but one master. Jeremiah xxiv. 6, 7, "For I will set mine eyes upon them for good, and I will bring them again to this land . and I will build them, and not pull them down ; and I will plant them and not pluck them up. And I will give them an heart to know me, that I am the Lord : and they shall be my people, and I will be their God: for they shall return unto me with their whole heart." Jeremiah xxxii. 37, " Behold I will gather them out of all countries, whither I have driven them in mine anger, and in my fury, and in great wrath ; and I will bring them again unto this place, and I will cause them to dwell safely : and they shall be my people, and I will be their God." Ezekiel xi. 19, 20, "And I will give them one heart, and I will put a new spirit within you ; and I will take the stony heart out of their flesh, and will give them an heart of flesh, that they may walk in my statutes, and keep my ordinances, and do them : and they shall be my people, and I will be their God."

SKETCH L.

Joshua xxiv. 17—31.

First, God's people are extremely ready to promise; they cheerfully covenant to serve the Lord.

Secondly, They render a reason. He is the Lord our God, who hath brought us and our fathers out of the house of bondage; he hath preserved us in all the way wherein we went; he hath driven out our enemies, and we will serve the Lord, for he is our God.

Thirdly, And Joshua said unto the people, Ye cannot serve the Lord: for he is an holy God; he is a jealous God; he will not forgive your transgression nor your sins. If ye forsake the Lord and serve strange gods, then he will turn and do you hurt, and consume you after that he hath done you good.

Fourthly, The people reply, Nay, but we will serve the Lord.

Fifthly, And Joshua said unto the people, Ye are witnesses against yourselves, that ye have chosen you the Lord to serve him; and they said, We are witnesses. Job xv. 6, "Thine own mouth condemneth thee, and not I, yea, thine own lips testify against thee." Luke xix. 22, "Out of thine own mouth will I judge thee."

Sixthly, Joshua made a covenant with the people the same day. And Joshua wrote these words in the book of the law of God, and took a great stone and set it up for a witness. Behold, this stone shall be a witness unto you, lest ye deny your God; so Joshua let the people depart every man to his inheritance.

Seventhly, This was Joshua's last act. After these things, Joshua, the son of Nun, the servant of the Lord died, and was buried in the border of his inheritance.

Eightly, And Israel served the Lord all the days of Joshua, and all the days of the elders, that survived Joshua: who had known the wonderful works which the Lord had wrought for Israel.

Remarks.

First, We have considered Joshua as a type of the Redeemer, in a variety of views; but the propriety of thus regarding him, is abundantly manifest in this closing scene. He exhibits to the people which he loved, the words and works of his God, and their God, and this is done for the purpose of inducing them to love, and consequently to serve the only true God. Secondly, He knew that they had, at that moment, strange gods in their possession. Thirdly, Things inanimate are produced as witnesses for God. The Almighty never leaves himself without a witness. The visible things of the creation testify of him. Lastly, Canaan or the promised land, is not a type of heaven; for the Cananite still remained in the land. Slay them not, said God, lest my people forget; but in heaven there will be nothing to annoy. Canaan is a striking figure of that rest into which the believer enters, consequent upon believing. And this rest, while he abideth here, is imperfect; the thorn in the flesh remains to buffet him, and thus he is kept humble, and thus his heart is taught to swell with gratitude, while he hears the God of his salvation declare— My grace is sufficient for thee. *In the beloved, thou art accepted.*

SKETCH LI.

Judges ii. 1—5.

First, Who are we to understand by the angel of the Lord? The Jews say, Some prophet; but christians more properly pronounce this angel, the angel of the covenant. Malachi iii. 1, "Behold I will send my messenger, and he shall prepare the way before me: and the Lord, whom ye seek, shall suddenly come to his temple, even the messenger of the covenant, whom ye delight in: behold he shall come, saith the Lord of hosts." Exodus xix. 19, "And when the voice of the trumpet sounded long, and waxed louder, and louder, Moses spake, and God answered him by a voice." Exodus xxxii, 34, "Therefore now go, lead the people unto the place of which I have spoken unto

154   SKETCH LI.

thee. Behold, mine angel shall go before thee: nevertheless, in the day when I visit, I will visit their sin upon them."

Secondly, I made you to go up out of Egypt and have brought you into the land which I sware unto your fathers; and I said, I will never break my covenant with you. Genesis xxiv. 7, "The Lord God of heaven which took me from my father's house, and from the land of my kindred, and which spake unto me, and that sware unto me, saying, Unto thy seed will I give this land: he shall send his angel before thee." Psalm lxxxix. 34, "My covenant will I not break, nor alter the thing that is gone out of my lips."

Thirdly, This angel of the covenant said, ye shall make no league with the inhabitants of the land. Deuteronomy vii. 2, "And when the Lord thy God shall deliver them before thee; thou shalt smite them, and utterly destroy them; thou shalt make no covenant with them, nor shew mercy unto them." 2 Corinthians vi. 16, "And what agreement hath the temple of God with idols? For ye are the temple of the living God, as God hath said, I will dwell in them, and walk in them, and I will be their God, and they shall be my people." Deuteronomy xii. 3, "And ye shall overthrow their altars, and break their pillars, and burn their groves with fire, and ye shall hew down the graven images of their gods, and destroy the names of them out of that place."

Fourthly, But saith the angel, ye have not obeyed my voice. Why have ye done this? Wherefore I also said, I will not drive them out from before you; but they shall be as thorns in your sides, and their gods shall be a snare unto you.

Fifthly, And it came to pass when the angel of the Lord spake these words unto all the children of Israel, that the people lifted up their voice, and wept. And they called the name of that place Bochim, and they sacrificed there unto the Lord. 1 Samuel vii. 6, "And they gathered together to Mizpeh, and drew water, and poured it out before the Lord, and fasted on that day, and said there, We have sinned against the Lord."

Remarks.

First, The invisible God has in a variety of instances manifested himself to his children, first as an angel, and secondly as a man. Secondly, These manifestations are for the purpose of bringing individuals to a sense of their transgressions: and of humbling them preparatory to their exaltation. Thirdly, When the people see and feel their errors, and supplicate God to have mercy upon them, he hears, and grants their request. Fourthly, We are hence encouraged, even in temporal evils, to look unto the Lord, to the great propitiation for sin, without whose blood shedding there could be no remission Lastly, All Israel will, by this angel of the covenant, be ultimately brought with weeping and supplication, home to God.

SKETCH LII.

Judges v. 1—11.

First, Consequent on the complete victory given by Jehovah, to the people of his election, Deborah and Barak utter a song of praise. Thus Moses, on a similar occasion, manifested his sense of divine goodness. Exodus xv. 1, " I will sing unto the Lord, for he hath triumphed gloriously : the horse and his rider hath he thrown into the sea."

Secondly, This victory was given by the Most High, for the purpose of avenging his people.

Thirdly, Deborah and Barak call upon kings and princes, to listen to the praises of their conquering God.

Fourthly, In this song of praise there is a brief recapitulation, of the acts of goodness, which God had vouchsafed toward them, even from their departure from Seir. (*Seir and Edom are the same.*) It was from Sinai to Canaan. Deuteronomy xxxiii. 2, " And he said the Lord came from Sinai, and rose up from Seir." Habakkuk iii 3, " God came from Teman, and the Holy One from mount Paran. Selah. His glory covered the heavens, and the earth was full of his praise." Isaiah lxiv. 3, " When thou didst terrible things which we looked not for, thou camest down, the mountains flowed down at thy presence."

Fifthly, The deplorable circumstances of the people when this deliverance was wrought, is described. The high ways were unoccupied, and the travellers walked through by-ways. The inhabitants of the villages ceased. They chose new gods, and war was in the gates: while among forty thousand Israelites neither shield nor spear were seen.

Sixthly, The heart of Deborah was toward the Governors of Israel, who offered themselves willingly, and for this she blessed the Lord. She calls upon those who rode upon white asses, who set in the elevated seats of judgment, to bear witness to the magnitude of divine goodness, in thus delivering Israel from the terrific power of the archers, who aimed to destroy them. "Rehearse," said she, "In the places of drawing water, the righteous acts of the Lord, even his righteous acts toward the inhabitants of his villages in Israel, then shall the people of the Lord go down to the gates."

Remarks.

First, Israel was an adulterous generation, they chose new gods, and thus plunged into all the calamities consequent upon desolating war. Secondly, The mercy of their omnipotent Creator, was manifest in their deliverance. Thirdly, A knowledge of the goodness of God stimulates to songs of thanksgiving and praise. Fourthly, The power of the Almighty is rendered more conspicuous, by the imbecility of the instruments he employs, and it thus becomes obvious that praise is not attributable to the creature. Not unto us, not unto us, but unto thy name, O Lord, be all the glory. Lastly, Every arrangement of Deity manifests what he will ultimately accomplish for his own glory, and for the good of his people. O that men would praise the Lord for his goodness, and for his wonderful works of creation, of preservation, and of redemption.

SKETCH LIII.

Judges xvi. 28—31.

First, Sampson was an eminent type of Christ in the circumstances attendant upon his birth, in the remarkable instances of his wonderful life, and more especially in his death. The death of Sampson was abundantly and most strikingly figurative of the sufferings and death of the Redeemer. The enemies of Sampson sported with his calamities; and how is the soul of the believer lacerated, when he beholds the Lord of universal nature, Mark xv. 17, 30, Deridingly clothed in purple, and a crown of platted thorns placed upon his sacred head! When he hears the chief priests mocking, and exultingly exclaiming, he saved others, himself he cannot save. Sampson in the last scene of his memorable life, appeals to the God of his salvation. O Lord God, remember me, I pray thee; thus did the struggling, agonized Saviour, lift his dying eyes to the divine Nature; " My God, my God, why hast thou forsaken me?" Father, into thy hands I commend my spirit.

Secondly, Sampson prayed he might die with the Philistines. Jesus Christ was numbered with transgressors. Mark xv. 28, " And the scripture was fulfilled, which saith, and he was numbered with the transgressors." Isaiah liii. 12, " Therefore, will I divide him a portion with the great, and he shall divide the spoil with the strong; because he hath poured out his soul unto death: and he was numbered with the transgressors; and made intercession for the transgressors."

Thirdly, The enemies which Sampson slew at his death, were more in number than all that he had slain in the course of his whole life. What did the Redeemer destroy in his death? 2 Timothy i. 10, " Our Lord and Saviour Jesus Christ, who hath abolished death, and hath brought life and immortality to light through the gospel." Isaiah xxv. 7, 8, "And he will destroy in this mountain the face of the covering cast over all flesh, and the veil that is spread over all nations. He will swallow up death in victory; and the Lord God will wipe away tears from off all faces; and the rebuke of his people shall he take away from off all the earth: for the Lord hath spoken it." 1 Corinthians xv. 54, " So when this corruptible shall have put on incorruption, and this mortal shall have put on immortality, then shall be brought to pass the saying that is written, Death is swallowed up in victory." But,

Fourthly, The Redeemer achieved more, abundantly more; he not only destroyed death, but him who had the power of death. Hebrews ii. 14, " Forasmuch then as the children are partakers of flesh and blood, he also himself likewise took part of the same; that through death he might destroy him that had the power of death, that is the devil." The power of death is taken from the adversary and given to the world's Saviour. All power in heaven and earth, is given to me, saith the God man—Can it be in better hands? The Lord of universal nature will do right. Death and the devil are the two pillars on which rest the misery and destruction of intelligent beings. The Philistines are the figures of the multiplied iniquities of mankind. The Redeemer laying hold of, and uprooting these pillars, the whole fabrick was demolished. At that eventful moment, Messiah, by being cut off, made an end of sin. The transgressions of mankind although searched for cannot be found, they are buried beneath the rubbish, they are like a great millstone whelmed in the depths of the sea. Such was the victory gained by him who led captivity captive, and who when he ascended up on high, received gifts for men, yea, even for rebellious men.

Fifthly, Sampson was a type of Jesus Christ, even in his burial. His brethren took him and buried him. Mark xv. 46, "And he brought fine linen, and took him down, and wrapped him in the linen, and laid him in a sepulcre which was hewn out of a rock." Luke xxiii 53, "And he took it down, and wrapped it in linen, and laid it in a sepulcre that was hewn in stone wherein never man before was laid."

Sixthly, The power of prayer is exemplified in the answer to the fervent petition of Sampson. The prayer of Sampson was the prayer of faith, and the prayer of faith is always answered. 2 Chronicles xx 12, "O our God, wilt thou not judge them? our eyes are upon thee." The prayer, the faith, of that righteous man, who is the head of every man, availeth much It is potent to procure the restitution of all things to exterminate evil from the universe.

SKETCH LIV.

1 Samuel xii.

First, Who were *God's people*, and who were *not his people?* The responses of the sacred oracles are infallible. We will inquire at the mouth of Moses, Exodus vi. 7, "And I will take you to me for a people, and I will be to you a God: and ye shall know that I am the Lord your God, which bringeth you out from under the burdens of the Egyptians." The prophet Jeremiah is also explicit and decisive, xiii. 11, "For as the girdle cleaveth to the loins of a man, so have I caused to cleave unto me the whole house of Israel, and the whole house of Judah, saith the Lord, that they may be unto me for a people, and for a name, and for a praise, and for a glory : but they would not hear." But there were who were not the people of God. Romans x. 19, " But I say did not Israel know ? First, Moses saith I will provoke you to jealousy by them that are no people, and by a foolish nation I will anger you."

Secondly, But who are now the people of God ? Blessed be the name of Jehovah, the sacred writers are still ready with their answers. Hosea i. 9, 10, "Then said God, call his name Loammi: for ye are not my people, and I will not be your God. Yet the numbers of the children of Israel shall be as the sand of the sea, which cannot be measured nor numbered; and it shall come to pass that in the *place where it was said unto them, ye are not my people ; there it shall be said unto them, ye are the sons of the living God.*" Luke ii. 10, 30—32, "And the angel said unto them, Fear not, for behold I bring you good tidings of great joy, which shall be to *all people*. For mine eyes have seen thy salvation, which thou hast prepared before the face of all people. A light to lighten the Gentiles, and the glory of thy people Israel." The suffrage of the apostle Paul is as usual, full and clear. Ephesians ii. 14, 16, " For he is our peace, who hath made both one, and hath broken down the middle wall of partition between us. And that he might reconcile both unto God in one body by the cross, having slain the enmity thereby." And verses 17, 18, 19, 20, "And came and preached to you who were afar off, and to them who were nigh. For through him we both have access by one spirit unto the Father. Now, therefore, ye are no more strangers and foreigners, but fellow citizens with the saints, and of the household of God. And are built upon the foundation of the apostles and prophets, Jesus Christ himself being the chief corner stone." This testimony is confirmed, Galatians iii. 28, " There is neither Jew nor Greek, there is neither bond nor free, there is neither male nor female, for ye are all one in Christ Jesus." Testimonies to this effect might be multiplied, but we hasten,

Thirdly, To inquire why the characters described are the people of God?

First, They are the property of God, because he created them. Genesis i. 27, "So God created man in his own image, in the image of God created he him." Deuteronomy xxxii. 15, 18, "Then he forsook God which made him, and lightly esteemed the rock of his salvation. Of the rock that begat thee, thou art unmindful, and hast forgotten God that formed thee." Psalm civ. 30, "Thou sendest forth thy spirit, they are created: and thou renewest the face of the earth." Psalm cxlviii. 5, "Let them praise the name of the LORD: for he commanded, and they were created." Isaiah xliii. 1, "But now, saith the LORD, that created thee." Malachi ii. 10, "Have we not all one Father? Hath not one God created us?" Ephesians ii. 9, "And to make all men see what is the fellowship of the mystery, which, from the beginning of the world, hath been hid in God, who created all things by Jesus Christ." Colossians i. 16, "For by him were all things created, that are in heaven, and that are in earth, visible and invisible." Revelations iv. 11, "Thou art worthy, O LORD, to receive glory, and honour, and power: for thou hast created all things, and for thy pleasure they are and were created."

Secondly, The human family belong to God, because he hath redeemed them. Exodus xv. 13, "Thou, in thy mercy, hast led forth the people which thou hast redeemed." Deuteronomy xv. 15, "The LORD thy God redeemed thee." Deuteronomy iv. 26, "I prayed, therefore, unto the LORD, and said, O LORD God, destroy not thy people and thy inheritance which thou hast redeemed." Deuteronomy xiii 5, "And redeemed you out of the house of bondage." Deuteronomy xxi. 8, "Be merciful, O LORD, unto thy people Israel, whom thou hast redeemed." Psalm xxxi. 5, "Into thine hand I commit my spirit: thou hast redeemed me, O LORD God of truth." Isaiah xxix. 22, "Therefore thus saith the LORD, who *redeemed* Abraham." Isaiah xliv. 22, 23, "I have blotted out, as a thick cloud, thy transgressions, and as a cloud, thy sins: return unto me, for I have redeemed thee. Sing, O ye heavens; for the LORD hath done it: shout ye lower parts of the earth: break forth into singing, ye mountains, O forest, and every tree therein: for the LORD hath redeemed Jacob." Hosea vii. 13, "Though I have redeemèd them, yet they have spoken lies against me." Luke i. 68,

"Blessed be the Lord God of Israel; for he hath visited and redeemed his people." Galatians iii. 13, " Christ hath redeemed us from the curse of the law." Revelations v. 9, " For thou wast slain and hast redeemed us to God by thy blood."

Yes, blessed be almighty God, help was laid upon one who was mighty; he sent redemption to his people. Hebrews ix. 12, " By his own blood, he entered in once into the holy place, having obtained eternal redemption for us." Christ Jesus hath bought, he hath paid the purchase for us; the right of redemption was in him. Exodus xv. 16, " Till thy people pass over, O Lord, till the people pass over which thou hast purchased." Acts xx. 28, " Feed the church of God, which he hath purchased with his own blood." Ephesians i. 14, " Which is the earnest of our inheritance until the redemption of the purchased possession." Deuteronomy xxxii. 6, " Is not he thy Father, that hath bought thee? Hath he not made thee, and established thee?" 1 Corinthians vi. 20, " For ye are bought with a price: therefore glorify God in your body, and in your spirit, which are God's." 2 Peter ii. 1, " But there were also false prophets among the people, even as there shall be false teachers among you, who privily shall bring in damnable heresies, even *denying the Lord that bought them*, and bring upon themselves swift destruction."

Thirdly, God hath established his right in human nature, because he hath preserved it. Nehemiah ix. 6, " Thou, even thou, art Lord alone; thou hast made heaven, the heaven of heavens, with all their host, the earth and all things that are therein, the seas and all that is therein, and thou *preservest them all*." Job vii. 20, " I have sinned; what shall I do unto thee, O *thou preserver of men?*" Psalm xxxvi. 6, " Thy righteousness is like the great mountains; thy judgments are a great deep: O Lord, thou *preservest man and beast*."

Thus, from a cloud of witnesses it becomes plain, that the whole human race belong unto him who created, who redeemed the lost nature, and who preservest the creatures he hath made. All souls, says God, are mine. It is true, we have sold ourselves for nought, and are ready to say, we have made a covenant with death, and with hell are we at agreement. But, saith God, by the prophet Isaiah, xxviii 18, " Your covenant with death shall be disannulled, and your agreement with hell shall not stand."

Fourthly, The consequences attendant upon being the people of God. Hebrews viii. 10, "For this is the covenant which I will make with the house of Israel after those days, saith the Lord; I will put my laws into their mind, and write them in their hearts: and I will be to them a God, and they shall be to me a people." Psalm cxlix. 9, "The Lord taketh pleasure in his people." This is another blessed consequence. Psalm cx. 3, "Thy people shall be willing in the day of thy power, in the beauties of holiness from the womb of the morning: thou hast the dew of thy youth." Isaiah lx. 21, 22, "Thy people also shall be all righteous: they shall inherit the land forever, the branch of my planting, the work of my hands, that I may be glorified. A little one shall become a thousand, and a small one a strong nation: I the Lord will hasten it in his time." Hebrews viii. 11, 12, 13, "And they shall not teach every man his neighbour, and every man his brother, saying, Know the Lord: for all shall know me from the least to the greatest. And I will be merciful to their unrighteousness, and their sins, and their iniquities will I remember no more. In that he saith, A new covenant, he hath made the first old. Now that which decayeth and waxeth old is ready to vanish away."

Fifthly, and lastly, We are to consider the advantages to be derived from belonging to God. Hosea ii. 15, "I will give her vineyards from thence, and the valley of Achor for a door of hope: and she shall sing there as in the days of her youth, and as in the day when she came up out of the land of Egypt." Zephaniah iii. 14—20, "Sing, O daughter of Zion; shout, O Israel; be glad and rejoice with all the heart, O daughter of Jerusalem. The Lord hath taken away thy judgments, he hath cast out thine enemy. In that day it shall be said to Jerusalem, Fear thou not; and to Zion, Let not thy hands be slack. The Lord thy God in the midst of thee is mighty; he will save, he will rejoice over thee with joy. I will gather them that are sorrowful for thy solemn assembly, who are of thee, to whom the reproach of it was a burden. Behold, at that time I will undo all that afflict thee. At that time will I bring you again, even in the time that I gather you; for I will make you a name and a praise among all people of the earth, when I turn back your captivity before your eyes, saith the Lord." John xiv. 13, 14, "And whatsoever ye shall ask in my name, that will I do, that the Father may be glorified in the Son. If ye ask any thing in my name, I will do it."

These are a few of the advantages contained in that vast charter of privileges granted to the people who were created and redeemed, and who are preserved by the God of heaven; for the Lord will not forsake his people, for his great name! because it hath pleased the Lord to make you his people. Blessed is the name of the Lord.

But, suffer me to ask, what effect these considerations should have upon us, who believe the truth as it is in Jesus? First, The knowledge of what God hath done for our souls, should put us in possession of undisturbed repose. We should cast every spiritual care upon him who careth for us. Secondly, We should unceasingly praise the Lord, both by *lip* and *life*, for the multitude and magnitude of his mercies. We should continually and unfeignedly say, not only the Lord be praised, but Lord what wouldst thou have me to do? Thirdly, These glorious discoveries should lead us, at all times, to consult our own interest in *every thing;* for in no way can we more effectually glorify God. Whether we are in the characters of husbands or wives, parents or children, masters or servants, in every character it is as much our *interest* as it can be our *duty*, to conduct with propriety. The ways of wisdom, the ways of virtue, are, at every period, ways of pleasantness, and all their paths are peace.

SKETCH LV.

2 Samuel xxiii. 1—4.

First, These, we are told, are the last words of David the son of Jesse. And what *were* the last words of this sweet singer of Israel? The spirit of the Lord spake by me, and his word was in my tongue. The Apostle Peter, Acts iv. 25, corroborates this testimony of David. "And when they heard that, they lifted up their voices to God with one accord, and said, Lord thou art God which hast made heaven and earth, and the sea, and all that in them is; who by the mouth of thy servant David hast said, Why did the heathen rage, and the people imagine vain things?"

Secondly, What did the spirit of God say to, or by this royal prophet? He characterized himself as the God of Israel. Exodus xx. 2, "I am the Lord thy God." God is the rock of ages.

Thirdly, God is the ruler over men; he is a just God. Isaiah xlv. 21, "And there is no god else beside me; a just God and a Saviour; there is none else beside me."

Fourthly, Emmanuel ruled in the fear of the Lord. This is the beginning of wisdom. Jeremiah xxiii. 5, 7, 8, "Behold, the days come, saith the Lord, that I will raise up unto David a righteous branch, and a king shall reign and prosper, and shall execute judgment and justice in the earth. Therefore, behold, the days come, saith the Lord, that they shall no more say, The Lord liveth which brought up the children of Israel out of the land of Egypt; but the Lord liveth, which brought out, and which led the seed of the house of Israel out of the north country, and from all the countries whither I had driven them; and they shall dwell in their own land."

Fifthly, And this branch shall be as the light of the morning. Proverbs iv. 18, "But the path of the just is as the shining light, that shineth more and more unto the perfect day." Yea, and he shall shine until it becomes evident, that he is the true light which lighteth every man that cometh into the world.

Sixthly, He shall be as a morning without clouds. Erst times our God was enveloped in clouds and darkness. Psalm xcii. 2, "Clouds and darkness are round about him;" but so luminous, so extensive will the clear shining of this sun of righteousness become, that he shall be as a *morning without clouds*.

Seventhly, He shall be like the tender grass springing out of the earth, and as clear shining after rain.

My attention has been recently called to a manuscript, in which there is a remarkable variation in rendering this passage. As the morning light shall Jehovah, the sun rise. Can we ever behold the rising sun, without recurring to the God of our salvation? How beautiful is the sun when bursting in all its splendour from the chambers of the east. How beautiful is the verdant earth, when illumined by the rays of the sun after the gently falling shower. So, just so, will the inheritance of God appear after his renovating word shall drop as the rain on the tender herb, and the showers upon the grass. Are not songs of praise and hymns of thanksgiving due to the God of our salvation?

SKETCH LVI.

2 Samuel xxiii. 5.

First, David's house and family were not so with God. Not as described in the preceding verses.

Secondly, Neither was the house of our spiritual David so with God, for all we like sheep have gone astray. But,

Thirdly, Yet he hath made with me, saith the royal prophet, an everlasting covenant. Of this covenant God speaketh by the mouth of the prophet Isaiah, xlix. 8, " Thus saith the Lord, in an acceptable time have I heard thee : and in a day of salvation have I helped thee : and I will preserve thee, and give thee for a covenant of the people, to establish the earth, to cause to inherit the desolate heritages. Hebrews viii. 8, " For finding fault with them he saith, Behold, the days come,' saith the Lord, when I will make a new covenant with the house of Israel, and with the house of Judah."

Fourthly, This covenant was indeed well ordered in all things. With respect to matter, manner, time and place, it was the work of the God of order : and in such infinite wisdom was it ordered, that it must be an enduring covenant. This is a most consolatory and elevating consideration : especially, when we investigate the covenant as described by Jeremiah, and by the apostle Paul. No wonder it is added :

Fifthly, And this covenant is sure. There are who give to the gospel trumpet an uncertain sound : few pretend to the faith of assurance, and indeed, as it respects the children of men, unstable in all their ways, no permanent conclusion can be drawn.

Sixthly, This, said the royal prophet, this, said that prophet of whom all the prophets have written, is all my salvation. Let us recur to the character of the speaker, the head of every man. I know, said he, the words I have received of my Father, are eternal life. This is all my salvation. The divinity is all the support of the humanity. But as this was all his salvation, so :

Seventhly, It was all his desire, Psalm lxxiii. 25, "Whom have I in heaven but thee? and there is none upon earth that I desire beside thee."

Eighthly, Although he maketh it not to grow; although this covenant was in the days of the son of Jesse, apparently upon the decline: yet the God of Israel declared that this covenant should grow, and prosper, and bring forth much fruit. Isaiah xi. "And there shall come forth a root out of the stem of Jesse, and a branch shall grow out of his roots." And the spirit of the Lord shall rest upon him, the spirit of wisdom and understanding, the spirit of counsel and might, the spirit of knowledge and the fear of the Lord. And he shall not judge after the sight of his eyes, neither reprove after the hearing of his ears. But with righteousness shall he judge the poor, and reprove with equity for the meek of the earth.

SKETCH LVII.

Psalm ix. 17.

The wicked shall be turned into hell, and all the nations that forget God.

First, Who are the wicked? Upon all occasions, especially upon those which involve difficulty, the holy scripture is our unerring guide, our never failing resource. Paul emphatically saith, And then shall that wicked be revealed, whom the Lord shall consume with the spirit of his mouth, and shall destroy with the brightness of his coming. Isaiah xlviii. 22, "There is no peace saith Jehovah, unto the wicked." Matthew xiii. 49, "At the end of the world the angels shall come forth, and sever the wicked from among the just."

Secondly, As sin is wickedness, wherever sin is found, it stamps the character of wickedness. All who are under the influence of the adversary are wicked; such were those religious characters among the people of God, who, with wicked hands, crucified the Lord of glory.

Thirdly, It should always be remembered that wickedness is not the work of God. It is the work of that wicked, of whom Paul spake, and to whom God spake in the garden of Eden, when he said, " Because thou hast done this, thou art cursed."

Fourthly, What doth the spirit of God teach us by the word hell? Commentators unite in assuring us that the term *scheol*, which we render hell, is literally the grave. Jacob says, I will go down into *scheol*, into hell, to my son mourning. If mischief befall him, says the same patriarch, ye shall bring down my grey hairs with sorrow to *scheol*, hell.

Fifthly, *Scheol* or hell, is sometimes represented as the state of departed spirits, as a state of anguish. Ezekiel xxxi. 16, " When I cast him, Pharaoh, down to hell." Again Chapter xxxii. 21, " The strong, among the mighty, shall speak to him out of the midst of hell." And verse 31, " Pharaoh shall see them, and shall be comforted over all his multitude." Again, Jonah ii. 2, " Out of the belly of hell or *scheol*, cried I, and thou heardest my voice." The Psalmist, speaking in his typical character, says, Psalm xvi. 31, " Thou wilt not leave my soul in *scheol*, hell, neither wilt thou suffer thine Holy One to see corruption." The apostle Peter, Acts ii. 31, Refers to this testimony. " He, seeing this before, spake of the resurrection of Chirst, that his soul was not left in hell, neither his flesh did see corruption." Thus, it is evident, the soul of the Redeemer was in hell, although it was not *left there*. It was in this hell, the spirits of those Antediluvians, were imprisoned, of whom the apostle Peter speaks, 1 Peter iii. 18, " By which also he went and preached unto the spirits in prison." And again, Chapter iv. 6, " For this cause was the gospel preached also to them that are dead, that they might be judged according to men in the flesh." Our Saviour in a variety of instances refers to this hell, as the state of soul and body, and the Holy Ghost by the apostle Peter emphatically says, 2 Peter ii. 4, "For if God spared not the angels that sinned, but cast them down to hell, and delivered them into chains of darkness to be reserved unto judgment."

Sixthly, Into this hell, the wicked, and all the nations that forget God shall be turned. Does not this comprehend every sinner? Who liveth and sinneth not? Does it not comprehend every unbeliever? But where is the *believer*, that was not once an *unbeliever?* This prophecy is fulfilled, or it is not. Our

Saviour said he came to fulfil the law, and the Prophets, and, if he did fulfil the law, and the *prophets*, when the sorrows of death compassed him about, when his soul was turned into hell, when the pains of hell gat hold upon him, then he fulfilled the law, and the prophets. In him the sinner died, for if one died for all, then were all dead. In him the wicked were turned into hell, and the scriptures were accomplished. But if you will not allow us thus to reconcile the scripture, if you still say the wicked, individually shall be turned into hell, with all the nations that forget God, I will join issue with your conclusion, and only remark, that these nations would remain in hell, through the wasteless ages of eternity, if Jesus were not the Saviour of *all men*, if they *continued to forget God.* But assuredly Jesus *is* the Saviour of all men, and assuredly all the nations of the earth will one day *remember* the God who made them. Hear the spirit of truth speaking by the mouth of the Psalmist. Psalm xxii. 27, " All the ends of the world shall *remember*, and turn unto the Lord: and all the kindreds of the nations shall worship before thee." All that the Father hath given unto me, saith the Saviour, shall come unto me. These nations cannot remain in hell, for they were *given by Jehovah to the Son*, and the Son declares, all that *was given unto him, shall come unto him*, and he informs us, Revelations i. 18, That he hath the keys of hell, and of death. The nations cannot continue, through all eternity in a state of darkness, and consequent misery, because *death* and *hell must deliver up* the *dead, which be in them, when both death and hell will be cast into the lake of fire*, which is the second, that is the last death. The nations that forget God will remember him again, when they will turn to him, and worship him: for, saith that God who gave himself a ransom for all, to be testified in due time, Hosea xiii. 14, " I will ransom them from the power of the grave; I will redeem them from death: O death, I will be thy plagues: O grave, *scheol*, I will be thy destruction." It is therefore the nations cannot remain in *scheol*, hell, because the ransomed of the Lord shall return to Zion, with songs, and because God, who cannot lie, declares, Revelations xxi. 4, " He will wipe away all tears from their eyes; and there shall be no more death, neither sorrow, nor crying, neither shall there be any more pain: for the former things are passed away."

There are perhaps, but two sorts of hearers, those who do, and those who do not believe. The first will see, and seeing they will believe, and believing they will rejoice, and most joyfully will they set their seals to the truth of God. The second will be angry, exceeding angry, and they will hasten to speak evil of that they do not understand. We are prepared for ill treatment, we expect it, but we will endeavour in patience to possess our souls. When we are reviled, we will not revile again, we ought not, for we are believers in, and servants of, a meek and lowly Master; and we are assured that at the period when there shall be no more pain, no more sorrow, no more death, we shall see and hear every creature which is in heaven, and on the earth, and such as are in the sea, and all that are in them, saying blessing, and honour, and glory, and power, unto him that sitteth upon the throne, and unto the Lamb forever, and ever, Amen, and Amen.

SKETCH LVIII.

Psalm xxviii. 9.

Save thy people, and bless thine inheritance: feed them also, and lift them up forever.

First, Who are God's people? The posterity of Abraham. Deuteronomy vii. 6, "For thou art an holy people unto the Lord thy God: the Lord thy God hath chosen thee to be a special people unto himself, above all people that are upon the face of the earth."

Secondly, The Gentiles are the people of God. Romans xv. 10, 12, "And again he saith, Rejoice, ye Gentiles, with his people. And again Esaias saith, There shall be a root of Jesse, and he that shall rise to reign over the Gentiles; in him shall the Gentiles trust."

Thirdly, And bless thine inheritance. What is the inheritance of our God? Psalm ii. 8, "Ask of me; and I shall give thee the heathen for thine inheritance, and the uttermost parts of the earth for thy possession." Psalm cxxvii. 3, "Lo, children are an heritage of the Lord."

Fourthly, The prayer of David, of our spiritual David, Save thy people. Save thy people from what? From sin. Matthew i. 21, "And she shall bring forth a son, and thou shalt call his name Jesus: for he shall save his people from their sins." John iv. 42, "Now we believe, not because of thy saying; for we have heard him ourselves, and know that this is indeed the Christ, the Saviour of the world." Secondly, Save thy people from death, which is the wages of sin. Christ Jesus hath abolished death, and brought life and immortality to light by the gospel. Thirdly, Save thy people from the curse of the law. Galatians iii. 13, "Christ hath redeemed us from the curse of the law, being made a curse for us." Fourthly, Save thy people from ignorance. They shall all be taught of God, they shall no more die for lack of knowledge, for they shall all know God from the least to the greatest, and to know God is life eternal. Then shall they be blessed, then shall they be lifted up forever.

SKETCH LIX.

Psalm xl. 6—8.

First, In what respect did not God require sacrifices and offerings? 1 Samuel xv. 22, "Hath the Lord as great delight in burnt offerings and sacrifices, as in obeying the voice of the Lord? Behold, to obey is better than sacrifice." Psalm li. 16, "For thou desirest not sacrifice, else would I give it: thou delightest not in burnt offering." Isaiah i. 11, "To what purpose is the number of your sacrifices to me, saith the Lord? I delight not in the blood of bullocks." Hosea vi. 6, "For I desired mercy, and not sacrifice, and the knowledge of God more than burnt offerings." Matthew xii. 7, "For if ye had known what this meaneth, I will have mercy and not sacrifice, you would not have condemned the guiltless."

Secondly, In what respect were sacrifices typical of the Redeemer? Hebrews ix. 12, "Neither by the blood of goats and calves, but by his own blood; he entered in once into the holy place, having obtained eternal redemption for us."

Thirdly, Jesus came to do the will of God, which will was the sanctification of the people, and the taking away their sin. Hebrews x. 10, "By the which will we are sanctified through the offering of the body of Jesus Christ once for all."

Fourthly, In the volume of the book it is written of me. Search the scriptures; for in them ye think ye have eternal life; and they are they which testify of me. In these scriptures, it will be found, that the law of God is within my heart, that I do indeed delight to do his will.

SKETCH LX.

Psalm xl. 12, 13.

First, Who is it that thus speaketh? Undoubtedly, Christ Jesus. Search the scriptures, said our Lord, they testify of me.

Secondly, What were the evils which compassed him about? There are two descriptions of evil. First, *Sin, this is said to be of the wicked one. Ye are of your father, the devil, for the works of your father you do.* Secondly, Suffering is an evil. Job ii. 10, "Shall we receive good at the hand of God, and shall we not receive evil?" Isaiah xlv. 7, "I form the light, and create darkness: I make peace, and create evil: I, the Lord, do all these things." To say that evil of this last description was sin, were to blaspheme God. But the Saviour could say, that by evils of both these descriptions, he was encompassed about. Isaiah liii. 3, 4, "He is despised and rejected of men: a man of sorrows, and acquainted with grief: and we hid as it were our faces from him; he was despised, and we esteemed him not. Surely, he hath borne our griefs, and carried our sorrows: yet we did esteem him stricken, smitten of God, and afflicted."

Thirdly, Mine iniquities have taken hold upon me. These iniquities were the Redeemer's, because committed by his body, of which he was the head; while, as an individual, he was *holy*, and *in him* was no sin. But Psalm xlix. 5, exhibits a complete explanation of our text. "Wherefore should I fear in the days of evil, when the iniquity of my heels shall compass me about." Thus were our iniquities acknowledged *his*, as *his righteousness* is said to be *ours*. Isaiah liii. 5, " But he was wounded for our transgressions, he was bruised for our iniquities: the chastisement of our peace was upon him; and with his stripes we are healed." 1 Peter ii. 24, " Who his own self bear our sins in his own body on the tree, that we being dead to sins, should live unto righteousness: by whose stripes we are healed." With strict propriety doth the Redeemer say, these iniquities are more in number than the hairs of my head; innumerable evils have compassed me about.

Fourthly, Therefore, my heart faileth. Father, if it be possible let this cup pass from me. He was dumb and opened not his mouth.

Fifthly, Be pleased, O Lord, to deliver me, make haste to help me. And he was heared when he prayed, Psalm lxxxvi. 13, " For great is thy mercy toward me; and thou hast delivered my soul from the lowest hell." Psalm xvi. 15, " For thou wilt not leave my soul in hell; neither wilt thou suffer thine Holy One to see corruption."

SKETCH LXI.

Psalm cxlv. 19—21.

First, Who are they that fear the Lord? They are those who are taught by the elucidating spirit of truth. Psalm xxv. 14, " The secret of the Lord is with them that fear him, and he will shew them his covenant." The fear of the Lord is the beginning of wisdom, and a sound understanding have all they who walk therein.

Secondly, What is the desire of those who fear God? Their desires are expressed in their prayers.

Thirdly, God will fulfil the desire of those who fear him. Whatsoever they ask, according to his will, they shall receive.

Fourthly, He will save them. I am God the Saviour, and beside me there is no God.

Fifthly, The Lord preserveth all those that love him, although their foes may be many and mighty, yet the Lord is *Almighty*, and the victory will be with him.

Sixthly, The sire of men and angels will destroy the wicked. 2 Thessalonians ii. 8, "And then shall that wicked be revealed, whom the Lord shall consume with the spirit of his mouth, and shall destroy with the brightness of his coming."

Seventhly, Psalm lxv. 2, the blessed consequence of this preservation, of this destruction is described. "O thou who hearest prayer, unto thee shall all flesh come." Isaiah xliv. 3, "For I will pour water upon him that is thirsty, and floods upon the dry ground; I will pour my spirit upon thy seed, and my blessing upon thine offspring" Joel ii. 28, "And it shall come to pass afterward, that I will pour out my spirit upon all flesh." No wonder then, that the mouth shall proclaim the praises of Jehovah, and that all flesh shall bless his holy name forever and ever.

SKETCH LXII.

Proverbs x. 24.

First, What is the wicked here spoken of? 2 Thessalonians, ii. 8, "And then shall that wicked be revealed, whom the Lord shall consume with the spirit of his mouth, and destroy with the brightness of his coming."

Secondly, What is the fear of this wicked? Matthew viii. 29, "And, behold, they cried out. saying, What have we to do with thee, Jesus, thou Son of God? Art thou come hither to torment us before the time?" Mark v. 7, "And cried with a loud voice, and said, What have I to do with thee, Jesus thou Son of the Most High God? I adjure thee by God, that thou torment me not." 2 Peter ii. 4, "For if God spared not the angels that sinned, but cast them down to hell, and delivered them into the chains of darkness, to be reserved unto judgment." Revelations xx. 2, "And cast him into the bottomless pit, and shut him up and set a seal upon him."

Thirdly, Who is the righteous? Romans iii. 10, "As it is written, there is none righteous, no, not one." Jeremiah xxiii. 6, "In his day Judah shall be saved, and Israel shall dwell safely: and this is his name whereby he shall be called, The Lord our righteousness."

Fourthly, What is the desire of the righteous? He desireth not the death of the sinner; he willeth that all shall be saved and come unto the knowledge of the truth. He was manifested to destroy the works of the devil.

Fifthly, The desire of the righteous shall be granted. Treasures of wickedness profit nothing; but righteousness delivereth from death.

SKETCH LXIII.

Isaiah i. 2, 3.

First, The magnitude of this subject may be estimated by the importance of the characters addressed—Hear, O heavens; and give ear, O earth. What are we to understand by the heavens? There seems to be a plurality of heavens. The aerial heavens, the starry heavens, the throne of God, and the seat of the blessed, inhabited by angels and the spirits of just men made perfect; these are solemnly called upon to hear what the Almighty is about to utter.

Secondly, The earth must also give ear; not any particular portion of the earth, in contradistinction to the general mass. Jeremiah xxii. 29, "O *earth, earth, hear* the word of the Lord." And chapter vi. 19, "Hear, O *earth:* behold I will bring evil upon this people, even the fruits of their thoughts, because they have not hearkened unto my words, nor to my law, but rejected it." Surely it cannot rationally be supposed, that the earth on which we tread, is thus solemnly called upon to hear the word of the Lord? Certainly not; it is human, it is animated earth, which in the beautifully figurative language of scripture, is thus commanded to hear.

Thirdly, Why are the heavens and the earth impressively enjoined to hear? *Because the* LORD *hath spoken.*

Fourthly, What are the heavens and the earth summoned to hear? Not the words of the creature, the doctrines and traditions of men—no, assuredly; it is the words of the LORD of heaven and earth, which all intelligent beings are commanded to hear.

Fifthly, What hath the LORD spoken? I have nourished and brought up children, and they have rebelled against me. The expression is remarkable. The *rebels were the children of God,* although in a state of rebellion. Ezekiel xvi. 6, 13, 14, 15, "And when I passed by thee, and saw thee polluted in thine own blood, I said unto thee when thou wast in thy blood, LIVE; yea, I said unto thee when thou wast in thy blood, LIVE. Thus wast thou decked with gold and silver, and thy raiment was of fine linen, and silk and broidered work; thou didst eat fine flour, and honey, and oil; and thou wast exceedingly beautiful, and thou didst prosper into a kingdom. And thy renown went forth among the heathen for thy beauty; for it was perfect through my comeliness which I had put upon thee, saith the LORD God. But thou didst trust in thine own beauty, and playedst the harlot because of thy renown, and pouredst out thy fornications to every one that passed by." Do you say, they were children before they rebelled, but not when they became depraved, lost, undone sinners? I deny that the sacred volume authorizes such an idea; and I appeal from your assertion to the Apostle to the Gentiles. Galatians iv. 5, 6, "Because ye are sons, God hath sent forth the spirit of his Son into your hearts, crying, Abba, Father Wherefore thou art no more a servant, but a son, an heir of God through Christ." Romans v. 8, "But God commendeth his love to us, in that while we were yet sinners Christ died for us." Colossians ii. 13, 14, "And you being dead in your sins and the uncircumcision of your flesh, hath he quickened together with him, having forgiven you all trespasses; blotting out the hand writing of ordinances that was against us, which was contrary to us, and took it out of the way, nailing it to his cross." Ephesians ii. 1, 5, 13, 16, "And you hath he quickened, who were dead in trespasses and sins. Even when we were dead in sins, hath quickened us together with Christ; by grace ye are saved. But now in Christ Jesus ye who sometimes were far off, are made nigh by the blood of Christ. And that he might reconcile both unto God in one body on the cross, having slain the enmity thereby."

Sixthly, Why did the people of God rebel against him? Because they were ignorant of the rock from whence they were hewn. Their knowledge was more confined, than that of the brute animals which fed on their grounds. The ox knew his owner, and the ass his master's crib, but Israel did not know; Israel was ignorant of the God who made him!

Seventhly, God the Lord was, nevertheless, the owner of these *rebellious*, these *ungrateful*, these *ignorant* people. They were the property of Emmanuel; he was their master, they were of his fold, the sheep of his pasture.

Eighthly, Although they were the people of God, they did not consider; and although they did not consider, they were his people But what was that which the people of God did not consider? They did not consider the character of him who made them, nor for what purpose they were made. They did not consider to what they were entitled; they did not consider the character of their adversary, nor how unequal he was to contend with the omnipotent Friend of sinners. Had they considered these things, they could never have been deceived; they would have walked with steady feet in the paths of *peace*, from which the highest felicity would have resulted. But as happiness was the aim and end of creation, the God who called the human family into existence for his own glory and their good, will not, cannot be disappointed. No individual ever hath, no individual ever can successfully resist the absolute will of almighty God.

SKETCH LXIV.

Isaiah i. 28.

First, Who are the transgressors, and who are the sinners? Were they of one nature? Why then, this mode of expression, transgressors and sinners?

Secondly, What is this threatened destruction? Is it the *eternal* ruin or death of the human family? If it be, God our Saviour will lose his offspring, that inheritance for which he hath paid a price all price beyond, and although all things were made for him, and by him, although in his human character, as the head of every man, all souls were given unto him, and he pledged his sacred word that none should ever pluck them out of his hands; yet he will *absolutely lose them*, lose those whom *he came to save*, lose those whom it is his *wish to save*, but whom man, *almighty man*, will not permit him to save. He, the word which was made flesh, cannot perform, what he was commissioned to perform, he has returned from an embassy which has proved nearly fruitless! Although the promise, the oath of God omnipotent, was engaged for his success. Although the Redeemer affirmed, *I have finished* what thou gavest me to do. But he was sent to be the Saviour of all men, the Saviour of the world, and it indubitably follows, if he has *not ransomed, if he has not saved all men, he did not finish the work he came to do*. But may not the sinner be destroyed, and the nature saved? If he may not, as *all have sinned*, no individual can be saved. If the sinner be destroyed and the nature saved, all must, all will be saved.

Thirdly, At what period was the destruction of the transgressors and the sinners together? When God prepared what, in the context he engaged to perform. " Ah, I will ease me of mine adversaries, and avenge me of mine enemies, and I will turn my hand upon thee, and purely purge away thy dross, and take away all thy tin, and I will restore thy judges as at the first, and thy counsellors as at the beginning: afterwards thou shalt be called the city of righteousness, the faithful city. Zion shall be redeemed with judgment, and her converts with righteousness." Then follows our text. "And the destruction of the transgressors and the sinners shall be together; and they that forsake the LORD shall be consumed." The transgressors and sinners were destroyed together, consequent upon which there shall be no more destruction; Psalm ix. 6, "O thou enemy, destructions are come to a perpetual end." Zechariah xiv. 11, "And men shall dwell in it, and there shall be no more utter destruction; but Jerusalem shall be safely inhabited." Thus are the scriptures fulfilled. "I came not to destroy the law, and the prophets, but to fulfil them." He, Jesus the Redeemer, finished the transgression, but in the same point of view that the transgression was finished, the *transgressors, and the sinners were destroyed.*

Fourthly, We are led from these considerations to contemplate with pious gratitude, and holy joy, the grand, the man restoring,

God honouring catastrophe, and we are as positive as we are of our existence, that Christ Jesus is the Lamb of God, that taketh away the sin of the world; that he will destroy the works of the devil, that he will be the destruction of hell. Hosea xiii. 14, " I will ransom them from the power of the grave; I will redeem them from death: O death I will be thy plagues: O grave I will be thy destruction." Indeed by his death, and in his death, the Redeemer destroyed both death, and the devil. 2 Timothy i. 10, " But is now made manifest by the appearing of our Saviour Jesus Christ, who hath abolished death, and brought life and immortality to light by the gospel" Hebrews ii. 14, " Forasmuch then as the children are partakers of flesh and blood, he also, himself, likewise took part of the same, that through death he might destroy him that had the power of death, that is the devil."

Fifthly, These are the true sayings of God. Can he be a believer, who refuses to admit the authenticity of the scripture? Can he who is not a believer escape condemnation? Is not the unbeliever condemned out of his own mouth?"He who believeth these true sayings of God shall never come into condemnation, shall never be ashamed, worlds without end. He hath passed from death unto life. He who doth *not* believe those true sayings of God cannot see life. The things which make for his peace are hidden from his eyes, and the wrath of God revealed from heaven against all ungodliness, abideth on him." Yea, let his character be ever so high in his own estimation, or in the opinion of his admirers, still the *wrath of God abideth on him; he is condemned, he has offended at least in one point, he is guilty of all, and his condemnation will continue until in his heart he accepts and believes those true sayings of God.* Yea, verily, for we have received these sayings from the living oracles of almighty God.

SKETCH LXV.

Isaiah i. 29, 30.

First, Who are those who shall be ashamed of the oaks? Undoubtedly those characters who were spoken of in the conclusion of our last subject; in the verse immediately preceding our text. Those who forsake the Lord, Jeremiah ii. 13, "For my people have committed two evils; they have forsaken me, the fountain of living waters, and hewn them out cisterns, broken cisterns, that can hold no water."

Secondly, These, saith the Lord, shall be consumed. Isaiah lxiv, 7. "For thou hast hid thy face from us, and hast consumed us, because of our iniquites."

Thirdly, What is intended by the oaks which they desired? The groves in which they performed their religious worship. The destruction of these places of worship, is pointed out in the thirteenth verse of the succeeding chapter. And upon all the cedars of Lebanon, that are high and lifted up, and upon all the oaks of Bashan. The devotional fervour of those Israelitish idolaters, is described, chapter lvii. 5, 6, " Inflaming yourselves with idols, slaying the children in the valleys under the clifts of the rocks; among the smooth stones of the stream is thy portion, they are thy lot; even to them thou hast poured a drink offering, thou hast offered a meat offering." Hosea iv. 13, " They sacrifice upon the tops of the mountains, and burn incense upon the hills under oaks, and poplars, and elms, because the shadow thereof is good:" The idolatry of the people of God is, in the language of scripture, denominated adultery and fornication. Jeremiah iii. 9, " And it came to pass through the lightness of her whoredom, that she defiled the land, and committed adultery with stocks and with stones."

Fourthly, But for all this shall they be ashamed and confounded. God speaking of his servants, contrasts them with unbelievers. Isaiah xlv. 4, " For Jacob my servant's sake, and Israel mine elect." All who are incensed against the redeemer shall be ashamed. Isaiah lxv. 13, 14, 15, "My servants shall rejoice, but ye shall be ashamed. Behold my servants shall sing for joy, but ye shall cry for sorrow. And ye shall leave your name for a curse unto my chosen." Again, chapter lxvi. 5, "Let the Lord be glorified, but he shall appear to your joy, and they shall be ashamed." Hosea iv. 19, "And they shall be ashamed because of their sacrifices." And Israel shall be ashamed of his own council; but my people, saith the Lord, by the prophet Joel, shall never be ashamed. Romans ix. 33, "Whosoever believeth on the Lord Jesus shall not be ashamed." And chapter x. 11, "For the scriptures saith, whosoever believeth on him shall not be ashamed." And now (says the apostle John,) little children abide in him, that when he shall appear we may have confidence, and not be ashamed before him at his coming. Thus the believer instead of being ashamed in the day of the Lord, will hold fast his confidence, and his rejoicing unto the end.

Fifthly, For ye shall be as an oak whose leaf fadeth, and as a garden that hath no water. What a blessing that Jesus is, the green fir tree, and that from him our fruit is found; that there is a river the waters of which can never fail; that on the banks of this river flourisheth the tree of life, bearing leaves that can never fade, clothed with living verdure for the healing of the nations. Revelations xxii. 2, What a never failing source of consolation to the philanthropic mind, are the declarations of the God of truth. The sixteenth chapter of Ezekiel is a luminous section in this treasury of divine discoveries. "Nevertheless I will remember my covenant with thee in the days of thy youth, and I will establish unto thee an everlasting covenant. Then thou shalt remember thy ways, and be ashamed when thou shalt receive thy sisters, thine elder and thy younger: and I will give them unto thee for daughters, but not by thy covenant; and I will establish my covenant with thee, and thou shalt know that I am the Lord; that thou mayest remember and be confounded and never open thy mouth any more, because of thy shame when I am pacified toward thee for all that thou hast done, saith the Lord God." Thus even the most obstinate shall be brought home, although it be with wailing and with supplication.

SKETCH LXVI.

Isaiah i. 31.

First, Who or what are we to understand by the strong? Not man assuredly, man is a worm, a vapour in his best estate, whose breath is in his nostrils. All flesh is grass, and the goodliness thereof as the flower of the field. Whenever man is spoken of as *strong*, it is either *spiritually* or *naturally*, if *spiritually*, he is only strong in the Lord; but he who is strong in the Lord cannot be intended in this passage. God is said to be a strong tower; he is called the strength of Israel, &c. &c. Our *adversary* is said to be *strong*. Luke xi. 21, "When a strong man armed keepeth his palace, his goods are in peace." The delusions of the adversary are said to be strong. 2 Thessalonians ii. 11, "And for this cause God hath sent them strong delusions that they should believe a lie." It is clear to my understanding, that the strong in our text intends the strong adversary, who as a roaring lion goeth about seeking whom he may devour.

Secondly, What are we to understand by the tow? It is written, Isaiah xliii. 17, "Which bringeth forth the chariot and horse, the army, and the power; they shall lie down together, they shall not rise; they are extinct, they are quenched as tow." Of flax men construct a most beautiful and profitable article, suitable for clothing for individuals of every description: tow is the refuse of flax, thrown away; and, saith the spirit, "every thing which tends to deceive, every delusion shall be *as tow*."

Thirdly, And the maker of it is as a spark. Who is the maker of it? Sin, we are assured, is the work of the devil. John iii. 8, "He that committeth sin is of the devil." Thus, as every thing God hath made is, with propriety, considered the work of God, so every thing made by the adversary is his work; and these his works shall be as tow, the refuse of flax, which is separated from flax, as the chaff is from the wheat.

But the maker of what is thus doomed to destruction shall be as the spark. Isaiah l. 11, "Behold, all ye that kindle a fire, that compass yourselves about with sparks; walk in the light of your fire, and in the sparks that ye have kindled. This shall ye have of mine hand, ye shall lie down in sorrow." But the spark and the tow shall both burn together, the worker and the work. Revelations xix. 20, presents a full, clear, and concise view of the last clause in our text. "And the beast was taken, and with him the false prophet that wrought miracles before him, with which he deceived them that had received the mark of the beast, and them that worshipped his image. These both were cast alive into a lake of fire burning with brimstone."

Ought we not with holy rapture, and devout gratitude, to prostrate before the Redeemer of men, to adore him for his abundant goodness, for his especial kindness to us, in thus irradiating our understandings, by that light which bringeth salvation, giving us to see by the luminous torch of faith, the wide spreading family of man, encircled in the arms of universal, of never failing goodness?

Fourthly, And none shall quench them. There is no figure in the Bible so frequently introduced, and so variously applied, as fire. God himself is represented under this figure. *Our God is a consuming fire.* Jeremiah xxiii. 29, "Is not my word like as a fire, saith the LORD." The ministers of God are said to be as flames of fire. *They shall be saved so as by fire.* The Apostle tells us this fire which results in salvation shall try every man's work. *If his work abide the test, he shall be rewarded, if not, his work shall be burned, and he shall suffer loss; nevertheless, he himself shall be saved, so as by fire.* Isaiah ix. 18, "For wickedness burneth as a fire; it shall devour the briers and thorns, and shall kindle in the thickets of the forest, and they shall mount up like the lifting of the smoke." Fire is frequently spoken of in the sacred volume as a purifier; indeed what element is so thoroughly cleansing, what particle of dross can endure its caustic heat? What saith the royal Psalmist? Psalm xii. 6, "The words of the LORD are pure words; as silver tried in a furnace of earth, purified seven times." Jehovah saith, Isaiah i. 26, "And I will turn my hand upon thee, and purely purge away thy dross, and take away all thy tin." Isaiah iv. 4, "When the LORD shall have washed away the filth of the daughters of Zion, and shall have purged the blood of Jerusalem from the midst thereof, by the spirit of judgment, and by the spirit of burning." Malachi iii. 2, 3, "But who may abide the day of his coming? And who shall stand when he appeareth? For he is like a refiner's fire, and like fuller's soap. And he shall set as a *purifier* and *refiner* of silver: and he shall purify the sons of Levi, and purge them as gold and silver, that they may offer unto the Lord an offering in righteousness." Matthew iii. 12, " The baptist, speaking of the Redeemer, impressively says, " Whose fan is in his hand, that he may thoroughly purge his floor, and that having gathered his wheat into his garner, he may burn up the chaff with unquenchable fire." The total and unextinguishable destruction of every thing which originated with the adversary, and finally of the adversary himself, will be the salvation of that nature in which the enemy hath sowed the seeds of every species of impurity. With this murderous foe, evil of every description commenced, and every evil shall end where it began. The auspicious period hastens, when the vision recorded in Revelations xviii. 20, shall be realized. And we shall see and hear the mighty angel, who grasping a massy stone, like a great millstone, shall cast it into the sea, saying, Thus with violence shall that great city Babylon be thrown down, and shall be no more found. Compare this passage with the testimony given, Revelations xvii. 5, " And upon her forehead." Whose forehead? Upon the forehead of this Babylon, " was a name written, Mystery, Babylon the great, the Mother of Harlots, and abominations of the earth." It is, consequent upon the destruction of Babylon, and its offspring, that John learned that there was to be *no more curse.* Revelations xxii. 3, That he learned that God would wipe away all tears from their eyes, that there should be no more death, neither sorrow, nor crying, that the former things were done away, and all things were become new. And that he heard every creature which was upon the earth, and which was in heaven, and such as were in the sea, and all that were in them, saying, " *Blessing, and honour, and glory, and power, be unto him that sitteth upon the throne, and unto the Lamb forever and ever.*

SKETCH LXVII.

Isaiah ii. 5.

First, **W**HAT is intended by the house of Jacob? By a house we understand, First, a place of residence. Secondly, The persons dwelling in the house. Acts x. 2, Cornelius feared God with his whole house. Hebrews xi. 7, By faith Noah prepared an ark to the saving his house.

Secondly, Jesus Christ, of whom Jacob was a figure, in whose person, both Jews and Gentiles are collected, the middle wall of partition being broken down, who is as much greater than the figure, as the whole is greater than a part, is the luminous substance of this figure.

Thirdly, The Gentiles were of this house before they were called. Galatians iv. 6, "And *because ye are sons, God hath sent forth the spirit of his Son into your hearts, crying, Abba, Father.*" It is God that calls upon his own house.

Fourthly, Hebrews iii. 4, "For every house is builded by some man; but he that built all things is God." It ought to be recollected, and with pious gratitude, that Joshua, speaking by the spirit of God, and being himself an illustrious type of Christ, decidedly declares, *As for me and my house,* we will serve the LORD. If the words of the spirit of truth are to be received with firm confidence, nothing doubting; if we yield full credit to the divine testimony; 1 Timothy v. 3, "If any man provide not for his own, and especially for those of his own house, he hath denied the faith, and is worse than an infidel:" I say, if we accept this decision, we shall rest assured, that Christ Jesus will indeed provide for his own house.

Fifthly, The master of the house invites every one of the family to walk in the light of the LORD. Isaiah viii. 20, "To the law, and to the testimony: if they speak not according to this word, it is because there is no light in them." Psalm viii. 19, "Blessed are the people that know the joyful sound: they shall walk, O LORD, in the light of thy countenance." Psalm cxix. 105, "Thy word is a lamp unto my feet, and a light unto my path." John viii. 12, " Then spake Jesus again unto them, saying, I am the light of the world." Jesus is the true light of the LORD, because God so loved the world, he gave them his Son; therefore, it is in this *true* light we are admonished to walk. Colossians ii. 6, " As ye have received the LORD Jesus, so walk ye in him." Let us walk in the light of the LORD.

Lastly, We are admonished to *walk* in him, to walk in the light of the LORD, not to *sleep* in him; when once we are in the way, we must *walk on*. The christian walks by faith, he does not *sleep* by faith. *Say to the people that they go forward;* be not weary; or if you be weary, *lean upon the Beloved.*

SKETCH LXVIII.

ISAIAH ii. 6—8.

First, GOD had forsaken his people. Romans xi. 12, " Now if the fall of them be the riches of the world, and the diminishing of them the riches of the Gentiles; how much more their fulness."

Secondly, Why hath God forsaken his people? " Because they be replenished from the east." The prophet Ezekiel, viii. 16, will aid us in comprehending what is intended by the east. " And he brought me into the inner court of the LORD's house, and, behold, at the door of the temple of the LORD, between the porch and the altar, were about five and twenty men, with their *backs toward the temple of the LORD,* and their faces toward the east; and they *worshipped the sun* toward the east."

Thirdly, And they please themselves in the children of strangers. Strangers were distinguished from the worshippers of the true God. Nehemiah ix. 2, " And the seed of Israel separated themselves from all strangers, and stood and confessed their sins, and the iniquities of their fathers." The Gentiles were considered as strangers. Ephesians ii. 12, " That at that time ye were without Christ, being aliens from the commonwealth of Israel, and strangers from the covenants of promise, having no hope and without God in the world." But God's people pleased themselves in these strangers to the covenant of promise.

Fourthly, God's people loved money, silver and gold; in fact, they loved the world, and the things of the world: their characters, and the consequences, are admirably described by the prophet Hosea, ii. 8, "For she did not know that I gave her corn, and wine, and oil, and multiplied her silver and gold which they prepared for Baal."

Fifthly, Their land is full of idols; of this fact our evangelical prophet speaks, chapter lvii. 5, "Inflaming yourselves with idols under every green tree, slaying the children in the valleys, under the clifts of the rocks." Jeremiah ii. 28, "But where are thy gods that thou hast made thee. Let them arise if they can save thee in the time of thy trouble; for according to the number of thy *cities* are thy gods, O Judah."

Lastly, God's people worship the work of their own hands, that which their own fingers have made. Revelations ix. 20, "And the rest of the men which were not killed by these plagues, yet repented not of the works of their hands, that they should not worship devils, and idols of gold, and silver, and brass, and stone, and of wood; which neither can see, nor hear, nor walk."

SKETCH LXIX.

Isaiah xiii. 9—12

First, What are we to understand by the day of the Lord? We will inquire at the sacred oracles. Malachi iv. 1, "For, behold, the day cometh, that shall burn as an oven; and all the proud, yea, and all that do wickedly, shall be stubble? and the day that cometh shall burn them up, saith the Lord of hosts, that it shall leave them neither root nor branch."

Secondly, What are we to understand by the destruction of the sinners of the land? on this head also we will draw our information from a sacred, from an infallible source. Psalm civ. 35, "Let the sinners be consumed out of the earth, and let the wicked be no more." Ezekiel xxxii. 7, "And when I shall put thee out, I will cover the heavens, and make the stars thereof dark; I will cover the sun with a cloud, and the moon shall not give her light." Luke xxiii. 44, 45, "And it was about the sixth hour, and there was darkness over the land, until the ninth hour. And the sun was darkened, and the veil of the temple was rent in the midst."

Thirdly, But in that day the world are to be punished for their evil. Revelations xiv. 19, "And the angel thrust in his sickle into the earth, and gathered the vine of the earth, and cast it into the great winepress of the wrath of God." Daniel ix. 24, 26, "To finish the transgression and to make an end of sins, and to make reconciliation for iniquity; for this shall Messiah be cut off, but not for himself." And I, said the Redeemer, if I be lifted up from the earth, will draw all men unto me. It was the knowledge of this truth, that constrained the Apostle to judge, *if one died for all, then were all dead.*

Fourthly, God will punish the wicked for their iniquity. 2 Thessalonians ii. 8, "And then shall that wicked be revealed, whom the Lord shall consume with the spirit of his mouth, and destroy with the brightness of his coming."

Fifthly, I will cause the arrogancy of the proud to cease. Isaiah ii. 17, "And the loftiness of man shall be bowed down, and the haughtiness of men shall be made low: and the Lord alone shall be exalted in that day."

Sixthly, Who is the man that, in that day, shall be more precious than fine gold, even a man than the golden wedge of Ophir? Job xxviii. 16, "It cannot be valued with the gold of Ophir, with the precious onyx or the sapphire." Proverbs viii. 19—23, "My fruit is better than gold, yea, than fine gold; and my revenue than choice silver. I lead in the way of righteousness, in the midst of the paths of judgment: that I may cause those that love me to inherit substance; and I will fill their treasures. The Lord possessed me in the beginning of his way, before his works of old. I was set up from everlasting, from the beginning, or ever the earth was." The learned, the wise, and the good, refer all these passages to Emmanuel; and, indeed, all the treasures of language are insufficient to describe a millionth part of the excellency of the Redeemer. Christ is not only more precious than the fine gold of Ophir, but more precious than the universe, and all the riches which the wide, the vast circle of the creation hath to bestow. And blessed be the divine Nature, this Saviour, this Redeemer, is the glorious, all perfect head of *every man.*

SKETCH LXX.

Isaiah xxvi. 19.

First, Who are these dead men? Romans v. 15, "*For if through the offence of one many be dead, much more the grace of God, and the gift by grace, which is by one man, Jesus Christ, hath abounded unto many.*" Ephesians ii. 1, "And you hath he quickened, who were dead in trespasses and sins.", Roman v. 12, "Wherefore as by one man sin entered into the world, and death by sin, and so death passed upon all men, for that all have sinned."

Secondly, These dead men are *God's dead.* "*Thy dead shall live.*" Ezekiel xviii. 4, "Behold, all souls are mine."

Thirdly, They shall live. 1John iv. 9, " In this was manifested the love of God towards us, because that God sent his Son into the world, that we should live through him." John xiv. 19, *Because I live, ye shall live also.*"

Fourthly, Who are they that constitute the dead body of the Redeemer? Ephesians ii. 14, 15, 16, "*For he is our peace, who hath made both one, and hath broken down the middle wall of partition between us ; having abolished in his flesh the enmity, even the law of commandments contained in ordinances ; for to make in himself of twain one new man, so making peace ; and that he might reconcile both unto God in one body by the cross, having slain the enmity thereby.*" Hosea vi. 2, "*After two days he will revive us: in the third day he will raise us up, and we shall live in his sight.*"

Fifthly, The exhortation, Awake and sing. But who are called upon to awake and sing? *They who dwell in the dust.* Psalm xxii. 15, " Thou hast brought me into the dust of death."

Sixthly, Why are those who dwell in the dust called upon to awake and sing? For the following reasons. First, For thy dew is as the dew of herbs. My doctrine shall distil as the dew on the tender herb. Secondly, The earth shall cast out the dead. Revelations xx. 13, "And the sea gave up the dead which were in it, and death and hell delivered up the dead which were in them." Hosea xiii. 14, "O death, I will be thy plague; O grave, I will be thy destruction."

SKETCH LXXI.

Hosea vii. 18.

First, Who is, upon this occasion, the speaker? The God of Israel, Jehovah. From the beginning of the world, God spake by the mouth of all his holy prophets. But his most holy will was, in an especial manner, manifested by that prophet, of whom Moses and the prophets had written; of whom every speaker testified, and whose harbingers they were. Exodus xx. 1, 2, "And God spake all these words, saying, I am the LORD thy God which have brought thee out of the land of Egypt, and out of the house of bondage."

Secondly, To whom does the God of Israel speak? To his redeemed. Hosea xiii 14, "I will ransom them from the power of the grave; I will redeem them from death."

Thirdly, What saith the Redeemer to those whom he hath redeemed? He pronounceth a woe upon them! Romans ii. 9, "Tribulation and anguish upon every soul of man that doeth evil; of the Jew first, and also of the Gentile."

Fourthly, Why was this woe pronounced? Of what evils did God complain? They had fled from the God who made them, who preserved, and who had redeemed them. "Destruction unto them, because they have transgressed against me: though I have redeemed them, yet have they spoken lies against me. Transgression is rendered more abominable, abundantly more heinous, *because found upon those whom Jehovah had redeemed.*" But were these people of God negligent respecting their religious duties? Isaiah xlviii. 1, 2, " Hear ye this, O house of Jacob, which are called by the name of Israel, and are come forth out of the waters of Judah, which swear by the name of the Lord and make mention of the God of Israel, but not in truth nor in righteousness. For they call themselves of the holy city, and stay themselves upon the God of Israel. The Lord of hosts is his name." Jeremiah ii. 12, 13, " Be astonished, O ye heavens, and be horribly afraid; be very desolate, saith the Lord. For my people have committed two evils; they have forsaken me, the fountain of living waters, and hewed them out cisterns, broken cisterns, that can hold no water " Isaiah l. 11, "Behold, all ye that kindle a fire, that compass yourselves about with sparks: walk in the light of your fire, and in the sparks that ye have kindled. This shall ye have of mine hand, ye shall lie down in sorrow." Matthew xxiii. 23, " Woe unto you, scribes and Pharisees, hypocrites! for ye pay tithes of mint, and anise, and cummin, and have omitted the weightier matters of the law, judgment, mercy, and faith: these ought ye to have done, and not to leave the other undone." Romans x. 2, 3, 4, "For I bear them record, that they have a zeal for God, but not according to knowledge. For they being ignorant of God's righteousness, and going about to establish their own righteousness, have not submitted themselves to the righteousness of God. For Christ is the end of the law for righteousness, to every one that believeth " Philippians iii 4, 5, 6, " If any man thinketh that he hath whereof he might trust in the flesh, I more. Circumcised the eighth day, of the stock of Israel, of the tribe of Benjamin, an Hebrew of the Hebrews; as touching the law, a Pharisee. Concerning zeal, persecuting the church, touching the righteousness which is in the law, blameless."

Fifthly, They had spoken lies against their Redeemer! *Every unbeliever speaketh lies against his Redeemer*, which Redeemer is the Holy One of Israel. First, John v 10, 11, " He that believeth on the Son of God, hath the witness in himself: he that believeth not, God hath made him a liar: because he believeth not the record, that God gave of his Son. And this is the record, that God hath given to us eternal life, and that this life is in his Son." "But," saith the Redeemer, " if any man hear my word and believe it not, I judge him not: for I came not to condemn the world, but to save the world." John iii. 17.

"For God sent not his Son into the world to condemn the world, but that the world through him might be saved." Were I, therefore, to declare unto you, that the Redeemer would not save the world, that he would condemn the world, would not this be speaking lies of the rock of *my*, of *your* salvation? If I should say, he would judge and condemn the unbeliever, that he would consign him, through the wasteless ages of eternity, to everlasting burnings, would not this be telling lies of the Redeemer? Of that God who hath graciously vouchsafed to say, he hath *concluded all in unbelief, that he might have mercy upon all?* And if I should, while thus declaring, thus giving the lie to the records of truth, profess myself a servant of, and a witness for God, would not this be a very great abomination? Would it not be, of all offences, the most abominable? And are not those, however they may be denominated among men, who thus give the lie direct to God Omnipotent, the most *heinous offenders?*

SKETCH LXXII.

Micah ii.

First, To perish is to die. Job xxxiv. 15, "All flesh shall perish *together*." Elihu probably spake by the spirit of prophecy, predicting the period at which our Saviour said, And I, if I be lifted up, will draw all men unto me. It was at that prodigious era, and at no other moment, *that all flesh perished together.* Christ Jesus did indeed die for all, and with him all died. But the Apostle Paul speaks of individuals *perishing*, for whom Christ *died.* 1 Corinthians viii. 11, " Through thy knowledge shall thy *weak brother perish, for whom Christ died.* This must certainly advert to a temporary death; for the purchase of Christ's blood cannot *finally be lost ; yet we see, that this weak brother, for whom Christ died, may perish, and that because I have eaten meat!* But, the Spirit saith, that Christ died for us, that whether we wake or sleep, we may be together with him. 2 Thessalonians ii. 10, "And with all deceivableness of unrighteousness in them that perish, because they received not the love of the truth, that they might be saved."

Secondly, There is no possibility of reconciling scripture testimonies, except we discriminate between the *salvation believed*, and the *salvation consequent upon believing*. The first, is like that all-sufficient Redeemer, by whom it was wrought out and completely finished; it is the same yesterday, to-day, and forever, enduring eternally, eternally abiding; yea, *although we believe not, Christ Jesus remaineth faithful*. If, like Peter, we should *deny* the LORD, whose purchase we are, still he will never *deny himself;* such is the character of the *first* salvation, of the salvation believed. But the *second salvation*, or the salvation *consequent on believing* this truth, is an operation of, or upon the mind of man; and *this salvation* is ever fluctuating, ever unstable, like the being with whom it is found.

SKETCH LXXIII.

ZECHARIAH ii. 10, 11.

First, To whom doth the Spirit speak? To the daughter of Zion; in other words, to the people of God dwelling in Jerusalem.

Secondly, Why is the daughter of Zion called upon to sing and rejoice? For the coming of the LORD. The people of God are described as looking out from the beginning with eager anxiety for the predicted Messiah; every faithful, every believing soul, waited for the consolation of Israel.

Thirdly, An additional reason is urged, why the daughter of Zion should rejoice and sing. Because I will dwell in the midst of thee, saith the LORD. When God was manifested in the flesh, when the Redeemer assumed the body prepared for him, then was this prophecy fulfilled. The divine Nature, dwelling in the human nature, is God the LORD dwelling in the midst of the human family.

Fourthly, There is yet another reason why the daughter of Zion should rejoice and sing; for many nations shall be joined to the Lord in that day. How many? We will consult the prophet Isaiah. His reponses to all our questions are full and unequivocal. Chapter ii. "And it shall come to pass in the last days, that the mountain of the Lord's house shall be established in the top of the mountain, and shall be exalted above the hills: and all nations shall flow unto it. And then will the Lord of hosts dwell in the midst of them, and all people shall know, that the Messiah is indeed the sent of God."

SKETCH LXXIV.

Matthew v. 3—7.

First, "Blessed *are the poor in spirit*" What is it to be poor in spirit? and who are those who are poor in spirit? Among men, those are denominated poor, who are destitute of what this world calleth good. But the words that Jesus spake, they are *spirit*, and they are *life;* they do not, upon this occasion, take cognizance of a man's standing in society, nor of the state of his finances. Blessed are the poor *in spirit*. Commentators inform us, that the poor in spirit are those who are *sensible* of their lost, undone state, of their manifold transgressions The poor in spirit then, are those who have no riches spiritually, they labour under great dejection, and they are ready to say with the wise man, Proverbs xiv. 13, "*Even in laughter my heart is sorrowful, and the end of mirth is heaviness.*" They do not say with the Laodiceans, in the Revelations, iii. 17, "I am rich and increased with goods, and have need of nothing: and thou knowest not that thou art wretched, and miserable, and poor, and blind, and naked." Such are the *poor in spirit*.

Secondly, What is the kingdom of heaven? Luke xvii 21, " Neither shall they say, Lo here! or lo there! for, behold the kingdom of God is *within you*." John i 26, " John answered, and said, I baptize you with water. but there standeth one among you whom you know not." *Jesus Christ himself is emphatically the kingdom of God;* and it is hard for those who fancy themselves opulent to enter into this kingdom; it is with extreme reluctance that they *deny themselves,* and putting on the Lord Jesus, are found clothed in his righteousness. Yet it pleased the divine Nature that *in him* all fulness should dwell.

Thirdly, How does the kingdom of God become the property of the poor in spirit? By the *love* of God, and the *gift* of God. For God so *loved* the world that he *gave* them his Son. If you say that the Son was given only to those who love the Father, we will inquire of the oracles of God, and the spirit of truth shall determine. 1 John iv. 10, "Herein is love, not that *we loved God,* but that *he loved us,* and sent his Son to be the propitiation for our sins." And if you still ask, but for the sins of how many was he the propitiation? The same beloved disciple replies, chapter i. 2, "But he is the propitiation for our sins, and not for ours only, but also for the sins of the *whole world.*"

Fourthly, "*Blessed are they that mourn.*" Who are they that mourn? Jeremiah iv. 28, "For this shall the earth mourn, and the heavens above be black: because I have spoken it." Chapter xii. 4, "How long shall the earth mourn, and the herbs of every field wither, for the wickedness of them that dwell therein?" Matthew xxiv. 30, "And then shall appear the sign of the son of man in heaven: and then shall all the tribes of the earth mourn."

Fifthly, The blessing. "*And they shall be comforted.*" Isaiah xl. 1, 2, "Comfort ye, comfort ye my people, saith your God. Speak ye comfortably to Jerusalem, and cry unto her that her warfare is accomplished, that her iniquity is pardoned, for she hath received of the Lord's hand double for all her sins." And chapter li. 3, "For the Lord shall yet comfort Zion; he will comfort all her waste places; and he will make her wilderness like Eden, and her desert like the garden of the Lord; joy and gladness shall be found therein, thanksgiving, and the voice of melody." Chapter lxi. 2, 3, "To proclaim the acceptable year of the Lord, and the day of vengeance of our God; to comfort all that mourn: To appoint unto them that mourn in Zion, to give unto them beauty for ashes, the oil of joy for mourning, the garment of praise for the spirit of heaviness."

Sixthly, By whom is this blessing to be communicated? Who is to speak comfort to the human mourner? Undoubtedly the *spirit of truth, who is to take of the things of Jesus, and show them to the sorrowing soul.* This spirit of truth is the comforter, the Holy Ghost. John xiv. 16, " And I will pray the Father, and he shall give you another Comforter, that he may abide with you forever ; even the Spirit of truth."

Seventhly, " *Blessed are the meek.*" And who, I pray, are the meek ? There are who are called meek. Moses is said to be the meekest of men. Numbers xii. 3, " Now the man Moses was very meek above all the men which were upon the face of the earth." Yet he was prevented from inheriting the earth, by the prevalence of his passions ; he could not enter the promised land, because he spoke unadvisedly with his lips at the waters of strife. In his wrath he slew the Egyptian, and in great wrath he break the tables which were inscribed by the finger of Deity. Well, then, if we cannot find among the sons of men, descending from Adam, by ordinary generation, an individual sufficiently meek to inherit the earth, let us see if we cannot find this meekness in *perfection* in the character of the *God man*. Zechariah ix. 9, " Rejoice, greatly, O daughter of Zion, shout, O daughter of Jerusalem : Behold, thy king cometh unto thee ; he is just, and having salvation : lowly, and riding upon an ass, and upon a colt, the foal of an ass." Matthew xi. 29, " Take my yoke upon you, and learn of me ; for I am meek and lowly in heart : and ye shall find rest to your souls." We pronounce, therefore, that it is Christ Jesus, and Christ Jesus only, who is *truly* and *perfectly* meek ; and it is *Christ Jesus, and Christ Jesus only, who shall inherit the earth.*

But, eighthly, What is the earth which this meek Saviour shall inherit ? Not the *inanimate earth on which we tread*. It is the nations of the earth. Ask of me, and I will give thee the heathen for thine inheritance, and the uttermost parts of the earth for thy possession. Every thing was made for, and by the Redeemer ; he is the heir of all things ; children are the heritage of the Lord ; and it is a glorious truth that the people are joint heirs with the Redeemer, to whatever the Redeemer is. Romans viii. 17, " And if children, then heirs, heirs of God, and joint heirs with Christ."

Ninthly, "*Blessed are they which do hunger and thirst after righteousness, for they shall be filled.*" Hunger and thirst after what righteousness ? Doubtless the righteousness of God, the righteousness described by Daniel, ix. 24, "To make reconciliation for iniquity, and to bring in *everlasting righteousness*." And by the Apostle Paul, Romans i. 17, " For therein is the *righteousness of God* revealed from faith to faith." The righteousness performed by him, in whom dwelt all the fulness of the God-head. The righteousness distinguished from the righteousness of the creature. Romans x. 3, "*For they being ignorant of God's righteousness, and going about to establish their own righteousness, have not submitted themselves unto the righteousness of God.*" This righteousness is called the righteousness of faith. Romans iv. 13, "For the promise that he should be the heir of the world, was not to Abraham or to his seed, through the law, but through the righteousness of faith; because it is the evidence of things not seen." This righteousness is called *the law of righteousness*, as contrasted with the righteousness after which the Jews sought. Romans ix. 31, "But Israel which followed after the law of righteousness, hath not attained to the law of righteousness." In the prophecy of Jeremiah, xxxiii. 6, the whole system is summed up—"Behold, I will bring it health and cure; and I will cure them, and will reveal unto them the abundance of peace and truth."

Tenthly, "*Those who hunger and thirst after this righteousness, shall be filled.*" By hunger and thirst, we are led to the contemplation of the human and divine Nature. Bread is given to the hungry, and water to the thirsty. Christ is the bread, the Spirit is the water. John vi. 33, " For the bread of God is he which cometh down from heaven, and giveth life unto the world." John vii. 38, 39, " He that believeth on me, as the scriptures hath said, out of his belly shall flow rivers of living water. But this spake he of the Spirit, which they that believed on him should receive." Every one *taught of God* hath this Spirit, which teacheth him to appropriate to himself the righteousness of the Redeemer, who is said to be the head of every man; while those, of a contrary description, are wells without water. 2 Peter ii. 17, " These are wells without water, clouds that are carried with a tempest, to whom the mist of darkness is reserved forever." But they who hunger and thirst after this righteousness, shall be filled. Isaiah lv. 1, " Ho, every one that thirsteth, come ye to the waters, and he that hath no money ; come ye, buy, and eat ; yea, come, buy wine and milk without money and without price."

Those who are filled, must of course be satisfied. Revelations vii. 16, "They shall hunger no more, neither thirst any more; neither shall the sun light on them, nor any heat."

Eleventhly, "*Blessed are the merciful: for they shall obtain mercy.*" What is mercy? The son of Jesse, and the man of Tarsus, gives us an answer to this question. It is an essential perfection among the attributes of God, which induces him to pity and relieve the miseries of his children. Mercy in man, although notoriously deficient in *quantity*, is the same in *quality*. The evangelist Luke, in the tenth chapter of his gospel, describes a certain Samaritan, who shewed mercy unto him who fell among thieves; and although we have considered the account of this traveller from Jerusalem to Jericho as a beautiful allegory, yet there are among men, who would, on a like occasion, have manifested mercy like that which is ascribed to the Samaritan.

Twelfthly, What is it to be merciful? To be *merciful*, is to be full of mercy. Are any among the fallen children of men full of mercy? Hosea iv. 1, "Hear the word of the LORD, ye children of Israel: for the LORD hath a controversy with the inhabitants of the land, because there is no truth, nor mercy, nor knowledge of God in the land." Doth the Redeemer of men possess this attribute of mercy in perfection? He does; God is merciful. Psalm lxii. 12, "Also unto thee, O LORD, belongeth mercy: for thou renderest to every man according to his work." God is merciful. He proclaimed himself merciful. Exodus xxxiv. 6, "And the LORD God passed by before him, and proclaimed, The LORD, the LORD God, merciful and gracious, long-suffering, and abundant in goodness and truth." Nor is the mercy of God opposed to his truth. Psalm lxxxv. 10, "*Mercy and truth are met together; righteousness and peace have kissed each other.*" Nor is the mercy of God limited. Psalm lxxxvi. 5, "For thou LORD, art good, and ready to forgive; and plenteous in mercy, unto all them that call upon thee." Nor will the mercy of the LORD ever fail. Psalm c. 5, "For the LORD is good, and his mercy is everlasting; and his truth endureth to all generations." It is also from everlasting. Psalm ciii. 17, "But the mercy of the LORD is from everlasting to everlasting upon them that fear him, and his righteousness unto children's children." It is by the union of mercy and truth, that iniquity is purged. Luke i. 72, 78, "To perform the mercy promised to our fathers, and to remember his holy covenant. Through the tender mercy of our God, the day-spring from on high hath visited us." Titus iii. 5, *" God saved us according to his mercy."*

Thirteenthly, What is the blessedness of the Redeemer? Psalm lxxii. 17, " His name shall endure forever: his name shall be continued as long as the sun, and men shall be blessed in him: all nations shall call him blessed." Psalm xlv. 2, " Thou art fairer than the children of men: grace is poured into thy lips: therefore God hath blessed thee forever." Luke xix. 38, " Saying, blessed be the king, that cometh in the name of the Lord; peace in heaven and glory in the highest." But how are men to be blessed, if the blessing be thus confined to the Redeemer? Ephesians i. 3, " Blessed be the God and Father of our Lord Jesus Christ, who hath blessed us with all spiritual blessings, in heavenly places in Christ Jesus." But what mercy did the Saviour need or obtain? Psalm lxxxix. 28, " My mercy will I keep for him forevermore; and my covenant shall stand fast with him." And in mercy shall the throne be established: and he shall set upon it in truth, in the tabernacle of David, judging, and seeking judgment, and hasting righteousness. Thus it will always be found, that the merciful are blessed; for they shall obtain mercy.

SKETCH LXXV.

Matthew v. 32—37.

First, Our Saviour not only directs, confirms, and enforces the law, but he refines, amplifies, and extends its precepts.

Secondly, *" Ye have heard that it hath been said by them of old times, Thou shall not forswear thyself; but I say unto you, Swear not at all."* James v. 12, " But above all things, my brethren, swear not, neither by heaven, neither by the earth, neither by any other oath: but let your yea be yea, and your nay, nay, lest ye fall into condemnation."

Thirdly, Swear not by heaven, for it is the throne of God; nor by earth, for it is his footstool. Isaiah lxvi. 1, " Thus, saith the LORD, the heaven is my throne, and the earth is my footstool."

Fourthly, Neither by Jerusalem; for it is the city of the great King. Psalm xlvii. 2, "Beautiful for situation, the joy of the whole earth is mount Zion, on the sides of the north, the city of the great King."

Fifthly, *Neither by thy head, for thou canst not change the colour of a single hair."* It is God alone that controlleth events; therefore let a persuasion of thy own imbecility keep thy mouth from swearing, and thy tongue from oaths. And

Sixthly, "*Let thy communication be yea, yea, nay, nay.*" 2Corinthians i. 17, 18, "When I, therefore, was thus minded, did I use lightness? Or the things that I purpose, do I purpose according to the flesh, that with me there should be yea, yea, and nay, nay? But as God is true, our word toward you was not yea and nay."

REMARKS.

First, That divine Being who gave the law, condescends to become its expositor. Secondly, The great Lawgiver designs to lead us to his blessed self. He is the husband of the creature whom he hath made; and in this character, he hates putting away. Thirdly, We are called to contemplate the nearness of the connexion between heaven and earth; the one is his throne, the other his footstool. Fourthly, There is a necessity of bridling the tongue; it is an unruly member. Lastly, The Redeemer directs, that our communications be simple, *yea* and *nay;* for whatsoever is more than this cometh of evil.

SKETCH LXXVI.

MATTHEW v. 38—42.

First, THE doctrine of retaliation was taught by the law given Moses. But our divine Moralist, teacheth us not to resist evil. Proverbs xx. 22, "Say not thou, I will recompense evil; but wait on the LORD, and he will save thee." Romans xii. 19,

"Dearly beloved, avenge not yourselves; but rather give place unto wrath: for it is written, Vengeance is mine; I will repay, saith the Lord." We are taught to recompense no man evil for evil, but as much as lieth in us, to live peaceably with all men.

Secondly, Jesus Christ teacheth us not only by precept, but by example. Isaiah l. 6, "I gave my back to the smiters, and my cheeks to them that plucked off the hair. I hid not my face from shame and spitting."

Thirdly, "*If any man will sue thee at the law, and take away thy coat, let him have thy cloak also.*" 1 Corinthians vi. 7, "Now, therefore, there is utterly a fault among you, because ye go to law one with another. Why do ye not rather take wrong? Why do ye not rather suffer yourselves to be defrauded?" 1 Thessalonians v. 15, "See that none render evil for evil unto any man; but ever follow that which is good, both among yourselves and to all men." 1 Peter iii. 9, "Not rendering evil for evil, or railing for railing, but contrariwise blessing."

Fourthly, *Whosoever shall compel thee to go a mile, go with him twain. Give to him that asketh thee, and from him that would borrow of thee, turn not thou away.*" Deuteronomy xv. 8, 10, "But thou shalt open thine hand wide unto him, and shalt surely lend him sufficient for his need, in that which he wanteth. Thou shalt surely give him, and thine heart shall not be grieved when thou givest unto him." Luke vi. "Give to every man that asketh of thee; and of him that taketh away thy goods, ask them not again. *And as ye would that men should do to you, do ye also to them likewise.* For if ye love them which love you, what thank have ye? for sinners also love those that love them. And if ye do good to them which do good to you, what thank have ye? for sinners also do even the same. And if ye lend to them of whom ye hope to receive, what thank have ye? for sinners also lend to sinners, to receive as much again. But *love* your *enemies*, and do good, and *lend, hoping for nothing* again; and your reward shall be great, and ye shall be the children of the highest: for he is *kind unto the unthankful and to the evil.*" Romans xii. 20, "Therefore, if thine enemy hunger, feed him; if he thirst, give him drink: for in so doing thou shalt heap coals of fire on his head."

REMARKS.

First, Do not let us, like the Jewish doctors, make these divine precepts void by our traditions. Secondly, Although these precepts may seem a violation of that law which ordaineth breach for breach, eye for eye, &c. &c. yet, in fact, it is not; for although *we must not exact*, he, Jesus Christ, freely gave; for he fulfilled the whole law, and was wounded for our transgressions. Thirdly, It is absolutely better to be silent under injuries, than *to be a plague to him who seeketh to be a plague to us*. Fourthly, If it be right to give to him that asketh, the Judge of all the earth will surely do right; *he will give to him that asketh*. Fifthly, He that doeth not as this divine Teacher directeth, is considered as a sinner. But would it not be blasphemy to charge the Teacher himself with these crimes?

SKETCH LXXVII.

MATTHEW v. 43, 44.

First, These words are not to be found in the Mosaic code. It was an inference drawn by the Jewish doctors from Exodus xxiv. 12, "Take heed to thyself, lest thou make a covenant with the inhabitants of the land whither thou goest, lest it be a snare in the midst of thee." But I say unto you, love your enemies. *Enemy* is contrasted with *friend*, love with *hatred*. See this divine precept exemplified. Luke xxiii. 34, "*Then said Jesus, Father, forgive them, for they know not what they do.*" And in Acts, vii. 60, "*And he kneeled down and cried with a loud voice, Lord, lay not this sin to their charge.*"

Secondly, "*Bless them that curse you.*" Romans xii. 14, "Bless them which persecute you: bless and curse not." 1 Corinthians iv. 12, "Being reviled, we bless; being persecuted, we suffer it; being defamed, we entreat."

Thirdly, *Do good to them that hate you, and pray for them that despitefully use you and persecute you.*

Remarks.

First, It is dangerous to trust to commentators; it is better to attend to our divine Master, who never teaches his disciples to do injury to any individual on any pretence. Secondly, The religion of Jesus Christ, is a religion of love, and that not in word only, but in deed and in truth; nor only to the meritorious as friends, but to the unworthy as enemies. Thirdly, We are thus taught, that it is injurious to charge the transgressions of men to the truth of God. Fourthly, An attention to the teaching of the Spirit will point out to us the difference between the doctrines of the Jews, of many who are styled christians, and the doctrine of God our Saviour. Both Jews and professing christians distinguish between the righteous and the unrighteous, exhibiting the one, as the object of the affection of God and all good men, and the other, as cursed even by God himself.

Lastly, Where are the christians, where is the moralist, who is, in every particular, conformed to these divine precepts? If an unerring individual is not to be found, are not these precepts a letter of condemnation to the whole mass of mankind?

SKETCH LXXVIII.

Matthew v. 45—48.

First, If we conduct as we are directed in the preceding verses, we are the children of our Father which is in heaven

Secondly, "*God maketh his sun to shine on the evil, and sendeth his rain on the unjust.*"

Thirdly, The love which we bear to them who love us, and the salutations which we render to our brethren, do not entitle us to thanks.

Fourthly, "*Be ye therefore perfect, as your Father in heaven is perfect.*" Ephesians v. 1, "Be ye therefore followers of God, as dear children." Colossians i. 28, "Whom we preach, warning every man, and teaching every man in all wisdom, that we may present every man perfect in Christ Jesus."

Remarks.

First, Does the Redeemer teach us to love our enemies, thus proving ourselves the children of our Father who is in heaven? *and will our divine Master give a precept which he will not enforce by example?* Assuredly not. And most incontrovertibly hath Jesus Christ proved his love to his enemies. But, secondly, Our Saviour directs us to be *perfect, as our Father who is in heaven is perfect.* Thirdly, Is it possible that we can, while we continue in this imperfect state, be thus perfect? Fourthly, The perfection inculcated is the perfection of God. Fifthly, Where doth this perfection exist? It exists only in Christ Jesus, who is, however, *the head of every man.* But, sixthly, For this perfection we were *individually* made, and to this perfection we shall *individually* be brought: for Emmanuel being the head of every man, is God our Saviour, and this God, this Saviour, this Redeemer, was manifested to take *away the sin of the world, and to cleanse us from all filthiness of flesh and spirit.*

Reflections upon the Lord's *Prayer.*

Our divine Master points out in the sixth section of St. Matthew's gospel the absurdity of the common practice of long prayers, cautions his disciples against expecting to be heard for their much speaking, and directs them, when they pray, to enter into their closets, and having shut their doors, to pray to their Father who seeth in secret.

The God-man also directs the *manner* of the prayer, which he wished his followers to adopt. "After this manner, therefore, pray ye. Our Father which art in heaven. Hallowed be thy name. *Thy* kingdom come. *Thy* will be done *in* earth, as it is *in* heaven. Give us this day our daily bread. And forgive us our debts as we forgive our debtors." It is observable, that although the disciples were commanded to enter into the closet and shut the door, to pray alone and in secret, yet they were directed to say, Our Father. The *christian* is not to consider himself *alone* when he addresses the throne of grace. He is not to say *my* Father, but, as we have the adoption of sons by Christ

Jesus, we should ever keep in devout and grateful recollection, this mighty blessing, this mysterious union, especially when addressing the divine Nature, the Sire of angels and of men, the creating God. If we ask not in the name of Emmanuel, we ask nothing; but thus asking, we do truly ask. It is an indubitable truth, that we are, and we ought always to believe we are, *ever together with* our common Head. And it is in this view that we cannot safely call any man Father, upon earth, for one is our Father, who is in heaven. But God doth not become our Father consequent upon our supplications. Certainly not; he was our Father before a single cry of distress passed our supplicating lips; and why, because he *was*, and *is* the *Father of Christ Jesus;* and, as the head of *every man is Christ*, and the head of Christ is God; so *every man* is allowed to view himself as a member of his glorious body (who for our sakes was numbered with transgressors) and thus to say, *Our* Father which art in heaven. Hence, although as descended from the first Adam, we are from *beneath*, yet as *allied* to the second Adam, we are from *above*. But for this grace we are indebted to Jesus Christ, without the shadow of merit resulting from our individual selves; and accordingly we are instructed, when entirely secluded from every other individual, to say, *Our Father.*

This our Father is in heaven, where nothing which defileth can enter. The accuser of the brethren cannot enter there. Heaven is a seat of peace and love, among the denizens of heaven no baleful spirit can obtain a place, no boisterous passion can find harbour there; much less can fury dwell in him who filleth the throne of mercy, who is the source of love, and from whom is derived never ending, still augmenting felicity. Thus, although Christ is in heaven, and we upon earth, distance is annihilated by an intimate union and combination of character, *for Jesus Christ is ever with us.*

"*Hallowed be thy name.*" This name was hallowed in the dress of Aaron, when on the emblematic mitre, was placed that plate, upon which was engraved, "*Holiness to the* Lord." Jesus Christ is our head; the hallowed name of the divine Nature resting upon him, *is God with us.* His name is holy. But we have nothing to fear from a holy name, although this be but a shadow; how much less then have we to fear from a Father whose name is holy. But his name is hallowed, and it is that hallowed name, which constitutes Christ Jesus, the Holy *One* of Israel. Reverend and holy is his name, *and his only.*

"*Thy kingdom come, thy will be done in earth as it is in heaven.*"

First, What is the kingdom of God? Christ Jesus is the kingdom of God? Luke xvii. 21, " Neither shall they say, lo here! or lo there! for, behold, the kingdom of God is within you." John the Baptist, as the immediate harbinger of Jesus Christ, preached or proclaimed the Redeemer as the kingdom of heaven. How vast is the magnitude of this kingdom. Thine, O LORD, is the greatness, and the power, and the glory, and the victory, and the majesty : for all that is in heaven and in the earth is thine ; thine is the kingdom, O LORD, and thou art exalted as head above all. The kingdom is the LORD's, and he is the Governor among the nations. The durability of this kingdom is equal to its magnitude. The iron, the clay, the brass, the silver, and the gold, were broken to pieces together, and became like the chaff of the summer threshing floor; and the wind carried them away, that no place was found for them: and the stone that smote the image became a great mountain, and filled the whole earth. "*Thy kingdom come,*" in the final descent of the Redeemer, in like manner as he ascended, *blessing his inheritance ; Thy will be done* IN *earth, as it is* IN *heaven. It is not the will of God that any should perish. It is not the will of our Father, which is in heaven, that one of his little ones should perish.* The LORD is not slack concerning his promise, as some men count slackness : but is long-suffering to us ward, *not willing that any should perish,* but that all should come to repentance. *It is the will of God* that all men should come unto the knowledge of the truth, and be saved. For the will of God is our sanctification ; God willeth that we should perform every good work, and abstain from every evil, and this will of God, Jesus Christ was appointed to execute. Then said I, lo I come, (in the volume of the book it is written of me) to do thy will, O God. By the which will, we are sanctified, through the offering of the body of Jesus Christ once for all. And, saith the world's Saviour, this is the Father's will, which hath sent me, that of all which he hath given me, I should lose nothing, but should raise it up at the last day. This is the will of him that sent me, that every one which seeth the Son, and believeth on him, may have everlasting life ; and I will raise him up at the last day. We are directed to pray, that this will of God may be accomplished, that it may be fully accomplished *in* earth as it is in heaven. The will of God is already done *in heaven, in the divine Nature ; our Head* hath ascended up on high, immaculate, *without the iniquity of his heels* , we are not, therefore, taught to pray that the will of God may be done *in heaven*, but that it may be *done in* earth *as it is in* heaven ; that it may be done in the whole of human nature, in the whole human family, in every individual ; that the will of God may be done in every individual, precisely as it is already done in their head, so that every man may be holy, even as God is holy. Hence, we are commanded, by the holy Spirit, to pray for all men. " I exhort, therefore, that, first of all supplications, prayers, intercessions, and giving of thanks, be made for all men ; for this is good and acceptable in the sight of God our Saviour, who will have all men to be saved, and to come unto the knowledge of the truth. For there is one God, and one Mediator between God and man, the man Christ Jesus ; who gave himself a ransom for all, to be testified in due time. This *one* Mediator, this glorious Redeemer, assures us, that whatsoever we ask, according to the *will* of God, we shall receive ; and hence, when the genuine believer supplicates for the salvation of all men, he asks in *faith, nothing doubting*."

" *Give us this day our daily bread* " It is not said, give us this day our *yearly bread*. It is good that man continues a dependent being. " Give me neither poverty nor riches ; feed me with food convenient for me : lest I be full and deny thee, and say who is the Lord ? Or, lest I be poor, and steal, and take the name of my God in vain. Having food and raiment, let us be therewith content. The *bread* which perisheth is a figure of the *bread of life*. The daily bread, for which we are taught to pray, is spiritual bread. " He gave them bread from heaven to eat. Then Jesus said unto them, verily, verily, I say unto you, Moses gave you not that bread from heaven, but my Father giveth you the true bread from heaven. For the bread of God is he which cometh down from heaven, and giveth life unto the world. Then said they unto him Lord, evermore give us this bread. And Jesus said unto them, I am the bread of life : he that cometh to me shall never hunger. The Jews then murmured at him, because he said I am the bread which came down from heaven. I am the bread of life. Your fathers did eat manna in the wilderness, and are dead. This is the bread which cometh down from heaven, that a man may eat thereof, and not die. I am the living bread which came down from heaven. If any man eat of this bread, he shall live forever: and the bread that I will give is my flesh, which I will give for the life of the world. The Jews therefore strove among themselves, saying, how can this man give us his flesh to eat? Then Jesus said unto them, verily, verily I say unto you, Except ye eat the flesh of the son of man, and drink his blood, ye have no life in you. Whoso eateth my flesh and drinketh my blood, hath eternal life, and I will raise him up at the last day. For my flesh is meat indeed, and my blood is drink indeed. He that eateth my flesh, and drinketh my blood, dwelleth in me, and I in him. As the living Father hath sent me, and I live by the Father: so he that eateth me, even he shall live by me. This is that bread which came down from heaven: he that eateth of this bread shall live forever." " *And forgive* us our debts as we forgive our debtors." Debts, trespasses and sins. These terms convey throughout the sacred volume similar ideas. "*Forgive us our debts.*" All who are directed to pray, are debtors or sinners; but as offenders are directed to supplicate for pardon only from God, it is clear that against God only have they offended, and to him only are accountable. Against thee only, said the royal prophet, have I sinned, and done this evil in thy sight. We are directed to pray that we may be forgiven, as we forgive others. Viewing Christ and the people, as making one complete whole; the christian man unites with the sweet singer of Israel, and faithfully saith, Thou hast forgiven the iniquity of thy people, thou hast covered all their sin. Selah. Thou hast taken away all thy wrath; thou hast turned thyself from the fierceness of thine anger; or he adopts the language of Isaiah, gratefully repeating, And the inhabitants shall not say, I am sick; the people that dwell therein shall be forgiven their iniquities; and he listens with devout love, gratitude, and admiration, to him who spake as never man spake, while he hears him declare that all manner of sin and blasphemy shall be forgiven unto men. Well doth the believer know, and boldly doth he assert, that the blood of Christ cleanseth from all sin; and adoring, he beholds the *Lamb of God who taketh away the sin of the world.*

"*And lead us not into temptation, but deliver us from evil, for thine is the kingdom, and the power, and the glory forever. Amen.*" What is temptation? Temptation is of two kinds; the one for *trial*, the other for the purpose of seduction; the one is of God, the other originates with the adversary. My brethren, saith the apostle James, count it all joy when you fall into divers temptations; and again, Let no man say when he is tempted, I am tempted of God: for God cannot be tempted with evil, neither tempteth he any man. To be led into temptation, and to be tempted, are not synonimous terms. Our Saviour was led up by the spirit into the wilderness to be tempted by the devil, but the arch fiend, after exhausting all his power, found him *superior to temptation*. The first Adam was not only *led into temptation but was tempted*, he became an easy victim to the allurements of our general mother, who was seduced by the tempter. Not so, Adam the second, firm and unyielding was the rock of our salvation. The Redeemer of the world was led up of the spirit into the wilderness to be tempted of the devil, *to be tried;* and thoroughly was he tried, yet not *tempted to evil.* The head of every man towered above every temptation. It is written, said Jesus, thou shalt not tempt the Lord thy God; get thee behind me Satan, for it is written, thou shalt worship the Lord thy God, and him only shalt thou serve."

This may be considered as the last scene of temptation. We never again hear of God's spirit leading the Saviour to be tempted. Having evinced his Omnipotence in the contention with the adversary, it was sufficient, and when we see that nothing short of Almighty power was requisite to defeat the adversary, we are convinced of the necessity of praying, *lead us not into temptation.* Trials justify, and necessarily originate supplication and prayer. Prayer is sanctioned both by the precept and example of Emmanuel. And he went a little farther, and fell on his face, and prayed, saying, O my Father, if it be possible, let this cup pass from me; nevertheless, not as I will but as thou wilt. Persecution on account of the truth, is a kind of temptation operating as a trial. Blessed be the man that endureth temptation: for when he is tried, he shall receive the crown of life, which the Lord hath promised to them that love him.

"*Deliver us from evil.*" Evil is of two kinds, sin and suffering. The heart of the sons of men are full of evil. Suffering is an evil. But shall we receive good at the hand of God, and shall we not receive evil? Shall a trumpet be blown in the city, and the people not be afraid? Shall there be evil in a city, and the Lord hath not done it? I form the light, and create darkness: I make peace, and create evil: I the Lord do all these things.

Yet we are directed to pray, without discrimination, that we may be delivered from evil.

"*For thine is the kingdom.*" There was given him dominion, that all people, nations, and languages, should serve him: his dominion is an everlasting dominion, which shall not pass away, and his kingdom that which shall not be destroyed. The kingdom is the Lord's: and he is the Governor among the nations. "And every creature which is in heaven, and on the earth, and under the earth, and such as are in the sea, and all that are in them, heard I saying, Blessing, and honour, and glory, and power, be unto him that sitteth upon the throne, and unto the Lamb forever and ever."

"*The power.*" And Jesus came and spake unto them, saying, All power is given unto me in heaven, and in earth. All power over angels. They are ministering spirits, and they fly to execute his commands. Over devils who tremble at the sound of his voice. Come out of him, said Jesus, even in the day of his humiliation, and instantly the devil quitted the mansion he had so long possessed and distressed. He bindeth the fallen spirits, and casteth them out, and he will finally confine them to outer darkness. All power is also given to him *in* earth, *that he may remove the covering from the face of all flesh, that he may open the understanding, and become eyes to the blind, ears to the deaf, and speech to the dumb. That he may turn men from the power of Satan unto God, that he may fill the earth, all animated earth, with the knowledge of his blessed self.*

"*The glory.*" "*Thine is the glory.*" And he said, I beseech thee shew me thy glory. And the glory of the Lord shall be revealed, *and all flesh shall see it together:* for the mouth of the Lord hath spoken it.

This glory shall be from everlasting to everlasting—Forever— Amen—So be it.

SKETCH LXXIX.

Fast Day.

Matthew vi. 16.

First, Hypocrites were punctual in their observance of fasts, because it was generally believed, that devout and honourable professors fasted, and that they were very abstemious, and very regular in this devotional act.

Secondly, They had their reward. They were admired, and held in high estimation by their brethren: they appeared unto men to fast, but they had forgotten the word of the Lord, by their prophet. Joel ii. 12, 13, "Therefore, also, now saith the Lord, turn ye to me with all your *hearts*, and with fasting, and with weeping, and with mourning: and rend your *hearts*, and not your garments, and turn unto the Lord your God; for he is gracious and merciful, slow to anger, and of great kindness." It appears that these hypocrites had not the most remote idea of the fast described by the prophet Isaiah, lviii. 5—7, speaking to those who fasted for strife, he says, or rather the spirit of God, speaking by the prophet, says, "Is it such a fast that I have chosen? A day for a man to afflict his soul? Is it to bow down his head like a bulrush? and to spread sackcloth and ashes under him? wilt thou call this a fast? Is not this the fast that I have chosen? to loose the bands of wickedness, to undo the heavy burdens, and to let the oppressed go free, and that ye break every yoke? Is it not to deal thy bread to the hungry, and that thou bring the poor that are cast out to thy house? when thou seest the naked that thou cover him, and that thou hide not thyself from thine own flesh?"

Thirdly, The disciples of our blessed Master paid no attention to this religious institution as it obtained among the Jews. Matthew ix. 14, "Then came to him the disciples of John, saying, Why do we and the Pharisees fast often, but thy disciples fast not?" But the Redeemer defended his disciples. "Can the children of the bride chamber mourn as long as the bridegroom is with them? But the days will come when the bridegroom shall be taken away, and then shall they fast."

Fourthly, The disciples of Jesus Christ cannot mourn while blessed by the light of the Redeemer's countenance. John xvi. 16, "A little while and ye shall not see me: and again a little while and ye shall see me, because I go to the Father." Matthew xxviii. 20, " Teaching them to observe all things whatsoever I have commanded you: and, lo I am with you alway, even unto the end of the world, Amen." It is unnecessary to multiply instances to prove that the soul cannot be afflicted which is cheered by the irradiating spirit, and presence of the Redeemer.

SKETCH LXXX.

Matthew vii. 7, 8.

First, The Redeemer teacheth his disciples to ask with holy confidence, and what is asked shall be given.

Secondly, The disciples are assured, if they seek they shall find.

Thirdly, They are commanded to knock and it shall be opened unto them.

Fourthly, Who are to receive? Every one who asketh.

Fifthly, Who are to find? He who seeketh.

Sixthly, Unto whom shall it be opened? Unto him that knocketh. The following scriptures will elucidate and corroborate our text. Genesis xxxii. 26—28, "And he said, let me go, for the day breaketh: And he said, I will not let thee go except thou bless me. And he said unto him, What is thy name? And he said Jacob. And he said, thy name shall be called no more Jacob, but Israel: for as a prince hast thou power with God and with men, and hast prevailed." Psalm cxviii. 5, " I called upon the Lord in distress: the Lord answered me, and set me in a large place." Psalm cxxiii. 2, " Behold as the eyes of servants look unto the hands of their masters, and as the eyes of a maiden unto the hand of her mistress; so our eyes wait upon the Lord our God, until that he have mercy upon us" John xiv. 13, " And whatsoever ye shall ask in my name, that will I do, that the Father may be glorified in the Son." John

xv. 7, "If ye abide in me, and my words abide in you, ye shall ask what ye will, and it shall be done unto you." John xvi. 23, "And in that day ye shall ask me nothing. Verily, verily, I say unto you, whatsoever ye shall ask the Father in my name, he will give it you." Hebrews iv. 16, "Let us, therefore, come boldly unto the throne of grace, that we may obtain mercy, and find grace to help in time of need." James i. 5, "If any of you lack wisdom, let him ask of God, that giveth to all men liberally and upbraideth not, and it shall be given him."

Remarks.

First, Every one is admonished to ask of God. Secondly, To ask in faith, he must believe; and believing *presupposes a promise, something to be believed, a promise made by one who is able and willing to perform.* Whoever comes unto God, must believe that he is. Thirdly, Every one must seek for what God has given, only *where it is;* and there he shall assuredly find it. Fourthly, There is *but one* door at which we must knock; but this will unquestionably be opened. I am the door, said the Redeemer; this door the Spirit openeth. Fifthly, As every one who asketh receiveth, then *Jesus asketh and shall also receive.* Sixthly, *He came to seek that which was lost, and verily he found it. He knocked, and the everlasting doors were opened unto him. He, this king of glory entered, entered* into life. And he said, I go to prepare a place for you; where I am, there shall ye be also.

SKETCH LXXXI.

Matthew vii. 9—12.

First, Or what man is there of you, whom, if his son ask bread, will he give him a stone? Or if he ask a fish, will he give him a serpent? Luke xi. 11, 12, "If a son shall ask bread of any of you that is a father, will he give him a stone? Or if he ask a fish, will he, for a fish, give him a serpent? Or if he shall ask an egg, will he offer him a scorpion?"

Secondly, Our Saviour considers the people as evil. There are two descriptions of evil, sin and suffering. The former description must be intended in this place; there is no medium between good and evil, and there is none *good but one.* Genesis vi. 5, "And God saw that the wickedness of man was great in the earth, and that every imagination of the thoughts of his heart was only evil continually. Nor, if we accept the testimony of the apostle Paul, were succeeding generations less reprehensible. Romans iii. 9, "What then, are we better than they? *No, in no wise: for we have before proved both Jews and Gentiles, that they are all under sin.*"

Thirdly, Although confessedly evil, yet they knew how to give good gifts unto their children.

Fourthly, The Redeemer pertinently asks, *How much more shall your Father, which is in heaven, give good things to those who ask him?* God is, truly, the giver of every good and perfect gift.

Fifthly, Therefore, all things whatsoever ye would that men should do to you, do ye even so to them.

Sixthly, For this is the law and the prophets. Matthew xxii. 39, "Thou shalt love thy neighbour as thyself." Luke vi. 31, "And as ye would that men should do to you, do ye also to them." Galatians v. 14, "For all the law is fulfilled in one word, even in this: *Thou shalt love thy neighbour as thyself.*"

Remarks.

First, We are all the offspring of God; and he loves us infinitely better than we, who are evil, love our children. Secondly, Every one of God's gifts are good; a good tree cannot bring forth evil fruit. Thirdly, For these good gifts, it becometh us to ask. Fourthly, *We are to do unto men whatsoever we would that men should do unto us;* and if we thus do, neither the law nor the prophets require more. Fifthly, Mankind have never, individually, kept this law, and, therefore, by *their deeds, can never be justified.* But sixthly, Jesus Christ was made under the law, and the prophets do all testify of him. I come not, said the Saviour, to *destroy the law* or the prophets, but to *fulfil them.* Seventhly, In order to fulfil the law and the prophets, *Jesus must do to every man, not what every man does to him, but what he would that every man should do.* We are commanded to love our neighbour as ourselves. The *Redeemer was made under this law, and he fulfilled it to the uttermost;* and his fulfilling this law is our life, our *eternal life*. It is, therefore, that the Saviour saith, *Because I live, ye shall live also.* Without Emmanuel, *God with us*, we can do nothing with the volume of inspiration, for indeed and in truth, it testifieth of him. Christ Jesus hath fulfilled the law, and he inheriteth the promises, and in him the promises are all *yea* and *amen to the glory of God the Father*.

SKETCH LXXXII.

Matthew vii. 13, 14.

First, The Redeemer invites, nay, commands us to enter in at the strait gate. This gate is the entrance into the way of life. What doth this figure exhibit? Undoubtedly Jesus Christ himself. John x. 1, 2, 7, 9, " Verily, verily, I say unto you, he that entereth not by the door into the sheepfold, but climbeth up some other way, the same is a thief and a robber. But he that entereth in by the door is the shepherd of the sheep. Then said Jesus unto them again, verily, verily, I say unto you, I am the door of the sheep. I am the door: by me if any man enter in, he shall be saved, and shall go in and out and shall find pasture."

Secondly, Narrow is the way that leadeth unto life, and few there be that find it. What are we to understand by *this way?* Our Saviour himself has answered this question. John xiv. 6, " Jesus saith unto him, *I am the way, and the truth, and the life:* no man cometh unto the Father but by me." But few there are who find this way: the fact is *there are none;* there are few who be perfect; *But are there any perfect except Deity,* except the God-man? Blind by nature, *we cannot* find the way. *But Jesus came to seek and to save those who were out of the way, those who were wildered and lost.* No man can know the things of God, but by the Spirit. But when the Spirit takes of the things of Jesus, and shows them to us, when he witnesseth with our spirits; in other words, when he takes us by the hand, and saith, this is the way, walk ye in it; we then go on, not only safely, but rejoicing.

Thirdly, *This way* leads unto life. What life? Undoubtedly life spiritual, life eternal, because *in this way is life, and this life is the light of the world.*

Fourthly, What are we to understand by the way of destruction? Isaiah lix. 7, " Their feet run to evil, they make haste to shed innocent blood: their thoughts are thoughts of iniquity; wasting and destruction are in their paths." The way of peace they know not; in other words, *they have not found Jesus*, but he hath *sought* and *found* them, and he will bring them *by a way that they did not know.* Romans iii. 16, " Destruction and misery are in their paths." Philippians iii. 19, "Whose end is destruction, whose god is their belly, and whose glory is in their shame, who mind earthly things."

Fifthly, Who are they that walk therein? Pharisees and Publicans.

Sixthly, Is this way of destruction eternal? I answer NO, assuredly NO; and I produce my evidences. Psalm ix. 5, 6, "Thou hast rebuked the heathen, thou hast destroyed the wicked, thou hast put out their name forever and ever. O thou enemy, destructions are come to a perpetual end." Psalm cvii. 20, "He sent his word and healed them, and delivered them from their destructions." Hosea xiii. 14, " I will ransom them from the power of the grave; I will redeem them from death; O death, I will be thy plagues; O grave, I will be thy destruction." Pain shall not be eternal; it had a beginning, and shall therefore have an end; but the soul of man is eternal, it is an emanation from the Deity, who is self existent. Yet, Romans viii. 22, " The whole creation now travaileth in pain." Revelations xvi. 10, " And the fifth angel poured out his vial upon the seat of the beast; and his kingdom was full of darkness, and they gnawed their tongues for pain." Again, chapter xxi. 4, "And God shall wipe away all tears from their eyes; and there shall be no more death, neither sorrow, nor crying, neither shall there be any more *pain.*

Remarks.

First, As there are but two ways, and we are at liberty to choose the best, it would be wisdom thus to do. O that men were wise. Secondly, If Jesus were not the new and the living way, if he were not the Omega, as well as the Alpha. Misery and destruction would be the eternal portion of the whole race of man.

SKETCH LXXXIII.

Matthew vii. 15—20.

First, Our blessed Master teaches his hearers to beware of false prophets. Many false prophets had arisen in Israel; no less than eight hundred and fifty at one time. Many also were predicted. Mark xiii. 22, " For false christs and false prophets shall rise, and shall shew signs and wonders to seduce, if it were possible, even the elect." 2 Peter ii. 1, " But there were false prophets also among the people, even as there shall be false teachers among you, who privily shall bring in damnable heresies, even denying the Lord that bought them, and bring upon themselves swift destruction."

Secondly, These false prophets were well spoken of by the people. Luke vi. 26, " Woe unto you, when all men shall speak well of you! for so did their fathers to the false prophets."

Thirdly, One reason why they were well spoken of and greatly admired, was their *appearance in sheep's clothing, while inwardly they were ravening wolves*. Thus did they conceal the ferocity of their dispositions under a cloak of gentleness, piety, and benevolence.

Fourthly, Our divine Master gives us infallible marks and evidences, whereby we may distinguish these false prophets, viz. their fruits. Do men gather grapes of thorns, or figs of thistles? But the false prophet, although highly estimated by the people, were no better than a thorn. Micah vii. 4, " The best of them is as a brier: the most upright is sharper than a thorn hedge." A good tree bringeth forth good fruit, but a corrupt tree bringeth forth evil fruit. Men are considered as corrupt trees. Genesis vi. 11, " The earth also was corrupt before God." Psalm xiv. 1, " They are corrupt, they have done abominable works; there is none that doeth good." To teach for doctrines the traditions of men, is bringing forth corrupt fruit. Hence, saith the Apostle, 2 Corinthians, iv. 5, "We preach not ourselves but Christ Jesus the Lord." The Redeemer of men was anointed to preach good tidings. Isaiah lxi. 1. And the fulfilment of this prophecy is recorded, Luke iv. 18. Listen to the apostle Paul, Romans x. 8, " The word is nigh thee, even in thy mouth, and in thy heart; that is, the word of faith which we preach." Let us not say, we cannot tell who are the false, and who are the true prophets; since they are designated by incontestible signs. Let us take care that in rejecting the prophet, we do not reject the man; that we do not preach false doctrine to the false prophet. but let us always remember, that he will *be saved, although his works will be burned.*

SKETCH LXXXIV.

Matthew vii. 21.

First, WHAT are we to understand by the kingdom of heaven? Sometimes the kingdom of heaven intends the Redeemer of men. Matthew iii. 2, " Repent ye, for the kingdom of heaven is at hand." Sometimes the people. Daniel vii. 14, "And there was given him dominion, and glory, and a kingdom, that all people and nations should serve him." Again, the kingdom of heaven intends the state and condition of the people. Romans xiv. 17, " For the kingdom of God is not meat and drink; but righteousness, and peace, and joy in the Holy Ghost." It is into this last community, as we presume that no man can enter, that doth not do the will of the Father which is in heaven.

Secondly, Who are entitled to enter into the kingdom of heaven, by a performance of the will of the Father? Surely, no *mere man.* Was Israel of old? Ask the prophet Hosea, viii. 1, " Set the trumpet to thy mouth. He shall come as an eagle against the house of the Lord, because they have transgressed my covenant, and trespassed against my law." Ask the apostle Paul, Romans ii. 13, " *For not the hearers of the law are just before God, but the doers of the law.*" Nay, let us make application to our blessed Master himself. Luke vi. 46, " And why call ye me Lord, Lord, and do not the things which I say."

Thirdly, Who then has done the will of God? Hebrews x. 7, "Then, said I, Lo I come (in the volume of the book it is written of me) to do thy will, O God." And was the will of the Father done? did the Father declare himself well pleased? Matthew iii. 17, "And lo, a voice from heaven, saying, this is my beloved Son in whom I am well pleased." Matthew xii. 18, "Behold, my servant, whom I have chosen; my beloved, in whom my soul is well pleased: I will put my spirit upon him, and he shall shew judgment to the Gentiles." Matthew xvii. 5, "This is my beloved Son in whom I am well pleased, hear ye him."

Fourthly, How then can we, who have broken the law of God, "*who have left undone the things which we ought to have done, and done the things which we ought not to have done*, enter into the kingdom of heaven?" I answer, Ephesians i. 6, "Because to the praise of the glory of God's grace, we are accepted in the beloved." 1 Corinthians i. 30, "But of him are ye in Christ Jesus, who of God is made unto us wisdom, and righteousness, and sanctification, and redemption." It is evident that it is not *saying* but *doing* which procures an entrance into the kingdom of heaven. It is evident that no human being, save the God-man, ever performed what God required; and it is as evident, the God-man, the head of every man, being made under the law, fulfilled the law in behalf of all those who had broken it. It is apparent that the righteousness of the Redeemer is as much the property of the sinner, as if he had performed it in his own individual person. And it is thus that the kingdom, the power, and the glory, all belongeth unto the Lord. If you should ask why did not Jesus Christ give us this information in his memorable sermon on the mount? I answer, he left this for his spirit to make manifest after his departure. John xvi. 26, "*But the Comforter which is the Holy Ghost,* whom the Father will send in my name, he shall teach you all things, and bring all things to your remembrance, whatsoever I have said unto you." Chapter xv. 16, He shall testify of me. Jesus Christ informed his disciples, that he had many things to say unto them, which they were not then able to bear. The Apostle speaks of growing in grace, and the knowledge and love of God. There are among the disciples of our Lord, children, young men, and fathers. Our Saviour, after his resurrection, explained to his disciples going to Emmaus, the things concerning himself. He made known to Peter in the vision of the sheet, what Peter never knew before, and thus taught him not to call unclean, what God had cleansed. The Redeemer left his desciples so ignorant, that when bursting the barriers of the grave, he appeared before them, they did not believe the testimony of their senses. They gave no credit to those with whom they had been accustomed to associate. And shall we dare to ask, why he did not teach them every thing at once? He directed them to search the scriptures, and he assured them that they testified of him. We have this day heard the testimony of these scriptures rehearsed in our ears. Beloved, believest thou the scriptures; I know that thou believest them.

SKETCH LXXXV.

Matthew vii. 22, 23.

First, To what day does the Redeemer advert? 2 Peter iii. 10, "But the day of the Lord will come as a thief in the night; in the which the heavens shall pass away with a great noise, and the elements shall melt with fervent heat, the earth also and the works that are therein shall be burned up."

Secondly, Who does the Saviour intend by the many who shall appear before him with a Lord, Lord, have we not prophesied in thy name, and in thy name cast out devils? 1 Corinthians xiii. 1, "Though I speak with the tongues of men and of angels, and have not charity, I am become as sounding brass, and a tinkling cymbal." Jesus said of those who believed, that in his name they should cast out devils. It is therefore that these boasters interrogate; have we not in thy name done many wonderous works? It is of such characters, the Apostle writes, 2 Thessalonians ii. 9, "Whose coming is after the working of Satan with all power, and signs, and lying wonders.

Thirdly, Then will I profess unto them, I never knew you. What is it to know? It is to approve, to acknowledge; *in every other sense, the Redeemer knew these people, for he had made them, and he knew them as workers of iniquity.* Psalm i. 6, "For the Lord knoweth the way of the righteous: but the way of the ungodly shall perish." Habakkuk i. 13, " Thou art of purer eyes than to behold evil, and canst not look on iniquity." *I never knew you in the characters you assume.*

Fourthly, He shall say, depart from me ye that work iniquity. Isaiah lix. 2, " But your iniquities have separated between you and your God, and your sins have hid his face from you." But, says God, Jeremiah xxxiii. 8, " I will pardon all their iniquties." Again, chapter xxxi. 34, " I will forgive their iniquities, and I will remember their sin no more." Hebrews viii. 12, " For I will be merciful to their unrighteousness, and their sins, and their iniquities will I remember no more." Isaiah liv. 8, " In a little wrath I hid my face from thee for a moment; but with everlasting kindness will I have mercy on thee, saith the Lord thy Redeemer." Yet all those *who exalt themselves* shall be debased, every high and lofty imagination shall be brought low; every self righteous boaster shall be ashamed and confounded; all their wonderful works shall be burned, they shall be judged and condemned; they shall call upon the rocks and mountains to fall upon them; they shall look on him whom they have pierced and mourn; upon him, the blood of whose covenant, they have trampled under foot, counting it an unholy thing. After all these things, the Redeemer of men shall manifest himself, and the word of Jehovah shall be accomplished: *they shall all know him from the least unto the greatest.* It is in this divinely consistent view, that the truth of God bursts forth with resplendent beauty. The deity appears faithful to himself; there is no *yea* and *nay*, mercy and truth hath met, and will meet together; righteousness and peace embrace each other.

SKETCH LXXXVI.

Matthew xii. 31, 32.

Wherefore I say unto you, all manner of sin and blasphemy shall be forgiven unto men ; but the blasphemy against the Holy Ghost shall not be forgiven unto men ; and whosoever speaketh a word against the son of man, it shall be forgiven him ; but whosoever speaketh a word against the Holy Ghost, it shall not be forgiven, neither in this world, neither in the world to come.

These words spake Jesus, the faithful and the true witness, and this same Jesus assures us, he spake nothing but that which he received of the Father, and do we not know that the words which the Redeemer spake are eternal life.

First, Let us enquire of the sacred oracles what is God ? God hath condescended to give us some idea of himself in the complex formation of the creature, man. Let us make man in our image ; the *plural* in the *singular*. Let *us*, in the plural, *make man* in the *singular*, in *our* image in the plural, and it is self evident that we can never lose *this* image of God. To know thee, the *only true God* is life eternal. As man was made in the image of God, we have only to analize the figure, and we shall be able to catch a glimpse of the substance. What is a man separated from his spirit ? When the body of a man is committed to the dust, the spirit returns to God who gave it. The character of God is given, Revelations i. 7, 8, " Behold he cometh with clouds : and every eye shall see him, and they also which pierced him : and all kindreds of the earth shall wail because of him. Even so, Amen. I am Alpha and Omega, the beginning and the ending, saith the Lord, which is, and which was, and which is to come, the Almighty."

"God," saith a learned commentator, " is one of the names which we give to the eternal, infinite and incomprehensible Being, the Creator of all things, who preserves and governs every thing by his almighty power and wisdom, and who is the only object of worship. The Hebrews generally give to God the name Jehovah. *He who* exists of himself, and gives being and existence to others; this is a name ineffable and mysterious, which denotes the eternity, immutability and independency of God, and the infallible certainty of his word and promises. The import of this name is opened and predicated of Christ. The devout Hebrews had such a veneration for this holy name, that they never pronounced it, but instead of it made use of that, of *Adonai*, which properly signifies my LORDS in the plural number; and of *Elohi*, *Eloi* or *Elohim*. They likewise call him *El*, which signifies strong, or *Shaddai*, whereby may be designed one who is self sufficient, or *Elion*, the Most High, or *Elsabaoth*, the God of hosts, or *Ja*, God: this name God, includes the whole trinity. God is a triune Being."

Thus are we enabled to trace a vestige of that character which none can find out to *perfection*.

Secondly, What doth this God declare unto us in the passage before us? Wherefore I say unto you, *all manner of sin and blasphemy shall be forgiven unto men*, but the blasphemy against the Holy Ghost shall not be forgiven unto men. I do not believe what professors in general say of this passage is true, but I know that the words of Jesus Christ are *at all times true words*. What infinite pains do men take to invalidate the testimony of God, to weaken the authority of divine revelation. This text is supposed to suit those professors of religion, who wish to make an essential distinction between God and Christ. The propensity to multiply gods is in the heart of man very powerful. Yet it is a precious truth that there is but *one God*, and that this *one God is the only wise God, our Saviour*. Those who would strip the Redeemer of his Divinity, assay to make Jesus Christ himself of their party, although the weapon by which they would dethrone the God-man; if they could succeed in their impious purpose, would inflict a deadly wound upon that eternal life of theirs, which is hid with Christ in God; would effectually destroy their hope of immortality; yet do they labour to establish this falsehood, as if all their hopes of happiness for time and for eternity were based thereon.

Is there any sin which is not against the Holy Ghost? Read John iv. 24, "*God is a spirit:* and they that worship him, must worship him in spirit and in truth." 2 Corinthians iii. 18, *Now the Lord is that spirit;* if there be a God out of Christ, he may be an implacable enemy, unwilling to forgive. *Blessed be God; the scriptures give no record of such a God.* We know, and are assured, that *God the Father, God the Son and God the Holy Ghost, are no more than different exhibitions of the same self existent, Omnipotent Being.* The gospel was first preached to every creature by the everlasting Father, unto Adam in the garden of Eden, the seed of the woman shall bruise the serpent's head, and afterwards unto Abraham; in thee, and in thy seed, all the families of the earth shall be blessed. It is confirmed by *God, manifested in the flesh,* and by all the teachings of the high Priest of our profession, yea, every act of his glorious life and suffering death serve to confirm the glad tidings of the gospel. John xii. 50, "And I know that his commandment is life everlasting: whatsoever I speak therefore, even as the Father said unto me, so I speak." This is, my friends, a divine discovery; read it, I beseech you, again, and again, and if God gives you faith to receive and believe it, you will then experience the teachings of God in his character of Holy Ghost. *All sins then, committed against God, are committed against the Holy Spirit,* for God is a spirit, the LORD is that spirit, and who will dare to say, he is not a Holy Spirit.

Thirdly, Why doth the Saviour say, *there is a sin which never can be forgiven unto the children of men.* I do not believe the Redeemer ever uttered such a sentence to any individual among the race of Adam; nay, in this oft-cited passage, he expressly says, *all manner of sin and blasphemy shall be forgiven unto men.* Were there no other sinners, except human sinners, we should lament that there was so much reason to call in question the truth of God, for could this be proved, the language of our text would apparently be a contradiction in terms, *all manner of sins and blasphemies shall be forgiven unto men;* but the sin against God hath not forgiveness. This may answer the purpose of those who do not admit the *divinity of Jesus Christ.* But the divinity of Jesus Christ is a scripture doctrine, and those who would dethrone the Redeemer, must not choose their weapons from the sacred armory: yet notwithstanding the abominable perversion of the sacred writings, which obtains in the world; it will always be true, that *God manifest in the flesh, is God almighty, that there is no other God, that every sin which is committed, is committed against God in his triune character,* and that passing by the nature of angels, he took upon him the seed of Abraham, dwelt on this earth by the name of Jesus Christ, and that the blood of Jesus Christ cleanseth the nature in which God was manifested from all sin ; let it be constantly remembered that all sins that are committed, are committed against God, the Holy God, the Holy Spirit, and the LORD is that Spirit. But we do not know that this cleansing blood was ever shed for *angelic sinners*, and as without shedding of blood there can be no remission of sins ; as the suffering Saviour when expiring for the sins of lost humanity passed by the nature of Angels; we must leave those offenders to the God who made them, well knowing that secret things belong to God, well knowing that the Judge of all the earth, and of every animated being will do right.

Wherefore, I say unto you, all manner of sin and blasphemy shall be forgiven unto men; but the blasphemy against the Holy Ghost shall not be forgiven unto men.

And whosoever speaketh a word against the Son of man, it shall be forgiven him : but whosoever speaketh against the Holy Ghost, it shall not be forgiven him, neither in this world, neither in the world to come.

Now, as we have proved from the sacred records, that there is no Holy Ghost except the son of man, and that the LORD is indeed and in truth *that spirit*, then our inference is demonstrable ; every sin committed against the Holy Spirit, is committed *against God*, and if the sin against the Holy Ghost cannot be forgiven, then no sin *can ever be forgiven*, and then what becomes of the declaration, *all manner of sins and blasphemies shall be forgiven unto men? and how doth the blood of Jesus Christ cleanse from all sin ?* David saith, against thee only have I sinned ; but those who are taught by God know, they have forgiveness of *sin*, *of all sin* by the blood shedding of Jesus Christ, that Christ is the propitiation for the sins of the whole world, and that remission of sins is by divine command preached to every creature ; nor can they believe that the servants of God were commissioned to go forth with a lie in their mouths.

Fourthly and lastly, We believe that the blood of Jesus Christ was not shed for the angelic sinner, we know that this prime angelic sinner is called in the sacred volume, the *man* who made the world a wilderness; we think that this sinner, and the sinners of the angelic nature, are the only sinners that can commit this unpardonable sin, or unpardonable sins, against the Holy Ghost. Mark the Evangelist seems to have this view of the text, chapter vi. 28, 29, That the Redeemer said, verily, I say unto you, *all sins shall be forgiven unto the Sons of men, and blasphemies wherewithsoever they shall blaspheme ;* But *he* that shall blaspheme against the Holy Ghost, hath never forgiveness, but is in danger of eternal damnation.

In this view, there is no contradiction in the divine testimony. All manner of sin and blasphemy is forgiven unto men, but the blasphemy against the Holy Ghost is not forgiven unto men, neither indeed can it be *committed by men ;* if it could, and if it could not be forgiven, then indeed there would be a sin from which the blood of Jesus Christ could not cleanse.* It is remarkable that the words *against* and *Holy*, are words supplied by the translator, and they are given in Italicks that there may be no hazard of deception in this particular. A learned Hebrew scholar once informed me, that a literal translation would thus word the passage ; *the sin of the Ghost shall not be forgiven,* and, he added, that he had seen old translations of the Bible, in which it was absolutely rendered, *the sin of the Ghost shall not be forgiven.* We do steadfastly believe, that the evil ghost, and the evil ghost only, *can commit a sin which cannot be forgiven,* and we will strenuously insist, *that all manner of sins and blasphemies shall be forgiven unto the sons of men, wherewith they shall blaspheme ; that the Lamb of God hath taken away the sin of the world, and that the blood of Jesus Christ cleanseth from all sin.*

Yet hath this evil ghost rendered many individuals, among the ransomed of the LORD, very unhappy from a fearful apprehension, that they had committed the unpardonable sin, *unpardonable sin !* What a sentence to be found upon the lips of the *Redeemed,* upon the lips of those for whose redemption the

---

*A respectable and modest Matron, who had recently tasted, that the LORD was gracious, firmly embracing the doctrine of God our Saviour, was followed by a reverend gentleman, who had long been her spiritual guide with much lamentation "O Catharine," he exclamed "how will you support this new and unfounded doctrine, what can you say to the *unpardonable* sin ?" "Only ask you," returned the believer, "What in your opinion is the difference between the *unpardonable* sin and other sins ? The ELECT you assure us can never commit an *unpardonable* sin, and to those who are not ELECTED ; every sin is *unpardonable.*
The Gentleman was a rigid Calvinist.

Lamb of God was slain, which Lamb of God was pledged to take away the sin of the world. But however strange, it is nevertheless true, and I have known many who have been made completely wretched in the dread of this sin, in the soul harrowing persuasion, that they either had or should commit this heinous transgression, and in consequence be consigned to never ending misery. I knew a lady, she was a resident in my native Island, who had continued through a series of revolving years, even to extreme old age, a pattern of every excellence which can adorn humanity. Virtue, religion and piety, these seemed natal in her bosom : but alas! for her, she attended an evening lecture, the subject under consideration was the unpardonable sin. She became impressed with an idea, that she had committed this unpardonable sin : no effort could eradicate from her tortured bosom this tremendous impression; she lost her reason, and died a complete maniac.

SKETCH LXXXVII.

Matthew xiii. 45, 46.

Again, the kingdom of heaven is like unto a merchantman seeking goodly pearls, who when he had found one pearl of great price, went and sold all that he had, and bought it.

First, What in this passage is intended by the kingdom of heaven? *Undoubtedly Christ Jesus.* But why so? Because it pleased the Father that in him all fulness should dwell, for he hath appointed a day in which he will gather all things into one. A kingdom is a multitude of human beings, congregating together, and submitting to the dominion of one individual selected from the people, and presiding over them. If a nation were ever so numerous, it could not be a kingdom except it were under the government of a king. The scriptures speak of an intellectual kingdom, consisting of righteousness, and peace, and joy in the Holy Ghost; but I am persuaded, the kingdom here spoken of is the Redeemer himself, and, as usual, I ground my confidence upon the sacred oracles. In Matthew, iii. 2, John Baptist as the harbinger of our Lord, when proclaiming the approaching Messiah, informed the people that the kingdom of heaven was at hand.

Secondly, Why is this kingdom of heaven likened unto a *merchantman seeking goodly pearls?* Because Jesus Christ was sent to *seek* and to *save* that which *was lost.* I am aware that it hath been said, the *Redeemer himself is the pearl of great price!* But with all due submission to authorities which I acknowledge highly respectable, I take leave to observe, that the figures selected, as emblematic of the Saviour, possess more intrinsick worth; Christ is a hiding place, he is a covert from the storm, he is the bread of life which cometh down from heaven, *but he is not spoken of as a pearl.* It is really astonishing that men who are, *humanly speaking*, both wise and good, should thus absurdly err; Christ, say they, is the pearl of great price, which the *miserable* sinner, in his unconverted state, must *seek, find and purchase.* But with what must this lost, undone sinner purchase this pearl? Why he must purchase it, *purchase Christ Jesus,* by parting with his sins, and if he could thus do, his would be the kingdom, the power, and the glory.

Thirdly, But what is this pearl of great price? Malachi iii. 17, "*They shall be mine,* saith the Lord of hosts, in that day when I make up *my jewels.*" Pearls are the individuals of the human family, and they have been purchased by the great merchantman.

Fourthly, But what is this one pearl of great price? Certainly the fulness of human nature, which Jesus came to seek. It was in search of this pearl, that he bowed his heavens and came down, and when he had found it, he gave or sold all that he had, and bought it. Yes, he purchased the people with his own blood, he gave his life a ransom for all; he was rich, but for our sakes he became poor, that we through his poverty might be made rich. How incalculable was the price which Jesus paid for this pearl. We are indeed *bought with a price, all price beyond,* and surely it is highly incumbent upon us to glorify God in our bodies, and our spirits, which are indisputably the property of God. We see the value which is set upon the human family, by the price which hath been paid for them, and we ought to rest, in the assurance, that Emmanuel will never willingly lose the purchase of his blood.

The names of the people are engraven upon precious stones, and it should be remembered, that the merchantman seeks the pearls, and not the pearls the merchantman. To him, therefore, belongeth the kingdom, the power, and the glory, worlds without end, Amen, and Amen.

SKETCH LXXXVIII.

Mark xiv. 21.

First, Our Saviour is denominated *the Son of man*. Mr. Cruden informs us, that the Redeemer is styled the Son of man in the four evangelists, about eighty times. That the almighty Father is the *child born*—the son of man—is a most elevating consideration. Jesus Christ a lineal descendant of the family of man! We have one origin! *God or the divine Nature is our common Father.*

Secondly, Jesus Christ was not the son of man precisely after the same manner that other individuals are the sons and daughters of men. Emmanuel is styled in the sacred volume, the seed of the woman, the only begotten of the Father. He was without sin. He could not say with the Psalmist, " In sin did my mother conceive me." produced by the power of the highest, he is called *holy, the Son of God*. When Jesus Christ is called the Son of man, the spirit teaches us that he is the Son of *every man*. So saith the prophet Isaiah, ix. 6, " To *us* a child is born, to *us* a son is given.

Thirdly. *The Son of man goeth indeed as it is written of him*. Where is it so written of the Redeemer? Psalm xxii. " My God, my God, why hast thou forsaken me? Why art thou so far from helping me, and from the words of my roaring? All they that see me laugh me to scorn, they shoot out the lip, they shake the head, saying, He trusted in the Lord that he would deliver him: let him deliver him, seeing he delighted in him. For dogs have compassed me: the assembly of the wicked have enclosed me: they pierced my hands and my feet. I may tell all my bones: they look and stare upon me. They part my garments among them, and cast lots upon my vesture." Isaiah liii. 3—5, 7—11, " He is despised and rejected of men; a man of sorrows, and acquainted with grief: and we hid as it were our faces from him; he was despised, and we esteemed him not. Surely he hath borne our griefs, and carried our sorrows: yet we did esteem him stricken, smitten of God, and afflicted. But he was wounded for our transgressions, he was bruised for our iniquities; the chastisement of our peace was upon him; and with his stripes we are healed. He was oppressed, and he was afflicted, yet he opened not his mouth: he is brought as a lamb to the slaughter, and as a sheep before her shearers is dumb, so he openeth not his mouth, He was taken from prison and from judgment: and who shall declare his generation? for he was cut off out of the land of the living: for the transgression of my people was he stricken. And he made his grave with the wicked, and with the rich in his death: because he had done no violence, neither was deceit in his mouth. Yet it pleased the LORD to bruise him; he hath put him to grief: when thou shalt make his soul an offering for sin, he shall see his seed, he shall prolong his days, and the pleasure of the LORD shall prosper in his hand. He shall see of the travail of his soul, and shall be satisfied: by his knowledge shall my righteous servant justify many; for he shall bear their iniquities."

But why was this immaculate, this Omnipotent Being *dumb* before his accusers? Why did he not look those rebellious individuals, whom he had commanded into existence, and whose life hung upon his word, into instant death? We are aware that he was perfect in meekness, and that the lowly Jesus had the humility, as well as the innocence of the lamb; this is one reason; but this is not all, there is yet another, and more powerful reason. The God-man well knew, that *strict justice had arraigned, that strict justice had produced him before the judgment seat.* Although the perfection of the divine nature, all the fulness of the God-head was his, in his individual character, yet he knew that he was the *responsible, the accountable head of every man;* that those numerous individuals which constituted the aggregate of the human family, from Adam to his youngest son were members of his mystical body; it was at this dread, this awful moment, that the *iniquity of his heels, the complicated iniquity of these wide spreading members, compassed him about, and it was therefore that he opened not his mouth, it was therefore that he was silent before the judgment seat.*

Fourthly, The Redeemer saith, *Woe to that man by whom the Son of man is betrayed.* Woe, says the celebrated lexicographer, Johnson, is grief, sorrow, misery, calamity. And, permit me to ask, is not woe the portion of every child of Adam? Psalm cxx. 5, " Woe is me, that I sojourn in Mesech, that I dwell in the tents of Kedar." Isaiah vi. 5, " Then said I, woe is me! For I am undone; because I am a man of unclean lips; for mine eyes have seen the King, the Lord of hosts." 1 Corinthians ix. 16, " For though I preach the gospel, I have nothing to glory of; for necessity is laid upon me; yea, woe is unto me, if I preach not the gospel."

But there are different degrees of sorrow; the soul is sometimes pierced by anguish, and the heart hath been broken by calamity. The sorrows now under contemplation, experienced by Judas Iscariot, were of the deepest dye. Woe was indeed unto that man! Perhaps his sorrows were only surpassed by the sorrows of him whom he *impiously* betrayed into the hands of his enemies.

Fifthly, *Good were it for that man if he had never been born.* It cannot be denied that these were the words of him, who spake as never man spake, and all whose words were words of truth, as well as grace. Hence it is concluded, and upon a *cursory* view, with some shadow of reason, that Jesus Christ could not be the Saviour of *this sinner*, and if he be not the Saviour of *this sinner*, consequently he is not the Saviour of *all men*. But the spirit of truth proclaimed, and still proclaims Jesus Christ the Saviour of *all men*, and this declaration is found upon the lips of all God's *holy prophets ever since the world began.* Are then the testimonies of God contradictory? By no means, a *house divided against itself cannot stand.* We confess that had there been no *possibility* of the ultimate felicity of Judas, if *he had never been born*, we should have been at a loss to reconcile this affirmation of the head of *every man*, of the *Redeemer of the world*, with other testimonies, although, even then we should have had full confidence that there was no *yea* and *nay*, no contradiction in sacred writ. But we boldly assert, that Judas Iscariot might have been a subject of redemption, might have entered into possession of complete felicity *without being born*, and if so, it would unquestionably have been *good for him if he had never been born*. Could he have been made a denizen of heaven, without being born, what darts of agony had missed his soul.

Is it not clear from the *manner* of our Saviour's expression, that Judas might have had an existence without being born into this state of suffering? It would have been good for *that man* if he had never been born, then he might have been a human being, *a man* without being born? Nay more, he might have possessed *good*, for it would have been *good*, or *good* were it for that man, if he had never been born; a *non-entity* is *neither susceptible of good nor evil*.

We repeat then, Judas Iscariot might have been saved, although he had never been born. Job iii. 3, "Let the day perish wherein I was born, and the night in which it was said, There is a man child conceived. *Why did I not give up the Ghost?* Why was not my birth prevented?" Jeremiah xv. "Cursed be the day wherein I was born: let not the day wherein my mother bear me, be blessed. Cursed be the man who brought tidings to my father, saying, A man child is born unto thee; making him very glad. Because he slew me not from the womb; or that my *mother might have been my grave.*" But, although both Job and Jeremiah thus spake, they knew that their Redeemer lived; they knew that in the righteousness of the LORD they were *owned, saved*, and *blessed*. Yet, for the purpose of avoiding the ills of life, they *deeply*, if not *unwarrantably* lament, that they had not yielded up the Ghost, and thus attained the port of blessedness ere ever they became tenants of pain, subjects of sin, and consequent sorrow. Had Judas Iscariot given up the Ghost before he was ushered into this state of being, he also might have been blest and happy; he would have been exempted from those agonizing sufferings, those scenes of sorrow, which were so great as to make him choose strangling rather than life. But we have seen, and experience teacheth us, that sufferings, lamentation and woe, are the lot of humanity; and although the lip of truth pronounced upon this unhappy man a peculiar woe, while we see this denunciation fulfilled, we cannot but look for the accomplishment of the rich promises of the gospel, which, considering the source from whence they proceed, *indubitably guarantee salvation to every son and daughter of Adam*. Well, then our Saviour, *the Saviour of all men*, may still be a God of truth and grace. The records found in Matthew xix. 28, and in Luke xxii. 29, 30, may still be faithful and true records. "And Jesus said unto them, Verily I say unto you, that ye which have followed me in the regeneration, when the Son of man shall sit in the throne of his glory, ye also shall set upon *twelve thrones judging the twelve tribes of Israel.* And I appoint unto you a kingdom, as my Father hath appointed unto me, that ye may eat and drink at my table, in my kingdom, and sit on thrones judging the twelve tribes of Israel."

Upon the whole, it must be admitted as an incontrovertible fact, that as they who *sit at odds, the attributes of Omnipotence are enemies to the perfection of God;* so, those who labour to render contradictory the testimonies contained in the sacred volume, *give a mortal stab, as far as is in their power, to the authority of sacred writ.* Can any thing be more derogatory to the honour of God our Saviour? Can any thing be more impious, more irreverent than to select *one part* of his most holy word *to confront or give the lie to another?* It is a well established fact, that Christ Jesus was delivered up for our offences, by the determinate purpose, council, and foreknowledge of God. Yea, the instruments were appointed, and the spirit of prophecy accurately described. Psalm xli. 9, "Yea, mine own familiar friend in whom I trusted, who did eat of my bread, hath lifted up his heel against me." Psalm lxix. 25, "Let their habitation be desolate, and none dwell in their tents."

That these references are strictly applicable to the immediate instruments of the crucifixion of our Lord, and *especially to Judas*, is beyond a doubt; and we are authorized to speak thus positively by the spirit of inspiration, which, in the first chapter of the Acts of the Apostles, decidedly sayeth, "Men and brethren, this scripture must needs have been fulfilled, which the Holy Ghost, by the mouth of David, spake before concerning Judas, who was guide to them that took Jesus. For he was numbered with us, and had obtained part of the ministry." For it is written in the book of Psalms, "Let his habitation be desolate, let no man dwell therein: and his bishoprick let another take."

Yet we see, that although our Saviour was delivered up to death by the determinate council of God, deep anguish of soul was, nevertheless, denounced upon the instruments of this astonishing transaction! The perpetrators of this important, this preconcerted deed, were haunted by remorse, by all the terrors of a guilty conscience. *I have sinned, said the wretched apostate, in that I have betrayed innocent blood.*

For God's works of providence, we pretend not to assign reasons; we only believe they are holy and wise, just and good, because they are the operations of infinite, of unerring wisdom.

Blessed are they who are exempted from temptation, or who are sustained in the trials which they may be called to endure. Blessed are they who are delivered from evil, or, as it is sometimes rendered, from the *evil one.*

Lastly, The genuine believer, the true christian will look forward with faith and joy, nothing doubting. He will anticipate the day of the LORD, as described by he prophet Isaiah, xxv. 6, 7, 8, 9.

As there can be no doubt that Judas was a lineal descendant from Adam, as we cannot learn that he was exempted from the grand charter of privileges, as it is asserted in holy writ, that the *devil entered into him in like manner as Satan entered into Peter*, stimulating him *throughout* the whole *guilty transaction;* and as, when the evil spirit was exorcised from his bosom, his agonies were undescribable; and as tears are to be wiped from all faces, we look forward with perfect confidence, expecting when the *burden of crimes will be removed even from the bosom of Judas*, when tears shall be wiped even from the face of Judas, and when the rebuke shall be taken, even from him who *betrayed his LORD and Master.*

Finally, Christians faithfully anticipate an era when there shall be no more pain; when he who sitteth on the throne shall say, Behold I make all things new. Write, said the Redeemer, for these are the true sayings of God. Glory, therefore, be unto his name for ever and ever.—Amen and Amen.

SKETCH LXXXIX.

Luke i. 38—45.

First, MARY, in the language of the believing heart, exclaims, Be it unto me according to thy word.

Secondly, Upon the departure of the angel she went immediately into the hill country to visit her kinswoman Elisabeth. This hill country was in the tribe of Judah, and it contained a city, appropriated to the sons of Aaron, of which house was Zacharias and Elisabeth.

Thirdly, Elisabeth, upon hearing the voice of Mary, was filled with the Holy Ghost, and with a loud voice spontaneously ejaculated, Blessed art thou among women.

Fourthly, Elisabeth piously addresses Mary, as the mother of her LORD. *Ye call me LORD and Master, saith the Redeemer, and ye say right, for so I am.*

Fifthly and lastly, Blessed is she that believed, for there shall be a performance of those things which were told her from the LORD.

If the communication made by the angel to Mary be not true, there can be no dependence upon what we are accustomed to receive as inspiration. If it be true, there can be no dependence upon those who seek to controvert the mysteries of our holy religion. Every one who doth not believe that Elisabeth was filled with the Holy Ghost, and that of course she was divinely inspired, uttering the words of truth, must rank with those unbelievers, who made God a liar. It is upon such infidels that all which is denounced upon the unbeliever must fall; upon them rests the sentence of *condemnation* or damnation, and such will be their portion, as long as they continue unbelievers. But every individual who believes the truth of God is assured, that *unbelief will ultimately know a period. That it will last no longer than that day of the LORD, when every eye shall see, and every tongue confess.*

SKETCH XC.

Luke i. 46—49.

First, UNDER the influence of the divine spirit, Mary speaketh of the Trinity in her own *person*. My *soul* doth magnify the LORD, and my *spirit* hath rejoiced in God my Saviour.

Secondly, Her language is the language of the faith of former ages. Genesis xxx. 13, "And Leah said, happy am I, for the daughters will call me blessed." 1 Samuel ii. 1, "And Hannah prayed, and said, My heart rejoiceth in the LORD, mine horn is exalted in the LORD," &c. &c. Psalm xxxv. 9, "And my soul shall be joyful in the LORD, it shall rejoice in his salvation." Habakkuk iii. 17, 18, "Although the fig tree shall not blossom, neither shall fruit be in the vines, yet I will rejoice in the LORD, I will joy in the God of my salvation."

Thirdly, Mary, under the influence of the holy spirit, speaketh of God as her Saviour, and her testimony perfectly corresponds with the testimony of the prophets and apostles. Isaiah xlv. 21, "And there is no God else beside me, a just God, and a Saviour." Psalm cvi. 21, "They forget God their Saviour, which had done great things in Egypt." 1 Timothy iv. 10, "We trust in the living God who is the Saviour of all men, especially of those that believe." Titus i. 3, "According to the commandment of God our Saviour." Again iii. 4, "But after that the kindness and love of God our Saviour toward man appeared." 2 Peter i. 1, "Through the righteousness of God our Saviour." Jude xxv. "To the only wise God our Saviour."

Fourthly, One reason why Mary magnified her Saviour, God, was, that God had regarded her low estate. 1 Corinthians i. 27, "But God hath chosen the foolish things of the world to confound the wise, and God hath chosen the weak things of this world, to confound the mighty." James ii. 5, "Hearken, my beloved brethren, hath not God chosen the poor of this world, rich in faith, and heirs of the kingdom which he hath promised to those that love him." But Mary urges a second reason, for magnifying her

God—From henceforth all generations shall call me blessed; unquestionably they shall, unquestionably they will.

Fifthly, For he that is mighty hath done to me great things; and holy is his name. Our subject furnishes an excellent specimen of divinity. It doth not afford the marrow of *modern* divinity, but it is a true example of *ancient, primitive* divinity, of the teaching of the holy Spirit. All who are under the influence of the spirit are thus taught. The teaching of the spirit which is contrasted to the spirit of truth, exhibits the reverse, and engenders glooms and impenitence. It is our duty and our interest, to give heed unto the teaching of the divine spirit, for faith cometh by the hearing of the word of God. Wherever these sacred truths are received, a correspondent spirit will be manifested, the spirit will rejoice. In what? In God the Saviour; and the soul will magnify, not itself, but Jehovah. Let us examine and prove ourselves by these testimonies, and if we be indeed *true believers*, we shall possess that peace which the world can neither give, nor take away.

SKETCH XCI.

Luke i. 50, 51.

First, The mercy of the Lord is on them that fear him from generation to generation. Job v. 11, "To set up on high those that be low; that those which mourn may be exalted to safety."

Secondly, The Lord hath shewed strength with his arm. What is the arm of the Lord by which he manifests his strength? The arm of the Lord is the man Christ Jesus; this appears from the following scripture testimonies. Isaiah xl. 10, "God will come and his arm shall rule for him. Verse 11, "He shall gather the lambs with his arm." Chapter li. 5, "Mine arm shall judge the people, the isles shall wait upon me, and on mine arm shall they trust. Awake, awake, put on strength, O arm of the Lord." Chapter lii. 10, "The Lord hath made bare his holy arm in the eyes of all the nations; and all the ends of the earth shall see the salvation of our God." Chapter lix. 16, "Therefore his arm brought him salvation." Those who are under the law are under the curse; they make *flesh their arm*, of whom the prophet Jeremiah saith, xvii. 5, " Cursed be the man that maketh flesh his arm." It is with the arm of the LORD that he showeth strength as a Creator, as a Redeemer, and as the Conqueror of death, and him that had the power of death.

Thirdly, The LORD scattereth the proud, in the imagination of their hearts. Isaiah ii. 12, " The day of the LORD of hosts shall be upon every one that is proud and lofty, and upon every one that is lifted up, and he shall be brought low." Chapter xiii. 11, "And I will cause the arrogancy of the proud to cease, and will lay low the haughtiness of the terrible." Jeremiah l. 31, 32, " Behold I am against thee, O thou most proud, saith the God of hosts: And the most proud shall stumble and fall, and none shall raise him up." James iv. 6, " God resisteth the proud, but giveth grace to the humble." The imagination of the proud heart shall be scattered like the wind blown bubble, in the midst of their vain conceits they shall be scattered, but in the meek and lowly Saviour they shall be gathered, when every high and lofty imagination shall be brought low, and the LORD alone exalted.

The spirit of God spake by the lips of Mary. The strength of the LORD exemplified in his mighty arm should never be forgotten, it should be the unceasing theme of our praise and thanksgiving. While contemplating this arm of the LORD, we feel ourselves strong in the God of our salvation, and in the power of his might. Before this arm of the LORD all opposition is prostrated; he hath destroyed death and him that had the power of death; he hath overcome the world, he is greater than our hearts. He that believeth this will not make haste. He will quietly wait and patiently hope for the salvation of our God. Almighty God increase our faith, confirm our hope, and build us up in love.

SKETCH XCII.

Luke i. 52—55.

First, God hath put down the mighty from their seats, and exalted them of low degree. 1 Samuel ii. 7, "The Lord maketh poor, and maketh rich; he bringeth low, and lifteth up."

Secondly, *He hath filled the hungry with good things.* Hence, our Saviour saith, Matthew v. 6, "Blessed are they which do hunger and thirst after righteousness, for they shall be filled." John vi. 35, " Jesus said unto them, I am the bread of life, he that cometh to me shall never hunger." Revelations vii. 16, "They shall hunger no more." But suppose the *enemies of God* should hunger? Romans xii 20, "Therefore, if thine enemy hunger feed him."

Thirdly, The rich he hath sent empty away. Undoubtedly the rich, the spiritually rich, are not able to appreciate the value of the bread of life. They would not know how much they were indebted to God for his goodness, while they did not *feel the want of a Redeemer.*

Fourthly, He hath holpen his servant Israel, in remembrance of his mercy. Isaiah xxx. 18, "And therefore will the Lord wait that he may be gracious unto you, and therefore will he be exalted, that he may have mercy upon you." Jeremiah xxxi. 4, 20, "Again, I will build thee, O virgin of Israel. Is Ephraim my dear son? Is he a pleasant child? For since I spake against him, I do earnestly remember him still, I will surely have mercy upon him, saith the Lord."

Fifthly, All these declarations are in perfect conformity with the promises made to Abraham and to his seed forever. God doeth in heaven and in earth, as in his sight seemeth good. He bringeth down the mighty, they are low; but he *exalteth them of low degree.* He *brings down,* that he may *bring up,* he *killeth,* that he may *make alive;* and the hungry are not left to make provision for themselves. It is *God himself,* saith Mary, *that filleth the hungry,* and that too with *good things;* and it is sufficient that they *are hungry,* for then they will relish the bread of God, which giveth life unto the world. But, as the whole need not a physician, so the full must be sent away until they become hungry. When they are hungry, they will be proper subjects of God's mercy; and although they may not remember God's mercy, God cannot forget his most splendid attribute.

Lastly, The mercy of God is boundless. It is that mercy which was spoken of to the fathers, which embraces all the nations, all the families of the earth.

SKETCH XCIII.

Luke i. 68—70.

First, UNDER the influence of the holy Spirit, Zacharias saith, *Blessed be the LORD God of Israel, for he hath visited and redeemed his people.* Thus we hear the holy Spirit again pronouncing, that the LORD God of Israel is the Redeemer. It *was clothed* in *the* garments of humanity, that the God of Israel visited and redeemed his people.

Secondly, In this *nature,* in the *house* of his servant David, is raised up to us an horn of salvation. The horn is emblematick of power. Moses speaking of Joseph says, his horns are like the horns of an unicorn. But the horn is not only emblematick of power, but of glorious power. God, says the prophet Habakkuk, came from Paran, and his brightness was as the light, and he had horns coming out of his head, and there was the hiding of his power.

Thirdly, But this glorious display of power is a manifestation of salvation. Psalm cxxxii. 17, " There will I make the horn of David to bud. I have ordained a lamp for mine anointed by redemption"—God manifested in the flesh is our Redeemer. Romans xi. 26, "And so all Israel shall be saved, as it is written, there shall come out of Zion the deliverer, and shall turn away ungodliness from Jacob." Thus the sacred oracles testify of Christ Jesus both as the Ransom and the Ransomer. *He gave himself a ransom for all.*

Fourthly, God hath spoken by the mouth of his holy prophets, which have been since the world began. Jeremiah xxxi. 10, "He that scattered Israel will gather him, and keep him as a shepherd *doth his flock.*" The fundamental principle of the religion of God in both dispensations is the *unity* and *oneness* of God; and therefore the divine and human nature are no more to be considered *two Gods*, than the *body* and *soul* are to be considered *two men*. For this reason we cannot acknowledge a *God out of Christ, we can acknowledge no God beside the Saviour.* All God's dealings with the children of men lead to, and will finally terminate in salvation; for this truth was taught by all God's holy prophets, and the gospel of God our Saviour is not *yea* and *nay*. No one can be considered a believer, who does not believe this truth. Those who believe the gospel of God our Saviour will love God in their hearts, and will consequently take pleasure in hearing his words and in doing his will, and they will manifest the cheerfulness of their obedience both by word and by deed, to the utmost of their power. They will delight in adorning the doctrine of God our Saviour.

SKETCH XCIV.

Luke i. 71—75.

First, That *we should be saved from our enemies, and from the hand of all that hate us.* Psalm cvi. 10, "And he saved them from the hand of him that hated them; and redeemed them from the hand of the enemy."

Secondly, *To perform the mercy promised to our fathers.* Acts iii. 25, " Ye are the children of the prophets, and of the covenant which God made with our fathers, saying unto Abraham, And in thy seed shall all the kindred of the earth be blessed."

Thirdly, *To remember his holy covenant; the oath which he sware to our father Abraham.* Genesis xxii. 16, " By myself have I sworn, saith the Lord, that in blessing I will bless thee, and in multiplying I will multiply thy seed as the stars of heaven."

Fourthly, That he would grant unto us, that we, being delivered out of the hand of our enemies, might serve him without fear. Hebrews ix. 14, "How much more shall the blood of Christ, who, through the eternal Spirit, offered himself without spot to God, purge your conscience from dead works, to serve the living God."

Fifthly, In serving God without fear, we shall serve him *in holiness and righteousness all the days of our lives.* Jeremiah xxxii. 39, "And I will give them one heart and one way, that they may fear me forever, for the good of them, and of their children after them." Ephesians iv. 24, "And that ye put on the new man, which, after God, is created in righteousness and true holiness." 1Peter, i. 15, "But as he which hath called you is holy, so be ye holy in all manner of conversation." The evil spirit, which is emphatically styled your adversary, and which is seeking to devour, would assuredly effectuate his purpose, had not the seed of the woman bruised his head. God mercifully bound himself by covenant to bruise the head of this serpent. God hath covenanted that his ransomed shall serve him, that they shall serve him for ever. But the service of God is a service of love. By faith the believer begins his heaven below. The *just*, the *justified* live by faith; faith is the evidence of things not seen, and the substance of things hoped for. God is not served, but *by faith; as it respects the creature, whatever is not of faith, is sin;* and this we know, that perfect love casteth out fear. We, said the first christians, have not received the spirit of bondage again to fear. The religion grounded on *fear*, cannot be the religion of God. But there is a *filial fear* of offending so good, so gracious a Redeemer; and this *fear* is only experienced by real believers. May we, my beloved friends, be blessed with a large portion of this *holy fear*.

SKETCH XCV.

Luke i. 76—79.

Fisrt, AND *thou child shalt be called the prophet of the highest.* Isaiah xl. 3, "The voice of him that crieth in the wilderness, prepare ye the way of the LORD, make straight in the desert a high way for our God." Malachi iii. 1, "Behold, I will send my messenger, and he shall prepare the way before me." Matthew xi. 10, "For this is he, of whom it is written, Behold, I send my messenger before thy face, which shall prepare thy way before thee."

Secondly, But why doth this prophet precede the Messiah? *To give knowledge of salvation unto his people by the remission of their sins.* God's people then were sinners, and their salvation is by the *remission* of their sins; and this remission could only be obtained by the shedding of blood. Luke xxiv. 4, 7, " And that repentance and remission of sins, should be preached in his name among all nations, beginning at Jerusalem." Romans iii. 25, " Whom God hath sent forth to be a propitiation through faith in his blood, to declare his righteousness for the remission of sins that are past, through the forbearance of God."

Thirdly, *Through the tender mercies of our God, whereby the day spring from on high hath visited us.* Psalm cxlv. 9, "The LORD is good to all, and his tender mercies are over all his works." Yea, verily, it is through the tender mercies of our God, that the day spring from on high hath visited us. Malachi iv. 2, " But unto you that fear my name, shall the sun of righteousness arise with healing under his wings." John Baptist was the prophet which ushered in this morning without a cloud, this day spring from on high.

Fourthly, For what purpose? *To give light to them that sit in darkness and in the shadow of death; to guide our feet into the way of peace.* Isaiah ix. 2, " The people that walked in darkness have seen a great light: they that dwell in the land of the shadow of death, upon them hath the light shined." Isaiah xlii. 6, 7, " I the LORD will give thee for a covenant to the people, for a light to the Gentiles, to open the blind eyes, to bring out the prisoners from the prison, and them that sit in darkness out of the prison house." Isaiah xlix. 9, " That thou mayest say to the prisoners, Go forth: to them that are in darkness, Shew yourselves." Isaiah lx. 1, " Arise, shine: for thy light is come, and the glory of the LORD is risen upon thee." Although all God's holy prophets testified of the Redeemer, yet was the Baptist greater than all, inasmuch as he pointed out the fulfilment of their prophecies. They said, Messiah *shall come;* John said, he *is come.* Behold the Lamb of God. John prepared the way of the LORD by preaching repentance; he did not give salvation to God's people, he only gave the *knowledge* thereof. This knowledge of salvation, is through the remission or forgiveness of sins. God's *people were* sinners, and the remission of their sins was only gained through the tender mercies of the God, against whom they had sinned. It was this tender mercy of God, which gave light and life to the world. God so loved the world he gave them his Son, and this Son is the light of the world, and this Son will lighten every man that cometh into the world. Those who set in darkness are in the shadow of death; but their feet shall ultimately be guided into the way of peace. All believers are thus circumstanced, even in this present world. As we have received the Redeemer as our peace, so let us *walk in him.*

SKETCH XCVI.

Luke ii. 8—14.

First, Why was this message sent, in the first instance, to shepherds? Shepherds were figures of the ministers of the gospel. Jesus himself, to whom, by the divine Nature, the words of life were given, was denominated the *Shepherd of the sheep.*

Secondly, They were watching their flock when the heavenly visitant appeared. Shepherds are watchmen; the sheep are a species of animals, that are not able to take care of themselves. Shepherds are, therefore, appointed by the owner of the sheep for three especial reasons: First, To *lead.* Secondly, To *feed.* And thirdly, To *protect* them.

Thirdly, *The shepherds were watching their flocks by night.* A learned commentator remarks upon this clause in our text, that these shepherds being engaged in the open air, watching their flocks by night, is a proof that the birth of the Redeemer could not have taken place in the *winter.* But this learned commentator did not recollect, that in those countries where wine and oil are produced, the *wintry* season is never severe; that it is sufficiently mild to admit of *flocks, with their attending shepherds, passing the night in the open field.* It was necessary this astonishing intelligence should be delivered in the *winter season*, and *in the night.* First in the *winter season*, inasmuch as in the beautifully figurative language of revelation, the *wintry season* is selected to delineate the barren and comfortless state of human nature, previous to the *dawning of the sun of righteousness;* before the promulgation of that doctrine which was to drop as the rain, as the small rain upon the tender herb, and the showers upon the grass. Hence in the gospel dispensation, the *winter* is said to be over and gone, the time of the singing of birds to be come, and the voice of the turtle to be heard in the land.

Again, It was necessary this God-honouring, this divine message, should be delivered *in the night.* The vicissitudes of day and night are, we know, occasioned by, and dependent upon the presence or absence of the sun. The darkness called he night, and the light called he day. When the Saviour was born it was a time of *darkness:* darkness covered the earth, and *gross darkness* the people. Thus the propriety of proclaiming these glad tidings *in the night,* becomes *self-evident.*

Fourthly, The angel of the Lord came upon them. The visibility of disembodied spirits or celestial beings, to those who are yet clothed in mortality, is admitted by some and denied by others. It is a subject which has been, in all ages, strongly contested. But to call in question the visibility of angels, is to call in question the *veracity,* in other words, the *divinity* of revelation, since there is no truth more clearly taught and established, throughout the sacred volume, even from its commencement. The vision of the ladder, which the patriarch Jacob witnessed, was designed to teach him, that through the instrumentality of these heavenly visitants, a constant communication betwixt heaven and earth should exist.

By what means celestial spirits render themselves to our astonished gaze, and why we do not always behold those myriads of beings, which, both when we sleep and when we wake, do constantly throng around us, with many other points equally inexplicable, must be considered as *secret things which belong to God.* But, that angels have appeared, that they have been seen by men, and have conversed with them, is revealed to us and to our children.

Fifthly, And the *glory of the* Lord shone round about them. Not the *glory of the angels;* for they had no *independent glory.* Some writers have supposed, that it was the native glory of the angels which shone so bright, like the face of Moses when he descended from the mount, and that to this glory the shepherds could not lift their eyes. But the Spirit of God asserts, that the *glory of the* LORD shone round about them. Here a question is naturally suggested. What is the *glory of the* LORD ? Moses once desired to see God; but instead of seeing God, he was informed, that God would cause his glory to pass before him. "And God placed Moses in the cleft of the rock, while his glory passed by. And the LORD descended in the cloud, and stood with him there, and proclaimed the name of the LORD, while his glory passed by him. And the LORD passed by before him, and proclaimed, The LORD, the LORD God, merciful and gracious, long-suffering, and abundant in goodness and truth, keeping mercy for thousands, forgiving iniquity, and transgression and sin; and that will by no means clear the guilty: visiting the iniquity of the fathers upon the children, and upon the children's children, unto the third and to the fourth generation." This was the glory of God; and there is a divine consistency in its shining round about the angel dispatched upon such an embassy. "And the glory of the LORD shone round about them, as the rainbow of the covenant surrounding the throne of grace." Figures of this nature are calculated to show the eternal duration of God's favour, as the ring placed upon the finger of the prodigal, which had neither beginning nor ending, so the glory of the LORD shone round about the angel, rendering visible the excellency of this glory in every possible direction. Are we not justified in pronouncing this *glory an appropriate appendage to a proclamation of the birth of the world's Saviour?* who being the Saviour of all men, his salvation, like the glory of the LORD, shone round about the world of mankind.

Sixthly, If this glory was the *glory of the* LORD, how came it to pass, that the shepherds were sore afraid? Fear is a passion by no means peculiar to the mind of man. All animated nature is more or less subjected to this passion. But man knowing more of himself, is more fearful than any other animal; and those who are apprized of their *danger*, without being made acquainted with their *Deliverer*, are consequently greatly alarmed, are, of necessity, *fearful* and *unbelieving*. But the fears of individuals respecting Deity, respecting their God and Father, are no evidence of a disposition in the divine Nature to injure them. Guilt is the parent of terror; but from a *reconciled* God, ought we to look for any thing which can originate or justify terror? When the glory of the LORD shone round about these shepherds, their fears were excited by their *ignorance of God*; and so, just so, when the sinful world shall behold their Saviour in the clouds of heaven, with power and *great glory*, they will be sorely afraid; not apprehending him to be their *Saviour*, they will call upon the rocks and mountains to hide them from the wrath of that *Lamb of God, who hath taken away the sin of the world.* Yet, in the Lamb, there is certainly no wrath, but the *fearful* and *unbelieving*, judge from their own *darkened* and *tormented minds.*

Seventhly, And the angels said unto them, *Fear not.* But why should they not fear? Had they not reason to expect as much wrath as grace? Certainly they had not. Why, were they not *sinners?* Undoubtedly they were, nor were they bid to banish their fears by reverting to a contemplation of their own rectitude. The angel did not say *fear not*, for behold I have found you in the path of duty, watching your flocks even in the night season. No consideration of this description was urged by this messenger of God. The only reason produced by this angelic preacher, why these poor affrighted shepherds should not fear, was based upon the message he was about to deliver. Fear not; for behold I bring you *good tidings of great joy which shall be to all people.*

What were these glad tidings of great joy, which were to be to *all people?* That they may be *saved if they would?* That there was a Saviour born unto *believers?* Do you not, my beloved hearers, know, that this was not the language of this celestial messenger?

But what were these glad tidings? *There is born unto you this day, in the city of David, a Saviour which is Christ the LORD.* This consideration was in truth, and indeed sufficient to banish, to annihilate their fears, for he could not be their *Saviour*, if they were never to be *saved;* he could not be the *Saviour* of any individual who was never *saved.* These tidings were indeed glad tidings of great joy. But were there no signs given by which these shepherds were to know whether they were saved or not? Signs were unnecessary, as we shall observe in the conclusion of our subject; indeed signs were given by which they might determine the identity of the Babe, whose birth was thus gloriously announced. Yet those signs were calculated rather to diminish than augment their faith. Ye shall find the Babe wrapped in swaddling clothes lying in a manger. These signs, to a people the wisest of whom believed, that the appearance of the Messiah would restore the pristine glory, and grandeur of the kingdom of Israel; nay, would place it in circumstances which should make it surpass its ancient splendour, whose ideas all centered in a terrestrial kingdom. To such individuals I say the appearance of a babe wrapped in swaddling clothes, and lying in a manger, exhibited no proof that the intelligence they had received was of divine origin. Poverty was stamped in legible characters upon the new born infant, upon his mother, and upon his supposed father. The prejudices of the Jewish nation were strong in favour of worldly grandeur. Yet the birth was strikingly announced; the character of the messenger was unquestionable. We know that nothing short of the *power* of God, can make a believer, and the *power* of God was upon this occasion wonderfully manifested, while, to corroborate the divine testimony, *suddenly there was with the angel, a multitude of the heavenly hosts praising God*, and *saying, Glory be to God in the highest, and on earth peace and good will toward men.*

Toward men. It appears that the shepherds conceived themselves included in this general description; they were men, and this was their title to the peace and good will descending from heaven. They hastened to Bethlehem, they were the first to do homage to the cradled infant, and they returned glorifying and praising God for all the things that they had heard and seen, which had been told unto them.

Let us, my beloved friends, unite with these believing shepherds in adoring our God in his state of humiliation; let us follow him worshipping, even from the manger through all the various scenes of his suffering, blameless life, till we see him taken down from the cross, till we behold him laid in the sepulchre. Let us follow him in imagination to those abodes of darkness, whither, as we are informed by the apostle Peter, he went to preach the gospel to those imprisoned spirits, who were sometimes disobedient in the days of Noah. Do we not see the sudden illumination of those prisoners of darkness? Do we not behold them leaping from their dungeons at the sound of their Redeemer's voice? Their preacher is Almighty, his doctrines are luminous, he speaks as never man spake, information must follow, they cannot but know God, their emancipation is certain, their chains are broken, and what heart but must congratulate those long-suffering, those finally liberated spirits?

Let us follow the Saviour in his triumphant resurrection. Let us transfer our affections to that heaven into which he has entered; let us prostrate before the throne of grace and devoutly say, Whom have I in heaven but thee? And there are none on earth that I desire beside thee. We, who have tasted that the LORD is gracious, have every incentive to love, to adoration and to praise; we have every incentive to gratitude, every motive to stimulate to the adornment of that doctrine, on which our future hopes of happiness are based. I conjure you, my dear hearers, my long loved friends, to be careful to add to your faith, virtue; let no one say in reference to you, *There, there*, so would we have it. Give not our adversary, or his adherents, reason to triumph over you; but give, I beseech you, give, I conjure you, give, I charge you, GIVE unto the God of your salvation, *your whole heart.*

SKETCH XCVII.

LUKE iv. 4.

First, To whom did our Saviour upon this occasion reply? To the grand adversary, who arrogantly dared even in the presence of Deity, to sanction his seductive wiles, by the authority of sacred writ.

Secondly, What advantage did he reap by his presumption? He learned, to his confussion, that man should LIVE. This declaration both tormented and surprised him; he had heard the Creator say, in the day thou eatest, thou shalt surely DIE, and although he knew himself to be a liar, he knew the Creator was a God of truth. Blessed be the name of this God of truth, *There was a way which this Vulture's eye had never seen.*

Thirdly, How could man, sinful man LIVE *by every word of God?* Was not the law the word of God? and is not this law said to be the ministration of DEATH?

But, Fourthly, For the consolation of every one, who is solicitous for the honour of God, and the felicity of man, and to the confusion of the adversary, and all those in whose paths are *misery and death;* let us once more listen to the Redeemer of men. John xii. 49, 50, "For I have not spoken of myself: but the Father which sent me, he gave me a commandment, what I should say, and what I should speak. And I know that his commandment is LIFE everlasting; whatsoever I speak therefore, even as the Father said unto me, so I speak."

I know, said Emmanuel, that this commandment is LIFE everlasting. The testimony of the royal Prophet, Psalm xix. 7, 8, 9, Beautifully illustrates and confirms the doctrine of our text. "The law of the LORD is perfect, converting the soul; the testimony of the LORD is sure, making wise the simple. The statutes of the LORD are right, rejoicing the heart; the commandment of the LORD is pure, enlightening the eyes. The fear of the LORD is clean, enduring forever: the judgments of the LORD are true and righteous altogether."

SKETCH XCVIII.

John i. 1—4.

First, In the beginning was the WORD, and the word was with God, and the WORD was God. We are informed that the WORD in Hebrew, *Dabar*, in Greek, *Logos*, is the eternal Son of God, the uncreated wisdom. The Evangelist, says a learned Commentator, to impress every reader with a sense of the dignity of Christ, as God, gives an account of his first existence, in quality of the logos or WORD of God, and Creator of the world. According to the Greek etymology, the word logos signifies the reason of God, or the wisdom of God. The eighth chapter of the Proverbs of Solomon contains a luminous and beautiful delineation of the God-man; and, saith our text, the word was God. The human nature of the Redeemer is styled the WORD; he being the express image of the Father, as our words are of our thoughts. Thus, the apostle Paul in his epistle to the Hebrews, chapter i. 3, "Who being the brightness of his glory, and the express image of his person, and upholding all things by the word of his power, when he had by himself purged our sins, sat down on the right hand of the Majesty on high."

Secondly, The Jews considered the Messiah as the WORD of God, and to this WORD they ascribed all the attributes of the Deity. They tell us that *Memra* or the WORD, which created the world, appeared to Moses on mount Sinai, to Abraham on the plains of Mamre, and to Jacob at Bethel. In fact, God has never manifested himself to the children of men, in any other character, and as a man, body, soul and spirit is but one man, so Father, WORD, and Holy Ghost is but one God. It was to exhibit God to the human family, in this character, that the gospel of St. Luke was written, and we embrace, as a first principle, that truth, which asserts that Jesus Christ is the *only wise God our Saviour*. Matthew i. 23, "And they shall call his name Emmanuel, which being interpreted is, God with us."

Thirdly, *All things were made by him, and without him was not any thing made, that was made.* Thus the word is the Creator. John i. 10. "He was in the world, and the world was made by him, and the world knew him not." Psalm xxxiii. 6, "By the word of the LORD were the heavens made; and all the hosts of them by the breath of his mouth."

Fourthly, In him was life, and the life was the light of men. Colossians iii. 4, "When Christ who is our life shall appear, then shall ye also appear with him in glory." Jesus Christ is indeed the light of men. John i. 9, "The true light which lighteth every man that *cometh into the* world." He is before all things, and by him all things consist. Finally, 1 John v. 11 "*This is the record, that God hath given to us eternal life, and this life is in his Son.*"

SKETCH XCIX.

John i. 18.

First, **W**HAT is God? He is a spirit; He is that *self created, self existent Being*, who in the beginning said, "Let *us* make man in our own image:" and in the image of God created he them, and called *their names Adam.* Thus was exhibited a figure of God manifest in the flesh, the divine in the human nature. He called *their names* Adam. The same name is named on them. HE shall be called the LORD our righteousness. SHE shall be called the LORD our righteousness. The *divine in the human nature, or the soul in the body.* No man hath at any time seen the soul. Exodus xxxiii. 20, "And he said thou canst not see my face; for there shall no man see me and live."

Secondly, What are we to understand by the only begotten of the Father? The only one of the human race, which was begotten by the divine Nature. Matthew i, 20, " But while he thought on these things, behold, the angel of the LORD appeared unto him in a dream, saying, Joseph, thou son of David, fear not to take unto thee Mary thy wife: for that which is conceived in her is of the Holy Ghost." Isaiah vii. 14, " Therefore, the LORD himself shall give you a sign: behold, a virgin shall conceive, and bear a son, and shall call his name Immanuel. Luke i. 35, " And the angel answered and said unto her, The Holy Ghost shall come upon thee, and the power of the Highest shall overshadow thee; therefore also that holy thing, which shall be born of thee, shall be called the Son of God." In the seventy-third verse of this memorable chapter, Zacharias refers to the oath which God sware to our Father Abraham, as recorded Genesis xxii. 16. The apostle Paul alludes to this promise, Romans i. 2, " Which he hath promised afore by his prophets in the holy scriptures.

Thirdly, The only begotten Son of God is said to be in the bosom of the Father. The Holy Ghost speaketh in the present tense. The only begotten Son, *which is in the bosom of the*

Father. John iii. 13, "And no man hath ascended up to heaven but he that came down from heaven, even the Son of man *which is in heaven.*"

Fourthly, The only begotten Son which is in the bosom of the Father. This is a figurative phrase. The bosom is that part of the body in which the heart is enclosed, and the affections are seated in the heart. It is while engaged in considering this and a variety of similar testimonies that the mind is prone to wander from the simplicity of truth. We can hardly forbear conceiving of the Father as a being constructed precisely as we ourselves are not attending to the figure which the Almighty hath manifested of himself, for although the soul has affections, it has no heart, no heart of flesh, but as manifested in the body; so the affections of the divine nature is manifested in the human nature, which is the body, that body which was prepared for the Redeemer; a body hast thou prepared for me, &c. &c.

Fifthly and lastly, No man can know the Father, but the Son, and those to whom the Son declares him. The only begotten Son which is in the bosom of the Father, he hath declared him. Emmanuel hath declared him. Emmanuel, the God-man, the divine and human Nature united. John xvii. 26, " And I have declared unto them thy name, and will declare it; that the love wherewith thou hast loved me may be in them, and I in them." How fraternal, how becoming the character of an elder brother is the reason affectionately rendered by the Redeemer—that the love wherewith thou hast loved me may be in them, and I in them. Chapter xv. 15, " Henceforth I call you not servants, for the servant knoweth not what his lord doeth, but I have called you friends, for all things that I have heard of my Father, I have made known to you." Gracious, ever gracious, ever condescending Redeemer, with what rapturous adoration shall we through the wasteless ages of eternity echo the loud hallelujah to thy glorious, thy emphatic name. Again Chapter vi. 45, our Lord saith, " It is written in the prophets they shall be all taught of God." How rational, how truly divine is the inference, " Every man therefore that hath *heard* and hath *learned* of the Father cometh unto me." Most luminous, most blessed is the divine Teacher whom by sweet and powerful constraint we shall all eventually approach. By his teaching we shall indeed be made wise unto salvation, for this *omniscient, omnipotent* Prophet, Priest and King is the true light, that *lighteth every man who cometh into the world. The light of the world.* GLORY BE TO GOD.

SKETCH C.

JOHN vi. 28, 29.

First, MEN arrogantly conceive themselves capable of doing the *works of God.* Matthew xix. 16, "And, behold, one came and said unto him, Good master, what good thing shall I do, that I may have eternal life?" Acts xvi. 30, " Sir, what must I do to be saved ?" Chapter ii. 37, " Men and brethren, what shall we do?" And in our text, *What shall we do that we might work the works of God ?*

Secondly, Jesus answered and said unto them, this is the work of God that ye *believe on him whom he hath sent.* This answer was given by him who spake as *never man spake.* But what are we to understand by believing on him whom God hath sent? God sent his Son into the world to destroy the works of the devil. Can we believe in Jesus Christ, and not believe this truth? And we have seen and do testify that the Father sent the Son to be the Saviour of the world. Can I believe in Jesus Christ, and not admit this *good report ?* " For I came down from heaven, not to do mine own will but the will of him that sent me." *What is the will of God?* The will of God is that *all men should be saved, and come unto the knowledge of the truth.* But the Redeemer came to *do* the will of him that sent him.

Thirdly, This believing on the sent Saviour is not the work of any created being, it is the work of God himself. God knoweth this, and it is therefore he saith, John xii. 47, " And if any man hear my words and believe not, I judge him not; for I came not to judge the world, but to *save the world.*" Faith is the gift of God. It is God who powerfully worketh this work of faith. No man can know the things of God but by the spirit of God. Paul may plant, and Apollos water, but it is *God who giveth the increase.*

SKETCH CI.

John vi. 67, 68.

Many of our Saviour's hearers left him, and thus leaving the rock of their salvation, attached themselves to lying vanities. This fact naturally originated this affecting question. *"Will ye also go away?* And the question produced the reply, *"Lord, to whom should we go? Thou hast the words of eternal life."* It is frequently affirmed by our adversaries that we shall not continue in our present sentiments, that we shall reject the doctrines we now embrace, that we shall turn back; but our reason for not turning back is the best possible reason. *Jesus hath the words of eternal life.* But we will inquire,

First, For what I pray you shall we turn back? *For eternal life?* Where have we life but where we are. Christ Jesus hath the words of eternal life. Shall we go from Christ to Moses, or can we desire to be again under the law? Hearken ye that desire to be under the law, do ye not hear the law? Galatians iii. 10, "For as many as are of the works of the law, are under the curse; for it is written, Cursed is every one which continueth not in all things that are written in the book of the law to do them." Shall we turn from the *master* to the *servant*, from the *blessing* to the *curse*, from the ministration of salvation and life, to the ministration of condemnation and death?

Secondly, Shall we turn from the Redeemer of the world to John? From the baptism of the one, to the baptism of the other?

Thirdly, Shall we turn from the glorious High Priest of our profession, to any who are in subordination to the traditions of men?

Fourthly, Shall we turn from the *righteousness of God*, which is by faith of Christ Jesus, unto the *righteousness found in the creature*, and the faith of the creature consequent thereon?

Fifthly, Shall we leave him who was *given by Jehovah* as a covenant to the people, and turn to *fabricating covenants for ourselves?* What, turn from an everlasting covenant to those enfeebled exertions, those fluctuating compacts in which there is no stability? Shall we adopt the conduct of the people described by Jeremiah, ii. 12, 13, when the heavens were called upon to be astonished, to be horribly afraid, to be very desolate, because the people of God had committed two evils; they had forsaken him, the fountain of living waters, and hewed them out cisterns, broken cisterns, which could hold no water. We are melted by this paternal enquiry, Is Israel a servant? Is he a home-born slave? Why is he spoiled?

What infatuation should we evince, were we to turn from the peace made by the blood of the cross, and from him who made that peace, and who is, therefore, *our peace*, which peace and which covenant can never be removed?

Sixthly, Shall we leave him who is made of God unto us sanctification, and turn to the santification exhibited by an imperfect creature? Shall we turn from the holiness we possess in Christ Jesus, which holiness *renders us perfect, even as our Father who is in heaven is perfect?* Shall we turn from this immaculate holiness, to the holiness found in a being who, in his *best estate, is vanity?*

Once we fed on husks; but we have returned to the house of our almighty Father, where there is enough and to spare; corn, wine, and oil in abundance; where there is enough for every child of Adam, and still there will be to spare. Shall we turn back to these husks, spending our money for that which is not bread, and our labour for that which satisfieth not? Shall we refuse to receive wine and milk without money and without price, even that wine which maketh glad the heart of God and man, which is the fruit of the true vine unadulterated, well refined on the lees, pure from those drugs used by wine merchants, who sell, at a great price, the wine of their own manufacturing, prepared from the fruit of the degenerate vine? Shall *we*, who, when babes were fed with the sincere milk of the word, having grown thereby, turn back to a gross compound of hypocrisy and self-conceit, which is a milk, not of the word of God that abideth forever, but of the doctrines and traditions of men? Shall we turn from that which is to be purchased without money and without price, and go back to that which, although destitute of real value, is yet sold at a very high price? Shall we turn from the love of God which thinketh no evil to the love of the creature, however alluring his blandishments, who is continually devising mischief? Made wise by experience, we are not now to be taught, that the imaginations of the human heart are evil, and that continually. Shall we, who have heretofore been imposed upon, who were once made to call in question the sufficiency, the all-sufficiency, and durability of the living fountain, and, under these impressions, sat about preparing, with abundant labour and much time, cisterns for ourselves, which, after a vast accumulation of expense, proved broken cisterns which could hold no water, shall we unwisely turn back to this worse than unprofitable labour? O, no; having drank of the never-failing spring, we indulge a hope, that it is not decreed we shall be so far deprived of our spiritual senses, as to act a part totally unbecoming the christian character.

We have found Jesus of whom Moses and the prophets testified, we have found a friend, an approved friend; we had formerly *many friends*, for we were supposed spiritually rich, and we have exchanged honourable proofs of mutual friendship; but we have found the friendship of this world vain and perishing.

When we confessed we were sinners, and that eternal misery was our due, when we frankly and unequivocally declared this truth, nay, more, when we boldly affirmed, that we accounted all things which we once imagined we possessed, (and which our very dear friends still boasted,) but dross, for the excellency of the knowledge of Christ Jesus the Lord, when we dared thus to think, thus to speak, we experienced that their friendship was not only vain, but vexatious. We discovered, that the *best* of these *once professing, once dear friends, was a brier; and the most upright amongst them, sharper than a thorn hedge.* We beheld our once affectionate friends, who had loved us in *word* almost as well as they loved themselves, we beheld those *very affectionate friends our most dangerous, most inveterate enemies!* When we affirmed, that the individuals, every individual of the human family, possessed every spiritual blessing in the seed of Abraham, the tongues once lavish in our praise, which seemed as dipped in oil when expatiating upon our virtues, were now, as if *set on fire of hell;* the poison of asps was under them, and their mouths were full of cursing and bitterness!!

Shall we then leave our *faithful* and *true* Friend, and turn back to those who are faithless and false? The Friend to whom we render the homage of our most pious affections, is the *sinner's*

Friend. Shall we who feel that *we are sinners*, leave this Friend and turn to the *adversary of sinners*, to the accuser of the brethren? The Friend with whom we are at length brought acquainted, is the same *yesterday, to-day,* and *forever;* with him is no variableness nor shadow of changing. He was the sinner's Friend, before the sinner knew it; indeed, before the sinner knew himself. He was the Friend of the helpless sinner, before the world was, and that, not in word only, but in *deed and in truth;* and, as a proof of his love, he gave them grace in Christ Jesus *before* the foundation of the world was laid; and from that period, this Creator, this Redeemer, this Preserver, this *Friend,* has been giving them, both in providence and in grace, unceasing proofs of his never-failing affection. Greater love hath no man than this, that he lay down his life for his friend. But this divine Friend, by whom we are called, and who hath made himself manifest unto us, has proved his love so strong, and that for his enemies, as to die for them while they were yet sinners! Shall we leave this Friend, and attach ourselves to *treachery* and to *fraud?* Never, never; forbid it thou never-failing Friend; forbid it thou who hast graciously said, I will never leave thee, nor forsake thee. When thou passest through the waters, I will be with thee, that they shall not drown thee; when thou passest through the fire, I will be with thee, that the flame shall not kindle upon thee.

Moreover, we have reasons, and very substantial reasons, for not leaving our Saviour and turning to any other. This divine Saviour has what no one ever had, what no one ever can have, *everlasting life. Thou hast the words of eternal life.* Could we find another God, or any being possessing his name, and were that being not an impostor, he would say, upon our application to him, "You are defeating your own purpose, you are missing your object, you are departing from the only-wise God the Saviour, in whom is life, and who is the light of the world, and you are turning to another, who, however benevolent in purpose, cannot save. I now, therefore, tell you, as there is no God beside the Saviour, and as there is no eternal life out of him, you would do well to hold fast the profession you seem to be quitting. I counsel you to return to your strong hold, to him in whom your life is hid; and I beseech you to rest in the assurance, that when Christ, who is your life, shall appear, you also shall appear with him in glory."

Again, Should we apply to Moses for life eternal, true to the dispensation which was committed to him, he would say, "Why come to me for life? I am but a servant; I have no abiding place in the house; I forfeited my own life, nor could gain admittance into the promised land. I could not bestow support even to the natural life. The Jews, indeed, imagined that it was I who gave them manna; but they grossly erred. It was their everlasting Father who gave them that bread, as the figure of himself, who is the true bread of God, that cometh down from heaven, giving unto the world eternal life. This, it was beyond my power to do." But, should we add, We demand of you what we shall do to be saved? He would naturally reply, "I have already told you; if you would enter into life, keep the commandments." But how must we keep them? "You must keep them with all your heart, with all your mind, with all your soul, and with all your strength; and you must continue thus to do, or be *written accursed:* for should you, in some unguarded moment, turn from your obedience, your former righteousness should not be remembered." But, upon this principle, if your testimony be *literally true*, we have gained nothing. "My testimony is, I assure you, literally true; the Jews, indeed, thought I did not mean what I said, and, therefore, undertook to give my words a construction, which never entered into my head or heart! Yet I declare to you, my words were always a picture of my thoughts." Well, then, we can expect nothing but death from you. "*It is granted; the law which came by me, was truly the ministration of condemnation and of death; and by the deeds of this law, no flesh living can be justified, nay, its administration communicates the knowledge of sin.*" Why then was it given? "My law, like every thing else, was made for him, of whom I spake unto the Jews, when I said, A prophet shall the LORD your God raise up unto you; like unto me, him shall ye hear." But how was this prophet like unto you? Is it not said of him, that he came not to condemn the world, but that the world through him might be saved? And is not his ministration said to be a ministration of life, while yours is described as the ministration of death? "He was like me in many respects, or rather I was, in many respects, made a likeness or figure of him."

"I was a leader of the suffering Israelites, leading them out of bondage, God made choice of me to bring them out; so was the prophet, of whom I spake, made a Leader and a Captain of salvation, to bring the children of men out of spiritual slavery and bondage, into liberty and rest. But you will do well to recollect the transaction which took place upon the mount of transfiguration, in the presence of Elijah and myself. Three of the disciples of the prophet, of whom I was a type, were desirous of building tabernacles for us, as well as for their Master, thus aiming to revive and perpetuate what God himself had buried. How solemn, how immediate, and how unequivocal was the reply; you, no doubt, recollect it; surely, it ought never to be forgotten; it was from Jehovah himself. Peter had said unto Jesus, Master, it is good for us to be here: and let us make three tabernacles; one for thee, and one for Moses, and one for Elias: *not knowing what he said*—When, lo! even while he thus spake, there came a cloud and overshadowed them, and they feared as they entered the cloud. And there came a voice out of the cloud, saying, *This is my beloved Son:* HEAR HIM. Will you not yield obedience to this gracious command? Will you not listen to his teaching, who says, Come unto me all ye that labour, and are heavy laden, and I will give you rest? My *burden was very heavy*, so heavy, that none of the fathers were able to bear it, but his burden is light. My yoke was very galling, but the yoke of the Redeemer is very easy; and the longer it is worn, the less oppressive it becomes. The ways of the Redeemer, are ways of pleasantness, and all his paths are peace. Return then to your *true rest*, for it is more glorious than my unyielding ministration. In one word, *I cannot give you life;* I am but a servant; I could not, if I would, make you free; but Christ Jesus is the Son, *and if the Son make you free, you will be free indeed*. Behold, he hath already delivered you from the curse of the law, and that, by submitting to it himself, by condescending to be *made a curse for you*. Go then, and do as I do, fall before his throne with humble gratitude, acknowledge your infinite obligations to him who was made under the law, of which I was the promulgator, that he may redeem you, and every other sinner adverted to in that law from its curse; and it is, therefore, that in him is life, and this life is the life of the world."

Again, to whom should we go? Shall we go to John the Baptist? John had, John has his disciples, as has Moses. What would this faithful servant of our gracious Master say unto us, were we to go from our common Redeemer, unto him? Would he not say, " Why comest thou to me ?" And should you reply, the Saviour himself did this, seeking baptism from thee, would he not say, " To my great astonishment he did, and I ventured to ask a reason for this humiliation, well knowing that I needed it of him who was in every respect my superior, the latchet of whose shoes I was not worthy to loose; but I submitted, when he answered, *Suffer it to be so now, for thus it becometh us to fulfil all righteousness*—In other words, as I was under the law, and was sent to baptize with water unto repentance, not to break but to fulfil the law, and thus by fulfilling, to become the end of it, whatsoever the law enjoined either preceptive or penal, either in its ceremonial or substantial character, he the Redeemer of men condescending to be *made under it, was bound to fulfil.*

" But, as Emmanuel included in himself the fulness of the human nature, being the second Adam, with strict propriety he said, *Suffer it to be so now, for thus it becometh us to fulfil all righteousness.* Thus, our common Saviour meekly replied, by rendering a reason why I should submit to his direction, which knowing him as I did, both in his *divine* and *mediatorial character*, I ought to have followed without a question. Yet, ever gracious, ever merciful, he acted in his accustomed manner, showing me unmerited favour. But, you will recollect, I informed the multitude who flocked to my baptism, that I must *decrease*, that I directed their attention to *him as the Saviour of the world, and that I called upon them to behold the Lamb of God who taketh away the sin of the world.* I gave those whom I baptized no reason to think they had any life or any true light in me, I told them I was not the master, I was no more than the harbinger of the true light, even with respect to my baptism; I said it was *water*, and unto repentance, but this could take away no more than the outward defilement of the flesh. I observed to my disciples that my superior should baptize with very different materials, that he should *baptize with the Holy Ghost and with fire, you* would do well to remember that I said I should *decrease*, and he should *increase.* As the increase of the sun's light seemeth to extinguish as it appears, the borrowed rays of the moon, so as the knowledge of the substance progressed, the figure would be less regarded.

" Washing with water, therefore, has become a beggarly element, it can do nothing more than put away the filth of the flesh.

It cannot furnish the answer of a good conscience, this can only be obtained by the resurrection of Jesus Christ from the dead. But we being in him, as his fulness, crucified with him, and in this baptism of his sufferings, buried with him in his death, we rise with him in his resurrection, in which resurrection we are presented without spot and blameless, having the answer of a good conscience toward God.

"But those who issued from the water, in which I baptized them, were still sinners before God. The water was not *powerful* to bestow either upon the baptized, or the *baptizer*; the answer of a good conscience either before or toward God; in one word, be assured, that in me as a baptizer, you have no life." Why then did our great Master say unto his disciples, Go ye into all the world, and teach all nations, baptizing them in the name of the Father, of the Son, and of the Holy Ghost? "With great propriety did our Saviour give this command. Yet he did not say, Go teach all nations, baptizing them in Jordan, or in any other *water*. He did not distinguish my baptism; but he said, baptize all nations in *my name*, in the name of the *Father*, *Son*, and *Holy Ghost*, that all the families of the earth may be as much in him, whether in the *character Father*, *Son*, or *Holy Ghost*, as all the members of the body of the individual baptized in the water, were in that water baptized. Agreeably to this testimony, you have heard the great Master say, I in them, and thou in me, that we may be made perfect in one; such too, was the gospel preached by Jehovah, unto Abraham our father, when he proclaimed and in thy seed shall all the families of the earth be blessed."

But is not believing mentioned as preceding baptism? "Not by St. Matthew; and thus runs the testimony as recorded by St. Mark, xvi. 16, He that *believeth and is baptized shall be saved, but he that believeth not shall be damned.* The *belief* of the gospel which precedes baptism, in like manner as the gospel preceded the accomplishment of what it foretold, when it was preached to Abraham, seems designed as the means of saving the mind or conscience, from the misery to which it is subjected, consequent upon unbelief. It should be observed, that the gospel, that is, the glad tidings of their restoration, was preached to every creature *before they believed;* it was preached for the purpose of rendering them believers, while the emancipation of the mind, from a sense of guilt and terror, was the result of that salvation, which could only take place on their embracing the truth; on their *believing* the gospel. If we would know who are those that are saved, upon commencing believers, the Redeemer himself informs us; And these signs shall follow them that believe; in my name shall they cast out devils; they shall speak with new tongues; they shall take up serpents; and if they drink any deadly thing, it shall not hurt them; they shall lay hands on the sick, and they shall recover.

As these were the parting words of our blessed Lord, in the moment of his being received up into heaven, we ought not to dispute them. Indeed it is impious to question the truth or consistency of any of the sayings of our Lord, for he spake at all times as never man spake. An adulterous generation is ever asking after a sign. Here are signs, infallible signs, marks and evidences of *true faith*."

Thus, it is abundantly plain, you can gain nothing by leaving Christ Jesus and his baptism, for John and his baptism. This or something of this nature would very probably fall from the lips of this devoted and faithful servant, this believing witness and harbinger of our divine Master, to any applicant who should contemplate leaving the rock of ages, and reposing on him who was at best *a reed shaken by the wind*.

Although the Apostles of our Lord were divinely taught, and consequently spake as moved by the Holy Ghost; although Paul might plant, and Apollos might water, yet they preached not *themselves, but Christ Jesus the Lord*. Should we therefore leave the Master, and turn to the servants, should we appeal to Peter and to John, they would answer, " Why refer to us? We are men of like passions with yourselves. We do nothing but in the name, and by the power of that Jesus, you are leaving;" should we call upon the Apostle to the Gentiles, he would reply, by pertinently asking, "Was Paul crucified for you? I am as you are, a sinner; once indeed, I imagined myself righteous, and, that as touching the law, my life was blameless, but now my eyes being opened, I see the vanity of all those expectations, which I so arrogantly cherished, while in the same moment, I was suffering in the want of what I now richly enjoy, that is, the assurance of understanding, that is, peace of conscience, and joy in the Holy Ghost, and that blessed confidence, that nothing could ever separate me from the love of God which is in Christ Jesus our LORD." This faithful servant would further say to every one, who would turn to him, saying, *I am of Paul.* " I beseech you, my friends, be as I am, for I am as you are. Are you sinners? So am I, nay, my transgressions surpass yours, for I am *the chief of sinners.* Yet have I redemption in the Beloved, which redemption is equally yours. If I am accepted in the beloved, so also is every individual of the human family. Am I complete in Christ Jesus? So are you. Did Jesus Christ put away my sin by the sacrifice of himself? *Remember he put away yours also.* Did he reconcile me unto himself by Jesus Christ? So, let me assure you, *precisely so,* was he reconciling *the world* unto himself, and the ministry, which God our Saviour was graciously pleased to commit unto me, was the ministry of reconciliation, viz. that God was in Christ reconciling the world unto himself, not imputing unto them their trespasses.

" It was, my enquiring friends, when you and I, and all mankind were like sheep going astray, that the LORD laid on him, Jesus, the iniquities of us all, that those accumulated and collected iniquities, being found upon him, the punishment and death which the law denounced upon the offender, might fall upon the head of every offender, *that the cause and effect might be forever removed.*

" Instead, therefore, of your leaving this blessed, this dear, this blessing, this ever blessing Redeemer, in whom you, and all the families of the earth are already blessed. Instead, I say, of your leaving him, the fountain of light, who hath died to redeem you, and coming to me, who am unequal of myself even to think a good thought, with whom evil, when I would do good, is ever present. Instead of an application so irrational, it is both your interest and your duty to turn from the *servant* to the LORD and *Master,* whose grace, is at all times sufficient for you, and, suffer me to entreat, to charge you, if you would possess that peace, which passeth understanding, to trust *solely* in the LORD Jesus, to trust in him as made of God unto *you,* exactly in the same manner, that he was unto *me* wisdom, that so neither you nor I may die for lack of knowledge; who is made of God unto *you,* and unto *me your fellow sinner?* Righteousness, that so through all eternity, we may inherit what the unrighteous never could inherit;

that is, the kingdom of God, which kingdom consisteth not in meats nor in drinks, but in righteousness, peace and joy in the Holy Ghost, who is made of God unto us in whom, that is, our flesh, dwelleth no good thing, *sanctification*, that so in him we may be presented before God, without spot, and blameless in love, and finally who is made unto us redemption; for, from ancient times he hath been manifested as the Redeemer, and when he condescended to clothe himself with our nature, as with a garment, it was that he might redeem us from all iniquity."

Christ Jesus hath finished his warfare, and when the Redeemer cried with a loud voice, it is finished, he immediately gave up the ghost, and thus having taken away the *sins of the world*, he appeared in the morning of his resurrection without sin unto full salvation. No wonder then, that joining issue with the apostle Peter, we uniformly and devoutly ask, " LORD *to whom shall we go? Thou hast the words of eternal* LIFE."

SKETCH CII.

John x. 36.

First, The Jews considered it blasphemy for the Saviour of the world, to call himself the Son of God. What I beseech you is blasphemy? Is it not speaking evil of God? Did the Jews consider it speaking evil of God for Emmanuel, the *God-head clothed in flesh, to call himself in his human character* the son of God? Father and Son are relative terms, Producer and Produced. The divine Nature produced the human Nature, and, therefore, the Deity assuming a robe of flesh accommodated himself to our understanding by styling himself, in several passages, the *son;* although in reference to the divine Nature, he elsewhere affirms, that the Father and he are one, and these important facts are *reconcileable* when we revert to the same Almighty being condescendingly exhibiting himself to the children of men in various characters.

But, Secondly, Our Saviour appeals to these accusing Jews in the verses immediately preceding my text. *Jesus answered them, Is it not written in your* law, *I said ye are gods ?*

If he called them gods, unto whom the word of God came, and the scriptures cannot be broken. "Say ye of him, whom the Father hath sanctified and sent into the world, Thou blasphemist, *because I said I am the Son of God.*"

In the eighty-second Psalm, Asaph affirms, " I have said, ye are gods, and all of you are children of the Most High: but ye shall die like men, and fall like one of the princes."

If it were not plasphemy to attach to the *mere children of men* the term God ; how strange was the accusation preferred against Emmanuel ! But our Saviour observes,

If I do not the works of my Father, believe me not. But if I do, though you believe not me, believe the works, that ye may know and believe, that the Father *is in me, and I in him.*

But the condescending, the benign Redeemer of lost men had said, *I and my Father are one*, and for this truth, the enraged multitude impiously stoned the God-man, the Redeemer of the world.

Thirdly, *Say ye of him whom the Father hath sanctified.* What are we to understand by the term sanctified? It is to separate or appoint any person or thing to any holy office or use. The first born under the law were sanctified. Exodus xiii. 2, " Sanctify unto me all the first born, whatsoever openeth the womb among the children of Israel, both of man and of beast; it is mine." The LORD is said to be sanctified, when his glory is made manifest to the work of his hands Numbers xx. 12, 13, " And the LORD spake unto Moses and Aaron, Because ye believed me not, to sanctify me in the eyes of the children of Israel, therefore ye shall not bring this congregation into the land which I have given them.

"This is the water of Meribah ; because the children of Israel strove with the LORD, and he was sanctified in them." The blessings of providence, the various gifts of God are sanctified The first epistle to Timothy iv. 4, 5, " For every creature of God is good, and nothing to be refused, if it be received with thanksgiving: For it is sanctified by the word of God and prayer."

VOL. III. 34

To separate or ordain any person or thing, as in our text, *say ye of him whom the Father hath sanctified, &c.*

Things animate and inanimate are said to be sanctified. God said unto Moses, Joshua vii. 13, "Up, sanctify the people, and say, sanctify yourselves against to-morrow; for thus saith the Lord God of Israel, There is an accursed thing in the midst of thee, O Israel: thou canst not stand before thine enemies, until ye take away the accursed thing from among you." In various parts of this book of Exodus, the breast of the wave offering, the altar, the tabernacle, &c. &c. are said to be sanctified.

Fourthly, The Son of God was sanctified before he was sent into the world. He was consecrated as the Lamb slain from before the foundation of the world, to be the Saviour of the world. Was he made holy? Was he not always pure, always holy? Was he not holy both in his conception, and in his birth? Did he then blaspheme in calling himself the Son of God, when even his figure, the figure of him who was to come, was called the Son of God, and when the offspring of the general head, even before they received the spirit, were considered sons of God? Galatians iv. 6, "*And because ye are sons*, God hath sent forth the Spirit of his Son into your hearts, crying, Abba, Father." Paul informs us, Romans viii. 14, "That as many as are led by the spirit of God, are the sons of God." Thus, it appears, that *before* and *after* they were led by the spirit of God, they were the sons of God, and it is unquestionably true, that the first man, the *earthy Adam*, was called the son of God, and that all his offspring are styled the offspring of God. *Have we not all one Father? Is not God the Father of the spirits of all flesh?*

Thus, to be made pure is to be sanctified. We are already sanctified in Christ Jesus. 1 Corinthians i. 2, "Unto the church of God which is at Corinth, to them that are sanctified in Christ Jesus, called to be saints, with all that in every place call upon Jesus Christ our Lord, both theirs and ours." But of him are ye in Christ Jesus, who of God is made unto us wisdom, and righteousness, and sanctification, and redemption; that according as it is written, he that glorieth, let him glory in the Lord. Thus are we, even at this period, *in Christ Jesus;* but when he who saveth his people from their sins shall appear, then shall we resemble him, even in our *individual characters.* Such is the testimony of Isaiah, Thy people also shall be all righteous, they shall inherit the land forever, the branch of my planting, the work of my hands, that I may be glorified. The Apostle, who is ever abundant in consolation, in his epistle to the Hebrews expresses himself in words, calculated to point out that great fundamental truth, which is the grand basis of our brightest hopes, *the union of the divine and human nature ;* for, both he that sanctifieth, and they who are sanctified, are all of one ; for which cause he is not ashamed to call them brethren.

And we echo, and re-echo this glorious truth, when this our brother shall come in the clouds of heaven, we, his people, shall assume his likeness ; yea, even these *vile bodies* shall be like unto the glorious body of the Son of God, according to the mighty working, whereby he is able to subdue all things unto himself.

SKETCH CIII.

JOHN xviii. 38.

Pilate said unto Jesus what is truth ?

First, IT is remarkable that while Pilate questioned the Redeemer, he waited not for an answer. But the salvation of Pilate, as a descendant of Adam, as a member of the sacred body of Emmanuel, was based upon the incontrovertible truth contained in an observation made by the Redeemer, chapter xiv. 6, " I am the way, and the *truth*, and the life."

Secondly, All the paths of the LORD are mercy and truth. God shall send forth *his mercy*, and his truth. Mercy and truth are met together. Psalm lxxxvi, " Thou, O LORD, art a God full of compassion, and gracious, long-suffering, and plenteous in mercy and truth."

Thirdly, God is in word and in deed a God of truth. Micah vii. 20, " Thou wilt perform the truth to Jacob, and the mercy to Abraham, which thou hast sworn unto our Fathers from the days of old." To this end, saith Jesus, was I born, and for this cause came I into the world, that I should bear witness unto the truth. Every one that is of the truth heareth my voice—Then follows our text. *Pilate said unto him what is truth?* Had Pilate waited for an answer, he might have heard the lip of truth repeat, *I am the truth.* He might, with the beloved disciple, John i. 14, have beheld his glory, the glory of the only begotten Son of the Father, full of grace and truth. Grace is connected with truth. Grace and truth came by Jesus Christ. Truth and peace are connected, and in Christ Jesus they are abundant. Isaiah xxv. 1, "O Lord, thou art my God, I will exalt thee, I will praise thy name; for thou hast done wonderful things; thy counsels of old were faithfulness and truth." Isaiah xxxix. 8, "Good is the word of the Lord which thou hast spoken. He said, moreover, for there shall be peace and truth in my days." Zechariah viii. 16, 19, " These are the things that ye shall do, Speak ye every man the truth to his neighbour; execute the judgment of peace and truth in your gates; Thus saith the Lord of hosts, the fast of the fourth month, and the fast of the fifth, and the fast of the seventh, and the fast of the tenth, shall be to the house of Judah joy and gladness, and cheerful feasts; therefore love the truth and peace."

Fourthly, *Jesus says, I am the truth.* The knowledge of this truth makes men free. Ye shall know the truth, and the truth shall make you free. If the Son make you free, you shall be free indeed. The Spirit of God is the Spirit of truth. Beloved, believe not every spirit, but try the spirits whether they be of God. The Spirit of God is called the Comforter. This Spirit witnesseth with our spirits. And, says the Evangelist John, first Epistle, v. 6, "It is the Spirit that beareth witness, because the Spirit is truth. For there are three that bear record in heaven, the Father, the Word, and the Holy Ghost: *and these three are one.*"

Fifthly, *Jesus is the truth*, Jesus is salvation, Jesus is life, Jesus is peace, Jesus is full of grace, full of mercy; he is our faithful and unchangeable Friend. Truth is not called wrath, nor death, nor damnation; and if it were the believing it would not give peace, nor joy, nor make the captive free.

Sixthly, Truth should be the constant theme of our public and private labours. I am determined, said the Apostle Paul, to know nothing among you, save Jesus Christ and him crucified. A preached gospel may be known, and when known, it will be believed; and the believer will find peace, and joy, and rest, will pass from death unto life, will love God, and will increase in good will unto man.

SKETCH CIV.

Acts i. 8, 9, 10, 11.

First, THE disciples were never invested with power until the Holy Ghost was given unto them, and then they had power to become the sons of God. John i. 12, "When thus empowered, they preach the word with holy and uniform energy." 1 Corinthians, ii. 4, "And my speech, and my preaching, was not with enticing words of man's wisdom, but in demonstration of the Spirit and of power." But the power which was bestowed upon them, was the power of God the Saviour, which was manifested in the working of miracles.

Secondly, Those who had received the Holy Ghost with power, were ordained witnesses unto God, unto the uttermost parts of the earth. These were the last words the Redeemer spake unto his disciples, either for their direction or comfort; he closed these instructions by blessing them, Luke xxiv. 50, 51, *"And he lifted up his hands and blessed them. And it came to pass, while he blessed them, he was parted from them and carried up into heaven."* The Redeemer was parted from them, *in the act of blessing them.* The sacred volume has registered three remarkable periods, when the blessing was, and is to be pronounced. First, in the garden of Eden, Genesis i. 28, "And God blessed them; and God said unto them, Be fruitful and multiply, and replenish the earth, and subdue it." Acts iii. 26, "God having raised up his Son, Jesus, sent him to *bless* you, in turning away every one of you from his iniquities." And the coming of Christ, thus to bless the human family, was said to be *glad tidings to all people.* The thirty-fourth verse, of the twenty-fifth of Matthew, is a confirmation of the universality of this blessing. *"Then shall the king say to them on his right hand, Come, ye blessed of my Father, inherit the kingdom prepared for you, from the foundation of the world."* The second luminous record preserved in the volume of inspiration is, when God himself preached the gospel to Abraham, saying, *In thee, and in thy seed, shall all the families of the earth be blessed*, this divinely consoling blessing was confirmed, both by the divine and human nature, by God Almighty as a Spirit, and as manifested in the flesh on a variety of occasions; and every concurring testimony is abundantly corroborated by the ascending Saviour, who, with lifted hands, closed his divine embassy by blessing his followers. The third glorious era is yet in future—" And, said the angels to the disciples, Ye men of Galilee, why stand ye gazing up into heaven? This same Jesus which is taken up from you into heaven, shall so come *in like manner as ye have seen him go into heaven.*" But in what manner did he ascend into heaven? We have seen, that while with uplifted hands he blessed them, he was parted from them, and carried up into heaven. 1 Thessalonians, iv. 16, " For the Lord himself shall descend from heaven with a shout, with the voice of the arch-angel, and with the trump of God: and the dead in Christ shall rise first." Thus will God the Saviour come in the clouds of heaven, with power and great glory; but his power and great glory will be displayed in the act of blessing, not cursing. In blessing every individual, which constitutes a part of the congregated nations; in blessing all the families of the earth with all spiritual blessings; *for in like manner as he ascended so shall he descend.* Such was, such is the Redeemer of men, who was anointed to preach the gospel to the poor, to heal the broken hearted, to preach deliverance to the captive, recovery of sight to the blind, to set at liberty those who are bruised, to preach the acceptable year of the Lord, and to comfort all who mourn.

SKETCH CV.

Romans ii. 4, 5.

First, It appears, that unbelievers despise the riches of God's goodness, although they profess to admire their own excellence.

Secondly, *Unbelievers* do not *know*, that the goodness of God leadeth them to repentance. The sentiments embraced by unbelievers are the reverse of this truth; they proclaim every where, that the grace of God prevents them from repenting, that the *grace of God is a licentious doctrine,* calculated to pervert the souls of men, to render them bad members of society, and to consign them to a place of never-ending misery in a future world! But, agreeably to our usual custom, we will enquire at the fountain of wisdom, the fountain of light. Isaiah xxx. " Now go write it before them in a table, and note it in a book, that it may be for the time to come, forever and ever. That this is a rebellious people, lying children, children that will not hear the law of the LORD; which say to the seers, See not; and to the prophets, Prophesy not unto us right things, speak unto us smooth things, prophesy deceits. Wherefore, thus saith the Holy One of Israel, because ye despise this word, and trust in oppression and perverseness, and stay thereon: therefore, this iniquity shall be to you a breach ready to fall, swelling out in a high wail, whose breaking cometh suddenly, in an instant; for, thus saith the LORD God, the Holy One of Israel, In returning and rest shall ye be saved in quietness, and in confidence shall be your strength: and ye would not. But ye said, No; for we will flee upon horses; therefore shall ye flee: and we will ride upon the swift; therefore, shall they that pursue you be swift. And, therefore, will the LORD wait, that he may be gracious unto you: and therefore, will he be exalted, that he may have mercy upon you: for the LORD is a God of judgment: blessed are all they that wait for him. And thine ears shall hear a word behind thee, saying, This is the way, walk ye in it, when ye turn to the right hand, and when ye turn to the left."

Thirdly, *But to those that despised the goodness of God not knowing that it led to repentance,* the apostle Peter informs us, Acts v. 32, Jesus Christ is, by the right hand of God, exalted to be a Prince and a Saviour, to give repentance, and forgiveness of sins.

Those who despise the goodness of God are represented as having hard and impenitent hearts. Indeed, this is the character given to the people of God throughout the sacred volume. Witness Exodus xxxiii. 3, " For I will not go up in the midst of thee; for thou art a stiff-necked people; lest I consume thee in the way." Exodus xxxiv. 9, "And he said, if now I have found grace in thy sight, O LORD, let my Lord, I pray thee, go among us; for it is a stiff-necked people; and pardon our iniquity and our sin, and take us for thine inheritance." Deuteronomy ix. 6, " Understand, therefore, that the LORD thy God giveth thee not this good land to possess it for thy righteousness, for thou art a stiff-necked people." Isaiah xlviii. 4, " Because I knew that thou art obstinate, and thy neck is an iron sinew, and thy brow brass." Ezekiel ii. 7, " And thou shalt speak my words unto them, whether they will hear, or whether they will forbear, for they are most rebellious " Acts vii. 51, " Ye stiff-necked and uncircumcised in heart and ears, ye do always resist the Holy Ghost : as your fathers did, so do ye."

Fourthly, These unbelievers are said to treasure up wrath against the day of wrath, which day of wrath is the revelation of the righteous judgment of God. Acts xvii. " God hath appointed a day in the which he will judge the world in righteousness by that man whom he hath ordained, whereof he hath given assurance unto all men, in that he hath raised him from the dead."

Fifthly, *In that day God will render unto every man according to his deeds.* Yet will not this retribution usurp the place or arrest the progress of his mercy. Psalm lxii. 12, " Also unto thee, O Lord, belongeth mercy, for thou renderest to every man according to his work." Proverbs xxiv. 12, " If thou sayest, behold we knew it not; doth not he that pondereth the heart consider it? and he that keepeth thy soul, doth not he know it? And shall not he render to every man according to his works?" Jeremiah xvii. 10, " I the Lord search the heart, I try the reins, even to give every man according to his ways, and according to the fruit of his doings." Chapter xxxii. 19, " Great in counsel and mighty in work : for thine eyes are open upon all the ways of the sons of men: to give every one according to his ways, and according to the fruit of his doings." Chapter xxvii. " Behold I am the Lord, the God of all flesh; Is there any thing too hard for me? Be not deceived, that which a man soweth he shall also reap." So, then, every one of us shall give account of himself to God? Certainly, every one shall be judged out of the things written in the books; and if any man's work abide, he shall be entitled to a reward—Moreover, the book of life shall afterwards be opened.

But, Sixthly and lastly, Upon recurring to these considerations, we should never lose sight of one plain, positive truth. The Judge himself, the Redeemer of the world, the Son of man, the God-man, whose work was before him, when he descended from heaven to seek and to save that which was lost, shall assuredly be *rewarded according to his work.* Dearly hath he earned, and he will most unquestionably possess all those souls which belonged unto the Father. Isaiah xl. 10, 11, " Behold the LORD God will come with strong hand, and his arm shall rule for him; behold his *reward is with him, and his work before him.* He shall feed his flock like a shepherd; he shall gather the lambs with his arm and carry them in his bosom." It was for this, that he might bring his ransomed home, that he tasted in the most ignominious form, the enanguished bitterness of death, for every man. See Hebrews xii. 2, where this glorious Author and Finisher of our faith is thus spoken of by the Apostle, who for *the joy that was set before him* endured the cross, despising the shame, and is set down at the right hand of the throne of God Nor will he be defrauded of any part of his recompense. Let us then be careful not to treasure up to ourselves wrath against the day of wrath, well knowing that our works must be tried, and that we shall receive the reward to which we shall be entitled, in its utmost extent; let us rejoice also that the man Christ Jesus shall likewise be rewarded, that his recompense will be full. But where would be his reward, if a single member of his body was to be consigned to never-ending sufferings? Children, said the Psalmist, are the heritage of the LORD. They are his recompense—a *reward* which he deemeth most precious. They constitute the lost nature of which the wandering sheep was an emblem, in pursuit of which he left the abodes of blessedness, and when he had found it, he layed it upon his shoulder rejoicing over it more than over the ninety and nine who had never strayed; more than over angels who had never lost their first estate. In such estimation doth the head of every man hold those individuals, which constitute the aggregate of his mystical body.

SKETCH CVI.

Romans ii. 16.

First, There *is a day when God shall judge the secrets of men.* Matthew xxv. 35, "For I was an hungred and ye gave me meat," &c. &c. &c.

Secondly, *And this judgment will be executed by Jesus Christ.* John v. 22, "For the Father judgeth no man, but hath committed all judgment unto the Son." We are aware that our Saviour saith, John xii. 47, "That if any man hear his words and believe not, he judges him not, because he came not to judge the world, but to save the world." The office of judge, and the office of Saviour, are distinct offices. The Redeemer in his descent, and abode upon this globe, was occupied in the great work of salvation, he did not then blend the character of a judge, but having fully accomplished the errand on which he was sent, he will, in the winding up of the great drama, be found upon the judgment seat, judging *every individual* who hath not *previously judged himself.* The words spoken by the Redeemer will be the test, and every mouth will be stopped before God. Such will be the process and final issue of the day when God shall judge the secrets of men by Jesus Christ. Thus saith our text, and its doctrine is corroborated by many passages. Acts x. 42, "And he commanded us to preach unto the people, and to testify that it was he which was ordained of God to be the Judge of quick and dead." Acts xvii. 31, "Because he hath appointed a day, in the which he will judge the world in righteousness, by that man whom he hath ordained; whereof he hath given assurance unto all men, in that he hath raised him from the dead." 1 Corinthians iv. 5, "Therefore judge nothing before the time, until the Lord come who will both bring to light the hidden things of darkness, and will make manifest the counsels of the heart, and then shall every man have praise of God." 2 Timothy iv. 1, 8, "I charge thee therefore before God and the Lord Jesus Christ, who shall judge the quick and the dead at his appearing, and his kingdom, Preach the word, &c. &c. I have fought a good fight, I have finished my course, I have kept the faith : Henceforth there is laid up for me a crown of righteousness, which the LORD, the righteous Judge, shall give me at that day: and not to me only, but unto all them that love his appearing."

Thirdly, This judgment doth not contradict the gospel, nay, it is in perfect unison with the gospel. Please to read at your leisure 1 Peter, Chapter iv. 5, 6, and Revelations chapters nineteen and twenty.

Fourthly, *If we judge ourselves we shall not be judged.* 1 Corinthians xi. 31, " For if we would judge ourselves we should not be judged." John v. 45, " Do not think that I will accuse you to the Father : there is one that accuseth you, even Moses, in whom you trust."

How excellent is the gospel plan ; the *judge* is the *Redeemer*, the *husband* the *Father*, the *elder brother* the *Head of every man.*

SKETCH CVII.

ROMANS xi.

First, WE do not hear the apostle Paul mentioned, until the close of the seventh chapter of Acts, while he is a spectator of the death of Stephen, and apparently consenting to his sufferings, for the witnesses laid down their clothes at his feet. In the succeeding chapter, he is described as making havock of the church, entering into every house, and committing men and women to prison. Of his lineage, and even his immediate parentage, we are totally ignorant; we only learn from himself that he was a Hebrew, both by father and mother, that he was of Tarsus, a city in Cilicia, a citizen of no mean city, that he was brought up at the feet of Gamaliel, that he was a zealous, devout man, in other words, a scholar and a religious observer of the law ; and he affirms, that he lived in all good conscience before God. Yet, although very devout, he was however very cruel, very vindictive, binding men and women, delivering them into prison, and persecuting them unto the death.

Secondly, The omnipotent power of God arrested this furious zealot in the midst of his persecuting career. He who verily thought, he ought to do many things contrary to the name of Jesus of Nazareth, who punished the christians in every city, who compelled them to blaspheme, and who was exceeding mad against them, even him, did the Almighty arm of the LORD arrest; while he yet breathed out threatenings and slaughter, a light from heaven shone round about him, and he fell prostrate to the earth. Do you not, my beloved hearers, imagine you are listening to the voice of the tender Redeemer; *Saul, Saul, why persecutest thou me?* Yea, verily, whatsoever is done to the *least of his brethren, to the smallest member of his body is done unto him.* Who art thou, LORD, said the terror struck delinquent? I am Jesus, whom thou persecutest. His agonized astonishment was now indescribably augmented, his heart melted, he was disposed to obedience, he was *slain, he died and was made alive.* The result was precisely what might have been calculated; LORD, *what wilt thou have me to do?* He was hastening to the city upon his persecuting errand; but he is directed thither for different purposes. " Arise, and go into the city, and it shall be told thee what thou shalt do". For three days he continued without sight or sustenance; but he was a chosen vessel unto God, ordained to bear his name before Gentiles and kings, and the children of Israel, and it was the good pleasure of God to show him how great things he must suffer for his name sake. " Inquire for one Saul of Tarsus, for *behold he prayeth.*" Forever blessed be the name of the *prayer hearing God.* Gracious heaven, what big emotions must have swelled the bosom of this man of Tarsus, when first he heard the voice of Ananias, when he listened to his address; could words have been more calculated to astonish, to console, and to elevate—? *Brother Saul,* the LORD, even Jesus, that appeared unto thee in the way, that thou camest, hath sent me that thou mightest receive thy sight, and be filled with the Holy Ghost. Mark how the christian spirit breathed forth in the words of Ananias. He did not say, *Jesus whom thou persecuted hath sent me;* but Jesus who appeared unto thee in the way as thou camest. Well, immediately the scales fell from his eyes, his understanding was illuminated, he arose and was baptized, and straitway he preached Christ in the synagogue, that he is the son of God, confounding the Jews, and proving that Jesus was the Messiah, the very Christ the Son of God. Such was the Apostle to the Gentiles. Is it wonderful that he magnified his office?

SKETCH CVIII.

1 CORINTHIANS XV. 28.

And when all things shall be subdued unto him, then shall the Son also himself be subject unto him, that put all things under him, that God may be all in all.

First, ALL *things shall be subjected unto him.* To whom? To him that did put all things under him. But who was it that did put all things under him? Certainly, Jesus Christ. Read the three verses immediately preceding our text, and the truth will stand confest, "For he must reign, till he hath put all enemies under his feet. The last enemy that shall be destroyed is death. For he hath put all things under his feet. But when he saith, all things are put under him, it is manifest that he is excepted, which did put all things under him." Then follows our text. *And when all things shall be subdued unto him, then shall the Son also himself be subject unto him, that did put all things under him (in other words, unto Christ Jesus) that God may be all in all.*

Secondly, What are we to understand by subduing? Undoubtedly bringing into subjection. But *bringing into subjection implies previous rebellion.* It is impious, therefore, to suppose that *this son,* to be brought into *subjection* was Christ Jesus. Was Christ Jesus in his individual character, ever in a state of *rebellion?* Yet we are told most irreverently, that at the final consummation of all things, we shall behold a universe of *Deists,* for *Christ Jesus* shall be brought into a state of *subjection ;* but such conclusions can only be formed by those who have never learned or who have forgotten, that the characters Father, Son and Holy Ghost are merely designed, as an accommodation to our limited understanding, and are but *various exhibitions* of the same *one eternal God.* And when all things shall be subdued unto him; an explanation of this clause in our text is furnished by St.

Matthew xiii. 41, "The Son of man shall send forth his angels, and they shall gather out of his kingdom all things that offend, and them which do iniquity." This is *subduing* the human earth, when from his kingdom, which is made up of all nations, and kindreds, and tongues, every thing that gives offence, and every one of those evil spirits, that have worked in the hearts of God's offspring is removed, then all things will be *subdued* unto God. The apostle Paul in his Epistle to the Philippians iii. 20, 21, repeats and confirms this glorious truth. "For our conversation is in heaven; from whence also we look for the Saviour, the LORD Jesus Christ: who shall change our vile body, that it may be fashioned like unto his glorious body, according to the working whereby he is able to *subdue all things unto himself.*"

Thirdly, *When all things are thus subdued unto himself, then shall the Son also be subject unto him, that did put all things under him.* We have already seen that it is Jesus, who put all enemies under his feet, and we have heard the Apostle affirm, that when he saith, all things are put under him, it is manifest *he is excepted*, who did put all things under him.

Then shall the Son also himself be *subject unto him that did put all things under him.* The offspring of God, the human family, was first exhibited in the singular character, in this character they sinned, and in this character they must be saved; accordingly we are admonished to have a *single eye*. Matthew vi. 22, "The light of the body is the eye: if therefore thine eye be single, thy whole body shall be full of light," And hence, Jesus Christ as the head of every man is called the light of the world and when all things shall be *subdued* unto him, who is the light of the world, then shall the Son also, who was made subject to vanity, be subjected to vanity no more. Human nature in the aggregate shall be brought into subjection to him, who is able to subdue all things unto himself, until that period partial reforms may take place, but the day of retribution will be the day of *final subjection*.

Fourthly, When the human family are thus individually and collectively subdued; it will not be the head only that will be filled with God, the whole body will be filled with God, for at this glorious era, God, or the divine nature, will be all in all. Ephesians i. 21, 22, 23, "Far above all principality, and power, and might, and dominion, and every name that is named, not only in this world, but also in that which is to come: and hath put all things under his feet, and gave him to be the head over all things to the church. Which is his body, the fulness of him that filleth all in all." Matthew xxviii. 18, "And Jesus came and spake unto them, saying, All power is given unto me in heaven and in earth." John i. 14, "And the word was made flesh, and dwelt among us, (and we beheld his glory the glory as of the only begotten of the Father) full of grace and truth." Colossians i. 18. "And he is the head of the body, the church: who is the beginning, the first-born from the dead: that in all things he might have the pre-eminence." Colossians ii. 9, 10, "For in him dwelleth all the fulness of the God-head bodily. And ye are complete in him, which is the head of all." Colossians iii. 11, "Where there is neither Greek nor Jew, circumcision nor uncircumcision, Barbarian, Scythian, bond nor free; but Christ is all, and in all." Read, my beloved hearers, the second chapter of the Hebrews, from the eighth verse to the close.

Fifthly, As the human nature was first put forth in God's image, so, at the final consummation of all things, this nature shall be restored to its original character. 1 John v. 20, "And we know that the Son of God is come, and hath given us an understanding, that we may know him that is true, and we are in him that is true, even in his Son Jesus Christ. This is the true God and eternal life." John xvii. 22, 23, "And the glory which thou gavest me, I have given them, that they may be one, even as we are one: *I in them, and thou in me, that they may be made perfect in one*; and that the world may know that thou hast sent me, and hast loved them as thou hast loved me." Thus will God be all in all; thus shall we be filled with the fulness of God. These are the true sayings of God. Blessed are those who have power given them to believe with their hearts, and to make confession to God.

SKETCH CIX.

2 CORINTHIANS, ii. 15, 16.

First, WHAT are we to understand by the Apostles being unto God a sweet savour of Christ, both in them that are saved, and in them that perish? That, as God had so loved the world as to give his Son to die for the sins of the world, it was a sweet savour unto him, that his servants should bear witness to this truth, and this grace, the fulness of which was in Christ, and as Jesus had by the grace of God tasted death for every man, it was pleasing to God that his apostles should constantly affirm, that Jesus Christ in giving himself a ransom for all was indeed the complete, unequivocal Saviour of all men. Hence, saith the apostle Peter in his First General Epistle, iv. 6, "For this cause was the gospel preached also to them that are dead, that they may be judged according to men in the flesh, but live according to God in the spirit."

God well knew that his eternal purpose was accomplished, that his beloved Son in whom he was well pleased, had made that expiatory sacrifice, which restored them who had perished, and thus knowing, he could not but regard with complacency, could not but accept as a sweet savour, the testimony which bore witness to the redemption of those who were saved, and to those who perished. Yes, the testimony of John is true, 1. 14, "And the word was made flesh and dwelt among us, (and we beheld his glory, the glory of the only begotten of the Father) full of grace and truth." The savour of the name of Jesus is always sweet to God whether manifested in the flesh, or seated at the right hand of his glory.

Secondly, Although to God they, the apostles, were a sweet savour of Christ both in them who were saved, and in them who perished; yet, to those who were in the state of death, who perished, they were the savour of death unto death, while to them who were saved, they were the savour of life unto life.

To those who judge agreeably to their own feelings, the testimony of life becomes the testimony of death, and they perish for lack of knowledge. *Perishing* is dying, a dead limb is *perished*. 1 Corinthians viii. 11, " And through thy knowledge shall the weak brother *perish* for whom Christ died ?" To those from whose eyes the things that make for their peace is hidden, the gospel is a savour of death unto death. If our gospel be hid, it is hid to them who are *lost ;* but blessed be God there are *none lost which shall not be found, there are none die, there are none perish, who shall not be made alive again—all have perished, all have died in Christ.* And if you would behold in one compendious view, the extensiveness of this death, the extensiveness of this salvation, turn to the second chapter of Paul's Epistle to the Hebrews. " But we see Jesus, who was made a little lower than the angels for the suffering of death, crowned with glory and honour, that he by the grace of God should taste death for every man. For both he who sanctifieth and they who are sanctified, are all of one : for which cause he is not ashamed to call them brethren. Forasmuch then as the children are partakers of flesh and blood, he also himself likewise took part of the same, that through death he might destroy him who had the power of death that is the devil; and deliver them who through fear of death were all their life time subject to bondage. For verily he took not on him the nature of angels ; but he took on him the seed of Abraham. Wherefore in all things it behoved him to be made like unto his brethren, that he might be a merciful and faithful high Priest in things pertaining to God, to make reconciliation for the sins of the people."

SKETCH CX.

Galatians vi. 7.

First, Our subject commences with an exhortation, *Be not deceived.* What are we to understand by deception ? A cunningly devised and cunningly managed artifice, or falsehood, by which the mind is effectually deluded and imposed upon

The first, who practised this art, was the grand deceiver, when, in the garden of Eden, he assailed and misled our general mother. But, it appears that the Father of mankind was not, at that eventful period, the victim of the adversary's wiles. 1 Timothy ii. 14, " And Adam was not deceived, but the woman being deceived was in the transgression." By this deceiver the nations are deceived. Revelations xviii. 23, " For by thy sorceries all nations were deceived." Even the Apostles were deceived. Titus iii. 3, " For we ourselves also were sometimes foolish, disobedient, deceived, serving divers lusts and pleasures, living in malice and envy, hateful, and hating one another."

Secondly, *God is not mocked.* What is it to mock? It is to hold up false lights, to delude by misrepresentation, by falsehood, to betray the confidence which was reposed in us.

Thirdly, *Whatsoever a man soweth that shall he reap* and *nothing else.* The sacred volume describes three characters as sowers. First, The man, Christ Jesus. But what hath the man Christ Jesus sowed? Matthew xiii. 27, " So the servants of the householder came and said unto him, Sir, Didst not thou sow good seed in thy field? From whence then hath it tares?" Secondly, The grand adversary, the man of sin. 2 Thessalonians ii. 3, 4, "Let no man deceive you by any means: for that day shall not come, except there come a falling away first, and that man of sin be revealed, the son of perdition; who opposeth and exalteth himself above all that is called God, or that is worshipped; so that he as God sitteth in the temple of God, shewing himself that he is God." This same arrogant man of sin, is a capital sower. He is that enemy, who, following the footsteps of the great husbandman, sowed tares among the wheat. Thirdly, Mankind individually are sowers, and the verse succeeding our text, describes the fate of these sowers. For he that soweth to his flesh, shall of the flesh reap corruption; but he that soweth to the spirit, shall of the spirit reap life everlasting. Thus we are taught *where,* as well as *what* we shall reap, and the life we shall reap, is eternal life, because it is in Christ. When Christ who is our life shall appear, we also shall appear with him. John vi. 33, " The bread of God is he which cometh down from heaven, and giveth life unto the world." Romans v. 18, " Therefore, as by the offence of one, judgment came upon all men to condemnation; even so by the righteousness of one, the free gift came upon all men unto justification."

It is thus the spirit teacheth my understanding. The almighty seed's man hath *sown the human nature, and he shall reap the human nature.* The man of sin *hath sowed tares, and he shall reap tares.* The individuals of human nature sow indiscriminately *good* and *evil*, and that which they sow, *they shall reap.* If their works be good, they shall be rewarded. If they be bad, the intense heat of the divine fire shall kindle upon them, and burning up the chaff, they themselves, by this very burning, be saved, so as by fire, when the Redeemer shall reap his harvest winnowed from every particle of chaff. Such is the doctrine of the *restitution of all things.*

SKETCH CXI.

2 Thessalonians ii. 11, 12.

The verse immediately preceding our text informs us why God sent the people strong delusions. *Because they received not the love of the truth, that they might be saved.* This leads us to enquire,

First, What we are to understand by the truth? Which it is not said, they *did not receive*, but simply they did not receive *the love of the truth.* Micah in the last verse of his prophecy, speaking of this truth, says, "Thou wilt perform the truth to Jacob, and the mercy to Abraham, which thou hast sworn unto our fathers from the days of old." Isaiah speaketh good things, chapter xxxviii. 17, "Behold, for peace *I had* great bitterness; but thou hast in love to my soul delivered it from the pit of corruption: for thou hast cast all my sins behind thy back." Jeremiah vi. 33, "Behold I will bring it health and cure, and I will cure them, and will reveal unto them the abundance of peace and truth." These are some of the features of that glorious *truth*, which unbelievers do not receive the love of.

The law came by Moses, but grace and truth by Jesus Christ. The law was true, but it was not the truth, *which was accompanied by mercy and grace;* strange as it may appear, the truth, which was replete with mercy and grace, was the truth which the people received not *in the love of it.*

Secondly, What is the consequence of this refusal? *God sends them strong delusion.* As far as I can determine, after the most diligent search, I do not think this term, *delusion,* occurs in more than one place in the sacred volume, our text excepted. In Isaiah lxiv. 4, it is thus written, "I also will choose their delusions, and will bring their fears upon them, because, when I called, none did answer; when I spake, they did not hear, but they did evil before my eyes, and chose that in which I delighted not." Thus, it is evident, that where there is not a *love of truth* predominating in the mind, God sends *strong delusions.* To this effect, saith the Lord by the prophet Hosea, iv. 17, "Ephraim is joined to idols; let him alone." Again 1 Kings xxii. 22, "And the Lord said unto him, wherewith? And he said I will go forth, and I will be a *lying* spirit in the mouth of all his prophets. And he said thou shalt persuade him, and shalt prevail also: go forth and do so."

This is a remarkable passage. The lying spirit offering himself to deceive by the mouth of the prophets, and the Lord said, thou shalt persuade, and shalt also prevail.

Thirdly, They are themselves deceived, for they *believe* a lie. What is a lie? Those who have seen the truth know the reverse of this must be a lie. If it be true that Jesus is the Saviour of all men, to declare he is not, is a lie.

Fourthly, The consequence of believing a lie. Our text informs us *all those who believe this lie, are the subjects of damnation; that they all might be damned, who believe not the truth.* They are not only damned for believing a lie, but they are damned for not believing the truth. And what is this damnation, which results from unbelief? It is condemnation, that they all might be condemned, who believed not the truth. John iii. 18, "He that believeth on him is *not condemned,* but he that *believeth not is condemned already,* because he hath not believed in the name of the only begotten Son of God." How long shall this condemnation continue? *It is, it will be coeval with the delusion.* How long will the delusion continue? Until the man of sin, the son of perdition be revealed. He who opposeth himself to, and exalteth himself above all that is called God, or that is worshipped, so that he as God, sitteth in the temple of God, shewing himself that he is God. When this is effected, then shall that which is written be accomplished. *The people shall be all taught of God.* Every man therefore that hath heard, *(and they shall all hear, every eye shall see, and every tongue shall confess)* and hath learned of the Father, cometh unto me. It is elsewhere written, and him that cometh unto me, *I will in no wise cast out,*

Taught, immediately taught by their Creator, taught by God himself—Can the delusion continue, especially when that wicked is removed, which the LORD shall consume with the spirit of his mouth, and destroy with the brightness of his coming? The prophet Isaiah informs us, that God will destroy the covering, cast over all people, and the veil that is spread over all nations. That it shall be said in that day, lo, this is our God: we have waited for him, and he will save us: this is the LORD; we have waited for him, we will be glad and rejoice in his salvation.

Amid a scene like this, can the delusion continue? Particularly as the *doer of the deed is separated from them,* as the God of this world will then have no more power to blind them, and, when they *see* and *believe* the truth, will the *condemnation for unbelief* be continued? Knowing God, will they not love God, and loving God, will they not *love the truth?*

It is evident from scripture testimonies, that this delusion, and its consequent condemnation or damnation, will continue as long as an unbeliever shall be found, until the consummation described in Revelations xxi. "And I saw a new heaven and a new earth: for the first heaven and the first earth were passed away; and there was no more sea. And I John saw the holy city, new Jerusalem, coming down from God out of heaven, prepared as a bride adorned for her husband. And I heard a great voice out of heaven, saying, Behold, the tabernacle of God is with men, and he will dwell with them, and they shall be his people, and God himself shall be with them, and be their God. And God shall wipe away all tears from their eyes; and there shall be no more death, neither sorrow, nor crying, neither shall there be any more pain: for the former things are passed away. And he that sat upon the throne said, Behold, I make all things new. And he said unto me, Write: for these words are true and faithful. And he said unto me, It is done. I am Alpha and Omega, the Beginning and the End. I will give unto him that is athirst of the fountain of the water of life freely."

Until this blissful period, the sufferings described in the eighth verse, will no doubt be realized, *darkness* is consequent upon *unbelief.* The fearful, and unbelieving, and the abominable, and murderers, and whoremongers, and sorcerers, and idolators, and all liars (all men, saith the sacred volume are liars) shall have their part in the lake, which burneth with fire and brimstone. But when they *have had their part in this lake, when unbelief is no more, when the veil shall be taken away, when the rebuke shall cease, when the knowledge of the* Lord *shall cover the earth, when death and hell shall be cast into the lake of fire, when there shall be no more death, neither sorrow nor crying, nor any more pain, the delusion will of course be destroyed, every individual will believe,* and consequently *every individual will love the truth :* the condemnation will cease, and the whole human family will find their honour their pleasure, the sum of their felicity, *in RIGHTEOUSNESS.*

SKETCH CXII.

1 Timothy iii. 16.

First, We acknowledge, with all the devotion and veneration, of which our natures are susceptible, the *mystery* of godliness, and we rejoice with joy unspeakable, that this adorable being, this omnipotent God was manifested in the flesh. But what are we to conceive of God? Is he not said to be *incomprehensible ?* Yet we may discern some vestige of his sacred footsteps, from the names by which he hath condescended to reveal himself. He is the Creator, all things were made by him. Proverbs xvi. 4, " The Lord hath made all things for himself. yea, even the wicked for the day of evil." 1 John i. 5, " This then is the message which we have heard of him, and declare unto you, that God is light, and in him is *no darkness at all."* 1 John iv. 16, " And we have known and believed the love that God hath to us. God is love; and he that dwelleth in love, dwelleth in God, and God in him." God is and must be, in the nature of things, *unchangeable.*

Secondly, God was *manifested in the flesh,* first in figure. Adam was the figure of him, who was to come. That the temple

SKETCH CXII. 287

at Jerusalem was a figure of the human nature, or the flesh in which God was manifested, is evident from the words of the Redeemer. John ii. 19, "Jesus answered and said unto them, *Destroy this temple, and in three days I will raise it up.*"

Thirdly, God was in *fact*, as well as in *figure manifested in the flesh*. Colossians ii. 9, "For in him dwelleth all the fulness of the God-head bodily." John xvii. 23, "*I in them, and thou in me, that they may be made perfect in one.*" John x. 30, "*I and my Father are one.*" Again, the Redeemer replied to Philip, "*Have I been so long with thee, and thou hast not known me?*"

Fourthly, In what flesh was God manifested? *In the human nature, or the second Adam.* 1 Corinthians xv. 45, "And so it is written, The first man, Adam, was made a living soul; the last Adam was made a quickening spirit." Isaiah speaks of the wonderful Counsellor, the mighty God, the everlasting Father, the Prince of peace, as the child born, the son given, and he affirms, that God hath wrought all our works *in us*, and the prophet Hosea iv. 2, gives us this remarkable information; "*After two days he will revive us, in the third day he will raise us up, and we shall live in his sight.*" Again, Isaiah vii. 14, "The LORD himself shall give you a sign: Behold, a virgin shall conceive, and bear a son, and shall call his name Immanuel." And, Matthew pronounces this scripture fulfilled, and adds, that the name Immanuel, when interpreted, *is God with us.*

Fifthly, To whom was God thus manifested in the flesh? First, To angels, they brought tidings of his birth. Luke ii. "And the angels said unto them, fear not, for, behold, I bring you glad tidings of great joy, which shall be to all people, and let all the angels of God worship him." The angels were the first preachers of the Redeemer's resurrection. Luke xxiv. 6, "He is not here, he is risen." Secondly, He was preached unto the Gentiles, and believed on, in the world, by every one taught of God. 1 John v. 20, "And we know that the Son of God is come, and hath given us an understanding, that we may know him that is true, and we are in him that is true, even in his Son, Jesus Christ. This is the true God and eternal life." And he hath been received into glory. This was witnessed by the men of Galilee, when they were assured, that in like manner as he ascended, so he should descend. And lastly, In the close of time, the grand catastrophe shall manifest God in the flesh to every human being. Jesus is upon the throne. Psalm xlv. 6, Thy throne, O God, is forever and ever; the sceptre of thy kingdom is a right sceptre." This God, of whom the Psalmist thus speaks, was God manifest in the flesh. Jesus is the judge, and the dead, small and great, shall stand before God. The whole human family shall be collected, and, finally, Revelations v. 13, " Every creature which is in heaven, and on the earth, and under the earth, and such as are in the sea, and all that are in them, shall unite to say, Blessing, and honour, and glory, and power be unto him, that sitteth upon the throne, unto God manifest in the flesh, and unto the Lamb forever and ever."

SKETCH CXIII.

Titus iii. 5, 6.

First, We are the saved of the Lord.

Secondly, Who are the saved of the Lord? 1 Timothy iv. 10, the Spirit answereth this question:—" For, therefore, we both labour and suffer reproach, because we trust in the living God, who is the Saviour of all men, especially of those that believe." Again, 2 Timothy, i. 9, 10, " Who hath saved us, and called us with an holy calling, not according to our works, but according to his own purpose and grace, which was given us in Christ Jesus, before the world began; but is now made manifest by the appearance of our Saviour Jesus Christ, who hath abolished death, and hath brought life and immortality to light by the gospel." Again, Galatians iii. 13, 14, " Christ hath redeemed us from the curse of the law, being made a curse for us; for it is written, Cursed is every one that hangeth on a tree. That the blessing of Abraham might come on the Gentiles through Jesus Christ, that we might receive the promise of the Spirit through faith."

But who were they, who were redeemed from the curse of the law? Undoubtedly those who were under the curse. Galatians iv. 4, 5, " But when the fulness of the time was come, God sent forth his Son, made of a woman, made under the law, to redeem them that were made under the law, that we might receive the adoption of sons." But, from what beside the curse of the law, are those who are saved, exempted? They are exempted from death. Romans vi. 23, "The wages of sin is death;" from which death Jesus Christ saved those individuals, who constituted the aggregate of his body, when, by suffering for them, he died for their sins, according to the scriptures. But, it will be asked, for whom did the Son of God suffer death? And who are they, who by the sufferings of Jesus Christ, are saved from the death which is the wages of sin? The spirit of God answers this question, Hebrews x. 10, "By the which will, we are sanctified, through the offering of the body of Jesus Christ *once for all*." 1 Timothy, ii 6, "Who gave himself a *ransom for all*, to be testified in due time." 2 Corinthians, v. 14, 15, "For the love of Christ constraineth us, because we thus judge, that if one died *for all, then were all dead*. And that he died for all, that they which live, should not henceforth live unto themselves, but unto him which died for them, and rose again." If there were any for whom Christ did not die and rise again, they, it seems, may live unto themselves. But to manifest beyond all contradiction, that Christ Jesus did *really*, and *truly save all men* from this death, by suffering it in their place, and to prove that this *all* includes as many as were, consequent upon transgression, subjected to death, we have only to consult the Apostle Paul, who thus decidedly expresses himself, Hebrews ii. 9, "But we see Jesus, who was made a little lower than the angels, for the suffering of death, crowned with glory and honour; that he, by the grace of God, should *taste death for every man*." And if it be possible to render this evangelical truth more clear, let us enquire at the mouth of the beloved disciple John, who, in his first general Epistle, chapter ii. verse 2, decidedly says, "And he is the propitiation for our sins, and not for ours only, *but also for the sins of the whole world*." As many as died in Adam, are saved from the death which was the wages of sin, in consequence of the second Adam dying for them; and the testimony which declared, the soul that sinned should die, is, in no sort, opposed to the restoration of the human family, *of the whole human family, for* mercy and truth have met together, righteousness and peace have embraced each other. God is, indeed, and in truth, a *just* God and a Saviour. Isaiah is full of this truth:—" Tell ye and bring them near; yea, let them take counsel together: who hath declared this from ancient time? Who hath told it from that time? Have not I the Lord? And there is no God else beside me; a *just* God and a *Saviour;* there is none beside me. Look unto me and be ye saved, all the ends of the earth: for I am God and there is none else. I have sworn by myself; the word is gone out of my mouth in righteousness, and shall not return, that unto me every knee shall bow, and every tongue shall swear."

But how is this salvation effected? First, Not by works of righteousness performed by us. What are righteous works? No doubt, works of righteousness, but not to be performed by *unrighteous characters,* any more than a corrupt tree can bring forth good fruit. Now, the Holy Ghost assures us, that it is written, there is none righteous, no, not one; that we all do fade as a leaf, and that our iniquities, like the wind, have taken us away.

As there are none righteous, no, not one, it is plain, that our righteousness can have nothing to do with this salvation. And, saith our text, not by works of righteousness which we have done. How then is our salvation accomplished? Right happy are we, that our comment is as infallible as our text. Ephesians ii. 4, 5, 8, " But God, who is rich in mercy, for his great love wherewith he loved us, even when we were dead in trespasses and sins, hath quickened us together with Christ; by grace ye are saved. For by grace ye are saved through faith, and that not of *yourselves; it is the gift of God.*" And that this faith, through which we are saved, is not the act of the sinner's mind, is abundantly evinced by the following considerations. Galatians ii. 16, " Knowing that a man is not justified by the works of the law, but by the *faith of Jesus Christ,* even we have believed in Jesus Christ, that we may be justified by the *faith of Christ,* and not by the works of the law; for, by the works of the law, shall no flesh living be justified. The Apostle affirms, that our salvation is not of works; and he adds a pertinent reason, *lest any man should boast.* And the testimony in our text is full on this head: The Spirit teacheth us, that we are saved, First, by the washing of regeneration; and secondly, by the renewing of the Holy Ghost, which was shed on us abundantly through Jesus Christ our Saviour. In our first generation, we are all as an unclean thing. Psalm li. 5, " Behold I was shapen in iniquity, and in sin did my mother conceive me."

The first act, therefore, in the work of salvation, was to wash or cleanse us by *regeneration*, that is, the *generation, generated over again*. This was effected when the second Adam was exhibited, clothed in garments of flesh; as the second Adam, he contained in himself the fulness of the lost nature. In him, as the second Adam, the lost nature was, in the sight of God, saved by the washing of regeneration. In this regeneration, our nature is cleansed; for that nature, procreated by the Holy Ghost, was conceived without sin. Thus we read—The Holy Ghost shall come upon thee, and the power of the Highest shall overshadow thee: therefore, also, that Holy Thing which shall be born of thee, shall be called, the Son of God. The head of every man, says a sacred writer, is Christ. Would not that be a monstrous birth, where the head should be born at one time, and the members of the body belonging to that head, at different periods? Had it not been the design of the just God and the Saviour, to commence our salvation in the conception, so that we may be REGENERATED and born over again, we can see no reason, why the second Adam did not descend as the LORD from heaven, in the fulness of the stature of a perfect man; but, having laid this plan, he did not abhor the virgin's womb, but was born of a woman, that so the fulness of the nature lost in the first Adam, in consequence of being by ordinary generation defiled, may be saved in the second Adam, in consequence of being in the second generation cleansed, washed, sanctified, and presented in him, an offering in a clean vessel, without spot, without wrinkle, or any such thing. This *regeneration* of our nature by the Holy Spirit, as related by the angel of the LORD to Mary, is the renewing of the Holy Ghost. Thus, it is not by works of righteousness which we have done, but according to his mercy he saved us, by the washing of regeneration, and renewing of the Holy Ghost. It is not *mending* or *repairing*, but *renewing our nature by the power of the Highest*. It is not putting a new piece in an old garment, but it is making *all things anew in Christ Jesus*. The prophet Jeremiah strikingly illustrates this subject—" Arise, and go down to the Potter's house, and there I will cause thee to hear my words. Then I went down to the Potter's house, and behold, he wrought a work on the wheels. And the vessel, that he made of clay, was marred in the hands of the Potter: so he made it again another vessel, as seemed good to the Potter to make it.

O, house of Israel, cannot I do with you as this Potter? saith the LORD. Behold, as the clay is in the Potter's hand, so are ye in mine, O house of Israel."

The whole house of Israel being compared to a potter's vessel, which vessel was marred in the hands of the potter, is like other scripture figures, apposite and most expressive. It does not appear, that the potter *cast away the clay*, assuredly not; but he made it again, *a nobler vessel, or another vessel*, as seemed good to the potter. Compare this passage with Ephesians ii. 10, "For we are his workmanship, *created anew in Christ Jesus unto good works, which God hath before ordained, that we should walk in them.*"

We hear of the *old Man* and the *new Man*. Ephesians iv. 22, 23, 24, "The old Man, *the first Adam*, the new Man, *the second Adam*. The old Man is corrupt, the new Man is after God, or in his likeness, created in righteousness or true holiness." Concerning the former conversation, we are exhorted to put off the former, and put on the latter, according to the spirit's teaching. Romans xiii. 14, "Put ye on the LORD Jesus Christ, and make not provision for the flesh to fulfil the lusts thereof." It is plain that this is an exhortation to receive the truth in the love of it, to live by faith in it, and *walking therein to add to our faith virtue*.

Agreeably to this renewal of the Holy Ghost, we hear him, that sat upon the throne, say, Behold I make *all* things new; and to shew that this declaration hath reference to the past, as well as the future, the Creator adds, It is done, I am the Alpha and Omega, the beginning and the end. Write, said he that sat on the throne, for these words are true and faithful—yea, verily, and they are precious words, faithful sayings uttered by the faithful and true. And if there be any thing on which we may rest our eternal hope, it is the good words of our God. The washing of regeneration, and renewing of the Holy Ghost; he hath shed on us abundantly through Jesus Christ. Abundantly is more than our wants demand. Psalm cxxxii. 15, "I will abundantly bless her provision; I will satisfy her poor with bread." John x. 10, "The thief, said our Saviour, cometh not but for to steal, and to kill, and to destroy; I am come that they might have life, and that they may have it more abundantly." To kill and to destroy, is the character of the adversary; but the friend, the Redeemer of the human family, descendeth to the earth, that we may have life, and that we may have it more abundantly. Not only the life forfeited, and lost in the first Adam, but as far superior as the heavens are to the earth, abundantly superior. Thus the Apostle, Romans v. 20, "Moreover the law entered, that the offence might abound: but where sin abounded, grace did much more abound."

But again, It is observable, that the Holy Ghost informs us, that this renewal is shed on us abundantly through Jesus Christ our Lord. This corroborates the doctrine, which bears testimony to the perfection of the work achieved by the Redeemer. God having so loved the world, as to give them his Son, has given with him all spiritual blessings. He hath blessed us abundantly with regeneration, and the renewal of the Holy Ghost, he hath shed these blessings upon us through Christ Jesus; this is the finished work of redemption, which is preached unto us, and which, believing with our hearts, we enter into rest, for we can no more come into condemnation.

But the question will be again and again repeated. Who are we to understand by the *us?* What *us* is intended? This question receives an answer from the spirit of truth, in Isaiah ix. 6, "*For unto us a child is born, unto us a son is given.*" God so loved the world, he gave them his son. The *us* then to whom the child is born, to whom the son is given, is the world of mankind.

Again, Matthew i. 23, "Behold a virgin shall be with child and shall bring forth a son, and they shall call his name Emmanuel, which being interpreted, is God with us." And this was glad tidings of good things unto all people. The prophet Hosea, vi. 10, clearly points out who the *us* are, that are saved by grace in our text. "After two days he will revive *us:* in the third day he will raise *us* up, and we shall live in his sight." Compare this text with Colossians ii. 12, "Buried with him in baptism, wherein also ye are risen with him, through the faith of the operation of God, who hath raised him from the dead." As from the concurring testimonies of sacred writers, it is abundantly evident, that both Jew and Gentile constituted the fulness of the body of the second Adam: so it is as evident, and from the same authority, that Jew and Gentile died in his death. When *I*, said our blessed Lord, am lifted up from the earth, I will draw *all men unto me.* This spake he signifying what death he should die; and it was this love of Christ, which constrained the Apostles to declare, that if one died for all then were all dead, but in the third day he raised the lost nature again, and it lived in the sight of the Creator.

Every arrangement for time and for eternity, results from the abundant mercy of God. The Holy Spirit informs us, by the Apostle James, ix. 17, "That the wisdom that cometh from above is full of mercy." This wisdom of God is exemplified in the plan of redemption. All the paths of the LORD are mercy and truth, unto such as keep his covenant and his testimonies. Psalm xxv. 10, "Thou, LORD, art good and ready to forgive, and plenteous in mercy unto all them that call upon thee."

Solomon assures us, Proverbs xvi. 16, "That by mercy and truth iniquity is purged; and that by the fear of the LORD, men depart from evil." And Isaiah beautifully says, "They shall not hunger nor thirst; neither shall the heat nor sun smite them: for he that hath mercy on them shall lead them, even by the springs of water shall he guide them. For the mountains shall depart, and the hills be removed; but my kindness shall not depart from thee, neither shall the covenant of my peace be removed, saith the LORD, that hath mercy on thee." The prophet Hosea, unites his suffrage, xiv. 3, "Ashur shall not save us, we will not ride upon horses, neither will we say any more to the work of our hands, Ye are our gods: for, in thee, the fatherless findeth mercy." The prophet Micah is on this list, vii. 18, "Who is a God like unto thee, that pardoneth iniquity, and passeth by the transgression of the remnant of his heritage? He retaineth not his anger forever, because he delighteth in mercy." And in the verse immediately succeeding, "He will turn again, he will have compassion upon us; he will subdue our iniquities; and thou wilt cast all their sins into the depths of the sea." I cannot forbear indulging myself, by passing on to the last verse in this prophecy: "Thou wilt perform the truth to Jacob, and the mercy to Abraham, which thou hast sworn unto our fathers from the days of old." In the thirty-second verse of the eleventh chapter of Romans, the Apostle Paul seems to sum up the whole business: "For God hath concluded all in *unbelief*, that he might have mercy upon all."

To conclude, it is observable, that *God's salvation* consists not in *our* conversion to God; nor is any change in us, according to the teaching of the Spirit of God, to be considered as the work of *regeneration*. The work of regeneration is a spiritual blessing, which we can have only in the seed of Abraham. But when the Spirit takes of the things of Jesus, and shows them unto us; when passing from darkness unto light, we come to the knowledge of him, in whom we have *redemption* and *regeneration*, and in whom we are *accepted*, and complete, perfect, and entire, lacking nothing; when the spirit of Jesus Christ witnesseth with our spirits, to these glorious truths, it is then we obtain peace and joy in believing; it is then we seek no longer for the living among the dead, for the new wine in the old bottles, nor for the new piece in the old garment. We then no longer stagger at the promises, through unbelief. We know, that in us, that is, in our flesh, dwelleth no good thing. We are no longer perplexed by the inconsistency of divine revelation. We behold in Jesus, in the *new Man*, in the *second Adam*, all things consist. The believer in Jesus Christ will acknowledge, that this change taking place in himself, *is not the truth, but a work of the spirit upon his heart, in consequence of the truth;* and this work of the Spirit, is to take of the things wrought out by Jesus, and show them to the soul. The change in his heart then, is in *consequence* of his seeing and believing the truth as it is in Jesus; it is *not* the *redemption*, the *righteousness*, nor the *sanctification*, but it is his embracing those glorious truths, which saves him from that indescribable anguish, to which he is heir, consequent upon his being a sinner, and from which he cannot be legitimately exempt, until he enters into rest, by *believing* the truth as it is in Jesus.

The genuine believer ceaseth from himself, he *denieth himself*, he no longer lives by sense, he doth not calculate according to the things which are seen, but he lives by faith, seeing what, to the eye of sense, is invisible. Viewing himself as a member in the body of the second Adam, he knows himself a subject of the *new birth;* he believes, that *all old things* are done away, and that *all things* are become *new;* and still living by faith, believing the word of the Lord, and viewing himself according to the unerring word of his God, a member of the body of Emmanuel, in life, in death, and in the resurrection, he understands the language of the spirit of truth, when he says, Reckon ye yourselves dead, indeed, unto sin, and alive unto God *by Jesus Christ*. Beholding himself thus blest, with all spiritual blessings in Christ Jesus, he enters *into rest*, ceasing from his own works as God did from his. God, as a Creator, when he saw the old creation finished, and *very good*, ceased from his work; and the genuine believer, beholding the completion of the *new creation*, and all *perfectly good*, enters into rest, and then, for the first time, understands what is intended by the *Sabbath*. Until this blessed period, he considered himself a partner with God, in the work of *regeneration* and *the new creation*, and that to complete both, he must do his part. But, at length, convinced of his extreme arrogance and presumption, he sitteth under the shadow of the *good tree* with inexpressible delight, and he keeps that Sabbath, in which he doth no *manner of work*. But, looking unto Jesus with grateful affection, he saith, *Thou, Lord, hast wrought all our works in us*. Believers, with devout gratitude, repeat after the Apostle, " It is not by works of righteousness done by *us*, that we are saved; but beholding that salvation, which was finished by those works of righteousness, that were wrought by him in our nature, in the *us*, to whom the child was born, and the Son given, they find joy unspeakable and full of glory." It is then impossible they can avoid loving God; for they know that *God is love*, not in word only, but in deed; and believing him to be in this character unchangeable, they trust in him at all times, not being afraid: and knowing, that God was in Christ reconciling the world unto himself, not imputing their trespasses unto them, they cannot discern any *just ground* for their continuing in a state of enmity against God, nor do they believe God is in a state of enmity with them. Why should God impute to them their trespasses, since Jesus has taken them upon himself? God will consider who was the doer of the deed, and he will consider who it was, that reconciled all things unto himself.

Believers, therefore, measure to every human being the same measure they measure to themselves. Whatever they may discover in themselves or in their fellow members in opposition to God, they consider as the seed sown by the enemy, and they hold it in utter abhorrence. They endeavour patiently to wait for the period, when the Lord of the harvest will give his angels charge to gather out of his kingdom, whatsoever gives offence; with those who do iniquity, they anticipate the era when these shall be utterly destroyed, and every individual seed sown by the

Son of man, the Son of God, the Saviour of the world, thus separated from every thing which can annoy from the spirits, which work, in the hearts of the children of disobedience, shall shine forth as the sun in the kingdom of the Father. They look earnestly and with joyful expectation, for the moment when they shall exchange the image of the earthly for the image of the heavenly, and be forever with the Lord. And of this blissful consummation they are perfectly assured, because *they know*, that Jesus Christ died for them, and for every man; that whether they wake or sleep, they may live together with him, who will thoroughly purge his floor, gathering his wheat into his garner, and burning up the chaff with unquenchable fire.

SKETCH CXIV.

1 Peter i. 22, 23.

First, Purification of soul, results from obedience to the truth, which is demonstrated by unfeigned love to the brethren, to those for whom the precious blood of Christ was shed, teaching us to measure the same measure to others, that we measure to ourselves. Acts xv. 9, " Put no difference between us and them, purifying their hearts by faith." Romans xii. 3, 4, 5, " For I say, through the grace given unto me, to every man that is among you, not to think of himself more highly than he ought to think; but to think soberly, according as God has dealt to every man the measure of faith. For as we have many members in one body, and all members have not the same office: so we, being many, are one body in Christ, and every one members one of another.

Secondly, Such universal benevolence is an incontrovertible evidence, that we are born again, not of corruptible seed, but of incorruptible, by the word of God which abideth forever. John i 13, " Born not of blood, nor of the will of the flesh, nor of the will of man, but of God" John iii. 3, " Jesus answered and said unto him, Verily, verily, I say unto thee, except a man be born again, he cannot see the kingdom of God."

SKETCH CXV.

1 Peter, iv. 18.

And if the righteous scarcely be saved, where shall the ungodly and the sinner appear?

First, Who are the righteous? Romans iii. 10, "As it is written, there are none righteous, no, not one." But where is it thus written? From whom did the Apostle Paul obtain his information? From the Son of Jesse. Psalm xiv. 2, 3, "The Lord looked down from heaven upon the children of men, to see if there were any that did understand and seek God. They are all gone aside; they are altogether become filthy; there is none that doeth good; no, not one."

Secondly, As the scriptures advert to righteous characters, we ought to believe that such characters do exist; yet we must embrace this testimony in a mode which may correspond with other testimonies; the word of God must not be held up as contradictory; the truth of God must not be controverted; the volume of inspiration must not make God a liar.

As none can be righteous in the sight of God, but those who keep the whole law, and as daily, if not momently experience, convinces us, that in many things every human being offends, it follows, that Jesus Christ, and Jesus Christ only, can be the righteous man of the scriptures; and that, as many as put on the Lord Jesus, are considered as righteous in his righteousness. Jeremiah iii. 6, "In his days shall Judah be saved, and Jerusalem shall dwell safely; and this is *his* name whereby he shall be called, *The Lord our righteousness.*" In the thirty-third chapter and sixteenth verse of this prophecy, the text is repeated, only changing the *masculine* for the *feminine*, "And this is the name wherewith *she* shall be called, The Lord our righteousness." There is a striking consistency, perfect coincidence, perfect truth, perfect beauty, and an exhaustless fund of consolation, in these corresponding passages. 1 Corinthians v. 21, "God hath made the Redeemer to be sin for us, who knew no sin, that we might be made the righteousness of God in him."

Thus, it is *in Christ Jesus*, that all the seed of Israel shall be justified and shall glory.

Thirdly, What are we to understand, by these righteous being *scarcely* saved? The word *scarcely*, undoubtedly intends, with much difficulty. But what is the salvation, that these righteous do with so much difficulty obtain? Not salvation from the curse of the law, nor from the wages of sin, which is death, nor from hell; these several salvations are the *free gift of God in Christ Jesus, in whom we are saved with an everlasting salvation*, nor shall we be ashamed or confounded, world without end, Isaiah xlv. 17. Yet there is a salvation consequent upon believing, in which these righteous are scarcely saved, because they are *scarcely believers*. It is in this view, that they are saved no longer than while they are believers; for no longer can they derive peace from a consideration of the righteousness, of the redemption, which they possess in Christ Jesus. There is a temporal, a spiritual, and an eternal salvation. All mankind are indebted to God for many temporal salvations; all mankind are indebted to God for eternal salvation, and all those who believe are indebted to God for spiritual salvation. In the first salvation, God acts as a God of providence; in the second, as a God of salvation; in the third, as a sovereign, showing mercy on whom he will show mercy. We have said, this last salvation is *consequent upon believing;* hence the Apostle Paul affirms, 1 Corinthians, xv. 1, 2, 3, " Moreover, brethren, I declared unto you the gospel, which I preached unto you, which also ye have received, and wherein ye stand; by which also ye are saved, *if ye keep in memory* what I preached unto you, unless ye have believed in vain. For I delivered unto you, first of all, that which I also received, how that Christ died for our sins, according to the scripture." Hence Paul exhorts his son Timothy, in his first Epistle to that preacher, iv. 16, to take heed unto himself, and unto his doctrine; and to continue therein; for, in thus doing, he should not only save himself, but those who heard him. But it is clear from scripture testimony, that Timothy could neither save himself, nor others from *eternal* damnation. This was the office of the Redeemer; and we say again, that it is from not distinguishing between the salvation wrought out, and completed by the Redeemer of the world, and the salvation which takes place in our hearts by the operation of the Comforter, the Holy Spirit; when he takes of the things which appertain to this finished redemption, and shows them to us, it is from the want of thus discriminating, that all the confusion respecting the scripture results. The believer is saved from condemnation, in the language of the translators, damnation, in consequence of believing; but if they, who, by putting on the LORD Jesus, are considered righteous, are *scarcely* saved, where shall the ungodly and the sinner appear?

Fourthly, Who are we to understand by the ungodly? Undoubtedly the fallen angelic nature. *Blessed is the man, that walketh not in the counsel of the ungodly.* In this ruinous path, Adam the first was a weary traveller: but the second Adam greatly victorious was able to say, *It is written, thou shalt worship the* LORD *thy God, and him only shalt thou serve.*

Fifthly, Who are we to understand by sinners? All who walk in the counsel of the ungodly, in consequence of which they are denominated ungodly men: but as the scriptures speak of the ungodly, and of sinners, it is proper that we also should discriminate: by sinners we presume is intended, those who continue in a state of unbelief, for this seems to be the only sin, which is now a source of condemnation, of that condemnation from which he that believeth is saved. This fact is supported by our Saviour. John iii. 18, " He that believeth on him is not condemned; but he that believeth not is condemned already, because he hath not believed on the name of the only begotten Son of God." 1 Corinthians xi. 32, " But when we are judged, we are chastened of the LORD, that we should not be condemned with the world." Again, John iii. 19, 20, 21, " And this is the condemnation, that light is come into the world, and men loved darkness rather than light, because their deeds were evil. For every one that doeth evil hateth the light, neither cometh to the light, lest his deeds should be reproved. But he that doeth truth cometh to the light, that his deeds may be made manifest, that they are wrought in God."

Sixthly, The apostolic question, Where shall the ungodly and sinner appear? 2 Corinthians v. 10, " For we must all appear before the judgment seat of Christ." Romans xiv. 10, " But why dost thou judge thy brother? Or why dost thou set at nought thy brother? For we shall all stand before the judgment seat of Christ." But although we must all appear before this seat of judgment, there will at that period be a very essential difference between the believer, and the ungodly, and the sinner. The apostle Paul directs us, 1 Corinthians xi. to judge ourselves, and we shall not be judged. Do ye not know, that the saints shall judge the world? Know ye not, that we shall judge angels? The volume of inspiration describes three characters in the final judgment. Believers, who having judged *themselves, shall not be judged*, who, seated with the judge, shall judge angels, the ungodly, which are the *fallen angels*, and the sinners, which make up the aggregate of the world. But the fate of these angels, and the human family will be very dissimilar. This, the living God, whom Paul declares to be the Saviour of all *men* in the close of the twenty-fifth chapter of Matthew clearly demonstrates, God having taken to himself our nature, and passed by the nature of angels, and who is emphatically styled the friend of sinners, when he shall judge them out of the things written in the books, when their mouths are stopped by conviction of the justice of their condemnation, when all the world stand *guilty*, GUILTY before him, shall then open the book of life, even the life of the world, at which luminous era, every son and daughter of Adam shall know him from the least of them, unto the greatest, know him, whom to know is life eternal, and thus taught of God, thus knowing him, every creature in heaven, on earth, and in the sea, shall unite in one grand hallelujah, saying, Blessing, and honour, and glory, and power unto him that sitteth upon the throne and to the Lamb forever and ever.

SKETCH CXVI.

REVELATIONS iii. 7.

First, WHO is the angel of the church of Philadelphia? Angel signifies a messenger bringing tidings, whether applied to individuals in heaven, or on earth. Revelations xxii. 9. "Then said he unto me, See thou do it not, for I am thy fellow servant, and of thy brethren, the prophets, and of them which keep the sayings of this book: worship God."

Secondly, By whom is the Evangelist directed to write unto the angel of the church of Philadelphia? To this question the volume of inspiration furnishes unequivocal responses. First, He is holy, one of the attributes of God manifest in the flesh. Isaiah i. 4, "They have provoked the Holy One of Israel." Psalm xvi. 10, "Thou wilt not suffer thine Holy One to see corruption." Luke iv. 34, "I know thee, who thou art, the Holy One of God." Whenever the people bear the character holy, they are considered as one with Emmanuel, who is made of God unto them sanctification.

Thirdly, He that is true. 1 John v. 20, "And we know that the Son of God is come, and hath given us an understanding, that we may know him that is true, and we are in him that is true, even in his Son Christ Jesus."

Fourthly, He hath the key of David. A key is an instrument which opens what was locked up, and concealed. Isaiah xxii. 22, "And the key of the house of David will I lay upon his shoulder, so he shall open and none shall shut; and he shall shut, and none shall open." The Jewish teachers are condemned for taking away the key of knowledge. Luke xi. 52, "Woe unto you, lawyers! For ye have taken away the key of knowledge; ye entered not in yourselves, and them that were entering in ye hindered."

Fifthly, He that openeth, and no man shutteth, and shutteth, and no man openeth. Isaiah xliv. 18, "They have not known nor understood, for he hath shut their eyes that they cannot see, and their hearts, that they cannot understand." Romans xi. 32, "For God hath concluded them all in unbelief, that he might have mercy upon all." Galatians iii. 23, "But before faith came we were kept under the law, shut up unto the faith, which should be afterwards revealed." But God the LORD openeth. Isaiah xlii. 7, "To open the blind eyes, to bring out the prisoners, and them that set in darkness, out of the prison house." For this purpose was the Redeemer given, for a covenant to the people, for a light of the Gentiles, and blessed be God, where he openeth no man can shut, the understanding which God illumines, no man can darken.

SKETCH CXVII.

REVELATIONS xi. 3—8.

First, AND *I will give power unto my two witnesses.* What are these two witnesses? The *law* and the *gospel.*

Secondly, Why are these two witnesses said to be *olive trees,* and *candlesticks,* standing before the God of the earth? Olive trees are emblematick of peace, and candlesticks of light.

Thirdly, What is intended by hurting them? *Wresting their testimony.*

Fourthly, What is the penalty to which those are subjected who hurt these witnesses? They must be killed by the fire, which proceedeth out of their mouth. Isaiah xi. 4, "And he shall smite the earth with the rod of his mouth, and with the breath of his lips shall he slay the wicked." Luke xix. 27. "But those mine enemies, which would not that I should reign over them, bring hither and *slay* them before me." Revelations xix. 21, "And the remnant were slain by the sword of him that sat upon the horse, which sword proceeded out of his mouth, and all the fowls were filled with their flesh."

Fifthly, These witnesses have power to shut heaven, and inflict plagues; alluding to Moses and Elias.

Sixthly, When was their testimony finished? Upon the cross. When the Redeemer of whom they testified, said, *it is finished.* Revelations xxi. 5, 6, "And he that sat upon the throne said, Behold, I make all things new, and he said unto me write: for those words are true and faithful. And he said unto me, it is done, I am Alpha and Omega, the beginning and the end."

Seventhly, And the beast that ascendeth out of the bottomless pit, shall make war against them, and shall overcome them, and kill them. The thirteenth chapter of this book, gives us an account of this beast. It is the spirit of anti-christ, which is opposed to the true Chrst, which warreth against the true Christ, and the multitudes which unite in opposition, overcome the witnesses, and the non-reception of the testimony of these witnesses is destroying or killing them *as witnesses*.

Eighthly, And their dead bodies shall lie in the streets of the great city, which spiritually is called Sodom, and Egypt, where also our LORD was crucified. It is observable, the *dead bodies of these witnesses were not buried;* and this proves they are not lost, their dead bodies are still in the street where Christ was crucified, which is spiritually, not naturally called Sodom and Egypt, the one bondage, the other sensual gratifications, both together including sin, and its consequences, which were both together crucified with Christ. *The witnesses still remain, although their testimony is refused,* and they are considered as a dead letter, they are however in the streets of the great city, and they shall still be preserved until they shall once more *stand before God.*

SKETCH CXVIII.

REVELATIONS xi. 9—13.

First, THEY of the people, and kindreds, and tongues, and nations, shall see their dead bodies three days and a half, and shall not suffer their dead bodies to be put in graves. They will not renounce *these two witnesses,* the *law* and the *gospel,* in other words, the *two testaments,* they still keep them in their streets, they are still called by their names, although they are *dead* bodies, to them a *dead letter,* yet they do not shroud them in graves, they still exhibit them to the public eye.

Secondly, And they that dwell upon the earth shall rejoice over them, and make merry, and shall send gifts one to another, because these two prophets tormented them that dwelt on the earth. They that dwell on the earth hail their emancipation from these two witnesses, the regulations established by the law and the gospel, were to them a source of suffering, and they are now merry at the expense of the ceremonial law, and those institutions, which they characterize as absurd, and they ridicule the idea of that gospel, which describes *Emmanuel, God with us or the Deity clothed in humanity.*

Thirdly, But after the expiration of three days and a half, the *spirit of life from God entered into these witnesses* or prophets, and, thus divinely reanimated, they stood upon their feet. We are informed in the sacred volume, that a thousand years are in the sight of God as a single day.

Fourthly, When the power of God was thus displayed in these witnesses, great fear fell upon those who witnessed this *new life*, that is, upon those which dwelt upon the earth.

Fifthly, And they heard a great voice from heaven saying unto the witnesses, Come up hither, and they ascended up to heaven, *to him of whom they testified*, in a cloud, in the presence and view of their enemies.

Sixthly, And in the same hour there was a great earthquake; the *earth*, the *human earth*, the family of man, trembling and quaking, and the tenth part of the city fell; and in the earthquake were slain of men seven thousand, the same number that had not bowed the knee to Baal, and the remnant were affrighted and gave glory to the God of heaven.

SKETCH CXIX.

Revelations xi. 14—19.

First, Our subject commences with the sounding of the seventh angel, which is called the third woe.

Secondly, Immediately after the sounding of this seventh angel, we hear voices in heaven, saying, The kingdoms of this world are become the kingdoms of our Lord, and of his Christ; and he shall reign forever and ever. This is an accomplishment of the prophet Daniel's prediction, chapter vii. 22, 27.

Thirdly, Consequent upon the kingdoms of this world becoming the kingdoms of our Lord, and his Christ, the four and twenty elders which sat before God on their seats, fell upon their faces and worshipped God. Why twenty-four elders? Because twenty-four is the combined number of the Patriarchs and Apostles. What was their attitude? They sat, in what place? Before God. What was their conduct at the sonorous utterance of the celestial voices? They fell upon their faces and worshipped God. In what manner? We give thee thanks, O Lord God Almighty, which art, and wast, and art to come; because thou hast taken to thee thy great power, and hast reigned.

Fourthly, And the nations were angry, and thy wrath is come, and the time of the dead, that they should be judged. Revelations xx. 12, "And I saw the dead, small and great, stand before God; and the books were opened, and another book was opened, which is the book of life: and the dead were judged out of those things, which were written in the books according to their works."

Fifthly, At this period, God's servants, the prophets, the saints, and them that fear the name of the Lord, both small and great, shall receive their reward. What is this reward? The answer of their prayers. Agreeably to the will of God, they have made supplication for all men, and they shall then see the salvation of all men.

Sixthly, God will destroy them that destroy the earth. What earth? Human earth, Adam and his posterity. Who is the destroyer? Our adversary, the devil, and all those hosts of infernals, who combine for the destruction of the human family.

Seventhly, At this period, and not until this period, the *temple* of God is opened in heaven? What are we to understand by the temple of God, which, upon this occasion, is to be opened in heaven? The twenty-second verse of the twenty-first chapter of this book, furnishes an answer to this question:—"And I saw no temple therein: for the Lord God Almighty, and the Lamb are the temple of it."

SKETCH CXX.

Revelations xxi 5.

First, Who is it that sat upon the throne? The Redeemer of men. Psalm xlv. 6, "Thy throne, O God, is forever and ever." Hebrews i. 8, "But unto the Son, he saith, Thy throne, O God, is forever and ever."

Secondly, The throne of the Redeemer is denominated a throne of grace. Hebrews iv. 16, "Let us, therefore, come boldly unto the throne of grace." This trait is expressive and perfectly in character, for him who is full of grace and truth. John i. 14, "And we beheld his glory, as the glory of the only begotten of the Father, full of grace and truth."

Thirdly, The Redeemer sat upon this throne. This intends his resting there, dwelling there, taking up his abode there.

Fourthly, What is the language of him, that sat upon the throne? Behold, I make all *things new*. We know, that all things were made by him and for him. Yet how extensive the depravity, how deep, how wide-spreading the ruin ushered in by the fall. But, saith he, who sitteth upon the throne, Behold, *I make all things new.*

Fifthly, God will make a new heart and a new spirit.

Sixthly, All things being made new, all old things must be done away. There will be no more sorrow, no more *death*, neither shall there be any more pain.

Seventhly, The everlasting Father, the Son given, the Redeemer of men, having made this important, this solemn declaration, enjoins it upon the Apostle to record it, and, benignly condescending, he adds as a reason:—"For these words are faithful and true."

SKETCH CXXI.

Revelations xxii. 1, 2, 3.

First, And he shewed me a pure river of water of life, clear as crystal, proceeding out of the throne of God and the Lamb. What is this river? Psalm xlvi. 4, "There is a river, the streams whereof make glad the city of God, the holy place of the tabernacles of the Most High." Zechariah xiv. 8, "And it shall be in that day, that living waters shall go out from Jerusalem, half of them toward the former sea, and half of them toward the hinder sea: in summer and in winter shall it be."

Secondly, In the midst of the street of it, and on either side of the river, was there the tree of life. Christ Jesus himself is this tree, this tree of life; and of this tree, the Spirit, by the mouth of the royal prophet, thus testifieth, Psalm i. 3, "And he shall be like a tree planted by the rivers of water, that bringeth forth his fruit in his season; his leaf also shall not wither; and whatsoever he doeth shall prosper."

Thirdly, The medicinal or restoring quality of this tree. And the leaves of the tree were for the healing of the nations. Mark iii. 15, "And to have power to heal sicknesses, and to cast out devils." In consequence of which,

Fourthly, There shall be no more curse. What is a curse? It is an execration or a supplication, that vexation, pain or torment, may overtake the object of our hatred. The supreme Being hath cursed first the serpent; secondly, the earth; and thirdly, the breakers of his law. Human beings bestow curses on each other, sometimes by divine appointment, as in Deuteronomy xxvii. But, more frequently, bad men, under the influence of the spirit of the adversary, curse each other after the manner of Shimei the son of Gera, who came forth cursing still as he came, 1 Samuel xvi. 5.

Fifthly, The Spirit of truth saith, there shall be no more curse; for the period hastens, when, instead of the curse, and contrasted therewith, the throne of God and of the Lamb shall be in it. Did the Spirit simply say, the throne of God shall be in it, or the throne of the Lamb shall be in it, we should not derive from the information such abundant felicity; but the throne of God and of the Lamb, is the union of the divine and human nature, and this union is our salvation. This throne is the seat of the King, as the head of the universe; it is the highest seat of regal power and dignity. Only in the throne, said Pharaoh, will I be greater than thou.

Sixthly, The servants of God shall serve him. Whether born in servitude, or bought, or conquered, or freely engaged, every individual of the human family is, in one or other of these points, the servant of God; and whether he is thus by birth, by purchase, by conquest, or by choice, he shall assuredly be brought into subjection.

SKETCH CXXII.

Revelations xxii. 4, 5, 6.

First, And they shall see his face. Under another dispensation this was impossible. Exodus xxxiii. 20, "And he said, Thou canst not see my face: for there shall no man see me and live." Why, in their individual characters, they were not pure in heart. Blessed are the pure in heart; for they shall see God. 1 John, iii. 2, "Beloved, now are we the sons of God, and it doth not yet appear what we shall be: but we know, that when he shall appear, we shall be like him, for we shall see him as he is."

Secondly, The name of God shall be upon their foreheads. Revelations iii. 12, "Him that overcometh will I make a pillar in the temple of my God, and he shall go no more out: and I will write upon him the name of my God, and the name of the city of my God which is New Jerusalem, which cometh down out of heaven from my God: and I will write upon him my new name." Revelations xiv. 1, "And I looked, and, lo, a Lamb stood on the mount Sion, and with him a hundred forty and four thousand, having their Father's name written in their foreheads." In the present state, they have worn the mark of the beast in their hand, and on their foreheads. Revelations xiii. 16, "And he caused all, both small and great, rich and poor, free and bond, to receive a mark in their right hand, or in their foreheads." But the name which they shall receive when they are before God, is a holy name; it appertaineth to him, who is called the Holy One of Israel, and the name whereby he shall be called is, The Lord our righteousness.

Thirdly, And there shall be no night there. Night is, literally, that portion of time when the sun is below our horizon; but it is, figuratively, mental darkness and ignorance. Romans xiii. 12, "The night is far spent, the day is at hand: let us, therefore, cast off the works of darkness, and let us put on the armour of light." Matthew xxv. 6, "And at midnight there was a cry made, Go ye out to meet the bridegroom." Night is expressive of adversity. Psalm xxx. 5, " Weeping may endure for a night, but joy cometh in the morning." Isaiah viii 22, " And they shall look unto the earth, and behold trouble and darkness, dimness of anguish." Psalm cvii. 10, "Such as sit in darkness and the shadow of death, being bound in affliction and iron." Night is descriptive of the power of the adversary. Luke xxii. 53, " When I was daily with you in the temple, ye stretched forth no hands against me, but this is your hour, and the power of darkness." Again, Night is emblematic of the power of sin. Colossians i. 13, " Who hath delivered us from the power of darkness, and translated us into the kingdom of his dear Son."

Fourthly, And they need no candle. What are we to understand by this candle? Ministers of the word. Matthew v. 14, 15, " Ye are the light of the world. Neither do men light a candle and put it under a bushel." Revelations i. 20, " The seven stars are the angels of the seven churches, and the seven candlesticks which thou sawest are the seven churches."

Fifthly, Neither light of the sun. Why is this? The sun was *created for a sign;* but when the substance is ever present, the sign will be unnecessary; the Lord God himself giveth them light.

Sixthly, And they shall reign forever and ever. In our mortal bodies sin reigneth ; but in a state of beatification, Jesus Christ and his righteousness shall reign forever and ever.

Seventhly, And he said unto me, these sayings are faithful and true. Revelations i. 1, " The Revelation of Jesus Christ, which God gave unto him, to shew unto his servant things, which must shortly come to pass ; and he sent, and signified it unto his angel by his servant John." Revelations xix. 9, " And he saith unto me, Write, Blessed are they which are called unto the marriage supper of the Lamb. And he saith unto me, These are the true sayings of God." Thus the Lord God of the holy prophets, sent his angel to shew unto his servants the things, which must shortly be done. Blessed, forever blessed be the name of the Redeemer of men

SKETCH CXXIII.

REVELATIONS xxii. 7, 8, 9.

THE first particular pointed out in our text, is the speedy accomplishment of the things promised, *Behold, I come quickly.*

Secondly, Blessed is he, who keepeth the sayings of the prophecy of this book.

Thirdly, And I, John, saw these things and heard them; and when I had heard and seen, I fell down to worship before the feet of the angel, that shewed me these things.

Fourthly, The admonition and testimony of the angel. *See thou do it not;* for I am thy fellow servant, and of thy brethren, the prophets, and of them who keep the sayings of this book: *Worship God.* This corresponds with the testimony of all God's sent servants.

Fifthly, *God is the only proper object of worship.* Exodus xxxiv. 14, "For thou shalt worship no other God." *Yet it appears that the Redeemer is a proper object of worship, of all adoration.* Matthew ii. 11, "The wise men worshipped him while he was cradled in the manger." Matthew viii. 2, "And behold, there came a leper and *worshipped him.*" Matthew ix. 18, "Behold there came a certain ruler and *worshipped him.*" Matthew xiv. 33, "They that were in the ship *worshipped him.*" Matthew xv. 25, "The woman of Canaan *worshipped him.*" Matthew xxviii. 9, "The disciples held him by the feet and *worshipped him.*" Matthew xxxviii. 17, "And when they saw him they *worshipped.*" In no instance do we learn, that the Redeemer rebuked these *worshippers.* We do not hear him say, *See thou do it not.* But this worship was not confined to his immediate disciples or cotemporaries. In the fifteenth chapter and fourth verse of this book of Revelations, we are thus taught, "Who shall not fear thee, O LORD, and glorify thy name? For thou only art holy; for all *nations shall come, and worship before thee.*" And Revelations v. 14, "And the four and twenty elders fell down and *worshipped him*, that liveth forever and ever." *These facts are incontrovertible proofs of the divinity of the God-man.* He is indeed the *only wise God our Saviour.* But this is only one from the mass of evidences. We could produce a thousand proofs. Blessed be God, to this consolatory truth, there are a cloud of witnesses. Blessed be God, that in this child born, in this everlasting Father, we live, move, and have our being.

SKETCH CXXIV.

Revelations xxii. 10, 11.

First, AND *he said unto me, seal not the sayings of the prophecy of this book ; Why ? For the time is at hand.*

Secondly, *He that is unjust, let him be unjust still, and he that is filthy, let him be filthy still.* Perhaps the best way of designating the unjust and filthy, is to advert to the contrast of those characters, the just and the spotless. Isaiah xxvi. 7, "The way of the just is uprightness : thou, most upright, dost weigh the path of the just." The paths, the ways of erring man, being thus tested by him, who is of purer eyes than to behold iniquity, we are not surprised to hear Job ask, Job ix. 2, "How should man be just with God ?" The apostle James decisively says, chapter ii. 10, "Whosoever shall keep the whole law, and yet offend in one point, he is guilty of all." And Jesus being the only *human individual*, who never offended in a *single point*, is the *only just, the only holy one.* But men are called just, this is by the righteousness of the just God, of the God-man, who was raised again *for our justification.*

Thirdly, What are we to understand by being filthy ? It is being defiled by sin, it is only a stronger mode of expressing the same melancholy truth ; nor is it a particular description of the human family, that are thus characterized ; listen to the prophet Isaiah, lxiv. 6, "All our righteousnesses are as filthy rags, we are all as an unclean thing." The prophet Zechariah, iii. 3, informs us, that even Joshua was clothed with filthy garments,

But man is not the only filthy being. God passeth over unclean spirits. Matthew x. 1, "And when he had called to him his twelve disciples, he gave them power over *unclean spirits* to cast them out." And he commanded the unclean spirits to quit their abode in the bosom of humanity.

Fourthly, The general judgment will convene two distinct races of intelligent beings, sheep and goats; these are figures of men and angels. The dead shall be raised incorruptible and glorious. But how can they be all righteous? Because Jesus Christ was manifested to destroy the works of the devil, because he is the Lamb of God, that taketh away the sin of the world, because he shall change these vile bodies, and fashion them like unto the glorious body of the Son of God; after which the individuals of the human family shall no more be unjust, filthy. But he that is unjust, shall be unjust still, and he that is filthy, shall be filthy still, and he that is righteous, shall be righteous still, and he that is holy, shall be holy still. Blessed be the name of our God, forever and ever.

SKETCH CXXV.

Revelations xxii. 12, 13.

First, And, *behold, I come quickly.* 2 Peter iii. 9, 10, "The Lord is not slack concerning his promise, as some men count slackness; but is long-suffering to usward, *not willing that any should perish, but that all should come to repentance.*" Habakkuk ii 3, "For the vision is yet for an appointed time, but at the end it shall speak, and not lie; though it tarry, wait for it; because it will surely come, it will not tarry."

Secondly, And my reward is with me. What is the reward of the Redeemer? Psalm cxxvii "Lo, children are the heritage of the Lord; and the fruit of the womb is his reward." But has God given every individual born of a woman to the Redeemer? John iii. 35, "The Father loveth the Son, and hath given all things into his hand." John xvi. 15. But will every individual thus given come unto Jesus? Is it not written, ye will not come unto me that ye may have life? The Redeemer affirmeth,

John vi. 37, " that all that the Father giveth shall come to him," and, he adds, " that those who come he will in no wise cast out." But may not the sovereign will of God finally consign them to perdition ? The testimony of Christ Jesus should invariably be considered as decisive, and to this question his answer is unequivocal. And this is the Father's will which hath sent me, that of all which he hath given me I should lose nothing, but should raise it up again at the last day. But doth the will of the Divine and human nature correspond respecting the reward that is with him ? John xvii. 24, " Father, I will that they also whom thou hast given me, be with me where I am ; that they may behold my glory."

Thirdly, I come quickly ; and my reward is with me, to *give every man according as his work shall be.* The Redeemer doth not say, he cometh to *pay* every man, then it would be wages, and as there is no man that liveth and sinneth not, the wages of sin being death, he must pay unto every man *death*. He doth not say, he cometh to give unto *some men*, but unto *every man*. But what are the works which will on that day be rewarded? Let us consult the sacred oracles of our God. Isaiah xxvi. 12, LORD, thou wilt ordain peace for us ; for thou also hast wrought all our works in us." But we will appeal to the great Shepherd and Bishop of souls. John xiv. 12, " Verily, verily, I say unto you, he that believeth on me, the works that I do shall he do also; and greater works than these shall he do ; because I go unto my Father." The reward of these works shall be great in heaven. But have all those who were given unto the Saviour these works in perfection ? Attend once more to the voice of the Redeemer of men, John xvii. 23, " I in them, and thou in me, that they may be made perfect in one ; and that the world may know that thou hast sent me, and hast loved them, as thou hast loved me." But are we not taught, that individuals will be rewarded according to their works? Assuredly we are. First, Jesus will be rewarded according to his works; all souls are his reward; and for these, despising the shame, he endured the cross. Secondly, the adversary, he who goeth about like a roaring lion, seeking whom he may destroy, shall be rewarded, according to his works. The evil which he thought to bring upon the human family, shall be brought upon himself. *Reward her even as she rewarded you, and double unto her double, ac-*

cording to her works; in the cup which she hath filled, fill to her double. Thirdly, The disciples of our LORD shall be rewarded, Hebrews xi. 26, "Esteeming the reproach of Christ greater riches than the treasures of Egypt, for he had respect unto the recompense of the reward." The preachers of the gospel have their reward, 1 Corinthians iii 8, 14, "Now he that planteth and he that watereth are one; and every man shall receive his own reward, according to his own labour. If any man's work abide which he hath built thereupon, he shall receive a reward." Believers of the truth as it is in Jesus, who give unto the poor, shall in no wise lose their reward. They who pray to their Father in secret have their reward The Saviour of the world assureth us, that he who receiveth a prophet, shall receive a prophet's reward. But as it is God that worketh in us both to will and to do, the reward is not of debt, but of grace. The way of the transgressor is hard. The ways of wisdom are ways of pleasantness, and all her paths are peace. Let us never be weary in well doing, for in due time we shall reap, if we faint not; let us always remember, that God is pleased with works of faith and labours of love, wrought in the name of Christ Jesus the LORD.

I have been asked what is intended by the eighteenth and nineteenth verses of the chapter which contains our text. If any man shall add unto these things, God shall add unto him the plagues that are written in this book. And if any man shall take away from the words of the book of this prophecy, God shall take away his part out of the book of life, and out of the holy city, and from the things which are written in this book. Perhaps it is less difficult to say, what this last declaration does *not* intend, than what it *does intend*. The eighteenth verse may be taken literally. An attempt to add to the testimony of God may multiply the sorrows of the audacious presumer But the loss which he who diminishes the words of the prophecy is to sustain, cannot design any *deduction from the reward of the Redeemer.* We cannot suppose that Emmanuel will lose any part of that, for which he endured the agonies of the cross He gave himself a ransom for all; he is the head of every man. *In the book of life all his members are written,* and it is impious to suppose, that the name of a single member of the body of Christ Jesus can be erased from the book of life! Perhaps the denunciation in this nineteenth verse is but another mode of expressing the latent truth contained in the parable of the talents. From him that hath not, shall be taken away, even that which he hath, or seemeth to have; and it shall be given unto him which hath the ten talents, that God may be all in all. This may be accomplished at that period, when those works of individuals which cannot stand the test, shall be destroyed, and they themselves saved so as by fire.

But whatever may be the design of this passage, I am satisfied, I am happy, that it is not a balance for, that it cannot cancel those reiterated promises which bear testimony to the salvation of all men, and which are abundantly multiplied in the oracles of my God.

SKETCH CXXVI.

Revelations xxii. 20.

First, We are to inquire of whom the Spirit speaketh; and it is abundantly apparent, that he speaketh of Jesus, of the Alpha and Omega, the first and the last; of Adam the second, of the Lamb of God who taketh away the sin of the world, of the head of the Church, of him who is the head of every man.

Secondly, Will he sustain these important characters, when he descends to judge the world? O, yes, assuredly he will; for he changeth not; Jesus Christ is the same yesterday, to-day, and forever. And when the risen Saviour ascended into heaven, and the disciples, with eager eyes, beheld his beatified elevation, it is recorded, that two men stood by them in white apparel, in other words, two angels of God, and addressing the disciples, said, "Ye men of Galilee, why stand ye gazing up into heaven? This same Jesus, which is taken up from you into heaven, shall so come in like manner as ye have seen him go into heaven."

Thirdly, *He which testifieth these things, saith, Surely, I come quickly.* This intelligence is to every believer in God our Saviour, glad tidings of good things. The Redeemer will come quickly, and he will accomplish, that which all his holy prophets have predicted. Listen to his own divine declaration. Luke iv. 18, 19, " The Spirit of the Lord is upon me, because he hath anointed me to preach the gospel to the poor; he hath sent me to heal the broken hearted, to preach deliverance to the captives, and recovering of sight to the blind, to set at liberty them that are bruised. To preach the acceptable year of the Lord.

Are there any who pretend to believe, that the Bible is the word of God, who will dare to say, that Christ Jesus will not continue the same; that he will not, at his second coming, descend to save the people from their sins, and to bless them? Are there any, calling themselves christians, who will dare to say, that when the seed of Abraham shall again be manifested to his brethren, he will be manifested to prove, that what he communicated to Abraham, and what that *Friend of God believed*, was not true? God forbid. To such glaring infidelity, we would not, we could not say—Amen.

Fourthly, "*Amen*"—This comprehensive word, we are told, is, literally, *so be it;* and hence it is added, "*Even so come*, Lord Jesus." Surely the voice of every genuine christian, is in unison with this supplication—*Even so come*, Lord Jesus; come thou philanthropic Saviour of all men; come, Lord Jesus, purge thy floor, and gather thy wheat into thy garner; come, thou glorious Redeemer, and separate between the precious and the vile; come, thou God-man, that the top-stone may be brought forth with shouting, crying grace, grace unto it. Thus closeth the Book of God.—The grace of our Lord Jesus Christ be with you all, Amen. It is remarkable, that the last verse of the Old Testament, terminates with the word curse; and the last verse of the New Testament, speaking better things, concludes with the grace of our Lord Jesus Christ. John i. 17, " For the law was given by Moses, but grace and truth came by Jesus Christ." The one is a dispensation of *cursing*, the other of *blessing*. The one a ministration of death, unto death, the other of life unto life. Therefore, the prophet Malachi, in the close of the Old Testament saith, lest I come and smite the earth with a curse. Therefore, the evangelist concludeth the sacred Oracles with this declaration, with this blessing. He which testifieth these things saith, Surely I come quickly: Amen. Even so come, Lord Jesus. The grace of our Lord Jesus Christ be with you all: Amen.

Reflections upon ROMANS ix. 27.

SALVATION, destruction, justification, condemnation; these are the themes of the christian theologian, and the numbers saved, and the numbers lost, employ their most profound research. Those, in whose paths are misery and destruction, rejoice when they discover in the book of God, any passages, which they imagine, establish those opinions, to which they are wedded. The apostle Paul in the twenty-seventh verse of the ninth chapter of his epistle to the Romans, particularly the latter clause of the verse, is frequently pressed into their service, " *A remnant shall be saved; though the number of the children of Israel be as the sand of the sea, a remnant shall be saved.*" The inference drawn by the advocates of destruction, is that ONLY, a remnant shall be saved. We are not solicitous to deprive them of whatever enjoyment they may derive from reading the scriptures; but we wish they would give such attention to the sacred writings, as might enable them to rest thereon, at least for their own support, that they would receive their own salvation from the hands of the bountiful, as genuine believers. A diligent investigation of the spirit's teaching, through the instrumentality of the man of Tarsus, would place them beyond a doubt, and give them to draw consolation from the only true source of comfort

It is very astonishing, that as the two salvations pointed out in the book of God, are so clearly and so unequivocally delineated, they are so often confounded, blended, misrepresented, and wrested to the destruction of that blessed peace, which passeth understanding. It is impossible to preserve the consistency of the sacred writings, without taking these two salvations into view, and if there be *no consistency*, if there be *contradiction*, it is equally impossible to obtain and preserve an *unwavering* faith. I have wondered much, that men, honest and sincere men, do not more accurately search the sacred writings. I have passed a large proportion of my life in searching the scriptures, and I appeal to God as a voucher of my truth, that I lie not, when I say those two salvations appear to me clearly, indubitably and most emphatically taught in that book, which we are told contains the only rule given by the faithful Creator, to direct our faith and practice. Commentators, celebrated commentators agree, that although the Jews were numerous as the sand of the sea, a remnant ONLY were destined to salvation, that the greater part should be for their unbelief, finally and *eternally damned*. Yes, I know that such is the opinion of a greater part of those who are falsely denominated the christian world. The simple idea *originated* and *supported* by these eminent writers, whose testimony is of far greater weight with the world, in general, than the testimony of the prophets and the apostles, is, that an omnipotent God, hath created millions of millions of human beings, with a purpose of consigning them to never ending torments, rescuing ONLY a little remnant, which by the plenitude of his sovereign power, he will preserve from everlasting burnings, There are, however, blessed be God, there are some according to the election of grace who still say, *let God be true, and every man a liar*.

What is this irrational and most tremendous doctrine propagated from the pulpit, and the press? Let me pause for a moment to examine. Is not the whole human family given by the divine nature to the Son, as the head of every man? Yea, saith the lip of truth, all that the Father hath, he hath given unto me; but, saith the commentator, a remnant ONLY of those, which were given unto Jesus, shall be saved; yet the Redeemer himself declares, *of all that thou hast given me, none of them are lost, save the son of perdition*.

The testimony of commentators has been aptly illustrated by the figure of a piece of cloth, presented to a connoisseur, who deliberately cuts off a remnant, and lays it by, to be saved or preserved, and commits the piece to the flames!!! Again, the family of man are said to be bought with a price, even the precious blood of the Son of God, and those, who make a *division in the God-head, represent God the Father, as destroying the piece, after the ransom had been paid by God the Son!*

I do not wish to deny, that the Apostle saith, *though the number of the children of Israel be as the sand of the sea, a remnant shall be saved;* but I deny that he saith, ONLY a remnant shall be saved. The two verses immediately preceding this oft-cited passage, render it, to my understanding, gloriously luminous. "As he said also in Osee, *I will call them my people, which were not my people; and her beloved, which was not beloved. And it shall come to pass, that in the place where it was said unto them, Ye are not my people; there shall they be called the children of the living God."* Then follows the passage in question, *Esaias also crieth concerning Israel, though the number of the children of Israel be as the sand of the sea, a remnant shall be saved.* What is this, but in other words, delivering his sentiments precisely as he afterwards delivered them in the eleventh chapter of this Epistle. " *And so all Israel shall be saved :* as it is written, There shall come out of Sion the Deliverer, and shall turn away ungodliness from Jacob. For this is my covenant unto them, when I shall take away their sins. As concerning the gospel, they are enemies for your sakes; but as touching the election they are beloved for the fathers' sakes. For the gifts and calling of God are without repentance. For as ye in times past, have not believed God, yet have now obtained mercy through their unbelief. Even so, have these also not believed, that through your mercy they also may obtain mercy. *For God hath concluded them all in unbelief, that he might have mercy upon all."* The Apostle hath selected these passages from the prophet Isaiah. I love to trace, to investigate scripture; and, as far as I am permitted, I am fond of tracing every thing to its source. Listen, O my soul, listen to the prophet as he himself speaketh. Isaiah x. 21, 22, " *The remnant shall return, even the remnant of Jacob unto the mighty God.* For though thy people Israel be as the sand of the sea, *yet a remnant of them shall return,* the consumption decreed shall *overflow with righteousness."* I confess the words *even* a *remnant* and *yet* a remnant, sound better to my ears, are more delightful to my soul, than *only a remnant,* and I have two reasons for my preference; first, I prefer the *divine* to human authority, and, secondly, if *even a remnant are saved,* it includes the whole piece, not a thread to be lost. Our evangelical prophet was of this opinion. " And it shall come to pass in that day, that the LORD shall set his hand again a second time, to recover the remnant of his people, which shall be left from Assyria, and from Egypt, and from Pathros, and from Cush, and from Elam, and from Shinar, and from Hamath, and from the Islands of the sea. And he shall set up an ensign for the nations, and shall assemble the *outcasts* of Israel, and gather together the dispersed of Judah from the four corners of the earth. Two or three berries in the top of the uppermost bough, four or five in the outmost fruitful branches, saith the LORD God of Israel; these also, when our God sets his hand a second time, shall be gathered in."

That the human family were and are very precious to the God who created them, is evinced by the astonishing price he hath paid for their redemption, and if he be *able* to preserve this dear bought purchase, can it obtain credit in any rational mind, that he will destroy the whole piece, reserving to himself only a remnant of that, for which he hath paid the price all price beyond.

I repeat, that I am sensible there are two salvations described in that book, which was dictated by the spirit of God. The one salvation is *spiritual* and *eternal*, the other is *temporal* and *immediate*. Those are very little acquainted with scripture, who have not ascertained this fact; and it is the ignorance thereof, which is the principal cause of that perversion of sacred writ, which obtains among mankind; and it is hence, that so many disconsolate beings remain in a state of unbelief and consequent condemnation. Instances of this temporal salvation are frequent. Noah and his house, Rahab and her house, &c. &c.

It is a delightful employment to search the scriptures, to draw water from these wells of salvation, to select those passages from the sacred volume, which proclaim the redemption of the betrayed, ensnared, and captivated nature; to bring from these mines of rich treasure, things *new* and *old*, both enlarges and elevates the spirit of the believer. The sacred volume is replete with testimonies of salvation, both for the body and the soul, both for time and eternity. Yet, in the present scene, the election only obtains the *knowledge* of salvation, and the rest, for *wise reasons are blinded;* in this sense a *remnant are saved*, but the time hastens, when all animated earth shall be filled with the *knowledge* of the LORD, and to *know God* is life eternal.

The prophecies were given by divine inspiration to the people of the Jews, and some have been ready to conclude, that the grace therein contained was confined to that people. Thus thought the Jews themselves, but they had no right thus to think, for even the prophets themselves assured them, that the God of Abraham, of Isaac, and of Jacob, was in deed and in truth, *the God of the whole earth.* The writings of the royal prophet are full to this purpose. Yet as the veil was upon the heart of the people of God, when they read Moses and the prophets, and as it is still continued upon the hearts of many of God's people, although we are ever looking forward to a day of transcendent light, yet do we frequently err, not knowing the scriptures. A serious attention to the scriptures would give us reason to expect, that darkness, such as has never yet been witnessed in our world, will abundantly prevail, before the second grand appearance of the Redeemer. But as we are told, God maketh darkness his pavilion, that he dwelleth in the storm, in the thick darkness, and that every eye shall see; when we recollect that the Being from whom we receive these assurances *cannot lie*, we do not surrender ourselves to lamentation and woe—We already see the *remnant* are saved, and we anticipate the era when all those individuals, however scattered, which constitute the whole of that nature, that composes the body in its aggregate, shall be full of light. I want nothing more than an attention to the scriptures to render me a believer in their divine author, except indeed the spirit, by which they were written, witnessing with my spirit to the truth thereof. No man can receive and understand the things of God, but by the spirit of God; but as faith cometh by hearing, it is necessary we hear this word, that bringeth salvation unto all men!

It is a blessed thing to know God. We are told, it is life eternal to know God, but certainly it is not life eternal to know God, except we know God as *he is*, the life of the world. It is a blessed thing to know God in this character, for in knowing him to be the life of the world, each individual of the world, who thus knows him, knows him to be his life, and each individual, thus taught, can say for himself, God is my life, and he whom God gives by his Spirit's teaching thus to know him, is an individual in that little remnant, who is saved *in consequence of believing*; but this not to the *exclusion* of the rest, for when *every eye shall see, then every heart will consequently believe.*

I am delighted and astonished, as I examine this divine treasury, to observe how many plain passages it contains, which testify of the *Creator*, as the *Saviour of the world!* I am, saith Jehovah, God the Saviour, and beside me there is none other, so that whatever *erring mortals* may apprehend from *God their Creator, God their Saviour*, he remembers his *own name*, and gives *this name*, as a reason for acting the part of a *Saviour*.

Be it known to you, not for your sakes do I do this, but for mine own *name sake*. Truly, it is said, God hath a name which is above every name, and to this name, when universally known, every knee shall bow, and every tongue confess. How the rich testimonies of my God cluster to my imagination—salvation is said to be of God, but this is not enough—corroborating testimony upon testimony immediately follows, until a cloud of witnesses pass in review. The name Saviour is appropriated to the Messiah, and it is as idle to ask of whom is the Messiah the Saviour, as it is to ask to whom doth the sun belong. We should be astonished to find this question seriously discussed among the learned. Who hath a right to enjoy the light of the sun; A disciple of our great Master, listening to such a conversation, would naturally observe, God maketh his sun to shine upon the *just* and upon the unjust.

It is an eternal truth that Jesus is, and that he was, the Saviour of all men, before the foundation of the world; but of this, the world are ignorant, they think of the Lamb of God as an adversary, and sometimes when they are very serious, religiously serious, they are afraid of him in that character; and it is from these fears that they believe that a *remnant is saved*. Trembling with apprehension, terrified mortals assay *to obtain an interest in Christ*; Alas, for them, how greatly are they misled! Would to God they knew, that their security rests upon this fundamental fact, that *Christ Jesus hath an interest in them*. The Divine nature gave the human nature, in all its fulness, to the Son, and the Son declareth, all that the Father giveth unto me, shall come unto me, and they who come, I will in no wise cast out; who then dare say, a remnant ONLY shall be saved? My people shall be willing in the day of my power, for it is written in the prophets, they shall be all taught of God; who, then, *dare say*, a remnant ONLY shall be taught of God? It is said by him of whom all the prophets have written, all who learn of the Father shall come unto me, and sooner or later, all shall learn of the Father, sooner or later, all shall come unto the Saviour, and all shall of course be saved; who, then, dare say, a remnant ONLY shall be saved? The fact is, every man who cometh into the world is already saved in the LORD, and in *consequence of this salvation*, men, all men will one day be *saved in themselves*, and when they are thus taught of God, thus saved, they will wonder they did not before believe : for, at the moment they commence *genuine believers*, they will acknowledge what they then believe was *as true before they believed as it ever was, or can be, at any given period.*

Blessed, right blessed are the people, who in this their day know the joyful sound ; they walk, O LORD, in the light of thy countenance. The Ephesians were children of darkness, they were Heathens, and without God in the world. Blinded and shut up in darkness.

One thing is clear, the man of Tarsus was a christian, and as the christian, hath received the LORD JESUS, so he walks in him. In fact, the christian man puts on the LORD JESUS as his righteousness, his holiness, and his redemption ; he needs no more, yet he wishes for more ; he wishes to be with, and like unto his God ; he wishes the whole body were even now saved *individually* from all consciousness of sin, even as the *remnant* is, in the present moment, saved ; and he pants for that era, when he shall realize the blissful scene described in the twenty-first chapter of Revelations, where the city had no need of the sun, neither of the moon to shine in it ; for the glory of God did lighten it, and the Lamb was the light thereof. This assuredly will be a catastrophe abundantly more to the honour and glory of God, than if the family of man were sent from the presence of God their Creator, God their Father, God their Redeemer, into regions of sorrow, into doleful shades, where peace and rest shall never dwell.

The doctrine of rewards and punishments is almost the coeval of time ; it has kept pace with every dispensation, and its date is truly ancient. Nor will the man of God's right hand, in any wise, lose *his reward.* But, what is the reward of the man of God's right hand ? Let us enquire of the Psalmist. Psalm cxxvii. 3, "Children are the heritage of the LORD, and the fruit of the womb is his reward." But, shall he lose this reward ? Did he not suffer upon the cross and endure the shame, in the hope of the recompense which was set before him ? And shall he not see the travail of his soul and be satisfied ? Will a remnant ONLY of his inheritance be his final portion ? Nay ; but his reward will be always with him. Lo ! I am with you always, is the language of Emmanuel, *God with us,* I will never leave thee nor forsake thee. Such is the language of the faithful Creator.

Mercy, saith this *faithful Creator*, shall be built up forever; it endureth forever; it goeth before the face of God forever. *The sins of the people are thrown behind the back of the Creator;* and, as God never turneth back, this divine Figure presents a glorious exhibition of his abundant goodness, of his abundant mercy to the children of men.

The creature can never fall lower, than the lowest. Jesus Christ was made in the likeness of *sinful flesh;* he was the *highest* and the *lowest.* There was no God above him, nor no man beneath him. I am, said Emmanuel, the Alpha and Omega. He is the foundation and the top-stone. And, in his character, will be made manifest, in presence of every creature in heaven, on earth, and in the sea, that perfect righteousness, which, as garment, shall cover *every member of that mystical body, of which he is the ever perfect, ever dignified, ever glorious head.* And in the day which approaches, will be revealed the salvation of the complete piece, of the whole family of man, when the whole of human nature, having *one new heart*, shall, from the fulness of *this one new heart*, ascribe to the world's Saviour, all might, majesty, power, and dominion, worlds without end: Amen and Amen.

Reflections upon John i. 45—51.

Philip findeth Nathanael, and saith unto him, We have found him, of whom Moses, in the law and the prophets, did write—Jesus of Nazareth, the Son of Joseph. And Nathanael said unto him, *Can there any good thing come out of Nazareth?* Philip said unto him, *Come and see.* Jesus saw Nathanael coming to him, and saith of him, Behold, an Israelite indeed, in whom is no guile. Nathanael saith unto him, Whence knowest thou me? Jesus answered, and said unto him, Before that Philip called thee; when thou wast under the fig-tree, I saw thee. Nathanael answered, and saith unto him, Rabbi, thou art the Son of God; thou art the King of Israel. Jesus answered, and said unto him, Because I said unto thee, I saw thee under the fig-tree, believest thou? Thou shalt see greater things than these. And he said unto him, Verily, verily, I say unto you, hereafter you shall see heaven open, and the angels of God ascending and descending upon the Son of man.

Is it not true, that the human species have, from the beginning, been divided into two classes, Pharisees and Publicans? All admit, that there is a God, and that this God is good. He is bountiful to the good, and to the good *only*, say the Pharisees. He is bountiful to *all*, say the Publicans. But, whether Pharisee or Publican, all agree, that it is both the duty and the interest of every man, of all descriptions of people, to *follow after, and to obtain virtue*. *The ways of wisdom are ways of pleasantness*, and the fragrant flowers of peace spring up in the paths of rectitude. Some, it is said, are good; and if some are good, the presumption is, that all may become good; and persons deeply conscious of the plague of their own hearts, look forward, however, to a period, when they shall become, in their own individual characters, even in this state of depravity, *perfectly righteous*, at least, as far as it respects themselves. Individuals, cherishing these ideas, are immeasurably happy, when they can press any passage in sacred writ into their service, on which to base their aerial superstructure. David, say they, was a man after God's own heart; and in their fondness for system making, they forgot that, as David was, *in reality*, a man black with crimes, the passage which describes him as a man after God's own heart, can only point to David's antitype. But, as I said, if they can draw but the shadow of reason from scripture, in support of their fancied excellence, they tenaciously adhere thereto, and that, in the face of a variety of plain testimonies, which expressly contradict their views. David experimentally describes the general corruption of mankind, particularly in the fourteenth Psalm:— "They are corrupt, they have done abominable works; there is none that doeth good The Lord looked down from heaven upon the children of men, to see if there were any that did understand and seek God. They are all gone aside; they are altogether become filthy; there is none that doeth good; no, not one."

The Apostle Paul is in unison with the Psalmist. Romans, chapter third, from the ninth to the conclusion of the twentieth verse, and to this testimony the Redeemer himself subscribes; and yet, when we hear of *good persons* and *good things*, it undoubtedly gives reason for expecting good; and the honest mind is confirmed in its ideas, although we hear the great Master decidedly pronounce, in the language of reproof, to the inquirer who approached him with a complimentary address —"*Good* Master, what shall I do to inherit eternal life? And Jesus said unto him, Why callest thou me *good*? None is good, save one, that is, God." The Redeemer knew, that this ruler of the people, did not acknowledge him to be what he *really* was, *Emmanuel, God with us*, and, therefore, he said unto him, why callest thou me good? there is none good but one, that is, God. But on this, and every similar occasion, we should do well to distinguish the species of excellence which we would imitate or describe. There is natural good, moral good, and spiritual good. This ruler of the people, attributed to our Saviour *spiritual good*, which could only belong to his *divine Nature*, which divine Nature was hidden from the view of the complimenter. How eager is our divine Master to set the inquirer right. " Why callest thou me good? Thou dost not know, that the Father and I are one. None is *good* save one, that is, God." Yet, there are who dare to affirm, that although the Redeemer was not the only wise God, he was, nevertheless, a *very good man*. Thus, they ignorantly make God, in our nature, a liar out of his own mouth.

Those who resemble this said ruler, are fond of conferring the character good, even in the superlative, upon sinful man; and it is in this spirit, they transfer the character, *an Israelite indeed, in whom there is no guile*, from the Redeemer, the *immaculate Redeemer*, to whom only it properly belonged, to Nathanael! I regard this as an astonishing instance of the prevalence, and ascendency of the pharisaical spirit over the minds of our fellow men. Let me carefully analyze this passage. One of our Lord's disciples meeteth a friend, and eager to communicate unto him a piece of intelligence, by which he himself was greatly elevated, saith unto him, "We have found him of whom Moses in the law and the prophets did write, Jesus of Nazareth, the son of Joseph, and we believe, he is the long expected, the promised seed, the Shiloh, he who will restore Israel " Nazareth was a town in Galilee of no reputation; the Jews entertained great contempt for the Galileans; and hence the propriety of Nathanael's question, " *Can any good thing come out of Nazareth?*" The Jews knew, that Messiah was to be that good *thing*, without a shade of evil, that he was to be, agreeably to the prophecies of their inspired writers, the *child born*, the *son given*, the *almighty Father, the mighty God, the Prince of peace*. Nathanael therefore could hardly forbear questioning, *Can this good thing, can any good come out of Nazareth?* Philip saith unto him, *Come and see*. Do not let prejudice so far tyrannise over your mind, as to prevent your seeing, examining and judging for yourself. The requst might have resulted from the soundest reasoning, and it was properly influential upon the simple, honest mind of Nathanael. He complied with the requisition of his friend, and immediately proceeded to visit the Nazarene, that he might by ocular demonstration settle this important point, whether this Nazarene was indeed that *perfect character*, which they were taught to believe, would distinguish the expected Messiah, that from the testimony of his own eyes, he might form a judgment by the appearance, by the conduct, by the power of Jesus of Nazareth, whether he were indeed the Messiah. As they drew near the subject of their conversation, the Saviour, to whom the secret recesses of every heart is open, and who was consequently acquainted with the purpose for which they approached him, called to Nathanael in whose mind *doubt* predominated, to *see and judge for himself. Behold your all perfect head, Behold an Israelite indeed in whom is no guile*. Yea, a sinless, guileless Being, although proceeding out of Nazareth.

This observation forcibly struck the mind of this *doubting man*; but how the master should know, that such were his doubts, greatly perplexed him. Whence knowest thou me, said Nathanael, that calling me by name, you bid me behold precisely such a character, as I supposed could not come out of Nazareth. Whence comes your knowledge of me, of my conversation with Philip, and of my doubts? Jesus answered and said unto him, Before that Philip called thee, when thou wast under the fig-tree, I saw thee. Thus was the whole soul of Nathanael interested and captivated. Had the conversation between Philip and Nathanael, *turned on the character of Nathanael*, and had this conversation convinced the Nazarene of the sanctity and guileless sincerity of the man, there would have been some rational ground for the idea, that the excellence spoken of was *proper to Nathanael*, and we might have concluded, that although as a man, he was a sinner; yet like some others among his fellow mortals, he was at least a *holy* sinner, and that the great master was *constrained in the face of his own testimony*, to render to Nathanael this tribute of praise.

Had, I say, the conversation between him and Philip, turned upon the excellence of Nathanael's character, without reverting to the individual, whom the Jews expected as the promised Messiah, there would have been some resemblance of propriety in the generally received opinion; but not a single sentence of this sort is recorded. Philip conceived, and he conceived justly, that he had made a most important discovery, that he had found him of whom Moses and the Prophets had written. It is observable, that when Jesus gave this disciple to understand, that he saw him under the fig-tree, he was, with the women of Samaria, convinced of the truth of Philip's report, for he answered and said unto him, " Rabbi, thou art the Son of God, thou art the King of Israel. But Jesus answered and said unto him, Because I said unto thee, I saw thee under the fig-tree, believest thou? Thou shalt see greater things than these; thou shalt have greater proofs of my divinity, thou shalt see heaven opened, and the angels of God ascending and decending upon the Son of man."

But Nathanael's goodness does not wound me; I am no more solicitous respecting him, than I am respecting any other individual among my fellow men. Yet it is of the last importance to me, that the excellence of his master's character should be established; because, upon the God-man, my life depends, and if it can be proved, that he has given a *contradictory* or *variant report*, before such a decision, my hopes of happiness would instantaneously vanish. Guile is guilt, sin. Jesus had said, there is *none good but God*. But if he said, Nathanael was *guileless*, *he then said he was without sin*; and what then becomes of the *consistency of his testimony*. But, if when he said, *behold an Israelite indeed, in whom there is no guile;* if we may venture to believe, that he then meant to correct the prejudices of Nathanael by a *reference to himself*, to call upon him, to acknowledge, that some *good thing* could come out of Nazareth, that he himself came out of Nazareth, although an *Israelite indeed, in whom was no guile*, then as our great high Priest *was holy, harmless, and undefiled*, the scriptures harmonize, the consisten-

Vol. III. 42

cy of the sacred volume is preserved, they are without contradiction.

It must be confessed, that the mistake which has obtained respecting this passage, is countenanced by the preposition *of*, in the text. Jesus saw Nathanael coming to him, and saith *of him*, the him repeated, without attending to the *previous conversation*, would, to a mind predisposed to consider Jesus Christ as celebrating the praises of Nathanael, induce a conclusion in favour of the received opinion. However, let this disciple be as meritorious and as guileless as he may, it is for my happiness, that the being, whom he acknowledged to be the Son of God, is the friend of sinners, and not in *word* only, but *in deed* and in *truth*. The friendship of Emmanuel is not like the friendship of the creature, it is powerful, it is life, it is godliness. In fact, Jesus is all-sufficient for me. Let but the teaching spirit take of the things of Jesus, and show them unto me, and I am completely blessed.

I should rejoice to see all the virtues, which either in fact or fancy, adorn human nature, continually increasing among mankind. But the virtues which adorn human nature in time or in eternity, are found in Christ-Jesus, and, blessed be the name of my God, all that is found in Christ Jesus belongeth unto me, and all that is found in me belongeth unto him. The character of Nathanael is distinguished, yet he *doubted*, and *he who doubteth*, says the sacred volume, *is damned*. With all the excellence then, which is attributed to this character, he *deserved damnation or condemnation;* yet he was saved *in* and by the Lord with an everlasting salvation. Although mankind have no particular interest in Nathanael as an individual, yet they will defend his character, even at the risk of robbing the Redeemer of his triumphant crown.

But I am persuaded this is not the design of God's children, who receive their ideas from tradition, and having thus received them, they mistake them for their own, and cherish them as the most precious truths; nor can they forbear distinguishing between the interests of morality, and the interests of Christ Jesus. May the spirit of truth lead our minds into all truth

Reflections upon JAMES v. 20, 21.

I HAVE often wondered, at the many attempts that have been made, both from the pulpit and the press, to set at odds the apostles, Paul and James. James, say they, is an Arminian, and Paul a Calvinist.

This subject formerly embarrassed me—but the spirit of peace, by pointing me to Jesus, hath led me into the knowledge of his truth. Paul and James were taught by the same spirit, but great confusion is made in the mind of professing christians for want of discrimination. The salvation begun, carried on, and completed by the Redeemer of the world, is one thing, it is the foundation—*other foundation can no man lay ;* it is the rock of ages, upon which the church is built; but the salvation wrought in us, when we believe, that this foundation *is* laid in Zion; the salvation which exempts us from that fear, which hath torment, which fear is the portion of the unbeliever; this salvation is distinct from the redemption which is in Christ Jesus; it is the superstructure, which is reared upon the foundation.

I am, saith the Saviour, the truth—and the fact is, there is no truth of permanent consequence, which is not found in the Redeemer. The truth as it is in Jesus is our life, our hope, our redemption. This truth is sufficient for every purpose, both for time and for eternity. In Christ Jesus all things consist; it pleased the Father that in him all fulness should dwell. Every one who is taught of God is acquainted with this truth, and it is therefore that as teachers of their fellow-men, they determine to know nothing among their fellow-men, save Christ Jesus, and him crucified.

This resolution becomes a fixed principle with every sent servant of the living God, and it is a fixed principle with every one that hath learned of the Father, to hear no other voice, than that of the good Shepherd.

> "They value not that doctrine, book or theme,
> That takes no notice of their LORD,
> Or leaves out his dear name."

Nor is it the name alone upon which the disciples of God our Saviour delight to dwell—No, it is what that name contains, which is, and will continue to be the theme of their rejoicing, worlds without end. Conscious that they are sinners, and having heard of a Saviour who is Christ the Lord, they listen to the glad tidings with holy joy. They believe there are many of God's children who know but little of the name that contains salvation, but they are persuaded that they know just as much as the God who made them, has seen proper to manifest unto them; but they rejoice exceedingly, when the gift of God is manifested to the children of men. His name shall be called Jesus, because he shall save his people from their sins.

> " Jesus, the name that lulls our fears,
> That bids our troubles cease,
> 'Tis musick in the sinner's ears,
> 'Tis life, and health, and peace."

Thus, the soul taught by the spirit of Jesus, whose office it is to take of his, and show it unto the people, rejoiceth evermore in the Lord, and the peace of his bosom passeth understanding. When he contemplates Jesus as the truth, when he believes, that in all that vast and mighty fulness of grace and truth, inherent in the Redeemer (in whom it pleased the Father all fulness should dwell) he hath an ample, a complete share; when he becomes confident, that *of his* fulness we all receive, and grace for grace, not as it is generally quoted, *out* of his fulness; it is then that his soul doth magnify the Lord; it is then that the genuine christian rejoiceth in God his Saviour. The christian *gathers* with Christ, he does not wish to unite either *directly* or *indirectly* with those who *scatter;* he is happy in knowing, that the Redeemer is ever with him, and he is at all times desirous to give unto the God-man the honour that is due unto his name. Here he is determined to join issue with the multitude, the innumerable multitude, described in the book of Revelations, sweet to his ear, sweet to his soul, is that God-honouring declaration, *Thou only art worthy, thou only art holy;* he is confident he loses nothing by this ascription, for he is assured, and believes, that there is no separate interest between the Head and the members, that if one member is honoured, every member partakes his full share of the honour; blessed with all spiritual blessings in Christ Jesus, partaking the faith, partaking the blessings of Abraham, he will continually *measure* the *same measure to every member of the human family which he measures to himself.* In this view, at least, he *loves his neighbour as himself.* But let me turn again to our Apostle—I am an admirer of this Apostle, but I could not yield him admiration, if he were not a disciple of Jesus Christ. Nay, he himself directs, that should he or an angel from heaven preach any other gospel, than that he had already preached, such erroneous individual should be accursed. Is not this a plain indication, that the apostles might possibly have preached another gospel? Man in his best estate is vanity, and so fully was the man of Tarsus convinced of this truth, that he seemed to be afraid of himself! for he assures us, that while he preached to others, he was necessitated to keep his own body under subjection, lest he himself should be a castaway.

The strong propensity manifested by professing christians to turn aside from the living and true God, to lying vanities, (and every thing of a religious nature, which doth not point to Jesus, is of this description;) I say, this strong propensity is surely passing strange. Preachers as well as hearers should be on their guard, for preachers themselves have hearts of unbelief. The first preachers seemed to be very sensible of this fact. Our blessed LORD was exempted from this, as from every other frailty, and when the enemy came to him he found nothing *in* him, therefore he gained no advantage over him. Not so his disciples: when the enemy approaches the most upright among his servants, he will always find something *in* them. There is a secret, a lurking foe in the fortress, always ready to deliver up the citadel to the besieging enemy. If our intentions be good, say they, nothing can be wrong. *Poor human nature,* while losing the power, did not lose the will. Pride frequently takes place of piety, and indeed the partition between pride and piety is so slight, that it is sometimes scarcely perceptible. But pride will manifest itself both in preachers and hearers. Preachers are called builders, workers together with God, and some of these builders sometimes think more highly of themselves than they ought to think, and it is a mercy that the everlasting Father is perfectly acquainted with all his children, that he remembers their frames, and considers they are but dust.

The Apostle addresses the people of God as brethren: yes, blessed be God, we have all one Father. *" Brethren, if any of you do err from the truth,* (these brethren had received the truth in the love of it, and yet they might err therefrom) *and one convert him."* There are a multitude of conversions; Saul was converted from one of the common people to one of the uncommon people, and a very sincere convert he was, continuing a long time in his converted state, and (as he conceived) he lived, as touching the law, *blameless.* But he was finally converted from a blind, bigotted Pharisee, to a consistent, luminous christian. Peter was converted from an irreligious fisherman, to a follower of Jesus. I say irreligious fisherman, because I believe he was not a religious man, because he cursed and swore, and because he spake falsely, in the hope of persuading those who charged him with being a disciple of the Nazarene, that he was not of his company. We are ready to say, if he had not been in the habit of swearing, he would not so easily have fallen into the practice; but Peter was afterwards converted. Jesus said unto him, Luke xxii. 32, " When thou art converted strengthen thy brethren."

God's children are often converted or changed; every degree in grace, attained while growing in grace, which every child of God does, may be considered as a new conversion, for they press on from what they *were,* to what they *were not,* even to the attaining the prize of their high calling. Sometimes they are converted by the spirit of God directly; sometimes by the same spirit indirectly; that is, through the instrumentality of God's servants. And the apostle James saith, *he who converteth a sinner from the error of his ways, shall save a soul from death.* We are frequently told of this kind of salvation, and are informed it is effectuated by God's ministers. But when a soul is converted from the error of his way, the instrument, if taught of God, will endeavour to keep out of sight, lest the glory which is due to the Creator should be given to the creature. Even in the performance of an act which produced a temporal salvation, such as restoring a cripple to the use of his limbs, the apostles scrupulously disclaimed every vestige of merit, and when the people regarded them with admiration, they immediately denied all title to praise, declaring they possessed no power in themselves. Acts iii. *In the name of Jesus of Nazareth, said Peter, rise up and walk.* Ye men of Israel why marvel ye at this? or why look ye so earnestly on us, as though by our own power or holiness, we had made this man to walk? The name of Jesus was, to these Israelites, an obnoxious name, yet, nevertheless, it was through faith in this name, the man became strong, whom they saw and knew; yea, the faith which was by Jesus Christ gave him perfect soundness in the presence of them all.

The conversions made by human beings, do not cover a multitude of sins. But when the great Master converts a soul from the error of his way, *he indeed* covers a multitude of sins; yea, he so effectually covers them, that when they are sought for, they shall not be found. The work of conversion is performed by our divine Master, better than by any of his servants; for Jesus converts them from the error of *their way*, by sending his Spirit to take of *his*, and show them unto the soul; and, thus the soul, embracing the better way, the way that is, verily, the truth and the life, is really saved from death. God's converts had a multitude of sins. One of God's children had so many sins, that they terrified him. Psalm xl. 12, "Mine iniquities have taken hold upon me, so that I am not able to look up; they are more than the hairs of my head." Beside these sins, there are *secret sins.* "Cleanse thou me from my secret faults." How often was this sinner converted! How many salvations did he experience! How replete with divine consolation is the assurance, that God will, in his own time, carry on, and with great power, this work of conversion, until the whole earth is filled with the knowledge of the Lord, as the waters cover the channels of the deep, making up the sea. And how happy, how blessed are they who are, by the grace of God, made use of, to turn many to light, from the power of Satan unto God. But these instruments will always say, *Not unto us, not unto us, but unto thy name be all the glory.*

It is remarkable, that the apostle James, v. 17, 18, speaking of the prophet of the Lord, says, "Elias was a man subject to like passions as we are, and he prayed earnestly, that it might not rain: and it rained not on the earth by the space of three years and six months. And he prayed again, and the heaven gave rain, and the earth brought forth her fruit." Yet the rain came not for his sake, who was a man subject to like passions with us. Elias was not the father of the rain; but the real Father of the rain, sends this blessing upon every character, upon the just, and the unjust, and his doctrines shall drop as the rain.

Again, Verse sixteen of this fifth chapter, "*The effectual fervent prayer of a righteous man availeth much.*" But who is a *righteous man?* The sacred volume informs us, there is no man who liveth and sinneth not. There is none righteous; no, not one, Romans iii. 10. And the assembly of divines have determined, that no mere man since the fall, is able to keep the commandments of God, but daily doth break them, in thought, word, and deed. Yet *there is a righteous character*, and *this righteous character* was clothed in humanity. 1John, ii. 1, "And if any man sin, we have an advocate with the Father, JESUS CHRIST THE RIGHTEOUS. The effectual fervent prayer of *this* righteous man, covereth a multitude of sins; it saveth the soul from death, it converteth a man from the error of *his way*, it bringeth him into that perfect way, which shineth more and more unto perfection. To say all in one word, it availeth much. But, for whom doth it avail? For whom doth the Redeemer pray? Read the seventeenth chapter of John, and abide by its decision:

First, *I pray for them: I pray not for the world, but for them which thou hast given me: for they are thine.*

Secondly, Neither pray I for *these alone, but for them also that shall believe on me through their word.*

Thirdly, That they all may be one as thou, Father, art in me, and I in thee, that they also may be one in us, that the *world may believe that thou hast sent me. When the world believes,* the world must of course be saved. And thus is accomplished to the ken of Deity, and thus will be accomplished, to the salvation of every individual, the *restitution of all things:* Amen and Amen, so be it. Come quickly, LORD Jesus; come quickly.

Some hints relative to the forming of a Christian Church, first published in 1791, *and now republished at the request of several respectable friends.*

Gloucester, July, 1791.

MY FRIEND,

WHEN I had the pleasure of meeting you in Boston, you requested that I would transmit to you, in writing, the substance of what I then delivered to you in conversation.

First, You ask me, what you, and your friends ought to do? I answer, do right as men, as members of civil society, and as christians. As men, as mere men, you must follow nature, or you will sink beneath the level of the beasts of the field. Vices of many sorts, are unnatural; they are solely the effect of habit. Swearing, drunkenness, and gaming, are of this description.

Secondly, You ought to act right as members of civil society. You cannot stand alone; living in, and members of a civil community, you must submit to those laws, which are enacted by the legislative body. If you deem existing laws too severe, you may avoid the rigour of which you complain, by a removal from the State. If you say, your interest will suffer in consequence of your departure, then it will be more for your interest to continue where you are; and you must be content to submit to a lesser evil, for the sake of a greater good; in other words, you must surrender, to the claims of government, a part of your property, for the security of the residue; you must then, if you consult your interest, to say nothing more, render obedience to the laws of the State, where they do not run counter to the laws of God and nature. We, in this State, and indeed the subjects of the Union at large, are peculiarly happy, that there are no regulations established among us, to which, as freemen and as christians, we cannot most cheerfully submit.

But, lastly, You are to perform your duty as christians. To be christians, you must be disciples of Christ Jesus; and to be disciples of this Master, you must be under his direction. Then are ye my disciples, saith the Saviour, if ye do whatsoever I command you.

You say, there are numbers in your neighbourhood, who profess the christian faith, who call themselves believers, and who, having heard with delight the voice of the good Shepherd, resolve they will not again attend to the voice of the stranger. Blessed be the name of the Redeemer, they are under no obligations so to do. You inform me, they cannot, consistent with their ideas of rectitude, contribute to the support of false teachers. Well, the mild government under which we live, has made ample provision for such conscientious persons; they are under no obligation to support, what they conceive a false religion. But, you suspect there are some, who value their money more than their religion; such persons are covetous, such persons are idolators, and for such characters the compilers of our Constitution have not made provision. The members of the Convention who formed our constitution, were of opinion, that religion of some sort or other, was a public benefit; and as neither public nor private advantage can be obtained in this world without some expense, our wise men thought it best to oblige every member of the community, to contribute to the support of the religion of his election, indulging serious, conscientious persons, with liberty to choose for themselves, and to dispose of their taxes to the support of their own teacher. This is all the liberty we have, and this, by many, is thought to be sufficient.

Permit me, then, in conformity to your request, humbly to propose, that as many of you as are real lovers of divine truth, should associate together in Church fellowship, state the articles of your faith in clear and concise language; and let all those who choose to subscribe thereto, mutually consent to have fellowship one with another. Let them meet together upon the first day of every week, for the purpose of worshipping God according to his divine appointment. If they have no one to preach the word of the kingdom unto them, let them read a portion of the scriptures which, accompanied by the Spirit of God, is sufficient to make them wise unto salvation. But you will say, "Suppose they have not that Spirit, in that case what are they to do?" I answer, if any lack wisdom, let them ask of God, who giveth unto all liberally, and upbraideth not. He will give the Holy Spirit to them who ask him. Do you ask, "Are there any inspired in the present day?" Assuredly there are. All men are under the influence of one spirit or another. All true believers are under the influence of the Spirit of the true Christ; all unbelievers are under the influence of the spirit of anti-christ. Are any acquainted with the things of God, they are indebted for this knowledge to the Spirit of God, who alone can take of the things of Jesus, and shew them unto us. Are there any real Universalists, they are made so by that Spirit of truth, which alone is able to lead them into all truth. Let, then, your brethren, if they are thus taught of God, supplicate the divine Presence and Favour; for, although God delighteth in doing us good, yet he will be inquired after; and he is a God that heareth and answereth prayer. Prayer indicates our trust in, and dependence upon him, in whom we have believed; and a declaration of this dependence, constitutes a part of the worship of God. Perhaps some will say, "They have not gifts; they know not how to pray;" but this is a very capital mistake. In many instances, indeed, we may not know *what* to pray for, but there are no individuals, in the wide family of earth or heaven, who do not know how to pray. Indeed, there are but few who know how to pray as the hypocrites, who make long prayers and abound in repetitions. Professors, in general, in their addresses to the throne of grace, seem to study more to please men than God. Is any among you afflicted, let him pray. A man who is really afflicted in the want of any thing, will not suffer in the want by which he is afflicted, because he cannot make use of what is called good language. Were he, in applying to a superiour, able and willing to assist him, to make use of very flowery language, his sincerity might justly be called in question. God be merciful to me a sinner, was more acceptable to God, than the much speaking of the Pharisee. David said, LORD, pardon mine iniquity, for it is great. Have mercy on me, thou son of David, is another prayer which answers the description of true prayer. Whoso cometh unto God, must believe that he is faithful, and a rewarder of such who diligently seek him; but it is him we must seek, and not the applause of men; yet it is the *latter* and not the *former*, which is sought by every one who can pray in private and not in public, or who can ask a favour of his fellow creature, and find it difficult to ask of God. Can we reasonably suppose, that the infinitely great and glorious God, is under the influence of much or fine speaking? The Searcher of all hearts, looketh only to the heart. If your hearts be right with God, then you will, when you meet together, come into his presence with thanksgiving, and into his courts with praise. But when you would sing the praises of the redeeming God, do not offer the sacrifice of fools, by singing what is not true, by singing your prayers, or by attending more to the sound than the sense, thus sing to the praise and glory of the singer. The religion of this world, is too often show and solemn mockery. Men pray to make an exhibition of their gifts; they sing to evince how well they have cultivated their voices and their ears; and few, in the present day, sing, but those who have learned, not of the Father of their spirits, but of some singing master. There should be order and regularity in all we do; and harmony in singing is good; but I would rather see a congregation unite in one key, in one part, while their hearts made melody unto the Lord, than a formal company of *mere singers*. Bass, counter, tenor, and treble, how accurately soever they might perform, if it was certain they attended only to the *manner* with unconsecrated hearts.

After singing a hymn of praise to God, you should address the throne of grace in prayer. Surely there are among you some, who may be able to speak to our common Father. If no more be said than simply, our Father, give us now we are met together in thy name, thy reviving presence. We lack wisdom; be graciously pleased to give us what thou seest we want; give us thy good spirit to guide us into all truth, and save us from the evil, that is in the world. We are met together, agreeably to thy divine direction, to search the scriptures; be pleased to commune with our spirits, and open unto us thy scriptures, that our hearts may burn within us. Send forth, O thou Lord of the harvest, labourers into thy harvest, and bring all men into the knowledge of the truth, that thy will may be done in their salvation. Bless our governours and rulers, and all conditions of men among us; enable us, and all who believe in the Saviour, to walk as children of light, that our light shining before men, they may be led to glorify thee, our heavenly Father. Surely, you will not find it difficult in some such way as this to address the God in whom we live, move and have our being. Our gracious God hath said, Ask and ye shall receive, seek and ye shall find, and whatsoever you ask, according to my will, you shall receive. When you have thus prayed, concluding with what we are taught to call the Lord's prayer; then let some one of the brethren read a portion of God's word, remembering always the words of our divine Master, who, when he bade us search the scriptures, assured us they testified of him; nor should we forget, that for the purpose of testifying of Jesus in his various characters, and of exhibiting a just idea of all his works; the sacred volume testifies also of many other persons, as of Adam, who was a figure of Jesus Christ; the second Adam of the deceiver, who beguiled our general mother, and who, in the character of a murderer, did the deed, which brought ruin and death on all the human race. Of two classes of fallen sinners, the angels who kept not their first estate, and the human nature, deceived by the former, and consequent thereon, apparently destroyed.

The scriptures give an account of a just God, who in the law which he gave by Moses, denounces death and the curse upon every one, who continueth not in all things written in the book of the law to do them; but in the same scriptures we have an account of the same God, manifested in the flesh, as the head of every man, made under the law, to redeem them that were under the law, being made a curse for them: and this revelation is that gospel, which is glad tidings to every child of Adam, because every child of Adam being once under the law, and a transgressor of the law, was consequently under the sentence of death, and subjected to the curse. Jesus having redeemed the human sinner by tasting death for every man, being the Saviour not of a few individuals only, but of all men; the gospel, which is a divine declaration of this truth, is indeed glad tidings to every fallen sinner. When we read in the scriptures of wrath, tribulation, death, &c. we know that God speaketh in his legislative character, as he was manifested by Moses, as the just God, who will by no means clear the guilty; but when we read of grace, mercy, and peace, of life, as the gift of God, of salvation began or completed, we know that the same God speaketh in the language of Zion, in the character of the just God and the Saviour. The one is the language of the law, the other is the language of the gospel. Whatever in any part of the scripture manifests sin, and the punishment due to sin, is the law: whatever exhibits Jesus as bearing the sin of the world, and suffering the punishment due thereunto, so making peace by the blood of the cross, is gospel: wherever I find the scriptures speaking of a reconciled God, well pleased for his (Jesus') sake, I find the gospel, the believing of which gospel, is accompanied by a salvation from all the misery, to which we are exposed, while we believe the law only, and not the gospel.

The Scriptures speak of a judgment *past*, and a judgment *yet to come*. The past judgment is, first, where the world was judged in the second Adam, according to the testimony of the Saviour, now is the judgment of this world, now is the prince of this world cast out, and death executed upon them, according to the righteous judgment of God. Secondly, Every one taught of God judges himself, and therefore he shall not be judged. Judge yourselves, and ye shall not be judged. The judgment *to come* is that last great day, when all who have not judged themselves, all unbelievers of the human race, and all the fallen angels, through whose influence unbelievers are held in a state of darkness and blindness, and who, as the deceivers of mankind, are reserved in chains of darkness unto the judgment of the great day; these shall then all be judged by the Saviour of the world. But the angelic, and the human sinner, shall then be separated; the one shall be placed on the right, the other on the left hand; the one addressed as the sheep for whose salvation the Redeemer laid down his life; the other as the accursed, whose nature he passed by. The human nature as the offspring of the everlasting Father, and the ransomed of the Lord, shall by divine power be brought into the kingdom prepared for them before the foundation of the world; the angelic nature will be sent into the fire prepared for the devil and his angels.

The scriptures lead us, by various and striking figures, to the contemplation of the Prince of peace, and to his contrast the prince of the power of the air. Sometimes these figures are taken from men; sometimes from things: every thing good is expressive of Christ and his salvation; every thing bad of the adversary and his destruction. The Prince of peace came to save human nature from the power and dominion of the devil and his works; he came to destroy the *latter*, that he might save the *former*. He was manifested to destroy the works of the devil, and he shall save his people from their sins. This indeed he hath done when he put away sin by the sacrifice of himself, and this he will do, when he shall give his holy angels charge, to collect every seed sown by the enemy in the human nature, that as tares, as evil seed sown by the evil one, they may be separated from the good seed, which when it was sown by the Son of man by whom all things were made, was pronounced very *good*, and will again be *as good*, when the evil, that came from the evil one, is separated from it. The Son of man, agreeably to the records of truth, shall take out of his kingdom; which kingdom will be composed of all nations, and kindreds, and people, and tongues, for the kingdoms of the world shall become the kingdoms of God, and of his Christ: out of this kingdom, I say, the Son of man will take out every thing that offends, and *those* who do iniquity.

There is nothing can give offence but sin, and sin is the work of the devil, of that spirit, which now worketh in the hearts of the children of disobedience; as then this evil spirit is the worker or doer of whatever gives offence, Jesus, as the the Saviour of the world, shall in the fulness of time separate from his kingdom both the *evil worker*, and his evil works; the evil workers in the characters of goats, the evil works in the character of tares.

When the sower of the evil seed, and all the evil seed sown, shall be separated from the seed which God sowed, then the seed which is properly the seed of God, will be like him, who sowed it, holy and pure, as God is holy and pure; when the veil shall be taken away, and the face of the covering from all people; every eye shall then see the Saviour as he is, and they who see him as he is, shall be like him; for the Redeemer is able to change even these vile bodies, that they may be fashioned like unto his own glorious body, according to the mighty working, whereby he is able to subdue all things unto himself. Thus stands the gospel of the grace of God, as revealed in the scriptures. It must be confessed, there are in the Bible many things, which may appear dark to us, our weakness is even infantile, and the prejudices of education tyrannise over the mind; the power of the adversary is great, and the purpose of God reserves the complete manifestation of himself to futurity. Our Saviour teaches us to look forward to a brighter day, when we shall attain a perfection of knowledge, knowing as we are known; here we know but in part; but blessed be our divinely gracious teacher, who in mercy hath made us acquainted with the purpose purposed on the whole earth, who hath assured us it is the will of God, that all men should be saved, and come unto the knowledge of the truth, while reason as well as revelation teaches us, that a being who is almighty, will do *all his pleasure*, and fulfil all his will. I wish, therefore, that as new born babes you may desire the sincere milk of the word, that you may grow thereby.

It is the business of him who deceiveth the nations, to keep the children of men in ignorance; they never would have seen the revelation of God, could he have prevented it, and when, by divine favour, the revelation was published in a living language; he made use of every art to persuade men, they were not to understand its divine author as he spake, so that upon this principle we are not the wiser for the given revelation, and when he can no longer hold us under his dominion in this way, his next device is to turn us from the plain, luminous truths of the law and the gospel, to the more dark and mysterious parts of revelation. I pray God to give you understanding, that you may not be ignorant of satan's devices.

After reading a portion of the sacred oracles, if any brother have a word of exhortation, let him deliver it; but let there be no contention, no disputation, have no fellowship with the unfruitful works of darkness.

After reading the word, give thanks to God, praying that you may be continually under his direction; sing a hymn of praise to your Redeemer, when some member of your association may, in the name of your Saviour, pronounce the concluding benediction.

You would, I say, do well upon the first day of every week, to establish such regulations. If you have a meeting-house, it is well; if not, any apartment consecrated to this employ will answer your purpose. The first churches of the living God, were thus convened in one house and another, as they found most convenient. Our God is not confined to places; wherever two or three are met together in his name, there God is, neither was it the place upon which the compilers of the constitution had their eye, it was the thing, it was piety, religion, and morality.

Piety, it is said, consists in that communion and fellowship between the spirits of men, and the Father of their spirits, with which they are indulged through our Lord Jesus Christ; or, it is more strictly a reverential adoration of Deity, a devotion of soul, and an earnest desire to be found in the paths of duty.

Religion is the assembling ourselves together, in a regular, orderly manner, at stated times, to worship God, and to receive instruction respecting the effectual and acceptable performance of duty.

Morality is the duty we owe to ourselves, to our families, to our brethren in the same faith, to our enemies, and to all mankind. In the practice of religion and morality, we adorn the doctrine of God our Saviour. A man may attend to the observance of religion and morality, and have no piety, but I presume no man can be pious, without attending to the practice of religion and morality.

If thus you conduct, you do, as I conceive, come up to the spirit and letter of our Constitution.

But you wish, when you are formed into a christian Church, to be made acquainted with your duty respecting ordinances, and on this head, also, the scriptures will afford you sufficient information and direction. As christians, you will not conceive yourselves bound to observe those ordinances contained in the Jewish Ritual, or what is commonly called the ceremonial law; but instead of all these, it has been thought by the generality of professing christians, that our divine Master has substituted the ordinances of baptism and the Lord's supper. Beside these, there are other ordinances, to which some professors of christianity tenaciously adhere, but baptism and the Lord's supper have, by a greater part of the religious world, been deemed an essential part of the christian religion. There are, however, a very respectable denomination of christians, which have totally rejected the external use, as well as the abuse of both these ordinances, and this they have done, from a full persuasion that the words of our common Master were *spirit* and *life*. Perhaps, there are not many in any denomination, who being able and willing to judge for themselves, will not agree with our Apostle, in considering ordinances merely shadows.

The Universalists, as christians, admit of but one baptism. The baptizer Christ Jesus, and the elements made use of, the Holy Ghost, and fire. Yet they believe, that John, by divine direction, baptized with water; but even this, though established by divine authority, they consider in the same point of view in which they are directed to consider a variety of other ordinances, that were established by the same authority; in that dispensation, they consider it merely as a figure. Water is a purifying element; but it can only remove external filth, it, however, goes as far as a figure can go, and very properly preceded that *one* baptism of our divine Master, which should effectually cleanse from all filthiness of flesh and spirit. Hence, he who baptized with water said, He that cometh after me is mightier than I; I indeed baptize you with water unto repentance; but he shall baptize you with the Holy Ghost and with fire.

We consider the ordinance commonly called the LORD's supper, as a very expressive emblem of the salvation of the human family in Christ Jesus. We are, however, informed, that this emblem may be used *worthily* or *unworthily*, and that he who eateth and drinketh *unworthily*, eateth and drinketh damnation or condemnation to himself; and we are furthermore taught, that the worthy receiver, in receiving, discerns the LORD's body, and that the unworthy receiver does not discern the LORD's body.

Yet, although the people called Universalists, associating as christians in church fellowship, generally adopt as their most reasonable service, this divinely expressive ordinance, yet, they do not hold themselves in subjection thereto, they are subject *to no shadows;* and while they hold this ordinance in the highest estimation, as an ordinance, yet they think the exercise of charity much greater, and are, therefore, determined that difference of mind or manners, respecting the use or disuse of this, or any other ordinance, shall never interrupt the gentle flow of their christian affection toward each other. On the whole, the people called Universalists determine, with the Apostle, to know nothing either as a *whole* or a *part*, directly or indirectly essential to their salvation, but Jesus Christ and him crucified.

Permit me again to caution you respecting your conduct, as a Church; let it appear to all, that you are under the influence of the spirit of God, and, as two or three, met together in any place in the name of the Saviour, constitute a Church, so, thus meeting and conducting with christian propriety, you will cause your light so to shine before men, as to oblige them to glorify your Father who is in heaven; But, as your peace and happiness will, in a great measure, depend on your conduct and character, let no individual have fellowship with you, but such as are seriously disposed to act a consistent part, to adorn the doctrine of God our Saviour—To adorn this doctrine is equally the interest and duty of every professor. Let no one take refuge under your name, merely from pecuniary motives; if you tolerate such proceedings, you will justly suffer as evil doers, and you will lose your glorying, you will be found resisting the powers that are ordained of God, and, as they are so very mild and gentle, in resisting them, you must expect censure and condemnation. Let every one who joins with you pay regularly into the hands of a Treasurer, what he would be obliged to pay to the parish Collector, and having thus legally made payment, let him be furnished with a certificate to produce when called upon by the Collector of parish rates. Do you say, that you should not have many to join with you on this principle? Better have none at all, than have them on any other principle; what advantage can you derive from associating with unprincipled men? Why should you bear the burden of such worthless characters? But, thus conducting, you will have none but real, honest, true believers, and one such a believer will be better than one hundred of a contrary character, and you will always find honesty the best policy; it will be advantageous to you both as members of society, and as christians. Possibly you will say, if we thus regularly pay as much as was demanded of us in the several parishes to which we have belonged, what are we to do with the money thus collected? Perhaps you may in time accumulate as much as if put out to interest; may enable you to support a minister without any additional charge, or you may accumulate sufficient to build a house for the worshippers of God; or you may be able to assist your suffering brethren, which is one of the first christian duties, and, I had almost said, worth all the rest. Your stock, however, will be continually increasing, and it will be the joint property of each of your members, you will by this means have none but the best men in your society; whereas, if you do not adopt some such plan, you will very probably have some of the worst.

There are, no doubt, many generous, well disposed men among you, who would be glad to hear the gospel preached in its purity; but as the poor have the gospel preached unto them, so the *poor in general* are the preachers of this gospel. They cannot go a warfare at their own expense, they must be helped on their way. If a preacher should visit you, in your present circumstances, he must be a burden on one, or a few individuals, but this is not right, why should the few act for the many? This is not reasonable, this is not just; we should be *just* as well as *generous;* but if you are connected in church fellowship with an increasing fund of your own, the necessary expenses attendant on a visit from a messenger of peace, could be defrayed out of the common stock. Do you say, the ministers of Jesus Christ having freely received, should as freely give; they should not sell the gospel, seeing they did not purchase it? your remark is just; it is a heinous sin to make merchandise either of the gospel, or the people to whom they are commanded to preach. But, although the messengers of peace have no right to sell the gospel, they are not obliged to give their time and the bread of their families to you; if they labour in sowing unto you spiritual things, it is a light thing that they reap at your hands carnal things; and, suffer me to add, if you do not consider the *former* more valuable than the *latter*, to preach to you, would, I fear, be to very little purpose.

But you say, "It is against the conscience of some individuals, to pay any thing for the support of any religion." There may be those who are of this description, and, perhaps, they would be glad to have it in their power, to avoid giving or paying any thing on any occasion; but it is never against the consciences of persons who thus express themselves, to receive all they can obtain in every way. Indeed, the very reason, why so many are loath to part with their property, operates in favour of their getting and keeping all they have a chance of grasping. But I have as much right to expect your people to come and till my land, and sow, and reap it for me, bearing their own expenses all the time, as they have to expect labourers to come among them, to labour for their profit, at their own charge. I confess it would give me, as an individual, and, I doubt not, many others, much gratification, to be able to go through the country preaching the word of the kingdom, bearing my own expenses; but, I am inclined to think, there would be as much pride as piety in this mode of procedure. He that laboureth in the gospel, should live by the gospel; besides, there is no evidence that our labours are beneficial, if we do not see the hearts of the people enlarged; no one ever became a believer of the gospel, but felt his heart enlarged; and if faith does not take place in the hearts of our hearers, then have we laboured in vain.

You have expressed a wish, that I would visit you; and it would give me pleasure to gratify you. I am solicitous to know if the spirit of my divine Master, has been taking of the things of Jesus and showing them unto you. A view of your order would exceedingly refresh my heart. I want to know how you are; I hear from many, that the doctrines of God our Saviour prevaileth much throughout the Union; but from some examples which have come under my observation, I am apprehensive, that he who was a liar from the beginning, has been practising upon the minds of the credulous, that under the name of the christian doctrines, he has imposed heresies as far from the scripture testimony of the everlasting gospel, as this arch deceiver can possibly fabricate. There may be as much anti-scriptural, irrational, inconsistent stuff, propagated under the name of the Universal, or, as some choose to term it, Murray's doctrine, as there can be under any other name. I have sometimes imagined, that a few dreamers have taken their ideas from our enemies; and, believing we defended those detestable doctrines with which our calumniators reproach us, they undertake to support them, though, in thus doing, they do as much violence to divine revelation, as any of the advocates for a partial salvation.

The adversary being convinced, that he cannot hurt the cause of truth by his own disciples, who are our inveterate foes, has, therefore, raised up some advocates for some truths, that, through their instrumentality, he may the more effectually injure the cause of truth, and still retain the ransomed of the LORD in his kingdom.

Permit me to point out a few of the errors, which are preached and received by some individuals who call themselves Universalists.

First, Because our Saviour hath finished the work which was given him to do for us men, and for our salvation, it is asserted that we, who are saved by the LORD with an everlasting salvation, have nothing at all to do! This is a vile, detestable error; it is contrary to reason as well as revelation. Indeed, whatever is opposed to reason, is equally opposed to revelation. It is true, we have not that to do in order to save ourselves, which was done by Jesus Christ; but, being completely saved in Jesus Christ, we have much to do. Ye are, saith the Spirit of truth, bought with a price; therefore, glorify God in your bodies and spirits, which are his. Let those who have believed, be careful to maintain good. Good what? Good *words*? No, truly; good *works*. But, in what respect can works done by us, be good? Can they be profitable to God? No; but they can be *pleasing to God*, because *profitable unto men*. In this view, they are *good works;* for, as all men are dear to, and beloved by the LORD, in doing good unto all, according to our ability, we may be said to glorify and please God. But, it is said by some, "We have nothing to hope in consequence of thus doing, nor have we any thing to fear from the neglect of acknowledged duties; the doctrine of rewards and punishments is a legal, and, therefore, in this gospel day, a justly exploded doctrine; we know that Jesus, being made under the law, hath redeemed us from the curse of the law, and, therefore, hath become the end of the law for righteousness, to every one that believeth." That Jesus was made under the law, for the purpose of redeeming them that were under the law, that he hath accomplished the work he came into the world to do, by redeeming the lost nature, that he is, indeed, the end of the law for righteousness to every one that believeth, are divine truths, which we are neither able nor willing to oppose. But, upon this truth of God, thus manifested, depends another truth. If Christ Jesus hath redeemed us, then we are not our own; we have one Master, we have one Father, the Redeemer of men; if we obey not this Master, if we walk not according to the direction of this Father, he will visit our transgressions with a rod; though we are, indeed, redeemed unto God by the blood of Jesus, if we sow to the flesh, we shall of the flesh reap corruption, for, whatsoever a man soweth, that shall he also reap. Though the human family do, indeed, constitute the fulness of the Saviour's body, they are delivered from condemnation, only while they walk not after the flesh, but after the Spirit; and though the faithfulness of the just God, as the Saviour, can never fail, yet he shall reward every man according to his works. That work of God which was wrought by the head of every man, will be rewarded by the eternal salvation of all men. The work of the *mere* creature, being, according to the nature of the creature, shall have its reward. If, therefore, the ransomed of the Lord, following the direction of their Lord and Master, act consistent with their character, shall they not be rewarded? Assuredly they shall; they shall be most amply rewarded; we have the promise of our blessed Master guaranteeing the reward. Whoso giveth even a cup of cold water to a disciple, shall have a disciple's reward. Whoso giveth unto the poor, lendeth unto the Lord; and look, what he layeth out shall be payed him again. God is not unmindful of our works of faith, and labours of love. What, because we cannot purchase heaven by our doings, or destroy death and hell by our labours, does it follow that we have, as dwelling in this world, nothing to hope and nothing to fear? Because Jesus died for all, are all, therefore, to live unto themselves? Nay; but he dying for all, all who live are, therefore, bound to live, not unto themselves, but to him who died for them. Let it, indeed, be proved that Jesus did not die for them, that they are not bought with a price, then they are still their own; and if they be their own, they may still live unto themselves. But no one of the human race hath a right thus to presume to live unto himself, inasmuch as Jesus gave himself a ransom for all, and, by the grace of God, tasted death for every man. Assuredly, my friend, the ransomed of the LORD will find it as much their interest as it is their duty, to glorify God in their bodies and their spirits, which are his; they will find it their interest, if they have much, to give abundantly; if they have little, to do their diligence, gladly to give of that little; for, thus doing, they will lay up for themselves a great reward.

The reward to which the man Christ Jesus is entitled, in consequence of the works he wrought, is the eternal salvation of Jew and Gentile, as his inheritance. So that all the Father had, being given unto him, they may be ultimately with him, to behold his glory.

Secondly, It has been affirmed, that the day of the LORD, commonly called the last day, or the day of judgment, is past. Our Saviour having said, "Now is the judgment of this world," such who are ever doing the work of the adversary, in proving one part of divine revelation false by another, affirm there can be no future judgment; those, who are taught of God, pursue a different method; they study to point out the consistency of divine revelation, in order to establish its authority. The scribe, instructed in the kingdom of God, rightly divides the word of truth; he clearly distinguishes between the judgment of all men, in connexion with their head, where the offended, divine Nature was the judge; and judging according to law, and eternal truth and justice, did not spare, but inflicted the threatened, deserved death, on the guilty world, so that, one dying for all, all were dead. I say, he who is taught of God, can readily distinguish between this judgment, and the judgment so frequently spoken of in divine revelation, as yet in future. In the former judgment, the whole human family were judged; but they were gathered into one. The angelic Nature is also spoken of in this judgment;

but in the singular character, the Prince of this world is cast out. But, in the future judgment, believers in Jesus Christ who have judged themselves, shall not be judged. Judge yourselves, saith the Holy Spirit, and you shall not be judged; but the rest of mankind will be the subjects of this judgment, when our Saviour shall be revealed from heaven in flaming fire, taking vengeance on them who know not God, and who obey not the gospel; and they shall then be punished with everlasting destruction, from the presence of the Lord and the glory of his power; the consequence of which shall be, they shall then be made to know God, and obey the gospel; for, although until this period they will, as unbelievers, suffer the punishment consequent on the revelation of the everlasting destruction, yet, it is not said, they shall be everlastingly punished with destruction. Were it possible to find a culinary fire that never could be extinguished, but which was, in the strictest sense of the word, everlasting or eternal; should any member of your body pass through that burning flame, though but a moment of time had been spent in thus passing through, yet, even in that moment, it would suffer the pain of eternal fire. Those who build on the foundation laid in Zion, wood, hay, stubble, their works shall be burned in this fire, and they, consequent thereon, shall suffer loss; but they, themselves, shall be saved, though it were as by fire. Were they, themselves, to be lost, being God's workmanship, then God would also suffer loss; but they, bad as they were, ignorant as they were of God, disobedient as they were in not obeying the gospel, (and surely they must be very ignorant of God, and very disobedient to the gospel, to build with such perishable materials,) yet they, themselves, shall be saved, as it were, by that fire in which the Lord Jesus shall be revealed, when he comes to take vengeance upon such characters.

Yes, the books shall be opened, and the dead, both small and great, shall be judged out of the things written in the books. Every mouth shall be stopped, and all the world become guilty before God; and while conscious of guilt, but ignorant of a Saviour, and that the Saviour is the only wise God who is *just even as a Saviour*, they shall call upon the rocks and mountains to fall upon them, that they may, beneath the covert of the falling mountains, be hidden from the wrath of the Lamb. But in this judgment, the Judge is the Saviour. Here all judgment is committed unto Jesus, because he is the Son of man, the Son of the offending, suffering, affrighted nature. In that future day, upon which God hath appointed the judgment, it is the Prince and the Saviour who is appointed to judge the world in righteousness, even that man whom the divine Nature ordained. Here, instead of head and members being judged together by the head of Christ, the divine Nature, the members are considered, in their distinct characters, as good and evil, or believer and unbeliever, as children of light or children of darkness, and judged by their own head, for the head of every man is Christ.

Again, The business of this judgment may be considered, in some sort, different from the former. *That*, was to suffer the wages of sin; *this*, after suffering the consequence of unbelief, which is the torment of fear, to stop every mouth, that the LORD alone may be exalted, and to bring every one into a state of willing obedience unto the gospel. In the former judgment, sin was put away from the lost nature, by the death or sacrifice of the Saviour as the second Adam, so that God may behold the once lost and polluted nature, as saved and pure in him. The last judgment is to bring each member into the same state in themselves. Once more, as in the *former* judgment, the prince of this world, who also is called the God of this world, was cast out, in the last judgment the whole of the angelic nature, who fell from their first habitation, and who are reserved in chains of darkness unto the judgment of this great day, will, in the character of goats placed on the left hand of the Shepherd of the sheep, be judged, and sent, as accursed, into the fire prepared for them. Then shall that wicked be revealed, whom the LORD shall consume with the breath of his mouth, and destroy by the brightness of his coming.

Thirdly, Some persons very seriously suppose, that all mankind will be on a level in the article of death. They conceive it cannot be otherwise, seeing that Jesus hath abolished death; and they believe, that in the dissolution of the body, the dust returns to the dust, and the spirit to God who gave it. But if Jesus, having abolished death, was sufficient to put all upon a level in death, it was sufficient to put all on a level in life also; but what is true in Christ, is one thing; and what is believed true, another. Peace and reconciliation with God, is the consequence of what is true in Christ Jesus. Peace of conscience, and joy in the Holy Ghost, is the consequence of what is true, as believed in our hearts. Neither in life nor in death, in the body nor out of the body, can any of the ransomed of the Lord be saved from misery, until they are made acquainted with God as their Saviour; and, although in death, the spirit does not descend with the body into the dust, and must be under the eye of the Father of spirits, yet where Christ is, that is 'in fulness of joy; they never can be, till they have peace and joy in believing. He who dies in unbelief, lies down in sorrow, and will rise to the resurrection of damnation, or, more properly, condemnation. Blessed are the people who know the joyful sound; it is they, and they only, that walk in the light of God's countenance. If this was not the case, where would be the necessity of preaching the gospel at all? If, in the article of death, every one for whom Christ died were made acquainted with him, and consequently, with the things that made for their peace, why trouble mankind, in life, about these matters? Why go forth as sheep among wolves, suffering every thing that the malice of blind zeal can inflict, in order to turn men from darkness to light, if the period to which we are all hastening, will effectually open the eyes of the understanding? If death destroys all distinctions, would it not be well to say, "Let us eat, drink, and be merry, for to-morrow we die?" "We are commanded to preach the gospel, and this is a sufficient reason why we should preach the gospel." Very true; but why are we commanded to preach the gospel? Is it not, that faith may come by hearing, and that, living by faith on the Son of God, we may finish our course with joy? But, if every one of the ransomed race are to be equally happy in death, then, although they did not live by faith, they, nevertheless, finish their course with joy, nor shall any individual arise to the resurrection of condemnation. This may be consolatory, but it is not scriptural. These Sectarians, aware of this error, support it by another, and, therefore, deny a future judgment.

Blessed, saith the Holy Spirit, are the dead, who die in the Lord, they rest from their labours. But if all are alike in death, it may be said, Blessed are the dead, who die in their sin, that is in unbelief, for they rest from their labours; but this cannot be, since it is only those, who believing the word of the gospel, put on the Lord Jesus, and having received him as their righteousness, sanctification, and redemption, so walk in him, that can be said to die in him. These, and these only, have part in the first resurrection, on whom the second death can have no power. These, in the resurrection, shall meet their Saviour with transport ; they shall rise to the resurrection of salvation ; they shall come to Zion with songs ; they shall rejoice, while the many who are, nevertheless, redeemed, yet unacquainted with the things, which make for their peace, and who rise in the second resurrection, shall be filled with anguish. It is from these unhappy, despairing beings, that the LORD God will wipe away all tears ; it is from these benighted beings, that the hand of divine benignity shall take away the veil. Those, who live and die in faith, shall have no tears to wipe away, no veil to remove. Tears, weeping, and wailing, will continue as long as unbelief, the procuring cause shall remain. These evils will be done away together, not in the article of death, but in the day of the LORD, when every eye shall see, and every tongue shall confess to the glory of the Father.

Fourthly, There are many, who, because the scriptures are said, and with the strictest propriety, to testify of Jesus, believe that they testify of nothing, or no one else ; hence under the influence of this error, they apply to the Saviour, what the Holy Spirit applies to the grand adversary. In defending these absurd notions, they sometimes blaspheme the name of Jesus, and cause the way of truth to be evil spoken of. There are in this class of men, some who will tell you, *that Jesus Christ was the man, who had not on the wedding garment ! ! !* And was consequently cast out into outer darkness ! ! ! Thus, I presume without design, they make a schism in the body of Emmanuel, they separate the BRIDEGROOM, the HEAD, the KING, from his BRIDE, his BODY, his KINGDOM ; they separate what God hath joined together, although on the continuance of this union depends our life ; for if we were not crucified and buried with Christ as his fulness, we shall never have a right to reign with him. There is something most horrid in fixing any character upon Christ Jesus, which indicates inherent pollution ; but there are among those expounders, to whom we advert, who are fond of making their hearers stare, and wonder at their ingenuity ; alas, poor souls, the subtle deciever is abundantly more ingenious than they themselves are, but they are not sufficiently acquainted with his devices.

The scriptures testify of the divine and human natures—of those natures united in *One*—of men and of angels—of good angels, who never fell—of angels who kept not their first estate, of believers in Jesus Christ, who glorify his name, of some who believe, but who make no open profession, because they love the praise of men, more than the praise of God, of wicked men, who have not the knowledge of God in all their ways, and of arrogant, self-righteous Pharisees, who, thank God, they are not like other men. Among this great variety, the man, who is under the influence of the spirit of truth, will find Jesus, as the skilful miner finds the vein of gold in the mountain.

The scriptures abound with striking figures, calculated to give us an acquaintance with the principal characters therein, and dreadful work will he make in explaining these figures, who hath not the spirit of the Saviour. The Redeemer of men is exhibited under the characters, Father, Brother, Friend, Prophet, Priest, and King, Shepherd, Sheep and Lamb, Light, Life, and Peace, Bread, Wine, and Water, Fruit, Balm, and Flowers. These, and many other characters and figures, by which Emmanuel has been pleased to make himself manifest all indicate grace, mercy and peace.

The adversary is represented under the character of a beast of prey, seeking to devour, a prince of darkness, a murderer, a liar, a deceiver, the accuser of the brethren, the vulture, the serpent, the goat; and when the people of God of old are said to have worshipped devils, they worshipped them in the form of goats; hence the fallen angels, in the twenty-fifth of Matthew, are represented under the figure of goats, while the human nature is represented under the figure of sheep. All we like sheep have gone astray. Under this figure of sheep there are, and will be, until the kingdoms of the world become the kingdoms of God and of his Christ, two characters. Sheep, that hearing the voice of the shepherd, follow him, and are denominated his sheep, and others who are not of this fold, who still wander in the wide waste wilderness, where there is no way; these other sheep, the hepherd and bishop of souls must bring in, that there may be one fold under one shepherd, that of all the Father gave him none may be lost, save the *son of perdition;* but this son of perdition was never the offspring of God: *God is not perdition.*

Fifthly, There are many, who willing to speak peace to themselves, where there is no peace, affirm, that it is not sinners, but sin, that will be brought to the judgment, that it is unbelief, and not the unbeliever, that is damned, that it is the sins, that are put on the left hand in the great day, to whom the judge is supposed to speak, but this is absolutely ludicrous. What is sin distinct from the subject? Or how can sin, in an abstract point of view, be the subject of rebuke or punishment? Upon this principal, our Saviour suffered in vain, nothing more was necessary, than to have laid our sins upon the cross, and made them suffer death; but every reflecting person must see and feel the absurdity of such stuff as this. Sins are never spoken *to*, they are frequently spoken *of*, and there are some very striking figures, by which they are represented, as the tares of the field, sown by the wicked one, while the sower of the seed, as an accountable, intelligent being, is the proper subject of the judgment; the seed is spoken of as offensive, and like other weeds given to the devouring flame. Sometimes the iniquities of our nature are spoken of as chaff, which closely cleaves unto the grain while growing, but is finally doomed to the consuming fire. Sometimes sin is spoken of as flesh, as dead flesh, as a body of sin and death, and in this character, the birds of the air are summoned to the supper of the great God, to eat the flesh of all men. Our Saviour, when explaining unto his disciples the parable of the sower, informed them, that the birds of the air were the wicked ones, they are at last called to feed on the carcases of the abominable and detestable things; bu I do not recollect, that, in any part of divine revelation, sin is spoken of in the character of an accountable being; we have already seen, there can be but two characters, the proper subjects of the judgment, angels and men: the one on the right, the other on the left hand of the judge, who is emphatically styled, the Saviour of the world.

We have, during a series of years, been charged with propagating the above absurd and truly *ridiculous fancies*. However, I conceived this folly was found only in the mouths, for I could hardly think it was in the hearts of our calumniators to believe, that there were any, who held such principles. I was induced to think, these falsehoods were laid to our charge, in order to prejudice the public against us, for as I never conceived of such a doctrine, as either *scriptural* or *rational* myself, so I never believed any one else did. But lately I understand, that this sentiment hath its advocates, and I have the mortification to learn, that these advocates rank with Universalists! Surely, surely, such teachers are not taught by the spirit, that dictated to the men of God, what stands recorded as divine revelation. We conceive, that in this particular at least they are yet to learn.

Sixthly, There are a class of Universalists more respectable than the former, who insist, that although all mankind will finally be saved, they have much to perform or to suffer, in order to *satisfy divine justice* before this event can take place. All, say these Universalists, who have not a *perfection* of holiness in themselves in the present state, all who are not in this distempered state, pure in heart, must, before they can see God in glory, pass through a purgatorial fire, and there suffer some thousands of years, until they have paid the utmost farthing of the debt they owed the just God, according as the account stands in the book of the law; but when they have suffered the unjust, for the unjust, then they shall come forth with pure hearts filled with fervent affection to him, who graciously condescended to let them pay their own debt. These are called Universalists, and indeed they are Universalists in the strictest sense of the word, for as they do not conceive it is the blood of Jesus, which cleanseth from all sin, so they imagine, that the same mode of procedure, which is adopted for the salvation of all men, will equally apply to fallen angels, and they therefore believe in the salvation of devils. That our Saviour passed by the nature of angels, and took upon him the seed of Abraham, makes, in the view of these Universalists, no difference, for as mankind must after all suffer for their own sins; devils can do the same, and therefore be saved in the same way. What God will do with the fallen angels, after they are sent into the fire prepared for them, I know not, " Men are the books we ought to read, the proper study of mankind is man."

We go no farther in our inquiries than our own nature; so far these Universalists accompany us; but leave us here, and we are better pleased to find them advocates for salvation in any way, than if they were labouring to prove the eternal ruin of the greater part of God's offspring. Yet we conceive these sectarians cannot, with any degree of propriety, be called Universalists on apostolic principles; nor does it appear, that they have any idea of being saved *by* or *in the* LORD with an everlasting, or with any salvation. It is difficult to know what they will have to thank God for, at last, they having *paid their own debt*, and satisfied divine justice in their own persons. I wonder not, that such Universalists as these are opposed, and with success by the partialists. Such Universalists have nothing to do with the ministry of reconciliation ; the doctrines of the atonement and acceptance in the beloved is out of their plan; such doctrines are considered by them as unfriendly to holiness; such Universalists as these, are as far from the doctrines of the gospel on one side, as their opponents are on the other. These are Pharisaical Universalists, Universalists, who are willing to justify themselves; and such Universalism as this will be much more acceptable to an adulterous generation, than the Universalism found in the ministry of reconciliation; to wit, *that God was in Christ reconciling the world unto himself, not imputing their trespasses unto them.* We are very much at a loss to account for the suffering of Christ at all on the plan adopted by these Universalists; he either suffered for the unjust, or he did not; if he did not suffer for the unjust, he must have suffered very *unjustly, inasmuch as he did not personally deserve sufferings,* he in himself being holy, harmless, and undefiled. If he did suffer for the unjust, he either satisfied divine justice, or he did not; if he did not, then his resurrection is not our justification, nor did he put away sin by the sacrifice of himself; then he cannot be the saviour of the world, or of any individual in the world ; nor can God be just, if he justifies the ungodly, and, of course, with respect to sinners, as their Saviour, he died in vain.

If he did satisfy divine justice, and make recconciliation for iniquity, then this man is our peace, and we have the atonement, and God is well pleased for his righteousness' sake ; then he hath redeemed us from the curse of the law, and is just although a Saviour. The inconsistent plan, adopted by this class of Universalists, is supported like all others of the same complexion by false views of some divine passages in the book of God. When they considered the tares and the goats as wicked men, sent into everlasting fire to do what Jesus Christ, by the grace of God, came to do, and which, by a single word, he can and will show them he hath done ; they must of course continue in this everlasting fire, until the business be done, until complete satisfaction be made.

The truth is, Jesus is even now the Saviour of all men, *especially of those who believe ;* all that was necessary on God's part for the complete salvation of all men, was finished, when Jesus accomplished what the prophets prophesied of him, saying, He shall finish transgression, he shall make an end of sin, he shall make reconciliation for iniquities, and shall bring in everlasting righteousness. Nothing more is now necessary, than for God to say, *let there be light*, and in a moment, in the twinkling of an eye, he can cause such a change to pass on his purchased possession, as shall make them like unto their glorified head. Yes, by a single word, he can, by the mighty power whereby he is able to subdue all things unto himself, change even these vile bodies, that they may be fashioned like unto his own glorious body. Why the Saviour does not do this now, I know not, any more than I know why he did not assume our nature a thousand years sooner than he did, or why he suffers any to pass out of this state of existence unacquainted with him, as their Saviour, living all their life time in bondage to the fear of death. All I can, all I ought to say, is, that the judge of all the earth does right, and will continue to do right. The ELECTION obtains, in this their day, the knowledge of the things, that make for their peace, and the rest are blinded. But we rest in full assurance, that the period will come, when every eye shall see, when the face of the covering shall be taken from all people, and the veil from all nations, when the earth shall be filled with the knowledge of the LORD, when they shall all know him from the least of them, unto the greatest of them; and to know God is life eternal.

Seventhly, and lastly, There are who call themselves Universalists, who, as the manner of some was in the apostolic age, forsake the assembling themselves together. These admit, that Jesus is the Saviour of all men, and that, therefore, all men are saved. These have not the assurance of understanding, these are not *heart* believers, these are mere *head* believers, their faith rests on the judgment of men; among these, are found some who profess Jesus, but, in works, deny him; these are wells without water.

Believers who do not believe *merely* because they have the gospel from men, but because they have it from the Spirit of God who taketh of the things of Jesus, showing them to the soul, and witnessing with the Spirit to the truth thereof, these are not wells without water; the spirit they have received, is, as a well of living water, springing up unto everlasting life.

Merely *head* believers, fancy themselves rich and increased in goods, and that they have need of nothing, except the gratification of their vicious appetites; these are among our greatest enemies; these defend truth precisely as the arch fiend would have them; these will not attend on the ministry of the word, where the disciples meet in the name of the Saviour, in order to hear what God the LORD will say unto them, but they will attend at the synagogues of Satan, where the slaves of the devil meet, there to be heard confirming the truth, as Peter denied his Master, with oaths and with curses. These are the scum of the Universalists; these serve Satan more effectually than his own disciples; or rather, they are his own disciples passing under the christian name, as spies, to betray the people under whose name they pass, into the hands of their enemies. The Apostle suffered more from such believers as these, than from all the rest of the world. It was in consequence of the prevalence of such examples, that so much was said on this subject in the Epistles. I pray God to preserve you from the evil that is in the world, and to direct you into the way of peace. O, let it never be forgotten by you, that it is only in the way of wisdom you can find peace.

I am more and more convinced, that it is only the spirit and power of God which can make a *consistent Universalist*. Do you ask me, what are the features of a *consistent Universalist*? I answer, a *consistent Universalist* is taught of God; and, under the influence of the divine Spirit, he is made acquainted with the law of God, by the deeds of which, he hath discovered no flesh living can be justified. Not that the doers of the law, are not entitled to justification. The doers of the law are, and shall be justified. But from an acquaintance with the exceeding breadth of the commandment, and the imbecility of human nature, the *consistent Universalist* is, with the compilers of the Shorter Catechism, convinced, that no mere man since the fall, ever kept the commandments of God, but daily doth break them in thought, word, and deed. He, therefore, considers all men, at all times, as sinners, and coming short of the glory of God; he believes, that man in his best estate, is vanity; and that all the righteousness found in the best of *mere* human beings, is but as a filthy rag. His knowledge of the law gives him the knowledge of sin; and the commandment, having come with power to his heart, it hath, indeed, been unto him the ministration of condemnation, and a killing letter. He hath been able to say with another Universalist, *I was alive without the law, but when the commandment came it slew me, and I died.* And he considers himself, with respect to making peace with God or satisfying the demands of the law, either in its preceptive or penal view, as dead.

A *consistent Universalist* is made to understand, that Jesus was, from everlasting, ordained to be the Saviour of all those who were exposed to the curse of the divine law, that in the fulness of God's time, he was made under the law, and that all that Christ Jesus did, and all he suffered, was considered by the great Lawgiver, as done and suffered by every man in his own person; and that every man is as much interested in what our Emmanuel did, as the second Adam, as they were in what was done by the first Adam. It is in this view, that he considers God as just in being his Saviour, as he would have been in his eternal damnation, if the Head of every man had never made reconciliation for iniquity. Believing that Jesus was delivered for his offences, and raised again for his justification, he has peace with God through the Lord Jesus Christ; and as this peace was made through the blood of the cross, he is persuaded it can never be broken; believing himself accepted in the Beloved, and complete in him, he is persuaded nothing can ever separate him from the love of God, which is in Christ Jesus; thus believing, he enters into rest, he ceases from his own works as God did from his; he never can come into condemnation. His heart condemns him not; he has, at all times, the answer of a good conscience toward God, by the resurrection of the Saviour from the dead. He does not consider himself under the law, any more than a woman considers herself under the direction or dominion of an husband, who is dead and buried. He considers himself in the condition of a woman, who, having buried one husband, is married unto another; this other and last husband, is Christ Jesus, whose name the believer bears, which is the new name given unto him, belonging to this one husband; to consider himself under the dominion of two husbands, would be to consider himself in the condition of an adulterous woman; but the *consistent Universalist* owns but one husband, and this Husband hates putting away.

The *consistent Universalist* is not afraid of death. He may be afraid of dying, but not of death; he is well assured, that Jesus hath abolished death, and that nothing now remains, but the shadow of death; and he is persuaded, that as he walks through the valley of the shadow of death, his Saviour will be with him; he is not afraid of the grand adversary; he believes his head is bruised, and that his power to kill is, therefore, destroyed; he cannot be afraid of hell, for his Saviour keeps the keys of death and of hell; he is assured his Saviour is the conqueror of both; and being persuaded, that all power in heaven and earth, is given to his Saviour, his Head, his Husband, his Father, his Brother, and his Friend, he discovers nothing in time nor eternity, to give him just cause of fear, that is, of tormenting fear. He is not under the spirit of bondage again to fear; he can serve God without fear all the days of his life. A view of the perfect love of God hath cast out all his slavish fear. But though the *consistent Universalist* has nothing to fear, he has every thing to hope; he lives in the hope of living with his Saviour to all eternity; and, experiencing the pain which is attendant upon the plague of the heart, he cherishes the cheering hope, that he shall shortly leave behind him this body of sin and death, and be clothed upon with his house from heaven. He lives in the hope, that all things shall work together for good, how evil soever they may, in this distempered state, appear. The hope of the *consistent Universalist* extends to the final salvation of the great family of man. He prays for this event, and he prays in hope, and his hope maketh him not ashamed; because the love of God is shed abroad in his heart, and he is convinced, that the love of God is boundless. The *consistent Universalist* views mankind as they are viewed by their everlasting Father; and this Father is, he is persuaded, no respecter of persons; he dare not, therefore, injure any of his Father's children on any pretence whatever; he never conceives he can render service to God, by injuring any individual among the children of men, either in word or in deed; he would be happy to have it in his power to do good unto all, but in an especial manner, to those who are of the household of faith, inasmuch as their character has placed them in circumstances, which render the aid of their brethren more abundantly necessary. If he meets with any thing injurious from man, though conscious he does not deserve it, he will not avenge himself, he will leave delinquents to the common Father of all. *A consistent Universalist* will do all the good he can for his own sake, being fully persuaded, that to be found in the paths of rectitude, is as much his interest as his duty. *A consistent Universalist* hates sin; but he loves human nature, and he will, as much as in his power lieth, live peaceably with all men; and he will keep his eye singly and constantly fixed on that holiness, without which no man can see the LORD.

Finally, A *consistent Universalist*, as a believer in, and a lover of God, ardently wishes to be pure, as God is pure. He is grieved to observe, that when he would do good, evil is present with him; so that frequently the good which he would do, he doeth not, and the evil which he would not do, that doeth he; yet he quietly waits, and patiently hopes for that blessed period, when, not only he, but every grain of his LORD's harvest, shall be thoroughly purged from every particle of chaff, from all filthiness of flesh and spirit; and thus purified, shall enter into that state, where nothing that defileth can follow him.

Thus have I aimed at giving you the information you appeared to desire; in thus doing, I have not studied elegance of style nor composition, nor the enticing words of man's wisdom. I have aimed at perspicuity; I have spoken to be understood, and, in the hope of obtaining my purpose, I have even risked tautology, giving line upon line, and precept upon precept. I have written for my plain, simple, honest, way-faring friends. If what I have written should have a tendency to lead your mind, or the minds of those with whom you associate, to a serious investigation, and should the result be your knowing and doing the will of God, we shall have reason to rejoice together; and that this may be the case, is the fervent prayer of yours, &c. &c.

JOHN MURRAY.

Thanksgiving Sermon, delivered at the Universal meeting-house, in Boston, February 19th, 1795. Published at the request of the hearers, and now republished in consequence of the solicitation of a respectable character.

PSALM lxix. 13.

I will praise the name of God with a song, and will magnify him with thanksgiving.

WHEN we consider the propriety of approaching the God of our salvation with songs of thanksgiving, and of swelling to his name the glad orisons of praise; we confess that our bosoms are fraught with the animating glow of hope, that on such a day as this, there are very few who are not impelled, by sentiments fully correspondent with the occasion, to join the general joy.

To be called upon by the illustrious head of the United States,* to have this call seconded and enforced by the venerable head of this Commonwealth, to be thus invited to celebrate the praises of the august and benificent Father of our spirits, thus powerfully directed, to render thanks to him for the manifold displays of his goodness and mercy, vouchsafed toward us, must in truth elevate our hearts, must originate the most sublime and pleasurable feelings, and induce us to resolve with the royal prophet, That we will *praise the name of God with a song, and magnify him with thanksgiving.*

The apostle James directs those who are merry to sing psalms; and David said, *I will praise the name of God with a song.* The knowledge of God is productive of peace, This is life eternal to know thee, &c. Acquaint now thyself with God, and be at peace. The knowledge of God, as manifested in his name, has a tendency to fill the heart with joy, which will burst forth in songs of praise. But what is this NAME, the knowledge of which inspires the soul with a resolution to celebrate the praise of God in songs? What is the NAME, which contains so much matter for praise, and for thanksgiving? When Moses, the servant of God, was appointed to deliver a message to, and be the deliverer of the

* WASHINGTON.

people of God, he requested the God by whom he was sent to inform him, what answer he should give the people, when they should ask by whom he was sent. The reply of Deity is remarkable. Thus shalt thou say unto the children of Israel, I AM hath sent me unto you, and God said moreover unto Moses, Thus shalt thou say unto the children of Israel, The LORD God of your fathers, the God of Abraham, the God of Isaac, and the God of Jacob, hath sent me unto you ; this is my name forever, and this is my memorial unto all generations. After this declaration, the prophet was taught to inform God's people, that the God of Abraham, of Isaac, and of Jacob, was the God of the whole earth, and when he bowed the heavens and came down, for the purpose of performing all the rich promises so emphatically made to the fathers; when he took on him our nature, he bore the name of Emmanuel, which being interpreted, is God with us! Believing, as we do, that God was manifest in the flesh, whatever name he sustains in that character, we are to consider as expressive of his nature. Thus the name Jesus contains salvation, not only from the *consequences* of sin, but also from *sin* itself, which is styled, by the sacred penman, the plague of the heart. But it may not be improper to point out a few of the names, by which the only wise God our Saviour is designated.

ADAM, 1 Corinthians xv. 45. EVERLASTING FATHER, Isaiah ix. 6. Eternal Life, 1 John v. 20. Faithful Witness, Revelations i. 5. FRIEND of sinners, Matthew ii. 19. HEIR of all things, Hebrews i. 2. PROPITIATION, John vi. 33. For the sins of the whole world, REDEEMER, Isaiah lix. 20. REFINER, Matthew iii. 3. The LORD our righteousness, Jeremiah xxiii. 6. SANCTIFICATION, 1 Corinthians i. 30.

These and many more names, by which the just God and Saviour is made manifest unto men, are calculated to inspire the soul with grateful affection, and to induce us to say in the language of the sweet singer of Israel, *I will praise the name of God with a song, and magnify him with* THANKSGIVING. God is love, he is that love, which thinketh no evil. Herein is the love of God, not that we loved him, but that he loved us, and gave himself for us.

Much is said in the records of truth of the *name of God*. Be it known unto you, saith the LORD, for mine *own name sake* do I do this. The redeeming God frequently makes mention of the honour of his name, upon which he will never suffer a stain, or even the shadow of an impeachment. As many as know the *name* of God will trust in him, and they, who trust in the name of the LORD, are not easily moved. The minds of those, who are staid upon the rock of ages, are kept in peace, and their spirits rejoice in God their Saviour. They sing with the spirit, and with the understanding also, and they *magnify the LORD with thanksgiving*. But there was a time when some of us thought, and there are many, who still think, that God is as effectually praised by the lamentations of corroding sorrow, as by singing and rejoicing. Surely such persons forget, that it is not the gloomy, but the cheerful servant, who does honour to his master. Yet it is in vain we call upon any one to be thankful until he be made fully sensible of his obligations to the Saviour of sinners. In order, therefore, that upon this auspicious occasion, we may render unto the LORD *unreserved thanks*, and thus unequivocally comply with the direction of those, who are so deservedly invested with authority. We will endeavour to point out, under the following heads, a few of the innumerable blessings, by which we are eminently distinguished.

First, Natural, secondly, civil, and thirdly, spiritual blessings.

First, Natural. We have abundant cause to thank God, that we are. There was a time when many of us might have been unable to determine, whether existence was *really* a blessing. Is there who could give God thanks for a being appointed to *endless sorrow?* We humbly conceive, it is hardly possible for any individual, to render to Deity the grateful incense of sincere praise, for a life, however eligible its present investiture, which must, or probably may terminate in exquisite and *never-ending* torment. But for us when we reflect that *infinite wisdom* could not have produced an order of intelligence without *any design*, that *Infinite goodness* could only entertain the most *benificent* design, and that *Infinite power* could not be *disappointed* respecting his benignant purposes, purposed in himself concerning the work of his hands. When we have the joint suffrages of the writers of revelation, even all God's holy prophets from the beginning of the world, together with the authority, of the assembly of divines, who, in answer to the first question in their Shorter Catechism, inform us, that *God's chief end in making man, was his own glory, and their good.* When we are moreover assured, that for the *pleasure* of the Creator, who taketh no *pleasure* in the death of the sinner; we are and were created, we cannot but adopt the language of the poet, and while gratitude expands and lifts the spirit, we join issue with him, and reverentially exclaim, Surely the *Creator had never created but to bless.* It is thus, under the influence of reason and revelation, that we joyfully believe, and when believing, in the name of our faithful Creator, we spontaneously praise him with songs of triumph, we extol that mercy, which endureth forever, and with the orisons of *thanksgiving, we magnify his goodness.* But we are blessed with many blessings, which serve to render this being, even in the present state, a well being.

First, Sight. This is an inestimable blessing, for which we are bound to give thanks to him, who made the eye; how innumerable are the blessings to which this blessing serves as an inlet. With the eye, we behold the wonders of God in the heavens above, and in the earth beneath, and rapt in filial wonder, and holy extacy we exclaim with the inspired bard,

"These are thy glorious works, Parent of good,
Almighty Father these," &c. &c.

With the eye we behold the reviving countenances of our beloved friends, inhaling from the transporting view, ineffable delight.

Secondly, Hearing. Is there, who can calculate the value of this blessing? It is at the same moment the vehicle of instruction and pleasure, it is a source of unbounded satisfaction, the avenue through which uncounted gratifications obtain admittance to the soul.

Thirdly, Speech. How great the magnitude of this mercy, how innumerable our obligations to the maker of our frames for the organ of speech; conversation is but another term for the highest felicity, of which our nature is susceptible; it is the stamina of social enjoyment, the medium through which the invisible becomes visible. The musick produced by the modulation of the human voice, is enchanting: how far doth its tones surpass all those, which have ever yet been drawn from instruments, constructed by the most skilful artist. Speech doth indeed proclaim the divinity of its Artist, and it is endowed with corresponding powers. It is frequently the harbinger of peace, and many have been redeemed from the grasp of despair by the heaven taught strains, which have issued from this distinguishing organ.

Fourthly, The use of our limbs. How invaluable is this blessing, how much are we indebted to him, who has furnished us with these useful members of our bodies, for the strength by which they are nerved, and for that agility, flexibility and ease, with which they are accommodated to the various purposes of life.

Fifthly, Health What would the whole world be without this prime source of felicity. Health may be compared to the sun in the natural world ; it gilds and beautifies every surrounding object, it tranquilizes and sooths the soul, and extorts, by its genial influence, even from the bosom of frigidity, the song of praise.

Sixthly, Reason. *The health of the mind.* This endowment is transcendently great ; its worth is beyond all utterance, nor is it possible too highly to appreciate its value. The Being who made, and who illumined the mind of man with this heaven-lighted lamp, is, indeed, worthy of all adoration. Reason secureth to our species, an indubitable superiority over every other part of animated nature; it enricheth us by the possession of the first of blessings, and it bestoweth a luminous hope of an ample harvest in reversion.

Seventhly, The earth, the sea, and the treasures produced by both. These loudly call for our grateful and unceasing acknowledgments to that Being, who causeth the earth to bring forth abundantly, who hath furnished it as a garden, liberally supplying it with whatever may serve to treat the taste, or smell, or sight, for food, for medicine, or delight ; who hath made the treasures of the deep our own, fashioning those seas, which seem to roll their waves, insurmountable barriers to all communication between the nations, as convenient paths for those commodious vehicles, which wafted forward by propitious winds more effectually produce reciprocal advantages, disseminating the conciliating idea of *universal brotherhood*.

But how little do we know of ourselves or our accommodations ; how very little of the parts that are most obvious. We dwell in a house, that is indeed admirably contrived both for ornament and use ; we look out at the windows, and obtain a confused prospect of surrounding scenes, while at home we are strangers ! Yet the most cursory or superficial view will give us to know, that we are *fearfully* and *wonderfully* made, that he who made us upholdeth us in life, that his goodness far transcendeth all description, and that it is therefore our most reasonable service, to celebrate his praises, who hath thus fashioned, and who still preserveth us, with the song of gratitude, *magnifying his name with thanksgiving.*

Let us not say, that the inestimable blessings, which have been so feebly sketched, are not peculiar to us, that we partake them in common with our species, and that therefore they do not call for our grateful acknowledgments. Are then the largesses of a benefactor lessened, because his munificence is as extensive as his power? What, because God is good unto all, shall we refuse to render him the tribute of thanksgiving? Because his tender mercies are over all his works, shall we refuse to raise to him the song of gratitude? What, depreciate the value of a blessing because it is enjoyed by others? Far, very far from every one of us, be such disingenuous, such illiberal, and selfish conclusions.

But the truth is, that we enjoy many discriminating mercies, and while it is a fact, that no individual is destitute of a call for thanksgiving; upon us the calls for gratitude are immeasurably accummulated. We can *see* the blind, we can *hear* the deaf, we can *talk* of the dumb, we can *walk* to the lame, we can visit the sick, we can pity the *maniac*, that poor unfortunate being, who pierced by the barbed arrows of affliction, is doomed to suffer all the tortures attendant upon " moping melancholy, and moon-struck madness." We can behold many, very many suffering in the want of those comforts, which we so richly enjoy, and the question is natural.—"Why are we not in a situation similar to that of those distressed sufferers, whom we contemplate?" With reverential gratitude our hearts should answer, It is of the LORD's free mercy alone, that we are not thus circumstanced; and we will therefore say with the Psalmist, *I will praise the name of God with a song, and magnify him with thanksgiving.*

Secondly, It is a very pleasing part of our duty, which enjoins us to give thanks to God for the blessings of civil government. Without that order, which is produced by government, we should hold the blessings of life on a very precarious tenure. Mankind, from the earliest ages, have seemed in some sort sensible of this important fact; the absolute necessity of civil arrangements is ascertained by experience, and various are the modes of government, which the wisdom of legislators hath devised.

Different modes have been allowed probationary terms, and approbated or condemned as they have been found capable of an accommodation with the circumstances and exigencies of mankind, and with the different periods during which they were operative.

The mode of government, which either by force or fraud, hath most generally prevailed in our world, is monarchical. Writers of distinguished eminence and great celebrity have conceived, that the mode of government, which is the most simple, is the best calculated to promote the true interest of society, and they have not hesitated to pronounce, that an absolute monarchy, being the least complex, would undoubtedly be the most beneficial, supposing the *prince a perfect man ;* but as man in his best estate is vanity, and there is no one completely good but God, no being, save the Monarch of heaven, can *safely be entrusted with unlimited power*. Men of reason and reflection have imagined, that the interest of society was promoted by substituting for an *absolute*, a *restricted* monarchy ; and this not fully answering the purposes of civil government, an aristocracy has been adopted ; thus destroying one tyrant by the establishment of a government, administered by a combination of tyrants ; and thus a few influential men impiously divide among themselves, the spoils of royalty, by which they aggrandize themselves and their descendants by the labours of the many.

The next mode of government is a democracy. The children of Israel, dazzled by the pageantry, which is an appendage of royalty, envied their gaudy neighbours, the possession of these gewgaws ; they sought to imitate them, and became clamorous for a king ; the prophet of the Lord laid before them the dreadful consequences, that would assuredly result from the regulation they so ardently solicited, and he expatiated in language the most emphatick, upon the glaring impropriety, and God dishonouring levity of rejecting the equitable domination of the only sovereign, who swayed the sceptre with an equal hand, who wore the crown for the general benefit, and whose administration was in every instance the result of infinite goodness, and infinite wisdom. The pride however of the Israelites got the better of their piety ; they rushed into the snares, which were laid for them, and by obtaining a king, fatally realized the prophetic prediction.

Perhaps no nation under heaven, at any period of time, hath had so much reason to praise the name of God with songs, and to *magnify him with thanksgiving*, as we, the inhabitants of these

United States. Planted here by the hand of the Most High, and even kings for a time (softened by that Being, in whose hands are all hearts) protecting fathers, our increase was rapid, until the nation, under whose shadow we grew, regarding with envy our growing greatness, devised means to render our prosperity subservient to their ambitious purposes. But that sovereign disposer of events, whose purposes are not to be defeated, and who still frustrates the artful devices of designing men, raised up among ourselves men, nerved by dauntless valour for our defenders, and he endowed them with that wisdom and true heroism, which enabled them to make a vigorous stand against the encroachments of arbitrary power. Threatened with the vengeance of incensed majesty, whose ministers prepared to execute his sanguinary decrees, and whose military veterans swarmed in our capitals, our people nevertheless felt themselves at home ; and they were almost universally strangers to fear.

It was at this period, in the time of the greatest danger, that the arm of the LORD was especially revealed in the choice, made by infinite wisdom of that illustrious character, who headed the virtuous band of patriot heroes. The leader of our armies, like the celebrated Roman chief, studied to gain the victory over his own and his country's foes, not by taking, but by preserving their lives. The breast of the patriot warrior was uniformly nerved by more than Fabian virtue, until at length, under the auspices of the protecting arm of the Almighty, a period was put to the lengthened scene of sorrow, by the commencement of peace.

Pausing for a moment, let us, at this period, take a retrospective view. Without money, justly appellated the sinews of war, without military materials, without internal strength or external aid ; strange as it may appear, the people were inspired with resolution to go forward : when the humane monarch of the Gallic nation beheld us with sympathizing concern, his aid was timely, his armies, his navy appeared on our land, and on our coast ; and we *sang praises to our God.* On the conclusion of the war, these armies, this navy *quitted our shores, and we magnified his name with thanksgiving.*

I am, my friends, aware, that these are subjects upon which I can give you no information ; but upon such a day as this, we may be allowed to retrace the splendid events, which illume our annals. It becomes us to summon the powers of recollection, to dwell upon the distinguishing goodness of him, who presideth in the heavens, that we may thus feel ourselves impelled with grateful joy to *praise the name of our God with a song, and to magnify him with thanksgiving.*

The illustrious chief, who led our patriot bands through all the rugged scenes of military life, conducted the victorious troops to a triumphant close, nor separated himself from the embattled hosts, until enwreathed with the blessings of peace, they were at liberty to seek her calm retreats. We mark with superior pleasure the intrepid warrior combining the sublime wisdom of the legislator with that skilful valor, which led our confederated bands to decisive victory; eminently qualified, he is judiciously placed at the head of the civil department, and he will point our citizens to those sure paths, in which they may secure the advantages contemplated from returning peace.

Peace attained, we fancied ourselves at the end of our labours, that we had already obtained the summit of that eminence, for which we are this day to *praise the name of God with a song, and to magnify him with thanksgiving.* But many revolving months rolled on before our wishes were crowned with a government, at once the boast and envy of the world.

Our government is not monarchical, it is not aristocratical, it is not democratical, but it is infinitely preferable to all, it is FEDERAL.

Our federal constitution, being a collection of constitutions, is on earth, what the galaxy or milky way, is in the heavens, where the combining lustre of the stars form one glorious splendor, which instead of diminishing the light of any particular luminary, adds to the transcendent brightness of the whole. How greatly are we indebted to the divine goodness for inspiring the same men with abilities to plan this government, to whom he had before given that intrepid valor and dauntless bravery, which procured and guaranteed our independence. Blessed above the nations of the earth in our local circumstances; more than three thousand miles removed from those ambitious Europeans, whose interest it would be to embarrass and interrupt our prosperity; our arms were no sooner laid by, than we were enabled to attend calmly to the important business of legislation, well knowing, that good government was the only sure means of ascertaining the enjoyment of the blessings of peace. Our government was not formed under the eye or influence of aliens, of open or secret enemies ; it was formed by ourselves, and fraternal confidence was the order of that auspicious era. Perhaps no period in the annals of time, hath marked a group of such illustrious characters assembled for deliberation replete with consequences so truly interesting, so extensively important. With ineffable delight, we recognize, as leaders of the meritorious band, a WASHINGTON, a FRANKLIN, an ADAMS, nor although the federal government resulted from the united wisdom of those heaven taught sages, although it was replete with excellence, yet it was not either by force or ingenious device pressed upon the people. The inhabitants of the several States, in their several capacities, were summoned to deliberate thereon. Wisdom dictated every step, and like every other work of God, the closer the survey, the fuller the investigation ; the stricter the scrutiny, the more were the beauties and excellence of the constitution discovered, until being supposed to possess all the good of every government without the evil, the true ore being separated from the dross, it was received with grateful transport, as heaven's last best gift to a world, which had long anticipated the mighty blessing. And for this we *will praise the name of God with a song, and magnify him with thanksgiving.*

But, alas ! Such is the nature of man in its present depraved state, that either through weakness or through wickedness some will endeavour to elevate themselves on the ruin of others ; thus as far as they are able interrupting the order of things, and breaking the peace of society. It was with deep regret, that we witnessed, even in this enlightened state, something of this sort. Our political horizon became clouded, its aspect was alarming, and we dreaded the effect of pernicious and innovating influence ; but the wisdom of a Bowdoin, and the lenient measures of a Hancock, (names which will be forever dear to the citizens of this Commonwealth) not only checked the progress, but, as we trust, entirely eradicated the evil.

The body politic has frequently been compared to the natural body. Our federal government contains the head and heart of this body ; the State governments may be considered as the members in their various descriptions, and as the blood, which is said to be the life of the creature, comes from the heart, and circulating to the extremities, returns to the heart again ; so, ever since the establishment of the federal government, the life of the body hath appeared in this direction, and it is to this, under God, that we owe the health and vigour of the body. But as the head and heart would be useless without the rest of the body, we are to give God thanks for the constitutions of government, which unite, and by their union establish liberty with order. Without this order it is obvious, that the existence of the FEDERAL GOVERNMENT would be no more, and hence the necessity of paying attention to the parts, for the preservation of the whole.

" When," saith our illustrious President, " we review the calamities, which afflict so many other nations ; the present condition of the United States affords much matter of consolation and satisfaction. Our exemption hitherto from foreign wars, an increasing prospect of that exemption, the great degree of internal tranquillity we have enjoyed, the recent confirmation of that tranquillity, by the suppression of an insurrection, that so wantonly threatened it, the happy course of our publick affairs in general, the unexampled prosperity of all classes of our citizens, are circumstances, which peculiarly mark our situation with indications of the Divine Beneficence toward us."

How pleasing these enumerations, how animating to hear the head of our government, after a review of the foregoing state of things, calling upon his beloved fellow citizens throughout the Union, to acknowledge with devout reverence and affectionate gratitude, their many and great obligations to Almighty God, and to implore him to continue, and to confirm to us the blessings we at present experience. How inexpressibly delightful to behold the heart of this truly great man, suitably and deeply impressed with sentiments so proper and so becoming. How alluringly persuasive his patriotic voice ; thus, in the language of paternal affection, inviting all religious societies, and denominations, and all persons whomsoever within the United States, although they may belong to no religious society or denomination, on this day to meet together, and render their sincere and heart-felt thanks to the great Ruler of nations, for the manifold and signal mercies, which distinguish our lot as a nation. Can we forbear persuading ourselves, that each individual attending to such precepts, and under the influence of such an example, will spontaneously and ardently call upon his spirit to bless the God of his salvation, crying with holy transport, "*Bless the* LORD, *O my soul, and forget not all his benefits.*"

To remember all the manifold mercies of Jehovah, would be impossible ; they are more in number than the hairs of our head ; they are the coevals of our existence, and every breath we draw is an added proof of immeasurable goodness. But it is indeed true, as has been frequently observed, that the most acceptable way of improving the mercies of our God is, to receive them with thanksgiving ; and it is undoubtedly incumbent upon us to engrave upon the memory as many of the innumerable benefits, which we derive from the inexhaustible source of divine munificence, as the limited conception of frail mortality can grasp.

Among the first of our temporal blessings, upon this occasion, we cannot but trace, (and it is with heart-felt gratitude,) we cannot but acknowledge, that divine interposition, which hath so graciously wrought for us the preservation of our peace, foreign and domestic. Inestimable are the blessings of tranquillity. Our sympathizing hearts have suffered from wars, although we were afflicted only by the hearing of the ear. How dreadful then to be drawn into the vortex of this desolating calamity, and how much are we indebted to the object of our filial reverence, who, in the hands of our God and Father, hath been made an instrument of preserving us from this great evil, and all the direful consequences, that follow in its train. But although foreign war is a calamity ever to be deprecated ; domestic or civil war combines a catalogue of yet greater ills : many of us have had an apportunity of forming some faint idea of this desolating evil among ourselves. But very faint indeed must be the idea we can form from any thing, which we have ever witnessed in this highly distinguished nation, when compared with what we have been informed of in other countries, both in ancient, and in modern times.

We were sometime since alarmed by the dread apprehension of the contagious spread of this desolating and truly shocking ravager ; but the timely suppression of this insurrection, as well as the *manner* in which it was suppressed, inspires us, upon this auspicious occasion, with unceasing gratitude. How must the patriotic mind, the federal bosom have swelled with conscious pleasure, to view so large a collection of virtuous citizens leaving the calm retreat of their peaceful homes, and marching forward in a cool, dispassionate manner, with the bright example of their beloved chief in their eye, and a measure of the same philanthropic benignity, that he in so great a degree (we had almost said without measure) possesses, in their hearts, determined to preserve the constitution, the laws, and if possible the people, who had violated them. See with what tender pity, with what mild compassion, the father of his country regards this deranged part of the family; see how like the Parent of the universe he conquers the refractory by love ; see how under the benign influence of true patriotism the political storm subsides, the sunny beams of serenity are restored, and the halcyon days of internal peace and security, consequent thereon, have commenced. Mark with what ineffable delight our virtuous citizens return to their homes, now more than ever endeared to them, while their hearts glow with secret satisfaction in the consideration, that the earth, over which they have passed, hath not drank in their brother's blood.

Is there who can behold a scene so elevating and impressive, without exclaiming with the Psalmist, *I will praise the name of God with a song, and magnify him with thanksgiving ?*

We have already observed, that the body politick has been compared to the natural body ; and as the natural body is subject to diseases, so also is the body politick; but if any part of the natural body is diseased, the disorder is by sympathy communicated to the whole ; thus, if one member suffers, all suffer ; yet these suffering parts hate not their own flesh, and an attempt will be made to remove the complaint without removing the disordered member. Passions too, it is said, are the elements of life, and perhaps these partial evils may indeed be productive of general good. Were it not, that the sea is frequently thrown into a tempestuous state by the force of the winds, it would become a stagnate mass of corruption ; and, although in consequence of storms and tempests, partial evils do succeed, yet the calamities, which would result from a perpetual calm, would be of infinitely greater magnitude.

Although our constitution of government may be, in the judgment of the wise and virtuous of both hemispheres, the nearest to perfection of any ever yet formed for the benefit of human nature ; yet, although the *nearest* to perfection, it may not be *perfect*, and although the men, who are, by divine providence, placed at the head of our government, may be as near perfection as any men in such circumstances ever were, yet they are not *perfect*.

In the present imperfect state, *perfection* is not the lot of humanity.

These considerations may give rise, in the bosom of many individuals, to feelings, that a judgment of charity may denominate a godly jealousy; they may admire and love our constitution so much, that their apprehensive minds may suffer in the dread of any change taking place in it, and agitated by those painful ideas, their consequent fears may form conjectures, that may exist no where but in their own imaginations; and as the evils apprehended are, in the nature of things possible, persons of this description, while they do no more than act the part of vigilant watchmen, are certainly excusable. It would however be well, as we suffer through life almost as much from imaginary, as from real evils, if such persons could dismiss their fears, and serve both their country and their God without fear, and in newness of life; at least it would be well, if they could avoid innoculating their brethren with this infection.

Yet, as the *rights of man are the rights of every man*, so every man has a right to think for himself, and if he will clothe his thoughts in decent language, he has a right to submit his views to the public eye. But, blessed be God, we are, as a people, well enough acquainted with the rights of man, to know that the charter of his rights endows no man with a right to do wrong.

On the whole, as difference of opinion hath existed, and will continue to exist among the individuals, which constitute the aggregate of mankind, and as our free constitutions admit of this difference, what have we to do, but mutually to agree to differ, well knowing that while we keep within legal bounds, our admirable constitution, like an indulgent parent, will spread over us its protecting wings.

Let us, then, my beloved friends, however we may be disposed to censure men or measures, leave it to the uninfluenced determination of a majority of free citizens, to approve or disapprove, agreeably to the direction of their best informed judgment.

Yet, as strength is established by union, and nothing can be more desirable than unity of spirit in the bond of peace, it is every man's *duty*, it is every man's *interest*, to exert himself for the promotion and establishment of peace. Blessed are the peace makers, they shall be called the children of God. But as opposition always begets opposition, so the mild influence of peaceful measures are the best calculated to beget and preserve peace; and it is, and always will be a truth, that a *soft answer turneth away wrath, while grievous words stir up anger.*

As our constitution is the boast of the unprejudiced part of the world, so it is the envy of the malignant, the ambitious, and the designing, both abroad and at home. Distinguished and highly blessed as we are, we cannot be without external and internal foes; and it is sometimes difficult for any, but him who trieth the reins, to determine, who is the genuine friend, who is the dangerous foe. But every lover of his country, when he beholds American citizens contending, acrimoniously contending with each other, experiences the same sensations, which agitated the bosom of Moses, when he beheld the strife of his brethren in Egypt, and, impelled by his feelings, he will involuntarily adopt the language of the Hebrew patriot. " Sirs, why do you thus, are ye not brethren?" Little do these contending parties know, how much their dissensions gratify the worst passions, and most unworthy part of their species.

But it is with inexpressible pleasure, that we are enabled to indulge the pleasing hope, that in this most respectable branch of the Union, these contentions will never be carried to any very injurious lengths. The good sense and amor patriæ of the citizens at large, will always oblige them to sacrifice private interests, and what is sometimes more difficult, private resentments, to *public good.* The virtuous mind gathers great consolation, while beholding men of every description, mixing together on public occasions, and looking with a benign aspect upon each other. This is the LORD's doing, and it is marvellous in our eyes, and we will therefore *praise his name with a song, and magnify him with thanksgiving.*

Blessed as we are, considering the uncertainty of human affairs, we cannot forbear humbly and fervently to beseech the great Author of these blessings, that he would vouchsafe graciously to prolong them to us, that he would imprint upon our hearts a deep and solemn sense of our obligations to him for them, that he would teach us rightly to estimate their immense value, that he would preserve us from the arrogance of prosperity, and from hazarding the advantages we enjoy by delusive pursuits, that he would dispose us to merit* the continuance of

* Though we may not *merit* ought from God, to whom we stand indebted for all we possess, yet we may have claims upon each other.

his favours, by not abusing them, by our gratitude for them, and by a correspondent conduct as citizens, and as men; that he would render this country more and more, a safe and propitious asylum, for the unfortunate of other countries, that he would extend among us true and useful knowledge, that he would diffuse and establish habits of sobriety, order, morality, and piety; and, finally, that he would impart all the blessings we possess, or ask for ourselves, to the WHOLE FAMILY OF MANKIND. How sublime is the reflection, that at this hour, those individuals who constitute in the aggregate the most favoured nation upon the globe, with their beloved chief at their head, are collected for the purpose of looking over the rent roll of their inheritance, with grateful hearts, acknowledging to whom they are indebted for all, saying with one voice, Not unto us, not unto us, but unto thy name, O LORD, be all the glory, at the same moment supplicating, and with fervour of devotion, not for themselves only, but for the residue of mankind. Surely, no day like the present ever exhibited such an epitome of that state of being, which only is more blessed than ours.

Thirdly, and lastly, We are to consider spiritual blessings.

While contemplating with grateful transport our natural and civil rights, and all those attendant blessings, which by divine favour we so richly enjoy, our bosoms swell with augmenting gratitude, when we recur to our religious rights and privileges; these are, of all others, the most valuable and best established *rights of man;* without these, all our other blessings would only serve to make life wretched, in the dread apprehension of death. The Father of mercies hath blessed the sojourners in the present world, with a rich inheritance, but it is defiled, and it fadeth away, while, in the seed of Abraham, we are blessed with an inheritance, incorruptible and undefiled, and that fadeth not away. Here our peace is liable to be broken, but the peace made by the blood of the cross, is that peace which passeth all understanding, and being the covenant of God's peace, it shall never be removed.

This state of things cannot be our rest, for it is defiled; but there is a rest remaineth for the people of God, where nothing that defileth can ever enter. As citizens of this world, notwithstanding the blessings which we enjoy, revelation and reflection teach us to expect tribulation; but as fellow-citizens with the saints, and of the household of faith, we look forward to uninterrupted pleasures in worlds beyond the sky.

Glancing over our spiritual blessings, I am constrained to pronounce them innumerable; in them we have the free gift of God, everlasting life; and for this we unite to *magnify* his most holy name. We are also bound to give thanks on behalf of all mankind, inasmuch as he who is our life, is also the life of the world. God so loved the world, that he gave them his Son, and this Son, thus given, gave himself a ransom for all; he died for the sins of the whole world, by the grace of God he tasted death for every man; he was delivered up to death for us. all; and it is therefore that he is the Saviour of all men, *to be testified in due time.* Is sin the source of sorrow? Christ Jesus was manifested to take away our sins, to redeem us from all iniquity, and to purify us to himself. Is the knowledge of God necessary to the enjoyment of God? They shall all know him, saith the Lord, from the least of them unto the greatest of them. Can no man know the things of God, but by the spirit of God? It is written, they shall be all taught of God. Are the people unwilling to come to God for life? They shall, saith God, be *willing in the day of my power.* Have they made a covenant with death, and an agreement with hell? Thus saith the Lord; Your covenant with death shall be *broken, and your agreement with hell shall not stand.* Have the people sold themselves for nought? they shall be redeemed without money. Does death and hell hold many, very many wretched captives? *Death and hell shall deliver up the dead;* the first shall be swallowed up of victory, and the second shall be cast into the lake of fire. O death, saith the Lord, I will be thy plague, O grave, *hades* or *hell,* I will be thy destruction. Do the kingdoms of the world wander after the beast? Do they worship this beast in the Church, in the State? *The kingdoms of this world shall become the kingdom of God, and of his Christ.* Does the whole creation groan and travail in pain together? *They shall be brought into the glorious liberty of the sons of God; and there shall be no more pain, for God, even our God, shall wipe away every tear from every eye.* Thus speak the oracles of God, thus spake the Faithful and True; And is it possible, that we can attend to such soul-satisfying sounds as these, than musick in its softest strains more sweet, without joining with the royal prophet, without adopting his language, and from the abundance of an overflowing heart, exclaiming, *I will praise the name of God with a song, and magnify him with thanksgiving?*

But while we contemplate the blessings secured to us by God our Saviour, we should not be unmindful of the privileges of a religious nature, by which we are distinguished in this present world. We have now no imperious, dogmatizing creed makers, availing themselves of their influence over the secular power, to enforce their opinions. We can now worship our God precisely according to the dictates of our own consciences. We can now, in our way to public worship, intersect the paths of our fellow men, without the smallest dread of censure, without encountering either the malignant glance or the supercilious sneer. We can now confess the ties of amity, although we do not worship in the same place, or entertain the same ideas of the object of our adoration. The philosopher of Verney, speaking of Pennsylvania, pronounced it the paradise of the globe; and rendering a reason for this decision, "There," said he, "every man thinks for himself, and he can publish his thoughts without terror. In that happy country, sects are so multiplied, and so various, that no one party can ever accumulate a number sufficiently large to trample upon the rest." Blessed be the God of our salvation, this vast advantage is not at this period confined to the State of Pennsylvania, but this salutary indulgence is now the inestimable privilege of the United States at large; and we are right happy to observe, that certain characters having lost the power to oppress, have also in a very great degree lost the inclination.

How astonishing the change which hath taken place in this country, and how friendly to the interests of society is this change; and should we continue in the way of peace, how great may be our improvements. It is rational, from present appearances, to indulge a hope, that our ministers will be ministers of peace, that they will approve themselves workmen who need not be ashamed; that, as followers of them who through faith and patience inherit the promises, they will, from the abundance of their believing hearts, declare the ministry of reconciliation, assuring every creature, that God was in Christ reconciling the world unto himself, not imputing unto them their trespasses, and calling upon them, in the language of unfeigned affection, thus beseeching them in Christ's stead, to be reconciled unto God, assuring them, as a further inducement to their being thus reconciled, that God the Saviour, although he knew no sin *personally*, was made sin for them, that they may be made the righteousness of God in him.

May we not rationally cherish hope, that under the influence of the spirit of our meek and lowly Master, whom they profess to serve, they will not only preach peace by the blood of the cross, but that they will, both by precept and example, lead their adherents into the way of peace, which is the way everlasting? May we not indulge a hope, that under the constraining influence of the love of Christ, they will lead their hearers to love God, who first loved them, and, as the chosen of God, to love one another with pure hearts fervently? Thus will the religion of God our Saviour appear to be what it really is, worthy of *all acceptation*. May we not, without being too sanguine, entertain an expectation, that the era approaches, when, instead of the odious distinctions of *orthodox*, and *heterodox*, of *democrat*, and *aristocrat*, of *federal* and *antifederal*, we may, as the children of one Father, as members of the same community, consider it as much our interest as our duty, to do good, and thus approve ourselves the children of our Father, who is in heaven.

Under such benign auspices, may we go on our way rejoicing, saying, Not on this day only, but on every future day of our lives, *I will praise the name of God with a song, and will magnify him with thanksgiving*.

And that this may be our mutual felicity, may God of his infinite mercy grant, through Jesus Christ our LORD, to whom be glory, now, henceforth and forever, Amen and Amen.

EXTRACTS FROM PAPERS CONTAINING MINUTES OF THE AUTHOR'S LIFE, WRITTEN BY HIMSELF.

EXTRACT FIRST.

This extract is taken from that period of the writer's life, when he was compelled, by the force of truth, to relinquish the traditionary religion, which had been given to him by education.

I HAD heard much of Mr. Relly, he was a conscientious and zealous preacher in the city of London. He had, through many revolving years, continued faithful to the ministry committed to him, and he was the theme of every religious sect. He appeared as he was represented to me, highly erroneous, and my indignation against him was strong.

I had frequently been solicited to hear him, merely that I might be an ear witness of what was termed his *blasphemies;* but I arrogantly said, I would not be a *murderer of time.* Thus I passed on for a number of years hearing all manner of evil said of Mr. Relly, and *believing all I heard,* while every day augmented the inveterate hatred, which I bore against this man and his adherents. When a worshipping brother or sister belonging to the communion, which I considered as honoured by the approbation of Deity, was drawn from the paths of rectitude by this deceiver, the anguish of my spirit was indescribable, and I was ready to say, *the secular arm ought to interpose to prevent the perdition of souls.* I recollect one instance in particular, which pierced me to the soul.

A young lady of irreproachable life, remarkable for piety, and highly respected by the tabernacle, congregation and church, of which I was a devout member, had been ensnared. To my great astonishment, she had been induced to hear, and having heard she had embraced the pernicious errors of this detestable babbler; she was become a believer, a firm and unwavering believer of universal redemption! Horrible! Most horrible! So high an opinion was entertained of my talents, having myself been a teacher among the Methodists, and such was my standing in Mr. Whitfield's Church, that I was deemed adequate to reclaiming this wanderer, and I was strongly urged to the pursuit. The poor deluded young woman was abundantly worthy our most arduous efforts.—*He that converteth the sinner from the error of his way, shall save a soul from death, and shall hide a multitude of sins.* Thus I thought, thus I said, and, swelled with a high idea of my own importance, I went, accompanied by two or three of my christian brethren, to see, to converse with, and if need were, to admonish this simple, weak, but as we heretofore believed meritorious female; fully persuaded, that I could easily convince her of her errors, I entertained no doubt respecting the result of my undertaking.

The young lady received us with much condescension and kindness, while, as I glanced my eye upon her fine countenance, beaming with intelligence, mingling pity and contempt grew in my bosom. After the first ceremonies, we sat for some time silent, at length I drew up a heavy sigh, and uttered a pathetic sentiment relative to the deplorable condition of those who live and die in unbelief, and I concluded a violent declamation, by pronouncing *with great earnestness, he that believeth not shall be damned.*

" And pray, Sir," said the young lady with great sweetness, " Pray Sir, what is the unbeliever damned for not believing ?"

What is he damned for not believing ? *Why he is damned for not believing.*

" But, my dear Sir, I asked what was that, which he did not believe, for which he was damned ?"

Why, for not believing in Jesus Christ to be sure.

" Do you mean to say, that unbelievers are damned for not believing there was such a person as Jesus Christ ?"

No, I do not; a man may believe there was such a person, and yet be damned.

" What then, Sir, must he believe, in order to avoid damnation ?"

Why, he must believe, that Jesus Christ is a complete Saviour.

" Well, suppose he were to believe, that Jesus Christ was the complete Saviour of others, would this belief save him ?"

No, he must believe that Christ Jesus is his complete Saviour, every individual must believe *for himself*, *that Jesus Christ is his complete Saviour.*

" Why, Sir, is Jesus Christ the Saviour of any *unbeliever ?*"

No, Madam.

" Why then should any *unbeliever* believe, that Christ Jesus is his Saviour, *if he is not his Saviour.*"

I say he is not the Saviour of any one, until he believes.

" Then if Jesus be not the Saviour of the *unbeliever*, *until he believes*, the unbeliever is called upon to believe a lie. It appears to me, Sir, that Jesus is the complete Saviour of *unbelievers*, and that unbelievers are called upon to believe the truth, and that by *believing*, *they are saved in their own apprehension, saved from all those dreadful fears*, which are consequent upon unbelief, upon a state of conscious condemnation."

No, Madam, you are dreadfully, I trust not fatally misled. Jesus never was, nor never will be the Saviour of any unbeliever.

" Do you think he is your Saviour, Sir ?"

I hope he is.

" Were you *always* a believer, Sir ?"

No, Madam.

" Then you were once an *unbeliever*, that is, you once believed that Jesus Christ was not your Saviour. Now as you say, he never *was* nor *never will be* the Saviour of any *unbeliever*, as you were once an *unbeliever*, he never can be your Saviour."

He never was my Saviour till I believed.

" Did he never die for you till you believed, Sir ?"

Here I was extremely embarrassed, and most devoutly wished myself out of her habitation. I sighed bitterly, expressed deep commiseration for those deluded souls, who had nothing but head knowledge ; drew out my watch, *discovered it was late*, and recollecting an engagement, observed it was time to take leave.

I was extremely mortified, the young lady observed my confusion, but was too generous to pursue her triumph. I arose to depart, the company arose, she urged us to tarry, addressed each of us in the language of kindness, her countenance seemed to wear a resemblance of the heaven, which she contemplated, it was stamped by benignity, and when we bid her adieu, she enriched us by her good wishes.

I suspected that my religious brethren saw she had the advantage of me, and *I felt* that her remarks were indeed *unanswerable;* my pride was hurt, and I determined to ascertain the exact sentiments of my associates respecting this interview. Poor soul, said I, she is far gone in error. True, said they, but she is notwithstanding a very sensible woman. Ay, ay, thought I, they have assuredly discovered, that she has proved too mighty for me. Yes, said I, she has a great deal of *head* knowledge, but yet she may be a lost, damned soul. I hope not, returned one of my friends, she is a very good young woman. I saw, and it was with extreme chagrin, that the event of this visit had depreciated me in the opinion of my companions; but I could do no more than censure and condemn, solemnly observing, it was better to avoid conversing with any of those apostates, and it would be judicious never to associate with them upon any occasion. From this period I, myself, carefully avoided every Universalist, and *most cordially did I hate* them. My ear was open to the public calumniator, to the secret whisperer, and I yielded credence to every scandalous report, however improbable. My informers were *good people*, I had no doubt of their veracity, and I believed it would be difficult to paint Relly and his connexions in colours too black; how severely has the *law of retaliation* been since exercised in the stabs, which have been aimed at my own reputation. Relly was described as a man black with crimes; an atrocious offender both in principle and practice. He had, it was said, abused and deserted an amiable wife, and it was added, that he retained in his house an abandoned woman, and that he not only thus conducted himself, but that he publicly and most nefariously taught his hearers, thus to dare the laws of their country, and of their God. Hence, said my informers, the dissipated and unprincipled of every class flock to his church; his congregation is astonishingly large, the carriages of the great block up the street, in which his meeting-house stands, and he is the idol of the voluptuous of every description.

All this, and much more was said, industriously propagated and credited in every religious circle. Denominations at variance with each other, yet agreed most cordially, in thus thinking, and thus speaking of Relly, of his principles, of his preaching, and of his practice. I confess I felt a strong inclination to see and hear this monster once at least, but the risk was dreadful!

I could not gather courage to hazard the steadfastness of my faith; and for many years I persevered in my resolution, on no consideration to contaminate my ear by the sound of his voice. At length, however, I was prevailed upon to enter his Church, but I detested the sight of him, and my mind, prejudiced by the reports to which I had listened respecting him, was too completely filled with a recollection of his fancied atrocities, to permit a candid attention to his subject, or his mode of investigation. I wondered much at his impudence in daring to speak in the name of God, and I felt assured, that he was treasuring up unto himself, wrath against the day of wrath; I looked upon his deluded audience with alternate pity and contempt, and I thanked God that I was not one of them. I rejoiced when I escaped from the house, and as I passed home, I almost audibly exclaimed, Why, O my God, was I not left in this deplorable, damnable state, given up like these poor, unfortunate people to believe a lie to the utter perversion of my soul? But I was thus furnished with another proof of my *election*, in consequence of my not being deceived by this detestable deceiver; and my consolation was of course exceeding great.

About this time there was a religious society established in Cannon-street, in an independant meeting-house, for the purpose of elucidating difficult passages of scripture. This society chose for their President a Mr. Mason, who, although not a clerical gentleman, was nevertheless of high standing in the religious world: frequent application was made to him in the character of a physician to the sinking, sorrowing, sin-sick soul. His figure was commanding, and well calculated to fill the minds of young converts with religious awe. When this company of serious inquirers were assembled, the President addressed the throne of grace in a solemn and appropriate prayer, and the subject for the evening was next proposed. Every member of the society was indulged with the privilege of expressing his sentiments for the space of five minutes, a glass was upon the table, which run accurately the given term. The President held in his hand a small ivory hammer; when the speaker's time had expired, he had a right to give him notice by a stroke on the table, round which the assembled members were convened. But if he approved of what was delivered, it was optional with him to extend the limits of his term. When the question had gone round the table, the President summed up the evidences, gave his own judgment, and having proposed the question for the next evening, concluded with a prayer.

At this society I was a constant attendant, and frequently was I gratified by the indulgence of the President, and the implied approbation of the society. It was on the close of one of these evenings, which were to me very precious opportunities, that the President took me by the hand, and requested me to accompany him into the vestry,—" Sit down, my good Sir, you cannot but have seen, that I have long distinguished you in this society, that I have been pleased with your observations, and I have given indisputable evidence, that both my reason, and my judgment approved your remarks." I bowed respectfully, and endeavoured to express my gratitude in a manner becoming an occasion so truly flattering.

" My object," said he, " in seeking to engage you in private, is to request you would take home with you a pamphlet I have written against Relly's Union ; I have long wondered, that some able servant of our Master hath not taken up this subject. But as my superiors are silent, I have been urged by a sense of duty to make a stand, and I have done all in my power to prevent the pernicious tendency of this soul destroying book."

Although I had, at this period, never seen Relly's Union, yet my heart rejoiced, that Mason, this great and good man, had undertaken to write against it, and from the abundance of my heart, my mouth overflowed with thankfulness.

" All that I request of you," said Mr. Mason, " is to take this manuscript home with you, and keep it until our next meeting. Meet me in this vestry, a little before the usual time. Read it, I entreat you, carefully, and favour me with your unbiassed sentiments." I was elated by the honour done me, and I evinced much astonishment at the confidence reposed in me. But he was pleased to express a high opinion of my judgment, abilities, and goodness of heart, and he begged leave to avail himself of those qualities, with which his fancy had invested me

I took the manuscript home, perused it carefully, and with much pleasure, until I came to a passage at which I was constrained to pause, *painfully to pause*. Mr. Relly had said, speaking of the record which God gave of his Son, *This life is in his Son, and he that believeth not this record, maketh God a liar;* from whence, inferred Mr. Relly, it is plain that God hath given this eternal life *in the Son,* to *unbelievers* as fully as to believers, else the *unbeliever* could not, by his *unbelief, make God a liar.* This, said Mr. Mason, *punning upon the author's name,* is just as clear as that this writer is an *Irish bishop.* I was grieved to observe, that Mr. Mason could say no more upon this momentous subject, nor could I forbear allowing more than I wished to allow, to the reasoning of Mr. Relly. Most devoutly did I wish, that the advantage in argument had rested with my admired friend Mason, and I was especially desirous, that this last argument should have been completely confuted. I was positive, that *God never gave eternal life to any unbeliever,* and yet I was perplexed to decide how, *if God had not given life to unbelievers,* they could possibly *make God a liar by believing that he had not.* My mind was incessantly exercised, and greatly embarrassed upon this question. What is it to make any one a liar, but to deny the truth of what he hath said? But if God had no where said, that he had given life to *unbelievers,* how could the *unbeliever make God a liar?* The stronger this argument seemed in favour of the grace and love of God, the more distressed and unhappy I became, and most earnestly did I wish, that Mr. Mason's pamphlet might contain something that was more rational, more scriptural than a *mere pun,* that he might be able to adduce proof positive, that the *gift* of God, which is everlasting life, was never *given to any but believers.* I was indisputably assured, that I myself was a believer, and right precious did I hold my *exclusive* property in the Son of God.

At the appointed time I met Mr. Mason in the vestry. " Well, Sir, you have read my manuscript, I presume?" I have, Sir, and I have read it repeatedly. " Well, Sir, speak freely, is there any thing in the manuscsript which you dislike?" Why, Sir, as you are so good as to indulge me with the liberty of speaking, I will venture to point out one passage, which appears to me not sufficiently clear. Pardon me, Sir, but surely *argument, especially upon religious subjects, is preferable to ridicule, to punning upon the name of an author.* "And where, pray, is the objectionable paragraph to which you advert?" I pointed it out, but on looking in his face, I observed his countenance fallen, it was no longer toward me. Mr. Mason questioned my judgment, and never afterwards honoured me with his attention. However, I still believed *Mason right, and Relly wrong ;* for if Relly were right, the conclusion was unavoidable, *all men must finally be saved.* But this was out of the question, utterly impossible; all religious denominations agreed to condemn this heresy, to consider it as a damnable doctrine, and what every religious denomination united to condemn, must be false.

Thus, although I lost the favour of Mr. Mason, and he published his pamphlet precisely as it stood when he submitted it to my perusal, yet my reverential regard for him was not diminished; I wished, most cordially wished success to his book, and destruction to the author against whom it was written.

In this manner some months rolled over my head, when, accompanying my wife on a visit to her aunt, after the usual ceremonies, I repaired, according to custom, to the bookcase, and turning over many books and pamphlets, I at length opened one that had been robbed of its title page, but in running it over, I came to the very argument which had excited in my bosom so much anxiety. It was the first moment I had ever seen a line of Mr. Relly's writing, except in Mr. Mason's pamphlet; I was much astonished, and turning to Mrs. Murray, I informed her, I held Mr. Relly's Union in my hand—I asked her uncle if I might put it in my pocket? "Surely," said he, "and keep it there if you please, I never read books of divinity; I know not what the pamphlet is, nor do I wish to know." As I put it into my pocket, my mind became alarmed and perturbed. It was dangerous, it was tampering with poison, it was like taking fire into my bosom—I had better throw it into the flames, or restore it to the bookcase; such was the conflict in my bosom. However, in the full assurance that the *elect were safe, and that although they took up any deadly thing, it should not hurt them.* I at length decided, to read the Union; and having thus made up my mind, I experienced a degree of impatience, until I reached home, when addressing the dear companion of my youth, I said, "I have, my dear, judged and condemned before I have heard; but I have now an opportunity given me for deliberate investigation." But, returned Mrs. M——, are we sufficient of ourselves? "No, my love, certainly we are not; but God all-gracious hath said, *If any lack wisdom let them ask of him who giveth liberally, and upbraideth not.* My heart is exercised by fearful apprehensions, this moment I dread to read, the next I am anxious to hear what the author can say. We will, therefore, lay this book before our God. There is, my love, a God who is not far from every one of us; we are directed to make our requests known unto him for all things, by supplication and prayer. God hath never yet said to any, seek ye my face in vain; we will, then, pray for his direction and counsel, and we may rest in the assurance of obtaining both." Accordingly, we entered our closet, and both of us, for we were both equally afflicted, prostrating ourselves before God, with prayers and tears besought him, the God of mercy, to look with pity on us; we were on the point of attending to doctrines of which we were not, we could not be judges, and we earnestly supplicated him to lead us into all truth. If the volume before us *contained* truth, we entreated him to show it unto us, and to increase our faith; if, on the other hand, it contained falsehood, we beseeched God to make it manifest, that we might not be deceived. No poor criminal ever prayed for life, when under sentence of death, with greater fervour of devotion, than did my labouring soul, upon this occasion, supplicate for the light of life to direct my erring steps. After thus weeping, and thus supplicating, we opened the Bible, and began to read this book, looking into the Bible for the passages to which the writer referred. We were astonished and delighted at the beauty of the scriptures, thus exhibited, it seemed, as if every sentence was an apple of gold in a picture of silver, and still, as we proceeded, the wonder was, that so much divine truth should be spoken by so heinous a transgressor; and this consideration was momently presented to my mind, as a reason why I should not continue reading. Can any thing good proceed from such a character? Would not truth have been revealed to men eminent for virtue? How is it possible discoveries so important should never have been made until now, and now only to this man? Yet, I considered, *God's ways were in the great deep*, he would send by whom he would send, *choosing* the *weak* and *base* things, to confound the *mighty* and the *strong*, that no flesh should glory in his presence. And, as my lovely wife justly observed, " I was not sure all I heard of Mr. Relly was true. That our Saviour had said to his disciples, they shall say all manner of evil of you *falsely*, and this may be the case in this instance. You have no personal acquaintance with Mr. Relly, nor do you know that any of those, from whom you have received his character, are better informed than yourself. I think it doth not *become us to speak or believe evil of any man without the strongest possible proof.*" All this was rational, I felt its full force, and blushed for my own credulity.

I proceeded to read; the Union introduced me to many passages of scripture, which had before escaped my observation. A student as I had been of the scriptures, from the first dawn of my reason, I could not but wonder at myself. I turned to Mr. Mason's book, and I discovered there a want of candour, and a kind of duplicity, which had not before met my view, and which perhaps would never have caught my attention, had I not read the Union. I saw the grand object untouched, and Relly had clearly pointed out the doctrines of the gospel. Yet there were many passages, that I could not understand, and I felt myself distressingly embarrassed. One moment I wished from my soul I had never seen the Union, and the next my heart was enlarged, and lifted up by considerations, which swelled my bosom to extacy. This was the situation of my mind during many succeeding months, and a large proportion of my time was passed in reading, in studying the scriptures, and in prayer; my opening mind was pressing on to new attainments, and the prospect brightened before me. I was greatly attached to my minister, a Mr. Hitchins, he was eminent in his line, and a most pleasing preacher; Mrs Murray was in the habit of taking down his sermons in short hand; we were delighted with the man, and exulted in considering him as a genuine gospel preacher. It happened that Mr. Hitchins took a journey into the county, and was absent on the Sabbath day. "Come, my dear," said I, " Our minister is out of town, let us avail ourselves of the opportunity, and hear the writer of the Union; this is a privilege, which few who read books can have, as authors are generally numbered with the dead, before their labours are submitted to the public eye." Her consent was always yielded to my solicitations; but we were terrified as we passed along, in the fear of meeting some of our religious brethren; happily, however, we reached the meeting-house without encountering any one, to whom we were known.

Mr. Relly had changed his place of worship, and we were astonished to observe a striking proof of the falsehood of those reports, which had reached us; no coaches thronged the street, nor surrounded the door of this meeting-house, there was no vestige of grandeur, either within or without. The house had formerly been occupied by Quakers; there were no seats, save a few benches, and the pulpit was framed of a few rough boards over which no plane had ever passed. The audience corresponded with the house; they did not appear very religious, that is, they were not melancholy, and I therefore suspected they had not much piety. I attended to every thing, the hymn was good, the prayer excellent, and I was much astonished to witness, in so bad a man, so much apparent devotion, for still, I must confess, the prejudices I had received from my religious friends, were prevalent in my mind. Mr. Relly gave out his text, "*Either make the tree good and its fruit good, or the tree corrupt and its fruit corrupt; for every tree is known by its fruit, a good tree cannot bring forth corrupt fruit, neither can a corrupt tree bring forth good fruit.*" I was immeasurably surprised; what, thought I, has this man to do with a passage so calculated to condemn himself? But as he proceeded. every faculty of my soul was powerfully seized and captivated, and I was perfectly amazed while he explained *who* we were to understand by the *good*, and who by the *bad trees*. He proved beyond contradiction, that a *good* tree could not bring forth any *corrupt fruit*, but there was no man, who lived and sinned not; all mankind had corrupted themselves, there were none therefore *good, no, not one*. No *mere man* since the fall, has been able to keep the commandments of God, but *daily* doth break them *in thought, in word, and in deed*. There was however one *good tree*, Jesus, he indeed stands as the apple-tree among the trees of the wood, he is that *good tree*, which cannot bring forth *corrupt fruit*. Under his shadow the believer reposeth, the fruit of this tree is sweet to his taste, and the matter of his theme constantly is, " *Whom have I in heaven but thee, and there is none upon earth, that I desire beside thee.*" I was constrained to believe, that I never until this moment heard the Redeemer preached, and, as I said, I attended with my whole soul. I was humbled, I was confounded, I saw clearly, that I had been all my life expecting *good* fruit from *corrupt trees, grapes on thorns, and figs on thistles*, I suspected myself, I had lost my standing, I was unsettled, perturbed and wretched; a few individuals whom I had known at Mr. Whitfield's tabernacle, were among Mr. Relly's audience, and I heard them say, as they passed out of the aisle of the church, I wonder how the Pharisees would like our preacher. I conceived this observation was aimed at me, and it increased my confusion. I wished to hear Mrs. Murray speak upon the subject, but we passed on, wrapped in contemplation, at length I broke silence—well, my dear, what are your sentiments? " Nay, my dear, she returned, what is your opinion?" I never heard truth, unadulterated truth before, as sure as there is a God in heaven, if the scriptures be the word of God, the testimony this day delivered is the truth of God. It is the first consistent sermon, I have ever heard. I reached home full of this sermon, took up the Union, read it with new pleasure, attended again and again upon Mr. Relly, and was more and more astonished. Mr. Hitchins returned home, but, as I conceived, very much changed, more inconsistent than ever. " No, my dear," said my wife, " it is you who are changed, he preaches, as I can prove by my notes, precisely the same, yet it is truly surprising, that his multiplied contradictions have until now passed without our observation."

Well, said I, what are we to do? Can we in future bear such inconsistencies, now that we are better informed? Suppose we keep our seats as usual, attending however one half of every Sabbath to the *preacher of Christ Jesus?* On this we immediately determined, and by this expedient, we imagined we might obtain the gratification of hearing the truth, without running the risk of losing our reputation, for well did we know, that as *professed* adherents of Mr. Relly, we could no longer preserve that *spotless fame we delighted to cherish.*

I now commenced the reading of the scriptures, with augmented diligence. The Bible was indeed a new book to me, the veil was taken from my heart, and the word of my God became right precious to my soul. Many scriptures, that I had not before known, pressed forcibly upon my observation; and many, that until now, I had not suffered myself to believe. Still the doctrine of *election* distressed me; unfortunately I had connected this doctrine of *election* with the doctrine of *final reprobation*, not considering, that although the *first* was indubitably a scripture doctrine, the *last was not to be found in, nor could be supported by revelation.* I determined to call upon, and converse with Mr. Hitchins, on this important subject. I found him in his study, encompassed about with the writings of great men. I wait upon you, Sir, for the purpose of obtaining help. The Armenians show me many scriptures which proclaim the universality of the atonement—I cannot answer them. What, my dear Sir, shall I do? " Why, Sir, the doctrines of election and of reprobation, are doctrines we are bound to believe, as articles of our faith, but I can say, with the Rev. Mr. Hervey, I never wish to think of them, except upon my knees. Never did I hear any one undertake to explain them, but he still further embarrassed the subject; one observation, however, is conclusive, and it never fails effectually to silence the Armenian. That if, as they affirm, *Christ Jesus died for all men, then assuredly all must be saved, for no one can be eternally lost, for whom the Redeemer shed his precious blood:* such an event is impossible. Now, as the Armenian will not admit a possibility that all will finally be saved, they are thus easily confounded."

This I thought was very good; it was clear as any testimony in divine revelation, that *Christ Jesus died for all, for the sins of the whole world, for every man*, &c. &c. and, even Mr. Hitchins had declared, that *every one for whom Christ died must finally be saved.* This I took home with me to my wife, she saw the truth that we were so well prepared to embrace, manifested even by the testimony of its enemies, and we were inexpressibly anxious to hear, and to understand.

We now attended public worship, not only as a duty, conceiving that we thereby increased a fund of righteousness, upon which we were to draw in every exigence, but it became our *pleasure*, our *consolation*, and our *highest enjoyment*. We began to feed upon the *truth as it is in Jesus*, and every discovery we made filled us with unutterable transport. I regarded my friends with *increasing affection, and I conceived, if I had an opportunity of conversing with the whole world, the whole world would be convinced. It might truly have been said, that we had a taste of heaven below.*

It was soon whispered in the tabernacle, that I had frequently been seen going to, and coming from Relly's meeting! This alarmed many, and one very dear friend conversed with me *in private* upon the subject, heard, what from the abundance of my heart, my mouth was constrained to utter, smiled, pitied me, and begged I would not be too communicative, lest the business should be brought before the society, and excommunication might follow. I thanked him for his kind caution, but as I had *conversed only with him*, I had hazarded nothing.

In a short time I was cited to appear before the society worshipping in Mr. Whitfield's tabernacle; I obeyed the summons, and found myself in the midst of a very gloomy company, all seemingly in great distress; they sighed very bitterly, and at last gave me to understand, that they had heard, I had become an attendant upon that monster Relly, and they wished to know if their information was correct. I requested I might be told from whom they had their intelligence? and they were evidently embarrassed by my question. Still, however, I insisted on being confronted with my accuser, and they at length consented to summon him, but I was nearly petrified, when I learned it was the identical friend, who had *privately conversed with me, and who had privately cautioned me,* that had lodged the information against me! Upon this friend I had called in my way to the tabernacle, confiding to him my situation, he said, he had feared the event, he pitied me, and prayed with me; but he did not calculate upon being *confronted with me,* and his confusion was too great to suffer his attendance. It was then referred to me, " was it a fact, had I attended upon Relly?" I had. " Did I believe what I heard?" I answered that I did—and my trial commenced. They could not prove me a breaker of those articles to which I had subscribed. I had, in no point of view, infringed the contract by which I was bound. But they apprehended, if I continued to approbate Relly, by my occasional attendance on his ministry, my example would become contagious; except, therefore, I would give them my word, that I would wholly abandon this pernicious practice, they must, however, unwillingly pronounce upon me the sentence of excommunication. I refused to bind myself by any promise; I assured them, I would continue to hear, and to judge for myself, and that I held it my duty, to receive the *truth of God* wherever it might be manifested. But Relly holds the truth in unrighteousness. I have nothing to do with his unrighteousness; my own conduct is not more reprehensible than heretofore. They granted this, but the force of example was frequently irresistable, and if I were permitted to follow, uncensured, my own inclination, others might claim the same indulgence, to the utter perversion of their souls. It was then conceded in my favour, that if I would confine my sentiments to my own bosom, they would continue me a member of their communion. I refused to accede to this proposal. I would not be under an obligation to remain silent. I must, as often as opportunity should present, consider myself as called upon to advocate truth.

The question was then put—Should I be continued a member of the society upon my own terms? And it was lost by only three voices. It was past one in the morning when I returned home to my poor, disconsolate wife, who was waiting for me; and when I entered her apartment, my spirits were so sunk, that throwing myself into a chair, I burst into tears. But the sweet soother of my every woe hastened to communicate that consolation she was so eminently qualified to bestow. "Now, said she, for the *first time*, you know what it is to suffer for Christ's sake, and you must arm yourself with fortitude to bear, what the adherents of Mr. Relly must always bear. Let us offer up thanksgiving and praise that it is no worse. *Fear not those who can only kill the body; these, however, have not power to kill the body;* it is true they can do more; they can murder our good name, which is rather to be chosen than life itself. But let us not fear, our God will be with us, he will preserve and protect us." Our hearts, however, were very full, and we wept and prayed together with great devotion.

A series of calamities succeeded; those whom I had esteemed my best and dearest friends, proved my most inveterate foes, and finding it impossible to reclaim us from what they conceived paths of error, they persecuted us with unceasing virulence; *presents* bestowed as tokens of affection in the days of confidence, where claimed as *legal debts*, and as the *law* allows not presents, I was arrested for the amount! I was betrayed into the hands of the bailiffs, by my religious friends, whom, had they exercised the *promised* forbearance, I could have paid to the utmost farthing. Thus heaven thought proper to keep us low, but our faith increased, and we cherished the hope, that maketh not ashamed, and even while struggling with difficulties, we enjoyed a heaven upon earth. We had a sweet little retirement in a rural part of the city, we wanted but little, and we had our wants supplied, and circumstanced as we were, we enjoyed as much as human nature can enjoy. One dear pledge of love, a son, whom my wife regarded as the image of his father, completed our felicity. But alas, this boy was lent us but one short year, and the health of my beloved companion was rapidly declining; only a few weeks, a few tremendous weeks rolled on, and as in speechless agony I kneeled by her bedside, I saw her breathe her last, she expired without a groan, and I was left to the extreme of wretchedness.

Here I close another period of my eventful life! What a sad reverse! A few short weeks since, I was in the most enviable circumstances, my situation was charming, my dwelling neat and commodious, my wife the object of my soul's devout and sincere affection, her lovely offspring swelling the rapture of the scene, a male and female domestic attached to our persons, and faithful to our interests, and the pleasing hope, that I should enjoy a long succession of these delights. Now I was alone in the world, no wife, no child, no domestics, no home, nothing but the ghosts of my departed joys; in religion, and religion only, the last resort of the wretched, I found the semblance of repose; religion taught me to contemplate the state to which I was hasting, my dreams presented my departed Eliza, I saw her in a variety of views, but in every view celestial; sometimes she was still living, but in haste to be gone; sometimes she descended upon my imagination an heavenly visitant, commissioned to conduct me home, and so much enjoyment did I derive from those dreams, that I longed for the hour of repose, that I might reiterate my felicity.

But religion was still my never failing source of consolation, I was full of the gospel, gladly would I have sacrificed my life, if I might thus have brought all men acquainted with the riches of the grace of the gospel of God, our Saviour, and my soul was often wrought up to a degree of extacy by the views, which divine revelation exhibited to my understanding; yes, I have experienced, that a belief of the truth disposes the mind to love God, and to do good to man, and that faith in the promises, is the best stimulous to that pure and undefiled religion, which consists in relieving the oppressed of every description, and so greatly was my heart affected by this divine religion, that I have in the midst of the streets in London been so entranced in contemplating its glories, that I have only been awakened to recollection by the jostling crowd, who wondered as they passed; yet, while in the fulness of my heart, I embraced every opportunity of expatiating upon the great salvation, every thing beside had lost the power to charm, or even tranquilize, and the torturing sensations I experienced, from reflecting upon past times, were not to be expressed; death had for me an angel's face, and I viewed this *sometimes king of terrors*, as my emancipating friend.

EXTRACT SECOND.

This extract embraces the period, during which the author was induced to quit his native shore ; and extends to his first introduction into America.

Having laid the companion of my youth, the wife of my bosom in the grave, my life seemed devoted to misery; I wept at all times, except when I turned my attention to the world, upon which I imagined I was verging; I wished the act of putting a period to a weary life, had ranked among the christian virtues; never did I more passionately long for any good than for the period, which was to put an end to my existence. I had but few acquaintance, I wished not to make new acquaintance, I was sick of the world, and all which it could bestow. The retirement of my lonely dwelling was most acceptable to me, and I abhorred the thought of expecting any thing like happiness in this world. Thus I passed weeks and months, and thus I verily believed I should finish my days, which, I cherished a soothing hope, were nearly numbered.

Through those sad scenes of sorrow, to which I was condemned, I had one friend, one earthly friend, from whom I derived real consolation. This friend was Mr. James Relly, the man who had been made an instrument in the hand of God of leading me into an acquaintance with the truth, as it is in Jesus. This kind friend visited me often, and in conversing with him, I found my heart lightened of its burden, I could better bear the pitiless storm, that beat upon me, when strengthened by the example of this son of sorrow; frequently we talked of the things of the kingdom, and Mr. Relly observing my heart much warmed and enlarged by these subjects, urged me to go forth, and make mention of the loving kindness of God. No, no, I constantly replied, it is not my design again to step forth in a public character. I have been a promulgator of falsehood, "and why not," he would interrupt, " a promulgator of truth? Surely you owe this atonement to the God, who hath lifted upon your understanding the light of his countenance." But no argument he could make use of, was sufficiently strong to excite in my bosom a single wish, that I had either inclination or capability for a character so arduous; my heart's desire was to pass through life, *unheard, unseen, unknown to all, as though I ne'er had been.* I had an aversion to society, and since I could not be permitted to leave the world, I was solicitous to retire from its noise and nonsense, I was indeed a burden to myself, and no advantage to any body else, every place, every thing served to make me more miserable, for they led my mind to the contemplation of past scenes, of scenes never more to return; such was the situation of my mind, when at the house of one of Mr. Relly's hearers, I met by accident a gentleman from America, I listened with attention to his account of the country, in which he had so long resided; I was charmed with his description of its extent, its forests, its lakes, its rivers, its towns, its inhabitants, the liberty they enjoyed, and the peace and plenty, which they possessed; I listened to every thing with astonishment, and toward the new world I turned my most ardent wishes; I communicated my desire to visit America, to my mother, to my brethren, I was ridiculed for entertaining a project so chimerical, what, cross the Atlantic! For what purpose? To whom would I go? What could I do? What object could I have in view? I was unable to answer any of these questions; I had not a single acquaintance in America, indeed, I had no wish to make acquaintance, I had nothing in prospect but a kind of negative happiness, I did not mean to commence a voyage in pursuit of bliss, but to avoid, if possible, a part of my misery.

For a considerable time, my mind laboured with my purpose, many difficulties interposed, I would have infinitely preferred entering that narrow house, which is appointed for all living, but this I was not permitted to do, and I conceived to quit England, and retire to America, was the next thing to be desired: nights and days of deliberation at length convinced my judgment, and I became determined upon my departure; my few friends urged me most ardently to let them apply to those, who had connexions in America, for letters of introduction or recommendation, no, by no means, this would most effectually defeat my purpose; I would rather not go than go thus. My object was to close my life in solitude, in the most complete retirement, and with those views, I commenced preparations for my voyage. I visited the brother of my departed wife, and I beheld both him and his children with the same eyes a dying person would have beheld them; tears frequently stole down my face, and a thousand thoughts, that served to harrow up my soul, crowded upon me; I was determined not to repeat this scene, and I bid them adieu; could I have done this upon a bed of death, how much happier should I have been.

The place I now occupied, to which I had recently removed, was extremely beautiful; it was in the vicinity of London, I had a fine garden, and a delightful prospect, but my better self had fled this globe, and with her fled my *soul's calm sunshine, every heart-felt joy*. I was extremely wretched; I spake to the master of a vessel, bound to New-York, I agreed for my passage, my heart trembled, it was worse than death. He fixed the time for my departure, every arrangement was made. My brother, my widowed mother, I met them in my parlour, it was torturing. " Sit down, my son," said my weeping parent; " my brother appeared a silent spectacle of sorrow, I know you, my child, too well to expect I can alter your resolution; it is now too late, to beseech you would reflect, I know you have long reflected, and I am astonished to find you still determined.

"You have a charming situation, your prospects are good, could you but make your mind easy, you might still be happy; why, then, this aversion to life"? I interrupted her by declaring, that the whole world would not, could not detain me longer in England, yet I passionately loved my country, and my few remaining friends shared my heart's best affections. This voluntary exile was worse than death, but I was impelled to go, and go I must. My poor mother threw her fond arms about my neck, " once more, said she, you leave me, but not now as before; then you left me in my native place, among my natural connexions; then too I had hope you would be restored to me again—but now," and she burst into tears; my heart was agonized, I entreated her to consider me as on the bed of death, nor again to think of me, as of a living son; be thankful, my mother, be thankful it is no worse, be thankful I have not fallen a victim to the despondency of my spirit: I leave you, it is true, but I leave you with your children, a son, a daughter, both kind and dutiful, and, what is better than all, I leave you in the hands, and under the care of a kind God, who hath said, I will never leave you nor forsake you. "But shall I hear from you, my son?" Do not, I entreat you, think of me as living; I go to bury myself in the wilds of America, no one shall hear from me, nor of me, I have done with the world, and prostrating myself in the presence of my mother and my God, with streaming eyes, and supplicating hands, I commended my soul, and all who were connected with, or allied to me, to that Being, who orders all things according to his own good pleasure.

I left my mother in an agony of affliction, and retired, but not to rest; my baggage had been sent on board ship in the morning, and, accompanied by my brother, we took a boat, and passed down to Grave's end, where I entered on board the vessel, that was to convey me to America, which in my *then judgment* was tantamount to quitting the world.

The vessel, however, did not immediately sail, I had an opportunity of going on shore again, and spending sometime at Grave's end. Fond of being alone, I ascended a lofty eminence, and sat me down under the shade of a wide spreading tree; here I had inclination and leisure for reflection. On one hand I beheld the wide ocean, my path to the new world, on the other the Thames, upon whose silvery surface many were passing to London.

My mind rapidly ran over the various scenes I had witnessed since my arrival in that great city I dwelt upon the good I had lost, never more to be recovered. My soul sickened at the recollection of my heavy bereavements, of the solitary situation to which I was reduced. I was going from a world in which I had some associates, and some friends, into a country where every individual was unknown to me! I was going on board a vessel, to the crew of which I was an utter stranger—all gloomy, truly gloomy. From one idea, however, I derived consolation; I might soon finish my course, and bid an eternal adieu to sorrow of every description. Yet I trembled at what was before me, I was fearful I was wrong; just at this period the wind shifted, the signal was made for sailing, but before I descended the eminence, I threw my eyes once more upon the surrounding scenes I felt destitute and forlorn, tears gushed in my eyes. My domestic felicity, my social connexions, the pleasure

I had derived from listening to the testimony of truth, these all rushed upon my recollection, until my heart was nearly bursting. I prostrated myself with my face to the ground, with streaming eyes, exclaiming, Oh, thou dear parent earth, thou much loved native soil, why not open and give me a quiet resting place in thy bosom. Oh, thou dear departed friend of my soul, hast thou no power to loose these chains that bind me to this state of being. Is there no eye to pity, no hand to help a wretched outcast? Can I not be indulged with death? But death comes not at call. In this situation I continued, bedewing the earth with my tears, until it pleased the kind God to speak peace to my tortured heart, and I seemed to hear a voice calling unto me, *Be of good cheer, your God is with you, he will never leave you nor forsake you, he is in the wide waste as in the city full. Be not afraid, when thou passest through the waters, I will be with thee, fear no evil, the friend of sinners will be with thee, and make thy way plain before thee, he will cause the desert to blossom as the rose. The young lions cry, and thy heavenly Father feedeth them. Thou art nearer and dearer to thy heavenly Father, than all the inhabitants of the deep, than all the tenants of the forests.* Thus did the spirit of grace and consolation comfort my afflicted heart, so that after bidding an affectionate adieu to the scenes of the morning, and of the meridian of my days, after taking what I believed an eternal leave of my dear native soil, of my friends and relatives, after dropping many tears to the memory of each, and last of all to the ashes of my dearer self, with an aching head, a pained heart, and eyes swelled by weeping, I hastened on board the vessel, and upon the ensuing morning, as we passed round Beachy head, I beheld the white cliffs of Albion. No language can describe my sensations, as those white cliffs receded from my view, as I took a last look of England! I retired to my cabin, covered my face, and wept until I was completely exhausted. But God was pleased to lift up the light of his countenance upon me, my voyage passed more pleasantly than I had calculated, and I was the happy instrument of contributing to the comfort of many on board. I was not sick upon the passage, and I became more than reconciled to my circumstances, and almost dreaded the thought of reaching our destined port.

I did not anticipate my fate on my arrival; I had determined upon nothing, and yet I was not distressed; a perfect indifference pervaded my soul. I had in my trunks many articles of clothing, more than I should want, for I did not calculate upon being many years an inhabitant of this globe. I had some money, I had my Bible, and a very large collection of the letters of my Eliza, in which I took much delight, and upon the whole, I fancied myself rather rich than otherwise; in this state of resignation, indifference, or insensibility, I passed the greater part of the voyage.

As we drew near the coast of America, I experienced none of those delightful sensations, which swelled my bosom on returning to England from Ireland a few years before, neither did I experience those terrifying apprehensions, for which there was such abundant reason, on advancing to an unknown country, without patron or friend. My mind was calm and unruffled, neither elated by hope, nor depressed by fear. I had attained precisely the situation for which I had supplicated heaven, when entering upon this untried state of being, humbly depending upon that God, who in every place was still the same unchanging friend of the creature whom he had made. I was, as it were, between two worlds, one I had tried, and finding it contained more of bitter than of sweet, I had turned from it with disgust. I advanced toward the other, without high-raised expectations, without fearful apprehensions.

I was pleased with the wonders of my God, as I beheld them in the great deep. I was amazed by the variety of inhabitants I saw, and yet how small a part could I trace. I was astonished at the number of birds I beheld all over the ocean. I thought if provision was made for them, I had no reason for fear. On a brilliant moonlight evening, our ship struck on something which threw us off our seats! What could it be, we were in the centre of the Western Ocean? We soon discovered it was a sleeping whale; we beheld too the water spout, so often described as a surprising phenomenon. Thus was my mind filled with wonder, and beguiled of its sorrows. We saw, also, a number of vessels on our way, some passing to the country we had left; my heart sighed as they pursued their course, and I frequently and audibly exclaimed, dear native country, never more to be seen by me, nor was this exclamation unaccompanied by a tear.

We were, as it was supposed, within three days' sail of New-York, when we met a vessel bound for England. Our merchant questioned the captain respecting the state of public affairs in America. The Americans had sometime before entered into the non importation agreement, and our merchant was anxious on account of the goods he had on board. The captain assured him, they had given up the agreement in Philadelphia, but that they adhered to it in New-York with great zeal. Our captain, therefore, received immediate orders to change the course of the vessel for Philadelphia; but when we had got near enough to this harbour, to take a pilot, the pilot informed us the reverse of the information we had received was the truth, upon which, the merchant determined to go as far as the city, there obtain a certainty, and if so, to proceed to New-York with all possible despatch. We were a considerable time passing up the Delaware, and upon a fine day, while we lay at anchor, the merchant proposed going on shore for the purpose of obtaining corn and fruit.

It was in the month of September, when we arrived in the Delaware; the country upon the banks of this fine river exhibited a most enchanting appearance, especially to those who had been for many weeks out of sight of land, and had never before seen these shores As we drew near the land, the woods, seeming to grow out of the water, had to me a very uncommon appearance; but every thing in this country was uncommon; we went on shore, and ascended a gentle rising, when entering into a small log house, I was astonished to see a woman preparing some excellent wild ducks for dinner—live in a log house and feed upon ducks! We past into her garden, where, amid its rich variety, my attention was arrested by a large peach tree loaded with the best fruit, bending to the earth! I was beyond expression charmed and delighted, and my heart bent with grateful affection to the kind Parent of all, for giving the inhabitants of this new world thus liberally to enjoy. When we reached Philadelphia, I was amazed to behold a city of such magnitude, in a country which I had considered as a wilderness. The captain mentioned it as a disappointment to me, that we had not put into New-York, as that was the place of my destination, but I requested him to make himself easy, as it was a matter of perfect indifference to me, upon what part of the country I landed, and if he could procure me a *private* lodging, I would go on shore in this city; this he told me he would do, but this he found, in the circle of his connexions, he could not do. He then proposed my going by land to New-York, this also I was willing to do, if he would let me know how. He would send and take me a place in the stage; the stage had been gone some time; he then proposed I should tarry in the vessel, and set out with him the next morning for New-York, to which arrangement I agreed. The other passengers left us in Philadelphia. The water was smooth, and our passage pleasant, until we were, as was supposed, near Sandy Hook, a dense fog then arose, which was sufficiently thick to prevent our seeing the end of our bowsprit. A sloop shot past us, and we inquired how far we were from Sandy Hook? The answer was *seventy* miles, but we understood *seven*, and we pressed on, and in a few moments were in the midst of the breakers; the vessel struck upon the bar, but passed over into a place, we afterwards found was called Cranberry Inlet. The fog now dispersed, and we discovered we were nearly on shore, our anchors, however, saved us, but we were greatly alarmed, and never expected to get off again. The sloop, with which we had spoken, entered this inlet before us, and was light. The captain proposed to engage this sloop to receive on board as much of our cargo as she could contain, thus by lightening his vessel, giving himself the only probable chance of getting off. This was effectuated, and night coming on, the captain, with many apologies, requested me to lodge on board the sloop, inasmuch as there were many valuable articles which he was afraid to trust, without a confidential person. To this I readily consented, and taking my Bible and my purse, I went on board the sloop. The captain's plan was, supposing the morning should present no prospect of getting off, to deposit the remainder of his cargo upon the beach, but if they should get off, we were immediately to follow, the goods were to be replaced, and the sloop dismissed. I went not to bed, and when the morning dawned, just at high water, the wind blowing from the shore, they got off, making a signal for us to follow, and with all possible despatch we prepared to obey, but the wind instantly shifting, drove us back, and they proceeded on to New-York, leaving us in the bay.

Upon examination, it proved we had no provisions on board, we were, therefore, necessitated to lock up the vessel, and go on shore in search of sustenance; it was the after part of the day before we could effectuate our purpose, when I went with the boatmen to a tavern, and leaving them there, pursued a solitary walk through the woods, which seemed to surround this place. My mind was greatly agitated. I was now in the new world, and in just such a part of this new world, as had appeared to me so desirable in prospect. Here I was as much alone as I could wish, and my heart exclaimed, *O, that I had in this wilderness, the lodging place of a poor way-faring man ; some cave, some grot, some place where I might finish my days in calm repose.* As thus I passed along, thus contemplating, thus supplicating, I unexpectedly reached a small log house, and saw a girl cleaning a fresh fish. I requested she would sell it to me. "No, Sir, you will find a very great plenty at the next house, we want this." The next house, what, this? pointing to one in the woods. "O no, Sir, that is a meeting-house." A meeting-house here, in these woods! I was exceedingly surprised. "You must pass the meeting-house, Sir, and a little ways further on, you will see the other house, where you will find fish enough." I went forward, I came to the door, there was indeed a large pile of fish of various sorts, and at a little distance stood a tall man, rough in his appearance, and evidently advanced in years. Pray, Sir, will you have the goodness to sell me one of those fish? "No, Sir." That is strange, to refuse me a single fish, when you have so many! "I did not refuse you a fish, Sir, you are welcome to as many as you please, but I do not sell this article, I do not sell fish, Sir, I had them for taking up, and you may obtain them the same way." I thanked him; "but," said he, "what do you want of those fish?" I informed him, that the mariners who belonged to the sloop at a distance, were at the tavern, and would be glad if I could procure them something for supper. "Well, Sir, I will send my man over with the fish, but you can tarry here, and have some dressed for yourself." No, it was proper I should see how they were accommodated. "Well, Sir, you shall do as you please, but after supper, I beg you would return, and take a bed with us, you will be better pleased here than at a tavern." I thanked him, and with much gratitude accepted his offer. I was astonished to find so much genuine politeness and good-natured urbanity, under so rough a form ; but on my return, my astonishment was greatly increased ; his room was prepared, his fire bright, and his heart open. "Come," said he, "my friend, I am glad you are returned, I have longed to see you, I have been expecting you a long while." I was perfectly amazed. What do you mean, Sir? "I must go on in my own way, I am a poor, ignorant man, I neither know how to read nor to write; I was born in these woods, and my father did not think proper to teach me my letters. I worked on these grounds until I became a man, when I went coasting voyages from hence to New-York. I was then desirous of becoming a husband, but in going to New-York, I was pressed on board a Man of War, and was taken in Admiral Warren's ship to Cape Breton. I never drank any rum, so they saved my allowance; but I would not bear an affront, so if any of the officers struck me, I struck them again, but the Admiral took my part, and called me his new light man. When we reached Louisburgh, I ran away, and travelled barefooted through the country, almost naked, to New-York, where I was known, supplied with clothes and money, and soon returned to this place, when I found my girl married; this rendered me very unhappy, but I recovered my tranquillity, and married her sister. I sat down to work, got forward very fast, constructed a saw mill, possessed myself of this farm, and five hundred acres of adjoining land. I entered into navigation, became the owner of a sloop, and have got together a large estate. But although I am unable either to write or to read, I am however capable of reflection; the sacred scriptures have been often read to me, from which I gather, that there is a great and good Being, to whom we are indebted for all we enjoy. It is this great and good Being who hath preserved and protected me through innumerable dangers, and as he hath given me a house of my own, I conceived I could not do less than to open it to the stranger, let him be who he will; and, especially, if a travelling minister passed this way, he always received an invitation to put up at my house, and hold his meetings here. This practice was continued for more than seven years, and, illiterate as I was, I used to converse with them, and was fond of asking them questions. They pronounced me an odd mortal, declaring themselves at a loss what to make of me: while I continued to affirm, that I had but one hope, I believed that Jesus Christ suffered death for my transgressions, and this alone was sufficient for me.

"At length my wife grew weary of having these meetings held in her house, and I determined to build a house for the worship of my God. I had no children, and I knew that I was beholden to almighty God for every thing, which I possessed, and it seemed right, I should appropriate a part of what he had bestowed for his service; my neighbours offered their assistance, but no, said I, God has given me enough to do his work without your aid, and as he has put it into my heart to do, so I will do; and who, it was asked, will be your preacher? I answered, God will send me a preacher, and that of a very different stamp from those, who have heretofore preached in my house. The preachers we have heard are continually contradicting themselves; but that God, who put it into my heart to build this house, will send one, who shall deliver unto me his own truth, who shall speak of Jesus Christ, and his salvation. When the house was finished, I received an application from the Baptists, and I told them if they could make it appear, that God Almighty was a Baptist, the building should be theirs at once. The Quakers and Presbyterians received from me similar answers. No, said I, as I firmly believe, that all mankind are equally dear to almighty God, they shall all be equally welcome to preach in this house, which I have built. My neighbours assured me I never should see a preacher, whose sentiments corresponded with my own; but my uniform reply was, that I assuredly should. I engaged the first year with a man, whom I greatly disliked, and we parted, and for some years we have had no stated minister. My friends often ask me, Where is the preacher of whom you spake? And my constant reply has been, he will by-and-by make his appearance. The moment I beheld your vessel on shore, it seemed as if a voice had audibly sounded in my ear, There, Potter, in that vessel cast away on that shore, is the preacher you have been so long expecting. I heard the voice, and I believed the report, and when you came up to my door, and asked for the fish, the same voice seemed to repeat, Potter, this is the man, this is the person whom I have sent to preach in your house!"

I was astonished, immeasurably astonished at Mr. Potter's narrative, but yet I had not the smallest idea it could ever be realized. I requested to know what he could discern in my appearance, which could lead him to mistake me for a preacher? " What," said he; " could I discern when you were in the vessel, that could induce this conclusion ; no, Sir, it is not what I *saw* or *see*, but what *I feel*, which produces, in my mind, a full conviction."

But, my dear Sir, you are deceived, indeed you are deceived, I never shall preach in this place, nor any where else.

"Have you never preached ? Can you say you have never preached ?"

I cannot, but I never intend to preach again.

"Has not God lifted up the light of his countenance upon you ? Has he not shown you his truth ?"

I trust he has.

"And how dare you hide this truth ? Do men light a candle to put it under a bushel ? If God has shown you his salvation, why should you not show it to your fellow men ? But I know, that you will, I am sure God Almighty has sent you to us for this purpose ; I am not deceived, I am sure I am not deceived."

I was terrified as the man thus went on, and I began to fear that God, who orders all things according to the council of his own will, had ordained that thus it should be, and my heart trembled at the idea; I endeavoured, however, to banish my own fears, and to silence the warm hearted man by observing, that I was in the place of a supercargo, that property to a large amount had been entrusted to my care, and that the moment the wind shifted, I was under the most solemn obligations to depart.

"The wind will never shift, Sir, until you have delivered to us a message from God in that meeting-house, which I have built for his honour."

Still I was fully determined I never would enter any pulpit as a preacher; yet being rendered truly unhappy, I begged I might be shown to my bed. He requested I would pray with them, if I had no objection. I asked him, how he could suppose I could have any objection to praying ? When he observed the Quakers seldom prayed, and there were others who visited him, who were not in the habit of praying. I never propose prayer, Sir, least it should not meet with the approbation of those with whom I sojourn, but I am always pleased when prayer is proposed to me. I prayed, and my heart was greatly enlarged and softened. When we parted for the night, my kind host solemnly requested, that I would think of what he had said. Alas ! He need not to have made this request ; it was impossible to banish it from my mind. When I entered my chamber and shut the door, I burst into tears; I would have given the world, that I had never left England. I felt as if the hand of God was in the events, which had brought me to this place, and I prayed most ardently, that God would assist and direct me by his counsel. I presented myself before him as a man bowed down by calamity; a melancholy outcast, driven by repeated afflictions of body and of mind, to seek refuge in *private* life, to seek solitude amid the wilds of America: thou knowest, said my enanguished spirit, thou knowest, O Lord, that if it had pleased thee, I should have preferred death as the safest, and most sure retreat, but thou hast not seen fit to indulge my wishes in this respect; in thy providence, thou hast brought me into this new world, thou seest how I am oppressed by solicitations, to speak unto the people the words of life, thou knowest, O God, that I am not sufficient for these things, thou God of my fathers, thou God of the stranger, look with pity on the poor lonely wanderer, now before thee. O thou, that sittest in the heaven, and rulest in the earth, and who assurest us, that a hair of our head cannot fall unnoticed by thee, O thou, who kindly directest thy poor dependent creatures, to acknowledge thee in all their ways, and to make their requests known unto thee in every time of affliction, behold thy poor dependent, supplicating thee for thy kind direction and protection; if thou hast indeed put it into the heart of thy servant, to demand of me the meanest and weakest of all, to whom thou didst ever give power to believe in the name of thy son, to declare unto him, and the people of this place, the gospel of thy grace, O God, in mercy prepare me, prepare me for so vast an undertaking, and let thy presence be with me; strengthen me, O Lord, by thy mighty spirit, and if it be not thy pleasure thus to employ me, for thou, O God, wilt send, by whom thou wilt send, graciously manifest thy will, that so I may not by any means be drawn into a snare. Thou art the sinner's friend, thou art the only friend I have. To thee, O thou compassionate Father of my spirit, encouraged by thy gracious promises, I make application. Pity, O pity the destitute stranger, leave me not, I most earnestly entreat thee, to my own direction.

Thus did I pray, thus did I weep through the greater part of the night, dreading more than death, even supposing death an object of dread, which for some years past it had ceased to be, the thought of engaging as a public character. On the one hand I discovered, that if there be a ruling power, a superintending providence, the account given by the extraordinary man, under whose roof I reposed, evinced its operations, that if the heart of the creature is indeed in the hand of the Creator, it was manifest, that God had disposed the heart of this man to view me as a messenger of God, sent for the purpose of declaring the council of his peace to his creatures; on the other hand, I recollected, that the heart is deceitful above all things, that the devices of the adversary are manifold, and that had it been the will of God, that I should have become a promulgator of the gospel of his grace, he would have qualified me for an object of such infinite magnitude

If I testified of Jesus according to the scriptures, I knew well upon what I must calculate, the clergy of all denominations would unite to oppose me, for I had never met with any individual of that order, either in the church of Rome or elsewhere, who were believers of the gospel, that God preached unto Abraham, that in Christ Jesus all the families of the earth should be blessed, nor did they, as far as I had known, embrace the ministry of reconciliation committed unto the Apostles, namely, that *God was in Christ reconciling the world unto himself, not imputing unto them their trespasses*, nor did they acknowledge the *restitution of all things, testified by all God's holy prophets ever since the world began*. To these doctrines, I supposed clergymen in this, as well as in the country I had left, united in their opposition; and, convinced that there were no enemies in the world, more powerful than the clergy, I trembled at the thought of stemming the full tide of their displeasure. I was persuaded that people in general being under the dominion of the clergy, would hate where they hated, and report what they reported; acquainted in some measure with human nature, and with divine revelation, I was certain, that if I appeared in the character of a real disciple of Christ Jesus, if I dared to declare the whole truth of God, all manner of evil would be said of me, and although it might be *falsely* said, while the *inventor* of the slander would be *conscious of its falsehood*, the greater part of those who heard would yield it credit, and I should become the victim of their credulity.

I knew how Mr. Relly had suffered in England, and the Apostles in Judea, and being a believer of the testimony of God, I was assured, if my doctrines were the same, my treatment would be similar. All this rose to my view, and the prospect was tremendous. Thus I passed the night, and the ensuing morning found me indisposed both in body and mind.

My good friend renewed his solicitations. "Will you, Sir, speak to me, and to my neighbours, of the things which belong to our peace?" Seeing only thick woods, the tavern across the field excepted, I requested to know what he meant by neighbours? "O, Sir, we assemble a large congregation whenever the meeting-house is opened; indeed, when my father first settled here, he was obliged to go twenty miles to grind a bushel of corn, but there are now more than seven hundred inhabitants within that distance." I was amazed, indeed every thing I saw, and every thing I heard amazed me; nothing except the religion of the people, resembled what I had left behind.

My mind continued night and day subjected to torturing reflections. I could not bring myself to yield to the intreaties of Mr. Potter, and still I urged the necessity of departing, the moment the wind would answer. Mr. Potter was positive the wind would not shift, until I had spoken to the people. I ardently desired to escape the importunities of this good man; the idea of a crowd, of making a public exhibition of myself, was intolerable to my desolate, woe-worn mind, and the suspense in which I was held, was perfectly agonizing. I could not forbear acknowledging an uncommon coincidence of circumstances. The hopes and fears of this honest man, so long in operation, yet he evinced great warmth of disposition, and was evidently tinctured with enthusiasm; but after making every allowance for these propensities, it could not be denied, that an over-ruling power seemed to operate in an unusual and remarkable manner. I could not forbear looking back to the mistakes made upon our passage, even to the coming into this particular inlet, where no vessel of this size had ever before entered, every circumstance combined to bring me to this house; Mr. Potter's address on seeing me, his assurance that he knew I was on board the vessel, when he saw her at a distance, all these considerations pressed with powerful conviction on my mind, and I was ready to say, If God Almighty has, in his providence, so ordered events, as to bring me into this country, for the purpose of making manifest the savor of his name, and of bringing many to the knowledge of the truth, though I would infinitely prefer death, to entering into a character which will subject me to what is infinitely worse than death; yet as I have not with me the issues of life and of death, am I not bound to submit to the dispensations of providence? I wished however to be convinced, that it was the will of God, that I should step forth in a character, which would be considered as obnoxious, as truly detestable. I was fully convinced it was not by the will of the flesh, nor the will of the world, nor by the will of the God of this world, all these were strongly opposed thereto; one moment I felt my resolution giving way, the path pointed out seemed to brighten upon me, but the next the difficulties from within and without obscured the prospect, and I relapsed into a firm resolution to shelter myself in solitude, from the hopes and fears, and the various contentions of men.

While I thus balanced, the Sabbath advanced, I had ventured to implore the God, who had sometimes condescended to indulge individuals with tokens of his approbation, graciously to indulge me upon this important occasion, and that if it were his will, that I should obtain the desire of my soul by passing through life in a private character, if it were *not* his will, that I should engage as a preacher of the ministry of reconciliation, he would vouchsafe to grant me such a wind, as might bear me from this shore before the return of the Sabbath. I determined to take the changing of the wind for an answer, and had the wind changed, it would have borne on its wings full conviction, because it would have corresponded with my wishes. But the wind changed not, and Saturday morning arrived. " Well," said my anxious friend, "now let me give notice to the neighbours." No, Sir, not yet, not yet; should the wind change by the middle of the afternoon, I must depart. No tongue can tell, nor heart conceive how much I suffered this afternoon; but the evening came on, and it was necessary I should determine, and at last, with much fear and trembling, I yielded a reluctant consent. Mr. Potter then immediately dispatched his servants on horse back, to spread the intelligence far and wide, and they were to continue their information until ten in the evening.

I had no rest through the night, what should I say, or how address the people? yet I recollected the admonition of our Lord. " *Take no thought what you shall say; it shall be given you in that same hour what you shall say.*" Ay, but this promise

ise was made to his disciples. Well, by this I shall know if I am a disciple. If God, in his providence, is committing to me a dispensation of the gospel, he will furnish me with matter without my thought or care. If this thing be not of God, he will desert me, and this shall be another sign, on this then I rested. Sunday morning succeeded, my host was in transports, I was—I cannot describe how I was; I entered the house, it was neat and convenient, expressive of the character of the builder. There were no pews, the pulpit was rather in the Quaker mode, the seats were constructed with backs, roomy, and even elegant. I said there were no pews, there was one large, square pew, just before the pulpit, in this sat the venerable man, and his family, particular friends, and visiting strangers. In this pew sat, upon this occasion, this happy man, and surely no man on this side heaven was ever more completely happy. He looked up to the pulpit with eyes sparkling with pleasure; it appeared to him as the fulfilment of a promise long deferred; and he reflected, with abundant consolation, on the strong faith which he had cherished, while his associates would tauntingly question, Well, Potter, where is this minister, which is to be sent you? "He is coming along in God's own good time." And do you still believe any such preacher will visit you? "O, yes, assuredly." Upon all this he reflected, and tears of transport filled his eyes; he looked round upon the people, and every feature seemed to say, "There, what think you now?" When I returned to his house, he caught me in his arms—"Now, now, I am willing to depart; O, my God, I will praise thee, thou hast granted me my desire. After this truth I have been seeking, but I have never found it until now; I knew that God, who put it into my heart to build a house for his worship, would send a servant of his own to proclaim his own gospel. I knew he would; I knew the time was come, when I saw the vessel grounded; I knew you were the man, when I saw you approach my door, and my heart leaped for joy." Visitors poured into the house; he took each by the hand. "This is the happiest day of my life," said the transported man. "There, neighbours, there is the minister God promised to send, how do you like God's minister?" I ran from the company, and prostrating myself before the throne of grace, besought my God to take me, and do with me whatever he pleased. I am, said I, I am, O Lord God, in thine hand, as clay in the hand of the potter. If thou, in thy providence, hast brought me into this new world, to make known to this people the grace and the blessings of the new covenant, if thou hast thought proper by making choice of so weak an instrument, to confound the wise, if thou hast been pleased to show to a babe, possessing neither wisdom nor prudence, what thou hast hid from the wise and prudent, be it so, O Father, for so it seemeth good in thy sight. But O, my merciful God, leave me not, I beseech thee, for a single moment; for without thee, I can do nothing. O, make thy strength perfect in my weakness, that the world may see that thine is the power, and that, therefore, thine ought to be the glory. Thus, my heart prayed, while tears of supplication bedewed my face.

I felt however relieved and tranquilized, for I had power given me to trust in the name of the LORD, to stay upon the God of my salvation. Immediately on my return to the company, my boatmen entered the house, the wind is fair, Sir; well, then we will depart, it is late in the afternoon, but no matter, I will embark directly; I have been determined to embrace the first opportunity, well knowing the suspense the captain must be in, and the pain attendant thereon.

Accordingly I set off, as soon as matters could be adjusted, but not until my old friend taking me by the hand said, You are now going to New-York, I am afraid you will, when there, forget the man, to whom your master sent you; but I do beseech you come back to me again as soon as possible; the tears gushed in his eyes, and regarding me with looks which indicated the strongest affection, he threw his arms around me, repeating his importunities, that I would not unnecessarily delay my return. I was greatly affected, reiterating the strongest assurances that I would conform to his wishes. Why should I not, said I, what is there to prevent me? I do not know an individual in New-York, no one knows me, what should induce me to tarry there? Ah, my friend, said he, you will find many in New-York, who will love and admire you, and they will wish to detain you, in that city. But you have promised you will return, and I am sure you will return, and in the mean time may the God of heaven be with you. Unable to reply I hurried from his door, and on entering the vessel, I found the good old man had generously attended to what had made no part of my care, by making ample provision both for me and the boatmen during our little voyage.

I retired to the cabin, I had leisure for serious reflections, and serious reflections crowded upon me ; I was astonished, I was lost in wonder, in love, and in praise ; I saw as plain as I could see an object of sense, that the good hand of God was in all these things ; it is, I spontaneously exclaimed, it is the LORD's doings, and it is marvellous in my eyes ; it appeared to me, that I could trace the hand of God in bringing me through a long chain of events to such a place, to such a person, so evidently prepared for my reception, and while I acknowledged the will of God manifested respecting my publick character, I at the same moment distinguished the kindness of God, evinced by his indulging me with a retirement so exactly suited to my wishes ; the house was neat, the situation enchanting, it was on the margin of the deep, on the side of an extensive bay, which abounded with fish of every description, and a great variety of water fowl. On the other side of this dwelling after passing over a few fields, (which at that time stood thick with corn)—venerable woods, which seemed the coevals of time, presented a "scene for contemplation fit—towering majestic, they filled the devotional mind with a religious awe." I reflected therefore with augmenting gratitude to my heavenly Father, upon the pressing invitation he had put it into the heart of his faithful servant, to give me, and I determined to hasten back to this delightful retreat, where nothing but the grandeur of simple nature in the surrounding objects, and the genuine operations of the divine spirit in the hospitable Master, awaited my approach.

I had not the least idea of tarrying in New-York, a moment longer than to see the captain, deliver up my charge, and receive my baggage, and I resolved to return to my benevolent friend by the first opportunity. And thus did I make up my mind. Well, if it be so, I am grateful to God, that the business is thus adjusted ; if I must be a promulgator of these glad, these vast, yet obnoxious tidings, I shall however be sheltered in the bosom of friendship, in the bosom of retirement. I will employ myself on the grounds of my friend, thus obtaining my own support, and health will be a concomitant, while I will preach the glad tidings of salvation, free as the light of heaven. The business thus arranged, my mind became reconciled to the will of the Almighty, and thus commenced another important stage of my various life.

NOTE.

The editor concludes the work of transcribing with regret, but these volumes have already extended far beyond her calculation. The papers, from which the extracts relative to the life of the author, are selected, are sufficient to complete a volume. These papers might be filled up, and made to constitute the fourth volume of this collection; and should the friends of the writer request, the sheets when corrected and completed, will be surrendered to their wishes, and they will be found to contain much to inform, and much to gratify the disciples of the Redeemer.

The probability is, that the eventful and useful career of the preacher will be closed among his chosen friends in this town; and taking a view of their acts of kindness, he is ready to say, "My lot is fallen unto me in a pleasant place, yea, and I have a goodly heritage."

FINIS.

BIBLIOLIFE

Old Books Deserve a New Life
www.bibliolife.com

Did you know that you can get most of our titles in our trademark **EasyScript**™ print format? **EasyScript**™ provides readers with a larger than average typeface, for a reading experience that's easier on the eyes.

Did you know that we have an ever-growing collection of books in many languages?

Order online:
www.bibliolife.com/store

Or to exclusively browse our **EasyScript**™ collection:
www.bibliogrande.com

At BiblioLife, we aim to make knowledge more accessible by making thousands of titles available to you – quickly and affordably.

Contact us:
BiblioLife
PO Box 21206
Charleston, SC 29413